HEMINGWAY'S

NEGLECTED SHORT FICTION

NEW PERSPECTIVES

HEMINGWAY'S
NEGLECTED SHORT FICTION

NEW PERSPECTIVES

Edited by

Susan F. Beegel

The University of Alabama Press

Tuscaloosa and London

First Paperback Edition 1992

The photograph on the cover is *Hemingway in Idaho, ca. 1960,* published courtesy of the
John F. Kennedy Library, Photographer Unknown.

∞

The paper on which this book is printed meets the minimum requirements of American
National Standard for Information Science-Permanence of Paper for Printed Library Materials, ANSI Z39.48-1984.

Library of Congress Cataloging-in-Publication Data

Hemingway's neglected short fiction : new perspectives / edited by
   Susan F. Beegel.
      p. cm.
   Includes bibliographical references and index.
   ISBN 0-8173-0586-6
      1. Hemingway, Ernest, 1899–1961—Criticism and interpretation.   2. Short
   story.   I. Beegel, Susan F., 1954–
   PS3515.E37Z625 1992
   813'.52—dc20   91-34441

British Library Cataloguing-in-Publication Data available

For Paul Smith

Contents

Editor's Note

This anthology contains 25 original essays on seldom-criticized Hemingway short stories, and seeks, by challenging the canon of oft-discussed Hemingway works, to extend our appreciation of a remarkably versatile author. *Hemingway's Neglected Short Fiction: New Perspectives* was originally published in the academic year 1989–90, and the months that followed its appearance marked a renaissance of interest in virtually all of Hemingway's short stories. Since its initial printing, this collection has been joined by two major contributions to the study of the short fiction.

Paul Smith's *A Reader's Guide to the Short Stories of Ernest Hemingway* (G. K. Hall, 1989) is an immensely useful reference work, providing a composition and publication history, compendium of sources and influences, and overview of the criticism for each of the 55 short stories Hemingway published during his lifetime. Smith's guide contains newly discovered contextual information, essential background material, and shrewd suggestions for future research. Its approach is democratic, according equal treatment to each short story and leaving canonical decisions to future scholars, while at the same time providing them with a wealth of information for making such decisions. The book is particularly valuable as it offers readers Smith's unequaled command of the Hemingway short story manuscripts.

Jackson Benson's anthology, *New Critical Approaches to the Short Stories of Hemingway* (Duke University Press, 1990), brings together 28 reprinted essays and five new articles on the short stories, as well as an overview and comprehensive bibliography of Hemingway short story criticism since 1975. Benson's selections encompass a variety of current critical approaches, and advance interpretations of both individual stories and groups of stories. The volume's bibliography is exemplary, its most valuable section listing criticism, explication, and commentary by individual story. An indispensable collection of recent criticism, and an essential bibliographic tool, Benson's anthology records the significant critical trends of the last decade, and promotes the originality of future scholarship by making the best that has been thought and said easy to consult.

A Reader's Guide to the Short Stories of Ernest Hemingway and *New Critical Ap-*

proaches to the Short Stories of Ernest Hemingway provide august company for *Hemingway's Neglected Short Fiction: New Perspectives.* Yet these three very different volumes enhance one another's usefulness, promising that the 1990s will be a particularly exciting decade for the study of Hemingway's short fiction. With new background materials, new command of manuscript collections, new reference works, new compilations of criticism, new bibliographic tools, and new essays all newly available, scholars and critics of the short stories now find themselves in an especially "target-rich environment."

Today we are better equipped than ever before to begin a major reassessment of Hemingway's short fiction. The essays gathered in this anthology provide a starting point for that reassessment, offering a multiplicity of new perspectives on long-overlooked stories—stories that, once neglected, are moving toward a new critical importance even as this paperback edition is printed.

Susan F. Beegel
1991

Acknowledgments

This anthology has involved the collaboration of 26 scholars, and I am deeply grateful to them all for their willingness to share their thoughts on Hemingway's neglected short fiction, and for their confidence in this project throughout the long months leading to publication. I am grateful, too, for the Hemingway Society's continuing efforts to foster the spirit of scholarly interchange and collegiality that alone makes such ventures possible.

All Hemingway scholars owe a debt of gratitude to John, Patrick, and Gregory Hemingway for their generous and enlightened administration of their father's literary estate. Special thanks are also due to the Ernest Hemingway Foundation, for permission to quote from Hemingway's unpublished manuscripts.

Many of the essays in this collection could not have been written without the cooperation of one or more libraries with Hemingway holdings. Our thanks to the Bancroft Library, the Humanities Research Center of the University of Texas at Austin, the John Fitzgerald Kennedy Library, the Lilly Library, the Princeton University Library, and the University of Wisconsin Library.

Certain names occur repeatedly in notes to the essays in this volume—Jackson Benson, Joseph DeFalco, Joseph Flora, Sheldon Norman Grebstein, Kenneth Johnston, Michael Reynolds, Paul Smith—creating a litany of the very best in scholarship of Hemingway's short fiction. These critics have given us a firm foundation for appreciation of the Hemingway short story; we anxiously await their future additions to that appreciation.

Finally, I have some personal thank-yous to tender as well. My gratitude to Paul Smith, for his always excellent and candid editorial advice. My deepest debt of all, however, is to my husband Wes, for his unflagging support. He has given unstintingly of himself to make this book a reality. And, after all, it was his idea in the first place.

Chronology

1899	Ernest Miller Hemingway born to Clarence and Grace Hemingway on 21 July in Oak Park, Illinois.
1917	Graduates from high school. Cub reporter for the *Kansas City Star*.
1918	World War I service as ambulance driver for the American Red Cross. Wounded on 8 July on the Italian front near Fossalta di Piave. Affair with nurse Agnes von Kurowsky.
1920	Reporter for *Toronto Star*.
1921	Marriage to Hadley Richardson. Moves to Paris on Sherwood Anderson's advice.
1922	Travels to Greco-Turkish War as *Toronto Star* correspondent.
1923	*Three Stories and Ten Poems* published by Robert McAlmon in Paris. Birth of son John.
1924	*in our time*, a collection of vignettes, published in Paris by Three Mountains Press.
1925	*In Our Time*, adding fourteen short stories to the earlier vignettes, published in New York by Boni & Liveright.
1926	*The Torrents of Spring* and *The Sun Also Rises* published by Charles Scribner's Sons.
1927	Publishes short story collection, *Men Without Women*. Marries Pauline Pfeiffer after divorcing Hadley Richardson.
1928	Moves to Key West, Florida. Birth of son Patrick.
1929	Father, Dr. Clarence Edmonds Hemingway, commits suicide in Oak Park. *A Farewell to Arms* published.
1931	Birth of son Gregory.
1932	*Death in the Afternoon*.
1933	Publishes short story collection, *Winner Take Nothing*.
1935	*Green Hills of Africa*.
1937	*To Have and Have Not*. Travels as war correspondent to the Spanish Civil War.

1938   Collaborates with Joris Ivens on *The Spanish Earth*, a film espousing the Loyalist cause. Publishes *The Fifth Column and the First Forty-nine Stories*.

1940   *For Whom the Bell Tolls*. Divorces Pauline Pfeiffer, marries Martha Gellhorn. Purchases Finca Vigía in Cuba.

1942   Edits *Men at War*.

1944   Meets Mary Welsh in London. With American troops in France and Germany as World War II correspondent. Participates in Allied liberation of Paris.

1945   Divorces Martha Gellhorn.

1946   Marries Mary Welsh.

1950   *Across the River and into the Trees*.

1951   Death of mother, Grace Hall Hemingway.

1952   *The Old Man and the Sea*.

1954   Receives Nobel Prize for Literature.

1960   Moves to Ketchum, Idaho. Mounting civil violence in Cuba. Hospitalized for uncontrolled high blood pressure, liver disease, diabetes, depression.

1961   Commits suicide in Ketchum house on 2 July.

1964   *A Moveable Feast* published posthumously.

1969   *The Fifth Column and Four Stories of the Spanish Civil War*.

1970   *Islands in the Stream*.

1972   *The Nick Adams Stories*.

1985   *The Dangerous Summer*.

1986   *The Garden of Eden*.

1987   *The Complete Stories of Ernest Hemingway: The Finca Vigía Edition*.

HEMINGWAY'S

NEGLECTED SHORT FICTION

NEW PERSPECTIVES

Introduction

Susan F. Beegel

How to define neglect? A short story is most obviously neglected when the criticism it has received has been insignificant in quantity and quality. Although nearly all of the short stories treated in this volume have been mentioned in numerous biographical and critical works attempting to provide a comprehensive view of Ernest Hemingway's life and work, many of these "mentions" have been little more than passing summaries or dismissals. Lengthy books on Hemingway will tick off a neglected short story in a single phrase, or, more copiously, with a sentence or two. A few examples should suffice:

> . . . "The Capital of the World," a fine story on the athlete-dying-young theme, with a setting in Madrid, and, as leading character, a boy from Estremadura. . . . [1]

> William Campbell, the drug addict in "A Pursuit Race," refuses to come out from under his bedsheet, too terrified to face whatever unnamed reality terrifies him. [2]

> [Hemingway's] fears about losing his vision during this disease [erysipelas] led to two minor stories about blindness: "Get a Seeing-Eyed Dog" and "A Man of the World," both published in the *Atlantic* in November 1957. [3]

> In "Homage to Switzerland," he trivialized his yearnings for Hadley in three vignettes that were supposed to be funny but weren't. [4]

Gertrude Stein prided herself on having told Hemingway that "remarks are not literature," and it is difficult to see how any number of remarks like those listed above can constitute significant critical literature on a story. [5] By this definition, then, a short story that has been very much "remarked on" but never analyzed in depth, a story with a bibliography like that below, may still be very much neglected.

A Day's Wait

Atkins, pp. 144–45.
Baker *(Artist)*, p. 134.
Baker *(Life)*, pp. 236, 246.
Bakker, pp. 40, 252.
DeFalco, pp. 53–54.
Dolch, pp. 104–5.
Flora, pp. 215–24.
Grebstein, pp. 8–10.
Hays, p. 25.
Hovey, pp. 43–44.
Killinger, p. 25.
Mahoney, item 18.
Shepherd, pp. 37–39.
Waldhorn, pp. 70–71.
Young, p. 286n.[6]

Despite the apparent length of the bibliography, no single critic, with the exception of Joseph Flora, has devoted more than two pages of consideration to this story, and 14 critics have produced a scant 21 pages among them— barely an essay.

Other stories defined as neglected for the purposes of this volume may have received an essay's-worth or so of attention. When such essays are themselves negligible, they add nothing to and may even detract from the critical stature of the stories they treat. Yet several of the stories repre- sented here have had the benefit of at least one excellent commentary, providing a system of interpretation that fully engages the work, makes a powerful case for its importance, and raises vital questions for future critics to address. I think particularly of essays like Robert Scholes's "Decoding Papa" on "A Very Short Story," Kenneth Johnston's "'Wine of Wyoming': Disappointment in America," Robert Fleming's "Perversion and the Writer in 'The Sea Change,'" and Paul Smith's "Some Misconceptions of 'Out of Season.'" Yet until now few if any critics have stepped forward to answer the challenges posed by these and other solitary fine essays on Hemingway short stories. And until seminal criticism engenders new growth, the work it treats may still be considered neglected.

By these definitions, a surprisingly large number of Hemingway's short stories are neglected. This volume contains 25 new essays treating more than 30 individual works, or about one-quarter of the author's entire output of short fiction, which Jackson Benson has estimated at 109 stories.[7] How- ever, many additional neglected stories must, of necessity, remain ne- glected here. For example, "After the Storm," "The Mother of a Queen," "Old Man at the Bridge," "A Canary for One," "Che Ti Dice La Patria?" and "One Reader Writes," stories available for more than 50 years as part of *The First Forty-nine Stories* collection are, sadly, among the missing. Missing too are the recently collected stories "The Good Lion," "The Faithful Bull," and "Nobody Ever Dies," as well as the Nick Adams stories "Summer People" and "The Last Good Country," resurrected by Philip Young from the Hemingway manuscripts in 1972. Nor does this anthology include consideration of stories like "I Guess Everything Reminds You of Something," "Black Ass at the Crossroads," and "Great News from the Mainland," posthumously published in 1987, or of still-unpublished stories like "A Lack of Passion," "A Room on the Garden Side," or "Indian Country and the White Army." In short, close to 50 percent of Hemingway's short fiction actually suffers from critical neglect, a sizable problem that this volume can only begin to address.

It is an odd state of affairs when one can enumerate so many neglected short stories by an author not particularly prolific of short stories—F. Scott Fitzgerald outpublished Hemingway in the genre by almost two-to-one— odder still when the author is universally acknowledged as a master of the form.[8] Many consider oft-criticized stories like "Big Two-Hearted River," "The Killers," "A Clean, Well-Lighted Place," "The Short Happy Life of Francis Macomber," "The Snows of Kilimanjaro," and *The Old Man and the Sea* among the best in American literature,[9] worthy to be ranked with Nathaniel Hawthorne's "Young Goodman Brown," Edgar Allan Poe's "The Fall of the House of Usher," Henry James's "The Turn of the Screw," Stephen Crane's "The Open Boat," and F. Scott Fitzgerald's "Babylon Revisited." The popular reputation of Hemingway's short fiction is, if anything, greater than its critical reputation. The phrase "a clean, well-lighted place" has become part of the English language like many a Shakespearean phrase before it, and doubtless as many American schoolchildren have read Hemingway's *The Old Man and the Sea* as Twain's "The Celebrated Jumping Frog of Calaveras County" or O. Henry's "The Gift of the Magi."

Dorothy Parker represents many readers who feel that Hemingway was principally gifted as a writer of short stories: "Mr. Hemingway's style, this prose stripped to its firm young bones, is far more effective, far more moving, in the short story than in the novel. He is, to me, the greatest living writer of short stories; he is also to me, not the greatest living novelist."[10] Harold Bloom agrees:

> Vignette is Hemingway's natural mode, or call it hard-edged vignette: a literary sketch that somehow seems to be the beginning or end of something longer, yet truly is complete in itself. . . . Much that has been harshly criticized in Hemingway . . . results from his difficulty in adjusting his gifts to the demands of the novel.[11]

Even those who believe that Hemingway's reputation must rest on his achievement as a novelist should concede that the short story was the crucible in which his celebrated style was formed. According to the author's personal mythology, he progressed from "one true sentence" to stories like "Up in Michigan," "Out of Season," and "My Old Man" as well as the *in our time* vignettes, revealing himself, like Jane Austen with her "little bit (two Inches wide) of Ivory," to be principally an artist of miniatures.[12]

Hemingway approached the writing of his first novel with dragging feet, perceiving it as an obligation to be fulfilled if he was to establish a literary reputation, an obligation at odds with his hard-won but still unrecognized achievement in the short story form:

> I knew I must write a novel. But it seemed an impossible thing to do when I had been trying with great difficulty to write paragraphs that would be the distillation of what made a novel. . . . I would put it off though until I could not help doing it. I was damned if I would write one because it was what I should do if we were to eat regularly. When I had to write it, then it would be the only thing to do and there would be no choice. Let the pressure build.[13]

The pressure did build. First, Maxwell Perkins wrote to express his admiration for the *in our time* vignettes, but added:

> I doubt if we could have seen a way to the publication of this book itself on account of material considerations: it is so small that it would give the booksellers no opportunity for substantial profit. . . . This is a pity, because your method is obviously one which enables you to express what you have to say in a very small compass.[14]

At almost the same time, George Doran rejected the longer *In Our Time* on similar grounds:

> Mr. Doran did not want to give the public a (with an initial) series of shocks in short stories altho he would be glad to do so in a novel and if I would write a novel they could publish this book as a second book, etc. All of which shows that publishing is a business and books of short stories are believed not to be saleable.[15]

Next, Horace Liveright accepted *In Our Time*, in the false hope of securing Hemingway's first novel by means of an option clause. Nevertheless, Hemingway could write to Perkins, who was also hoping to acquire a novel, that:

> Somehow I don't care about writing a novel and I like to write short stories . . . so I guess I'm a bad prospect for a publisher anyway. Somehow the novel seems to me an awfully artificial and worked out form but as some of the short stories are now stretching out to 8,000 to 12,000 words, maybe I'll get there yet.[16]

When the revolutionary short stories of *In Our Time* earned high praise from F. Scott Fitzgerald, Edmund Wilson, Ford Madox Ford, and Ezra Pound, as well as claims that "Hemingway's first novel might rock the country," when Alfred Knopf and Harcourt, Brace, and World joined in vying with Boni & Liveright and Charles Scribner's Sons for the right to publish that novel, sight unseen, there was no longer any choice.[17] *The Sun Also Rises*, composed "during two concentrated and intensely creative months" in 1925, was the result.[18] The novel *did* rock the country, perhaps in part because it was a novel by a writer whose natural mode was vignette. On first reading the manuscript in May 1926, Perkins observed to Fitzgerald that, "When you think of Hemingway's book you recall scenes as if they were memories—glorious ones of Spain, & fishing in a cold river, & bull-fights, all full of life and color; and you recall people as hard & actual as real ones. That is the way you remember the book."[19] More than 60 years later, at least one contemporary critic is still echoing Perkins's initial judgment, "*The Sun Also Rises* reads now as a series of epiphanies, of brilliant and memorable vignettes."[20]

To understand why Hemingway's short stories are neglected, one must first understand that the genre itself is often neglected in favor of the novel. The recent *Columbia Literary History of the United States*, for example, surveys developments in "poetry, drama, criticism, and the novel" without recognizing the short story as a genre.[21] Turning to the *1987 MLA International Bibliography*, we find 28 essays on 6 novels by Hemingway, but only 12 essays on 15 of his short stories. The same volume shows 21 essays on 4 novels by Nathaniel Hawthorne, versus 21 essays on 14 short stories; 39 essays on 5 novels by Mark Twain, versus 1 essay on a single story; 7 essays on 2 novels by Stephen Crane, versus 1 essay on a single story; and 6 essays on 2 novels by F. Scott Fitzgerald, versus 2 essays on 2 short stories. While these writers were powerful novelists, they were strong short story writers as well, and the relative numbers of essays do not reflect either the quantity or quality of their efforts in short fiction. Edgar Allan Poe's reputation, on the other hand, rests almost entirely on his talent as a short story writer. He wrote only one novel, the incomplete and derivative *Narrative of Arthur Gordon Pym of Nantucket*. Yet the *1987 MLA International Bibliography* shows 3 essays on *Pym* versus 21 essays on 13 short stories. With the exception of "The Fall of the House of Usher," no single short story by Poe attracted more than half as much critical attention as his lone novel.

Why does the academy thus undervalue the genre in which Hemingway most excelled, the genre that was the spawning ground of his novels? Hemingway's struggle to break into commercial publishing suggests that critical neglect of the short story may have something to do with the exigencies of the literary marketplace. The ivory tower's neglect of the short story may be symptomatic of its infection with commercial values, with the notion that bigger is always better, or at least more profitable. As Perkins, Doran, Knopf, and Liveright each strove to tell Hemingway in their various ways, virtually any novel is more profitable than the most excellent and ground-breaking collection of short fiction. Short story collections are generally shorter than novels—*In Our Time, Men Without Women,* and *Winner Take Nothing,* for instance, all fit comfortably between the covers of *For Whom the Bell Tolls*—and are therefore more expensive to print and more difficult to market at an attractive price, a daunting prospect for anyone funding a publishing venture. The reasons why the term "blockbuster," originally "a bomb capable of destroying a city block," has become synonymous in our culture with "bestseller," the reasons why Sidney Sheldon and Danielle Steel are so commercially successful, are the reasons why publishers actively discourage short story collections by authors who have not first achieved a bestselling novel. Dorothy Parker describes the syndrome:

> Any bookseller will be glad to tell you, in his interesting *argot,* that "short stories don't go." People take up a book of short stories and say, "Oh, what's this? Just a lot of those short things?" and put it right down again. Only yesterday afternoon, at four o'clock sharp, I saw and heard a woman do just that to Ernest Hemingway's new book, *Men Without Women.* She had been one of those most excited about his novel. Literature, it appears, is here measured by a yardstick.[22]

In addition to this general contempt for the genre, there are other, more particular reasons for critical neglect of more than half of Hemingway's short stories. To begin, 50 years after the publication of *The Fifth Column and the First Forty-nine Stories,* we still have no definitive, complete edition of Hemingway's short fiction. Macmillan's 1987 anthology, the so-called Finca Vigía edition of *The Complete Short Stories of Ernest Hemingway,* is not the answer. Far from complete, it contains unannotated and unreliable texts of less than 60 percent of Hemingway's actual short story output, while presenting heavily edited fragments of unpublished novels as short stories. To date, we lack a carefully researched and edited text that collects and arranges in chronological order of their composition all of Hemingway's efforts in the genre, both previously published and otherwise.

Inaccessibility, then, is one cause of neglect. As of this writing, as many as 15 Hemingway short stories, or fragments of short stories, remain unpublished. Only during the last year or so, while the present volume was in progress, did changes in the executorship of Hemingway's literary estate permit photocopying of manuscripts in the John Fitzgerald Kennedy Library's extensive Hemingway collection. Prior to this decision, only those researchers with the funds to travel to Boston, the dedication to copy manuscripts by hand, and the luck to be granted permission to cite them in scholarly publications (or the daring to pirate them) have been able to produce studies of Hemingway's unpublished short fiction. Such studies have been few, and his unpublished short stories remain neglected by definition.

Uncollected works are almost as inaccessible and therefore nearly as neglected as unpublished works. Few critics, for instance, are willing to rummage in back files of *Double Dealer*—if their libraries possess back files of *Double Dealer*—to produce an article on "A Divine Gesture" for readers who have never seen the story and are not likely to see it. If "Big Two-Hearted River" had never been collected, had never made it out of the little magazine, *This Quarter*, there is no doubt it would be a neglected, if not virtually unknown short story today. Critical essays find only as many readers as the literature they treat.

While posthumously published anthologies like *The Nick Adams Stories* and the Finca Vigía edition have eased the problem of inaccessibility a great deal by making a number of previously unpublished or uncollected short stories more widely available, they have introduced another problem—the unauthoritative text. The silently and carelessly edited posthumous Hemingway books that Scribner's produced, for quick sale to an unwitting general public rather than to meet rigorous scholarly standards, contain a number of pitfalls for the unwary. "Summer People" is a case in point. In the version printed in *The Nick Adams Stories,* Nick stands up after making love to Kate in rough blankets beneath the hemlocks and says, "You've got to get dressed, slut."[23] The story's manuscripts reveal that the insult is a typesetter's misreading of the heroine's nickname—"Stut." According to Paul Smith, the Finca Vigía edition corrects this egregious error but does not replace the entire page of text accidentally or deliberately dropped from "Summer People" in *The Nick Adams Stories.*[24] Because Hemingway scholarship lacks conscientiously edited texts of such stories, the responsible researcher cannot approach them without a great deal of spadework among the manuscripts and proofs, a necessity that discourages study.

Unpublished, uncollected, unauthoritative. The words alone indicate why it is so easy to neglect some stories. After all, Hemingway himself chose not to publish or collect them, to lend his countenance to their first or continued appearance in print. A usually exacting craftsman, one who accused Fitzgerald of "whoring," of publishing slick magazine stories for the money alone, the young Hemingway would withhold the still unpublished "A Lack of Passion" because it "wasn't good enough" and "wouldn't come right."[25] The aging Hemingway, with lucrative magazine offers readily available and ever-increasing financial obligations, occasionally lowered his standards, as he accused Fitzgerald of doing, to publish embarrassments like "The Good Lion" in *Holiday* or "Nobody Ever Dies" in *Cosmopolitan*. However, he did not compound the offense by anthologizing such material, and seems to have retained a lifelong distinction between stories that were worthy of permanent preservation in hardcover collections and stories that were good enough only for ephemeral appearance in magazines. Such stories may, arguably, deserve comparative neglect. Their chief value seems to reside in the light they shed on Hemingway's development as an artist, the background they provide for understanding his more important work.

The truly difficult question before us, however, and the one this volume makes the most strenuous effort to answer, is why solid Hemingway stories available for more than 50 years should still be neglected today. First, it is important to remember that, given what Norman Mailer has called the necrophilia of critics, an author cannot be canonized until he is dead, and Hemingway has been dead only 27 years.[26] Despite the popular recognition early granted him, his acceptance by literary salons during his youth, and even his anointment by the Nobel Prize Committee and the academy in his declining years, Hemingway's reputation has not been immune from the process of canonization after his death. The conservative pace of that process may be partly responsible for the neglect of more than half of his short fiction.

While the living artist may be the object of savage critical attack, the dead artist destined for canonization quickly becomes the object of almost religious veneration. As Mailer would have it, critics "murder their writers, and then decorate their graves."[27] Hemingway himself commented wryly on this phenomenon in *Death in the Afternoon:*

> Joselito was admitted to be very good in the press, but it was pointed out that he was only able to place banderillas on one side, the right (the bulls of course were very small), he insisted on that; that he killed holding the sword so high that some said he pulled it out of his hat . . . and . . . he was hooted, whistled at and had cushions thrown at him the last day he fought in Madrid. . . . The next day . . . he was killed at Talavera de la Reina . . . and at once became in the press, and remains, the greatest bullfighter of all time.[28]

Canonization by definition requires hagiography, the writing of worshipful or idealizing criticism. A savage attack on a living artist is, after all, only a bad review. But dead authors are not reviewed, they are "interpreted" in academic essays, where savage treatment can call into question the raison d'être of the essay itself. Without tradition, custom, or usage to justify their interest in an author undergoing canonization, critics tend to spend a great deal of time validating the author's worth.

That validation seems to require demonstration of an artist's moral values, his participation in the humanistic traditions of Western culture, in the values of Greek and Latin antiquity that have led us, over the centuries, to call canonized works "classics." Here is John Silber, president of Boston University, addressing the Greek Orthodox Diocese of North and South America on "Our Hellenic Heritage":

> When we recognize that all men, rich and poor alike, face essentially the same end—that is, that all of us die—and that the problems posed by higher religion and by ethical systems have been those of seeing how defeat can be transformed into victory through a variety of spiritual and moral movements, we will confront religion and ethics in a profoundly different light; in the light of the humanities.[29]

Silber's address could easily be an early work of Hemingway criticism, for example, Arthur Waldhorn discoursing on *The Old Man and the Sea:*

> *The Old Man and the Sea* is . . . a story about the inevitable doom facing all "joined by the necessity of killing and being killed." Doom is not, in Hemingway's vision, to be identified with defeat. All creatures share doom. Knowing this breeds humility in man, the reverence Santiago feels for the marlin alive and dead. Defeat means yielding to doom without a struggle, abandoning, in effect, the pride that makes it worthwhile to be a man. "You killed him for pride and because you are a fisherman," Santiago says. He kills, then, because not to do so would have meant defeat, and "man is not made for defeat. A man can be destroyed but not defeated."[30]

Waldhorn's Santiago belongs with Silber's "heroes of Homer," asking "along with St. Paul, 'O death, where is thy sting? O grave where is thy victory?'"[31]

The Old Man and the Sea is, by such conventional definitions, Hemingway's most obviously classic work. It is no accident that this novella or long short story should have precipitated Hemingway's Nobel Prize, Western culture's most distinguished literary award, itself a promise of canonization, given only to authors who produce works of "ideal tendencies."[32] Witness the profoundly moral language of Hemingway's Nobel Prize citation, which praises the author for overcoming the "brutal, callous, and cynical" tendencies of his early career to produce a literature of "heroic pathos," distinguished by its "natural admiration for every individual who fights the good fight in a world of reality overshadowed by violence and death."[33]

Similar moral language pervades the years of Hemingway biography and criticism immediately following the author's death, as if critics were striving to erase the Nobel committee's apparent doubts about the author's wholehearted participation in the canonical business of "affirming life."[34] Hemingway the man was first and foremost a wounded veteran of World

War I, returning in his art again and again to the scene of his battle trauma, seeking control of a fear of his own mortality learned in the harshest possible way. Hemingway's great theme was courage, an existential courage emphasizing the importance of living with dignity in the face of a hostile or indifferent universe, of taking responsibility for one's smallest actions, and of "holding tight" in the face of death. For such critics, Hemingway's fiction is full of "code heroes" who practice these values: Ole Andreson calmly awaiting his assassins, Nick Adams counting the beads of wilderness rituals to ward off whatever "tragedy" awaits him in the swamp of memory, the old man seeking a clean, well-lighted place against the night, Francis Macomber finding the courage to confront a charging Cape buffalo, Harry reassuring his wife that death is "very easy" and "a bore," Santiago insisting that "a man can be destroyed but not defeated." It is a world of "tutors" and "tyros" as well, where Ole Andreson instructs Nick, Nick instructs his sons, the old waiter instructs the young waiter, Wilson instructs Macomber, Harry instructs his wife, and Santiago instructs Manolin in the all-important art of "holding tight."

Such theorizing provides an extremely important and compelling view of Hemingway's life and work and has been essential to his canonization, identifying as it does so well the locus of ethical experience in his fiction. If, as John Steinbeck has observed, it is true that "Great writing has been a staff to lean on, a mother to consult, a wisdom to pick up stumbling folly, a strength in weakness, and a courage to support sick cowardice. And how any negative or despairing approach can pretend to be literature I do not know,"[35] then perhaps "The Killers," "Big Two-Hearted River," "A Clean, Well-Lighted Place," "The Short Happy Life of Francis Macomber," "The Snows of Kilimanjaro," and *The Old Man and the Sea,* at least as we have interpreted them to date, deserve their exalted rank in the pantheon of American short stories.

Yet such ideas have been a Procrustean bed for Hemingway's fiction in the hands of less adept critics who have striven to cut all of his stories to fit this model or discarded them in frustration when they refused to fit. Here we have a major reason for the neglect of many important and long-available short stories. Who is the code hero in "Out of Season," "Wine of Wyoming," "A Natural History of the Dead," "Alpine Idyll," "Get a Seeing-Eyed Dog"? Who is the tutor and who the tyro in "Up in Michigan," "Mr. and Mrs. Elliot," "A Simple Enquiry," "The Mother of a Queen," "The Sea Change"? What values are being taught? Where is the theme of courage and holding tight in *The Torrents of Spring* and "Homage to Switzerland"? Such short stories have been neglected because they do not fit the heroic paradigms we have created, the ethical models we have produced to canonize Hemingway's work and validate our own criticism.

Recent events, however, suggest that Hemingway's canonization is at last complete. In the years following her husband's death, Mary Hemingway, in consultation with Charles Scribner's Sons, refused to contemplate publication of "anything that would risk reduction of the author's stature."[36] Of late, however, as Mary's long, final illness and death in November 1986 deprived Scribner's of her guidance, the firm has apparently come to feel that Hemingway's stature is secure enough to sustain publication of anything—no matter how unorthodox, unfinished, and unrevised. While the first 24 years after Hemingway's death saw the publication of just six posthumous volumes—*A Moveable Feast* (1964), *By-Line: Ernest Hemingway* (1967), *The Fifth Column and Four Stories of the Spanish Civil War* (1969), *Islands in the Stream* (1970), *The Nick Adams Stories* (1972), and *Ernest Hemingway: Selected Letters* (1981)—or one book every four years, in the last two years Scribner's has hastily published four books by Hemingway: *The Dangerous Summer* (1985), *Dateline: Toronto* (1985), *The Garden of Eden* (1986), and *The Complete Short Stories* (1987).

Publication of *The Garden of Eden,* in particular, has prompted a swing in the critical pendulum, suggesting that the academy now joins Charles Scribner's Sons in feeling that Hemingway is sufficiently secure on his pedestal to withstand public exposure of his art's less than ideal tendencies. Perhaps because it is a novel, the posthumous *Garden of Eden* has forced critics to confront for the first time themes of homosexuality, perversion, and androgyny present throughout Hemingway's career in short stories like "Mr. and Mrs. Elliot," "A Simple Enquiry," "The Sea Change," and "The Mother of a Queen," widely available for at least 50 years. Suddenly, and with little sense of irony, critics are struggling to reconcile the well-known novelist of

> In the late summer of that year we lived in a house in a village that looked across the river and the plain to the mountains. In the bed of the river there were pebbles and boulders, dry and white in the sun, and the water was clear and swiftly moving and blue in the channels. Troops went by the house and down the road and the dust they raised powdered the leaves of the trees. The trunks of the trees too were dusty and the leaves fell early that year and we saw the troops marching along the road and the dust rising and leaves, stirred by the breeze, falling and the soldiers marching and afterward the road bare and white except for the leaves.[37]

with the newly discovered novelist of

> He had shut his eyes and he could feel the long light weight of her on him and her breasts pressing against him and her lips on his. He lay there and felt something and then her hand holding him and searching lower and he helped with his hands and then lay

back in the dark and did not think at all and only felt the weight and the strangeness inside and she said, "Now you can't tell who's who can you?"

"No."

"You are changing," she said. "Oh you are. You are. Yes you are and you're my girl Catherine. Will you change and be my girl and let me take you?"[38]

as they have never struggled to reconcile the heavily promoted short story writer of

Holding the muleta, with the sword in his left hand widening it in front of him, he called to the bull.

The bull looked at him.

He leaned back insultingly and shook the wide-spread flannel.

The bull saw the muleta. It was a bright scarlet under the arc-light. The bull's legs tightened.

Here he comes. Whoosh! Manuel turned as the bull came and raised the muleta so that it passed over the bull's horns and swept down his broad back from head to tail. The bull had gone clean up into the air with the charge. Manuel had not moved.[39]

with the long-neglected short story writer of

Elliot had taken to drinking white wine and lived apart in his own room. He wrote a great deal of poetry during the night and in the morning looked very exhausted. Mrs. Elliot and the girl friend now slept together in the big mediaeval bed. They had many a good cry together. In the evening they all sat at dinner together in the garden under a plane tree and the hot evening wind blew and Elliot drank white wine and Mrs. Elliot and the girl friend made conversation and they were all quite happy.[40]

Publication of *The Garden of Eden* has performed at least one service for Hemingway's neglected short fiction—the *inaccrochable* is no longer *inaccrochable;* in fact, it is rather fashionable.[41] Critics need no longer shun with distaste stories about "those whose sexual inclinations are aberrant."[42] Yet instead of encouraging a broader vision of Hemingway's art that might incorporate its full diversity, the novel has, at least temporarily, merely prompted a critical shift from hagiography to iconoclasm and a new, nearly prurient interest in Hemingway's life. Instead of pursuing the old machismo-oriented criticism that made Hemingway the poet laureate of courage and manliness and his women characters "divine lollipop[s]," the latest critical fashion is to view Hemingway himself as a "divine lollipop," smother-loved in flowered bonnet and ruffled baby dress, and his women characters as surrogate mothers dispensing "erotic privileges" to male protagonists.[43] *The Garden of Eden* has created a school of Hemingway criticism heavily indebted to Max Eastman's savage 1934 review, "Bull in the Afternoon," where everything the author ever wrote about courage and *pundonor* becomes "a wearing of false hair on the chest."[44]

One would at least expect Kenneth Lynn, Hemingway's most contro- versial biographer and the best-known practitioner of the new school with its psychosexual emphasis, to turn to long-neglected stories like "Mr. and Mrs. Elliot," "A Simple Enquiry," "The Sea Change," and "The Mother of a Queen," where he might ostensibly discover something about Heming- way's very real interest in homosexuality and androgyny. Perhaps it is an index of how pervasive patterns of neglect have become that Lynn has chosen instead to pursue such themes through canonical short stories or not at all. "Big Two-Hearted River" is now about a boy "being thrown out of his parents' summer cottage," "Snows of Kilimanjaro" about Grace Heming- way's "ancient criticism" to "'stop trading on your handsome face, to fool little gullible girls, and neglecting your duty to God and your Saviour Jesus Christ,'" and "The Killers" about Hemingway's resentment at having been dressed as his sister Marcelline's twin during babyhood.[45]

Big two-hearted fiction, ranging from

> He took all his pain and what was left of his strength and his long gone pride and he put it against the fish's agony and the fish came over onto his side and swam gently on his side, his bill almost touching the planking of the skiff and started to pass the boat, long, deep, wide, silver and barred with purple and interminable in the water.[46]

to

> He dreamed that Tom's mother was sleeping with him and she was sleeping on top of him as she liked to do sometimes. He felt all of this and the tangibility of her legs against his legs and her body against his and her breasts against his chest and her mouth was playing against his mouth. Her hair hung down and lay heavy and silky on his eyes and on his cheeks and he turned his lips away from her searching ones and took the hair in his mouth and held it. Then with one hand he moistened the .357 Magnum and slipped it easily and sound asleep where it should be. Then he lay under her weight with her silken hair over his face like a curtain and moved slowly and rhythmically.[47]

It is not surprising that Hemingway criticism itself has been equally two- hearted, swinging from hagiography to iconoclasm. Yet no single critical approach, no unified theory of this author's life and work, can encompass the emotional range of his art or reduce the complexity of its vision to readily comprehensible slogans. Both Hemingway's life, which has achieved the status of myth, and his fiction, too often interpreted in the light of that mythic life, deliberately resist closure and consensus. Perhaps the best Hemingway criticism should do so as well.

There is a small body of diverse and worthwhile criticism on Heming- way's short stories between the extremes of hagiography and iconoclasm. Paul Smith, in his "Critical Essays on the Short Stories, 1976–1988," cites several recent books and a handful of essays "that promise to re-orient . . . criticism of the stories."[48] He records how the opening of the author's manuscripts and the adoption of poststructuralist approaches have refreshed critical perspectives on Hemingway's canonical short fiction. Yet Smith is quick to point out that "recent criticism of the stories has often repeated, or, at best, inched forward the criticism of the previous two decades," and that "a winnowing review of the critical articles since 1975 to find those that have advanced Hemingway criticism of the stories into the 1980s or considered previously neglected works leaves less than one might expect."[49]

Two forthcoming books, slated for publication in 1989, should make significant contributions to the tentative reassessment of Hemingway's short fiction begun in the last few years. Jackson Benson is currently enlarging his 1975 compendium of criticism on the short stories and updating its comprehensive bibliography. Paul Smith's *A Reader's Guide to the Short Stories of Ernest Hemingway* will contain a chapter on each of the 55 stories published in Hemingway's lifetime, treating the sources of the story, its composition, publication, and critical history. His book, like Benson's, will indicate new directions for study and greatly contribute to the ease of pursuing them.[50]

To these two efforts, this anthology adds 25 new, never-before-published essays covering more than 30 neglected stories. The stories treated span the author's career, from an apprentice fiction ("The Mercenaries," 1919) to his last short story ("A Man of the World," 1957), with the largest number drawn from the 1920s and 1930s to give proportionate emphasis to Hemingway's most productive years in the genre. The stories treated also represent a broad spectrum of problems with neglect. Some have been ignored because they are intensely experimental ("Homage to Switzerland," "A Natural History of the Dead," the bullfighting vignettes), some because of their grotesque subject matter ("Alpine Idyll," "The Mother of a Queen"), some because of persistent biographical misreadings ("Out of Season," "Mr. and Mrs. Elliot"), some because their context has been inadequately understood ("Banal Story," the Spanish Civil War stories, *The Torrents of Spring*), some because their manuscripts have only recently become accessible ("A Very Short Story"), some because they do not fit stereotypical views of Hemingway's major themes ("A Day's Wait," "Wine of Wyoming," "The Capital of the World"), some because they have just been published ("The Mercenaries," "On Writing," "African Story"), and some because they have just been collected ("Get a Seeing-Eyed Dog" and "A Man of the World"). The neglect of a handful ("Light of the World," "Up in Michigan," "A Pursuit Race") seems entirely arbitrary.

Readers will find a wide array of critical approaches represented here. Although Hemingway traditionally does not attract theorists, some of these essays bring the techniques of Continental linguistics, Marxism, deconstruction, metafiction, psychoanalysis, and semiotics to bear on the fiction. Others use the more conventional approaches of biographical, textual, contextual, thematic, and source study to illuminate stories, appropriate as some of these works are so neglected that they have never had the benefit of even a close reading until now.

This volume's goal, then, is not to construct a conveniently holistic but necessarily reductive single view of the life and work through the neglected short fiction. Rather, it is to use these short stories, stories neglected for years precisely because they defy facile interpretations, as avenues for exploring the many complexities of Hemingway's art. While the careful reader will find a number of patterns emerging to unite these essays and the stories they treat, the 25 different points of view represented here may sometimes challenge or even contradict one another. Individually, these scholars have made Hemingway's neglected short stories yield fresh meaning; collectively, they have defied consensus and closure as vigorously as the fictions they discuss. This multiplicity of new perspectives on Hemingway's neglected short fiction should broaden, rather than narrow, our appreciation of his art, just as it should expand, rather than contract, our canon of his oft-criticized short stories.

In *Death in the Afternoon,* Hemingway wrote, "[the whore] wouldn't have anything to do with the dwarf, he was full size except that his legs were only six inches long, and he said 'I'm a man like any man,' and the whore said 'No you're not and that's the trouble.'"[51] Like the dwarf, the neglected short stories discussed here are full size except that they are told in fewer words. Truncated, grotesque, freakish, even sexually abnormal, these are not stories like any stories, and that's the trouble. Yet their trouble is also their unique interest. Perhaps it is time criticism abandoned a squeamish insistence on physical and moral conformity in literature and embraced Hemingway's dwarves.

Notes

1. Carlos Baker, *Hemingway: The Writer as Artist,* 4th edn. (Princeton: Princeton UP, 1972) 149.

2. Arthur Waldhorn, *A Reader's Guide to Ernest Hemingway* (New York: Farrar, Straus and Giroux, 1972) 22.

3. Jeffrey Meyers, *Hemingway: A Biography* (New York: Harper & Row, 1985) 439.

4. Kenneth S. Lynn, *Hemingway* (New York: Simon and Schuster, 1987) 410.

5. Gertrude Stein, *The Autobiography of Alice B. Toklas* (1933), in *Selected Writings of Gertrude Stein,* ed. Carl Van Vechten (New York: Vintage, 1962) 207.

6. This bibliography of criticism on "A Day's Wait" has been compiled from bibliographies by Jackson J. Benson, ed., *The Short Stories of Ernest Hemingway: Critical Essays* (Durham: Duke UP, 1975) and Paul Smith, *A Reader's Guide to the Short Stories of Ernest Hemingway* (Boston: G. K. Hall, 1989). Its sole purpose is to indicate at a glance how little attention this short story has received. For complete references to the works indicated, see the collected bibliography that concludes this volume.

7. Benson, 332–75.

8. Jackson Bryer, introd., *The Short Stories of F. Scott Fitzgerald: New Approaches in Criticism* (Madison: U of Wisconsin P, 1982) xi-xii.

9. Because Hemingway himself regarded *The Old Man and the Sea* as a "very long" short story rather than a novella, I will follow suit for the purposes of this volume. See Ernest Hemingway to Maxwell Perkins, 7 Feb. 1939, in *Ernest Hemingway: Selected Letters, 1917–1961*, ed. Carlos Baker (New York: Charles Scribner's Sons, 1981) 478–79.

10. Dorothy Parker, "A Book of Great Short Stories" (1927), in *The Portable Dorothy Parker* (New York: Penguin, 1978) 460.

11. Harold Bloom, introd. *Ernest Hemingway's* The Sun Also Rises: *Modern Critical Interpretations* (New York: Chelsea House, 1987) 4.

12. Jane Austen to J. Edward Austen, 16 December 1816, in *Jane Austen: Letters, 1796–1817*, ed. R.W. Chapman (London: Oxford UP, 1975) 189.

13. Hemingway, *A Moveable Feast* (New York: Charles Scribner's Sons, 1964) 76.

14. In A. Scott Berg, *Max Perkins: Editor of Genius* (New York: Pocket Books, 1978) 109.

15. Hemingway to Gertrude Stein and Alice B. Toklas, 20 January 1925, in *Letters*, 147.

16. Hemingway to Perkins, 15 April 1925, in *Letters*, 156.

17. See Carlos Baker, *Ernest Hemingway: A Life Story* (New York: Charles Scribner's Sons, 1969) and Scott Donaldson, "The Wooing of Ernest Hemingway," *American Literature* 53.4 (January 1984): 695.

18. William Balassi, "The Writing of *The Sun Also Rises*, with a Chart of Its Session-by-Session Development," *The Hemingway Review* 6.1 (Fall 1986): 65.

19. Perkins to Fitzgerald, in Donaldson, 703.

20. Bloom, 4.

21. Emory Elliott, introd., *The Columbia Literary History of the United States* (New York: Columbia UP, 1988) xxi.

22. Parker, 459.

23. Hemingway, "Summer People," in *The Nick Adams Stories* (New York: Charles Scribner's Sons, 1972) 227–28.

24. Conversation with Paul Smith. 7 September 1988.

25. See Hemingway, *A Moveable Feast*, 155; *Death in the Afternoon* (New York: Charles Scribner's Sons, 1932) 273; and to Perkins, 17 August 1927, Princeton University Library.

26. Norman Mailer, "First Advertisement for Myself" (1959), in *The Long Patrol: 25 Years of Writing from the Work of Norman Mailer,* ed. Robert F. Lucid (New York: World, 1971) 160.

27. Mailer, 160.

28. Hemingway, *Death in the Afternoon,* 242–43.

29. John R. Silber, "Our Hellenic Heritage," *Bostonia* 62.6 (November–December 1988): 29.

30. Waldhorn, 192–93.

31. Silber, 29.

32. Baker, *Life,* 528.

33. In Baker, *Life,* 528.

34. Norman Mailer shares such doubts, finding the affirmative qualities of *The Old Man and the Sea* fraudulent. In "First Advertisement for Myself," Mailer writes:

    > As a capsule criticism: *The Old Man and the Sea* is cheered for being an affirmative work, a triumph of the human spirit, etc., etc. But a work of affirmation must contain its moment of despair—specifically, there must be a bad moment when the old man Santiago is tempted to cut the line and let the big fish go. Hemingway avoided the problem by never letting the old man be seriously tempted. Like a giant (but not like a man) Santiago just hung onto the fish—perhaps he knew that *Life* magazine was going to provide him with all the affirmation he needed.

35. John Steinbeck, *Journal of a Novel: The* East of Eden *Letters* (New York: Viking, 1969) 115–16.

36. Philip Young and Charles W. Mann, *The Hemingway Manuscripts: An Inventory* (University Park: Pennsylvania State UP, 1969) ix.

37. Hemingway, *A Farewell to Arms* (New York: Charles Scribner's Sons, 1929) 3.

38. Hemingway, *The Garden of Eden* (New York: Charles Scribner's Sons, 1986) 17.

39. Hemingway, "The Undefeated," *The Short Stories of Ernest Hemingway* (New York: Charles Scribner's Sons, 1966) 258.

40. Hemingway, "Mr. and Mrs. Elliot," *Short Stories,* 164.

41. Of course, *inaccrochable* is Gertrude Stein's famous adjective for the censorable "Up in Michigan." "'It's good,' she said. 'That isn't the question at all. But it is *inaccrochable.* That means it is like a picture that a painter paints and then he cannot hang it when he has a show and nobody will buy it because of course they cannot hang it either.'" In Hemingway, *A Moveable Feast,* 15.

42. Waldhorn, 228.

43. Francis Hackett coined the "divine lollipop" phrase to describe Catherine Barkley in "Hemingway: *A Farewell to Arms,*" *Saturday Review of Literature* (6 August 1949): 32–33. See Lynn, 387 on "erotic privileges."

44. Max Eastman, "Bull in the Afternoon" (1934), in *Ernest Hemingway: The Man and His Work,* ed. John K. M. McCaffery (New York: Cooper Square, 1969) 71.

45. Lynn, 103, 430, 112.

46. Hemingway, *The Old Man and the Sea* (New York: Charles Scribner's Sons, 1952) 94.

47. Hemingway, *Islands in the Stream* (New York: Charles Scribner's Sons, 1970) 343–44.

48. Paul Smith, "A Partial Review: Critical Essays on the Short Stories, 1976–1988," in *The Short Stories of Ernest Hemingway: Critical Essays,* ed. Jackson Benson, rev. edn. (Durham: Duke UP, forthcoming).

49. Smith, n.p.

50. Publication information on Benson's forthcoming book appears in note 48, on Smith's in note 6.

51. Hemingway, *Death in the Afternoon,* 273.

1

"The Mercenaries":
A Harbinger of Vintage Hemingway

Mimi Reisel Gladstein

This anthology begins with Mimi Reisel Gladstein's consideration of a very early short story, "The Mercenaries," written in 1919, when Hemingway was just 20 years old, but unpublished until 1985, when Peter Griffin included the piece in his biography, Along with Youth: Hemingway, The Early Years. *Because Hemingway wrote "The Mercenaries" when his sole writing experience was that of cub reporter for the Kansas City* Star; *well before his Paris apprenticeship to Gertrude Stein, Ezra Pound, James Joyce, and others, the short story offers an excellent opportunity to study a Hemingway as yet unmolded by the literary influences that were to shape his career. Gladstein takes advantage of this opportunity. In the midst of the youthful melodrama of "The Mercenaries"—the story features a duel over a signora with "eyes like inkwells and full red lips"—Gladstein discovers many themes, character types, plot lines, and stylistic devices destined to characterize Hemingway's best work in future, and locates the author's essence in his juvenilia.*

A distinguishing feature of recent Hemingway study is the proportion of attention being paid to the writer's early life and writing apprenticeship. Two major recent biographies are dedicated solely to the period prior to his marrying Hadley Richardson, shortly after his twenty-second birthday: 1985 saw the publication of Peter Griffin's *Along With Youth: Hemingway, The Early Years,* and Michael Reynolds's *The Young Hemingway* followed in 1986.[1] Both studies add much to our understanding of the factors and forces that contributed to the maturation of the young man who was to create a revolution in twentieth-century literary style.

Along With Youth has particular appeal for readers who do not normally have access to special collections and unpublished materials because it includes five previously unpublished Hemingway short stories. These are "The Mercenaries—A Story," "Crossroads," "Portrait of an Idealist in Love," "The Ash Heel's Tendon," and "The Current." Griffin calls "The Mercenaries" the best of the lot.[2] He tells us little more about it except that it was rejected by both *Redbook* and *Saturday Evening Post*.

Griffin's placement of the story in his text indicates that it was written shortly after Hemingway's return from Italy and before Agnes von Kurowsky broke their engagement, written perhaps as part of his plan to earn a nest egg for their forthcoming marriage.[3] Evidence from the manuscripts themselves suggests a later genesis. Item 572 in the Ernest Hemingway Papers at the John Fitzgerald Kennedy Library is headed with a 602 State Street, Petoskey, Michigan address. This item is definitely identified as an Ernest Hemingway typescript. Hemingway was not in Petoskey until October of 1919.[4] Agnes's rejection letter came much earlier, in March of that year. A second, more carefully typed manuscript, item 573, is headed with a 600 N. Kenilworth, Oak Park, Illinois address. In all likelihood this is a later version as it contains corrections inked in on item 572. There are also differences between the text as Griffin publishes it and the Kennedy Library manuscripts.[5] Griffin does not provide any information about the rationale for his editorial revisions.

Whatever its correct dating and exact text, "The Mercenaries" was not among the works that Hemingway took with him to Paris. After the story was rejected twice, he withdrew it from circulation and never worked with it again, even after what Kenneth G. Johnston calls the "fortunate loss" of all of his typescripts and manuscripts in the Paris train station.[6] Hemingway's decision to withdraw the story from circulation is evidence of his early editorial astuteness and judgment. The quality of "The Mercenaries" is not equal to that of the writing Hemingway did a few years later. Still, while I agree with Robert W. Lewis's evaluation of the story as an interesting apprentice work, I cannot agree with his dismissal of it as one that "hardly adumbrates Hemingway's published work of *In Our Time* five years later."[7] What is most interesting about "The Mercenaries" is the way it prefigures not so much *In Our Time* specifically, but many of Hemingway's other short stories and novels. One can argue that, for all its faults, "The Mercenaries" anticipates many of its author's prevailing themes, character types, and plot lines. While lacking technical sophistication and that stylistic economy that characterizes vintage Hemingway, it is still interesting not only as juvenilia but also as a harbinger of what was to come.

Like many quintessential Hemingway stories, "The Mercenaries" is a tale of men without women. Its characters are indicative of the kinds of characters who would continue to populate the Hemingway world. As early as 1919 we find that Hemingway did not often choose to focus on the activities of ordinary individuals who would be familiar to the average reader. Like the bullfighters, big-game hunters, and demolitions experts of future fame, the characters in "The Mercenaries" are engaged in death-challenging enterprises. In this case, the main characters are the soldiers of fortune named in the title. The behavior of a French artillery lieutenant named Denis Ricaud is more reserved and genteel than that of his American companion, Sergeant Perry Graves, and that of the narrator, one Rinaldi Rinaldo, an Italian-American who has spent three years in Italy during the war. We learn nothing about these characters from the narration; everything we know is revealed dramatically through the dialog, a technique Hemingway was to use most effectively later.

Another element characteristic of later stories already in place in this early effort is the de rigueur drinking scene, complete with discussions of the relative merits of various alcoholic beverages, indicating the relative sophistication of the various characters. The most hardened of the mercenaries orders absinthe for all, and although Rinaldi identifies it as "that smooth, insidious, brain-rotting mixture," he makes no effort to countermand the order.

Rinaldi is a name that appealed to Hemingway. He resurrected it twice in his published fiction, most notably in *A Farewell to Arms*, but also earlier in *in our time*.[8] In "The Mercenaries" Hemingway uses the name for his narrator, who does little other than listen. The character who bears that name in the sketch in *in our time* is also a listener, this time "a disappointing audience" for Nick's assertion of "a separate peace." The Rinaldi of *in our time* makes no comment when Nick tells him "We're not patriots," although he may in fact be unable to reply as he is wounded, lying face down in the dirt, "breathing with difficulty." Likewise, the Rinaldi of "The Mercenaries" makes no response to Perry Graves's question after the story of Graves's duel with Il Lupo, although as narrator he tells us that he was thinking about "how this leather-faced old adventurer had matched his courage against admittedly one of the most fearless men in Europe" (111).

The matter of Rinaldi's name is one of the unaccountable editorial changes Griffin makes from the Kennedy Library manuscript. In the original the character is called Rinaldi Rinaldo; Griffin's version changes the name to Rinaldi Renaldo, a change that affects the pronunciation and also makes the name different from the name Hemingway would use later for the Italian doctor in *A Farewell to Arms* and the wounded Italian soldier in *in our time*. Manuscripts at the Kennedy Library suggest that Hemingway meant

the name to be the same in all three places. The reason for Griffin's altera-
tion of Hemingway's spelling is not given, although it seems an intentional
revision as Griffin also changes an *i* to an *e* the first time Graves mispro-
nounces the name and calls Rinaldo "Risolvo." Here Griffin changes Risolvo
to Resolvo.

In some ways, the narrator of "The Mercenaries" and Jake Barnes in
The Sun Also Rises function similarly. Jake brings his friends to Pamplona
where he is obviously one of the cognoscenti. In the course of the story, the
friends and the reader gain knowledge about and entrance to the world of
bullfighting and its attendant rituals and ceremonies. Jake's friends are suffered at the Hotel Montoya because of Jake. Montoya, who serves as the
high priest of the aficionados, has concluded that Jake has *afición,* and
therefore Jake is invited where ordinary American tourists are excluded.
Rinaldi in "The Mercenaries" is also one of the cognoscenti. He is allowed
to pass through the dining room full of neobohemians and enter the rear
room where the hardened soldiers of fortune gather. This he does because
he is "recognized favourably" by Cambrinus. In "The Mercenaries" it does
not matter if one is known or unknown to the group; being passed by
Cambrinus gains one ready access to the back room. Ricaud and Perry
immediately invite Rinaldi to join them because he is "armed with a smile
from Cambrinus himself" (105). What Hemingway accomplishes here and
what he was to do again in *The Sun Also Rises* is create a sense of an
in-group.

Part of the appeal of Hemingway's writing is the opportunity it gives
the reader to participate in a world totally unlike the mundane or everyday.
In "The Mercenaries," the appeal of the exotic and the dangerous is used
blatantly in the first sentence as the reader is invited to learn about "pearl
fishing in the Marquesas," "employment on the projected Trans Gobi Desert Railway, or the potentialities of any of the hot tamale republics" (104).
This is not a world for the fainthearted. Similarly, the first sentence of the
first story in the collection *In Our Time,* "On the Quai at Smyrna," immediately evokes the horror of war: "The strange thing was, he said, how they
screamed every night at midnight." The first of the interchapters or
sketches is also set in war, in unfamiliar terrain, in this case the Champagne.
While the majority of the *In Our Time* stories take place on native ground,
almost all of the interchapters are set on foreign turf and have to do with
death.

The nature of bravery is a major theme running through Hemingway's
work, and "The Mercenaries" establishes an early genesis of this theme. In
much of Hemingway's fiction, the measure of a man is the way he faces
death, whether it be in battle, in the bullring, hunting big game, or alone
on the vast ocean. Francis Macomber, Ole Andreson, Pedro Romero,

Robert Jordan, Colonel Cantwell, and Santiago come easily to mind. The centerpiece of "The Mercenaries" is the story of how Perry Graves and Il Lupo face the prospect of sudden and violent death and what that means about each one's courage. If they were the only characters faced with mortality in the story, "The Mercenaries" would be less interesting than it is. There is, however, another important death-facing character in the story, and in that character's reaction to the story of the duel between Graves and Il Lupo there is an intimation of Hemingway's more mature narrative techniques and characterizations.

In their dismissal of "The Mercenaries," most critics have neglected the character of Denis Ricaud. Reynolds calls the story "a barracks-room tale" that communicates "none of the fear or horror that Hemingway discovered in Italy."[9] Reynolds does not mention the role played by Ricaud in the story. Neither Paul Smith nor Robert W. Lewis discusses Ricaud. Yet, Ricaud is in many ways the most intriguing character in the story. Rinaldi's character is a cipher. The reader does not learn why he is at the Café Cambrinus or what his future plans are. We learn only that his grandfather was Italian and that he himself was not in the artillery. He is there mainly as a device for getting the story told.[10] Sergeant Perry Graves is a poorly realized character, a cartoon cutout created to retell the fantasy Hemingway made up for Chink Dorman-Smith to account for the week he spent with Jim Gamble in Taormina.[11] His characterization is inconsistent, and the failure of the Graves character may well account for the failure of the story.

Ricaud is another matter. In his assessments and telling comments, he prefigures such characters as Count Mippipopolous in *The Sun Also Rises* and even Count Greffi in *A Farewell to Arms*. Like Mippipopolous, Ricaud has patrician manners that stand in opposition to the drunken gaucherie and carelessness of those about him. In *The Sun Also Rises*, though Brett labels the Count as "one of us," the Count's behavior while they are drinking and dining together is quite different from hers. In Jake's apartment she flicks her ashes on the rug until she sees Jake notice it and then asks for an ashtray. The Count does not take out his cigar until ashtrays are present, and then he takes it out of a heavy, pigskin cigar case. He cuts the cigar with a gold cutter, having first offered a cigar to Jake. In "The Mercenaries," Graves offers Rinaldi a package of cheap cigarettes, shoving them across the table at him. Ricaud politely suggests that Rinaldi might prefer one of his cigarettes. He offers them out of a "monogrammed cigarette box," which he slides across the table with his "small, well-manicured hand" (105). As if the difference in class between Graves and Ricaud were not made clear enough by this initial action, later in the story Graves indicates that his taste in cigarettes is symbolic of his status in life. In explaining why he was demoted to sergeant from his wartime rank of captain, Graves says, "I was an officer, but not a gentleman. I could command a battery, but I've got a rotten taste in cigarettes" (108).

While characters like Jake are trying to learn "how to live," the Count has already gotten "to know the values." Having lived through seven wars and four revolutions, the Count enjoys himself with good food and wine and company. His quiet sense of self is juxtaposed with the frenetic frustration of Jake's circle. In "The Mercenaries," Ricaud's comment after Graves's story anticipates Count Mippipopolous's contention that having "lived very much" has allowed him to "get to know the values." Ricaud, who provides the only penetrating commentary in the story on the question of bravery, uses the word "standards" instead of the word "values." In Ricaud's explanation, "It is a question of standards" (111). Having died in his imagination a thousand times during his wartime experiences and expecting that he will imagine many more deaths before he is buried, Ricaud understands the character of Il Lupo, whose bravery is called into question by his behavior in the duel with Graves. Il Lupo has behaved courageously in war, bringing the Austrian ace Von Hauser "back alive to the Italian lines, his guns jammed, his observer dead in the cockpit" (107). Ricaud understands the problem to be one of imagination. The American has "courage without imagination," a quality that Ricaud calls "a gift."

Ricaud's assessment, which most commentary has ignored, raises this story above the level of barracks-room bravado. The technique of judging a character by that character's response to a story or situation is used in vintage Hemingway. An analogy can be made to "The Killers," where the impact on Nick of Ole Andreson's situation is crucial to interpreting the theme of the story. "The Mercenaries" is also similar to both "The Killers" and *The Sun Also Rises* in that it anticipates the "don't think about it" motif. Ricaud's problem is that he thinks too much. He does not have the gift of a lack of imagination. Ricaud is not taken in by Graves's simple definition of bravery, nor can he accept Graves's dismissal of the danger they will be facing.

In the conversation prior to his telling of his meeting with Lupo, Graves's drunken posturing focuses on the forthcoming role that he and Ricaud will play as officers in the Royal Republican Peruvian Army in a conflict with Chile. The job pays well, $200 per month in gold, and Graves sees it as a "Peruvian doughnut." Griffin tells us that the expression was Schio slang for "duck soup."[12] Smith also explains that it is slang for a simple task, "a piece of cake."[13]

Hemingway used the expression in a letter to Howell Jenkins, written from Petoskey in December of 1919. In the letter Hemingway describes his forthcoming job as a hired companion for Ralph Connable, a job that would leave his days free, give him the run of the Connables' Toronto mansion, pay all his expenses plus $50 a month, as "This Toronto thing looks like the original Peruvian Doughnuts."[14] Obviously then, the phrase suggests a cushy situation. However, much more is suggested in Graves's harping on the doughnut theme than his being a "propagandiste" to himself about how easy the next assignment will be.

Graves's use of the word "doughnut" in the place of key words in various patriotic expressions brings to mind techniques Hemingway would use in other works to underline his prevalent theme of distrust in abstractions, particularly those that glorify war; he returns again and again to the emptiness of words. Nowhere is this stated more succinctly than in Frederic Henry's narration in *A Farewell to Arms* when he says, "Abstract words such as glory, honor, courage or hallow were obscene besides the concrete names of villages, the numbers of roads, the names of rivers, the numbers of regiments and the dates."[15] If anything, the attack on abstractions is more subtle here because it is not stated directly. Graves starts his harangue by substituting the word "doughnut" for the word "flag" in the call to rally round the doughnut. He uses it the same way as he exhorts his group to follow the doughnut. He then substitutes "doughnut" for "country" in "Viva la doughnut." A pun follows as Graves promotes the "Peruvian doughnut" and puts down "Chile concarne."[16] Ricaud is puzzled and inquires about the meaning of the doughnut, but rather than respond, Graves continues his wordplay.

The bitterness hits a little closer to home when his next statement uses "doughnut" in place of "democracy" in the slogan that took the United States into World War I. "Make the world safe for the doughnut" is an obvious play on the rationale for the war as one that would "make the world safe for democracy." Graves goes on to use "doughnut" in place of crucial words in a number of other patriotic slogans such as "Don't give up the doughnut" ("Don't give up the ship") and "Remember the doughnut" ("Remember the Maine"). After asking to be wrapped in the doughnut (flag), Graves stops his chanting to comment ironically on the ineffectiveness of the "slogum." In this scene Hemingway anticipates "A Clean Well-Lighted Place," in which the word "nada" is substituted for key words in the Lord's Prayer to convey the sense of nothingness that replaces the comfort of religion. In "The Mercenaries" the word "doughnut" is used to convey the meaninglessness of patriotic slogans.

The "doughnut" passage is layered with meanings and foreshadows a crucial component of Hemingway's mature style—his method of word or phrase repetition to heighten meaning and to add a touch of bittersweet humor. The "irony and pity" section of *The Sun Also Rises* comes to mind, as does Bill Gorton's affection for stuffed dogs. Besides using "doughnut" to replace key words in patriotic slogans, Hemingway also invokes the connection between doughnuts and doughboys, the nickname for American infantry soldiers in World War I. It is a connection made in Mrs. Elizabeth Bacon Custer's book, *Tenting on the Plains: or Gen'l Custer in Kansas and Texas* (1887). Hemingway owned the book; Reynolds lists it among the books on Hemingway's own Key West inventory.[17] In this book, Mrs. Custer defines a doughboy as a small round doughnut served to sailors on shipboard, generally with hash. Doughnut and doughboy are yoked in "The Mercenaries" when Graves uses the expression, "Peru expects every doughnut to do his duty," playing on Nelson's famous signal to his fleet before the Battle of Trafalgar: "England expects every man to do his duty." An important component of the irony in "The Mercenaries" is the bitter situation in which these survivors of World War I found themselves. Demoted to the position of soldiers-for-hire for countries they care nothing about, they have lost even the illusions that the doughboys carried with them into World War I.

Ricaud's misunderstanding of Graves's bitter humor points up the differences in their character and nationality. Ricaud is unaware of the slang term. He thinks the doughnut must be the national symbol of Peru. Graves's wordplay here implies that his understanding of the situation may be deeper than is apparent from his behavior. Hemingway has Graves replace patriotic terms with a word for something with nothing in its center, something hollow at the core. When Graves and Ricaud go to fight for the doughnut, they go to fight for something with nothing as its center. Graves's use of the term in past patriotic slogans implies that maybe all battles have been fought over nothing. The doughnut section of the story suggests that Graves may have more imagination that Ricaud gives him credit for when he says in a later passage that Americans have courage without imagination.

While Graves seems to be dismissing the danger of their forthcoming assignment by comparing it to Peruvian doughnuts, Ricaud is too wise in the ways of the world to dismiss the danger of this "little war." Ricaud, like Jake Barnes, Frederic Henry, and Robert Jordan after him, understands the absurdities of war, the ironic jokes that fate can play. His tone is full of sarcasm when he says, "Perhaps a joke war, eh?" (112). He knows that one can die just as dead in a joke war as in a real one, just as Hemingway knew one can be blown up when passing out chocolate as well as when leading a charge. Ricaud is also sensitive to the fact that he does not know anything about the country he is being paid to serve, the country in which he may die. He mentions the fact that neither he nor Graves knows enough about the country "at whose disposal we have placed our swords" (107). Graves takes him literally, commenting that he does not know how to use a sword, and it is that reference to swordplay that prompts the Il Lupo story, the narrative-within-the-narrative that is the centerpiece of the story. Still, in interpreting "The Mercenaries," one should not ignore Ricaud's commentary before, and more important, after Graves's narrative. That commentary helps to lift the story momentarily above the slick-magazine level about a tale of sexual and physical competition.

Graves is a less satisfactory character. The narrator describes him as a gaunt, leather-faced, old adventurer, but Graves's behavior and conversation are often puerile. At times he seems unable to hold his liquor, missing the point of Rinaldi's questions and Ricaud's comments. His behavior shows none of the control or hardened cynicism one would expect from an experienced mercenary. Then, in the midst of his drunken tirade, he is reminded of his postwar experience in Italy and tells how he bested the greatest of the Italian aces. It is a boastful tale, complete with the arrogant gesture of stopping to drink a cup of coffee before his exit after humiliating Il Lupo. Unaccountably then, after his story, when Ricaud proposes a toast to his bravery, Graves responds "embarrassedly" with "Aw, say, Napoleon!" (112).

The ambiguities in Graves's characterization are heightened when he begins to tell his story. His description of the countryside as he rides to Taormina indicates his sensitivity to color. "Lemon orchards" and "orange groves" line the hillsides, their fruit "shining through the green leaves and darker green of olive trees" (108). This description of the vegetation is followed by one of the beauty of the "old stone houses" and the "blue" and "purple" of the bay and far coast. He makes a distinction between the blue of this bay and that of the Bay of Naples, this bay being bluer. In Graves's words, "everything" is "all color," and the countryside is "so pretty that it hurts to look at it." Later, when he pictures the dinner scene, he describes the wine as "like melted up rubies" (109).

But Hemingway's Graves is inconsistent in his diction and in his behavior. At times he is made to seem a crude barbarian, mutilating cigarettes and the English language, describing a meal as "no short order chow." Still, he knows what to call an *antipasto di magro* though he says it is made up of "all kind of funny things." He describes every course of the dinner in careful detail and likens the fish to "those soft-shelled crabs you get at Rousseau's in New Orleans" (109), leaving the impression that he is used to good restaurants and good food.

If Hemingway's inconsistencies are not enough, Griffin adds to the problem with one of his unaccountable editorial revisions. Before the doughnut diatribe, Graves is calling for a toast against Chile. Here the original manuscript reads, "They are a bad lot, those Chillies!" Griffin has inserted the word "not" into Graves's sentence so that it reads "They're not a bad lot, those Chillies!" In the previous paragraph, Graves has proposed that each man drink a toast against Chile, beginning with Ricaud's "A bas

Chile!" and ending with his "To hell with Chile!" Griffin also capitalizes the "H" in hell. In the original manuscript, the movement is clear. Graves proposes negative toasts against Chile in various languages; he calls Chileans a bad lot, and then responds to the question, "Ever been there?" with the assurance that even though he has never been to Chile, they are "a rotten bad lot those dirty Chillies." All this hectoring against Chile causes the more worldly-wise Ricaud to smile and comment that Graves is making propaganda for himself, quite understandable as both Ricaud and Graves are going off to fight for Peru against Chile, two countries about which they know nothing. Having Graves contradict himself in the middle of his diatribe might create an interesting ambiguity, but the note of complexity does not originate in Hemingway's text.

Some of Graves's prejudices are hard to interpret as his character is presented so ambiguously. On the one hand, Hemingway obviously means him to be a hero, a brave man who faces down the greatest ace in Italy. On the other hand, he is presented as a crude lout who takes advantage of a case of mistaken identity and knowingly does what a gentleman like Ricaud would not do. He also continually insults his colleague Ricaud by referring to him as Napoleon, even after Ricaud corrects him. He is "unmoved" by Ricaud's correction. When Rinaldi introduces himself, Graves responds "Wop?" He then proceeds to address Rinaldi by an ever-changing barrage of ethnic-sounding alternatives to his real name. He calls him Risolvo, Risotto, Riscossa, Disporto. In trying to assess Hemingway's attitude toward Graves, one is beset by some of the same problems readers have encountered in assessing Mike Campbell's antisemitic remarks in *The Sun Also Rises*. Does Hemingway think this behavior is acceptable? Is it part of good-old-boy, drunken dialog? Ricaud and Rinaldo are presented as positive characters, so when Graves treats them badly, his character is seen as less attractive. Ricaud's good manners and intelligent commentary, although he misunderstands at points, are contrasted with Graves's drunken belligerence. Ricaud's commentary calls into question even the quality of Graves's bravery as ensuing from lack of imagination. Still Ricaud does call for a toast to Graves as one who makes the bravest ace in Italy look like a coward.

Another minor problem is a lack of firm control of point of view. During Graves's narrative-within-the-narrative, another narrator unaccountably intrudes with a description of Graves's face and voice. Graves also loses the narration when an omniscient narrator inserts an explanatory sentence to signal the reader that the control of the situation had shifted "from the handsome Lupo to Perry Graves" (110). This sentence could not have been uttered by any of the characters in the story.

In sum, the inconsistencies of characterization, problems with tone, and slippage in point of view are main reasons that "The Mercenaries" does not succeed. Still, for all its lack of artistic control, it remains an interesting harbinger of the Hemingway to come.

Notes

1. Both Griffin and Reynolds project three volumes when their biographical studies are completed.

2. Peter Griffin, *Along with Youth: Hemingway, The Early Years* (Oxford: Oxford UP, 1985) 104.

3. In Griffin's book, on the page before "The Mercenaries," there is a letter to Bill Horne written in early February of 1919 expressing Ernest's longing for Ag. This is followed by a couple of paragraphs about Ernest's earning some money by speaking about his war experiences and beginning to write seriously. Griffin names "The Mercenaries" as one of the stories Hemingway wrote in February. Following "The Mercenaries," Griffin places a discussion of the events that led up to the rejection letter from Agnes.

4. Carlos Baker does not mention "The Mercenaries" in the list of works he discusses in his biography—*Ernest Hemingway: A Life Story* (New York: Charles Scribner's Sons, 1969) 65, 84. Instead, he lists a fragment titled "Wolves and Doughnuts" which was written on the back of a letter to Howell Jenkins dated from Petoskey, 20 December 1919. The fragment, with only a word or two changed, contains the first paragraph and most of the first sentence of a second paragraph of "The Mercenaries." The title suggests that Hemingway already had the body of the story in his head as it refers to things that are not discussed in the first paragraph. The fragment may be further evidence that the story was written at a date later than Griffin's placement of it since it is on the back of a letter written very late in the year.

5. Unless there are other projects underway to republish this apprentice fiction or incorporate "The Mercenaries" in another anthology, the version Griffin published in *Along with Youth* will stand as the most accessible text. The reader should be warned that the published text is different from Hemingway's text. Griffin makes editorial revisions about which he does not warn the reader. Granted that in most cases the revisions are minor, part of the interest in reading an unpublished apprentice piece is in seeing the product raw. Griffin's minor revisions are mostly matters of punctuation. He adds commas, changes commas to periods, inserts hyphens and possessives, capitalizes, and moves commas within quotation marks. One could hardly quibble with his decision to make these changes, although it would have been better form if he had noted his intention to do so. I will discuss more telling changes, changes that significantly influence meaning, in the text of my essay.

 In his review of Griffin's book, Robert W. Lewis describes it as "marred by many errors" and details some of Griffin's misquotations, solecisms, typographical errors, and his erratic use of *sic*. Lewis suggests that anyone doing serious research will have to go back to the originals. See "Hemingway's Lives: A Review," *The Hemingway Review* 7.1 (Fall 1987): 45–62. For my study of "The Mercenaries" I used items 572 and 573 from the Ernest Hemingway Papers at the John Fitzgerald Kennedy Library. However, for the greater ease of most readers, the page references for quotations from "The Mercenaries" will refer to Griffin's text.

6. Kenneth G. Johnston, *The Tip of the Iceberg: Hemingway and the Short Story* (Greenwood: Penkevill, 1987) 2. However, Paul Smith questions Hemingway's account of the

loss of his manuscripts in "Hemingway's Apprentice Fiction: 1919–1921," *American Literature* 58.4 (December 1986): 574–88.

7. Lewis, 46.

8. Michael Reynolds suggests that Hemingway found the name Rinaldo Rinaldi in *With British Guns in Italy,* Hugh Dalton's account of his experiences on the Italian front. See Reynolds's *Hemingway's First War: The Making of* A Farewell to Arms (Princeton: Princeton UP, 1976) 150. Reynolds concludes that Hemingway may have learned of the book from "Chink" Dorman-Smith in the early 1920s. Dalton's book was published in 1919, and "The Mercenaries" was written in that same year. If Hemingway did not learn of the book until the 1920s, it seems unlikely as the source for the name Rinaldo Rinaldi. *With British Guns in Italy* is not listed in Reynolds's subsequent work, *Hemingway's Reading, 1910–1940* (Princeton: Princeton UP, 1981). Perhaps someone Hemingway met in Italy bore a similar name, or perhaps the repetition of basically the same sounds in first and last names appealed to a man who had an affinity for nicknames.

9. Reynolds, *The Young Hemingway* (Oxford: Basil Blackwell, 1986) 125.

10. Smith classifies Hemingway's apprentice fiction by its setting: Chicago, Italy, or Michigan. "The Mercenaries" is classified with seven other Chicago stories and sketches. Smith notes that in these stories the narrator plays the role of an intermediary between the audience and unfamiliar scenes and characters, as well as the role of "the privileged reporter retelling the tale of an old hand" (576–77). Michael Reynolds in *The Young Hemingway* also notes that Hemingway's use of a point-of-view character who is a detached narrator is evidence of a "growing awareness of technique" (125).

11. See Smith, 578 and Reynolds, *The Young Hemingway,* 126 for details of the story Hemingway told Dorman-Smith. In *Ernest Hemingway: A Life Story,* Baker recounts Hemingway telling a similar story to Luman Ramsdell and Dutch Pailthrop in Petoskey (66). In the Petoskey version the scene is the Riviera, and the duel is stopped by the woman.

12. Griffin, 129.

13. Smith, 575.

14. *Ernest Hemingway: Selected Letters, 1917–1961,* ed. Carlos Baker (New York: Charles Scribner's Sons, 1981) 30.

15. Ernest Hemingway, *A Farewell to Arms* (New York: Charles Scribner's Sons, 1929) 185.

16. Here Griffin uses a lower case "c" in the "Chile" of "Chile concarne." This makes Hemingway's pun less obvious.

17. Reynolds, *Hemingway's Reading,* 115.

2

Uncle Charles in Michigan

Susan Swartzlander

Susan Swartzlander's essay on "Up in Michigan" moves us into the dynamic years of Hemingway's Paris apprenticeship. Begun late in 1921, "Up in Michigan" is the earliest Hemingway short story of enduring quality. Yet "Up in Michigan" remained essentially unpublished until 1938. The short story's censorable sexual content was at fault, and too many of today's critics have continued to avert their eyes from the callous sacrifice of Liz Coates's virginity on a splintering Michigan dock. Swartzlander's detailed and sensitive exploration of "Up in Michigan's" simplicity of plot and complexity of style reminds readers of this story's power. She moves us toward a new appreciation of Hemingway's indebtedness to James Joyce, and specifically to Joyce's "Uncle Charles Principle," a way of using diction and syntax to reflect multiple characters in a single, third-person, omniscient narrative voice. In the process, Swartzlander demonstrates Hemingway's easy mastery of such literary lessons, and his own striking ability to integrate the subjective and objective elements of a narrative into a scene that "reverberates with emotion."

"Up in Michigan," one of the first short stories Ernest Hemingway wrote, appeared in *Three Stories and Ten Poems*, a limited edition of 300 copies that was published in Paris in 1923. The story was not reprinted until 1938 when it was included, slightly revised, in *The Fifth Column and the First Forty-nine Stories*. The work was neglected for 15 years because of publishers' fears over censorship, not because the story was deemed unimportant juvenilia. Kenneth Lynn reports that it was on the strength of "Up in Michigan" and "Out of Season" alone that Robert McAlmon published the early collection.[1] Writing to Maxwell Perkins on 14 February 1927,

Hemingway explained that Horace Liveright's refusal to publish "Up in Michigan" in *In Our Time* influenced Hemingway's decision to change publishers. "Up in Michigan I am anxious to print—it is a good story and Liveright cut it out of In Our Time. That was the reason I did not want to stay there." Hemingway was particularly pleased with the way the story explored a relationship: "I think it is publishable and it might set Mr. [Allen] Tate's mind at rest as to my always avoiding any direct relation between men and women because of being afraid to face it or not knowing about it."[2]

In a 1936 letter to Ivan Kashkin, Hemingway insisted that "Up in Michigan" was a valuable story: "It is a very good story" (*Letters*, 431). Hemingway believed that the story was one "that influenced many people" (*Letters*, 468). He particularly singled out Morley Callaghan, claiming that Callaghan had rewritten it "many times in saleable terms" (*Letters*, 431). In a letter to Perkins, Hemingway called the story "Morley's source book" (*Letters*, 327). Arguing again for inclusion of the story in a collection, Hemingway told Perkins in 1938 that "Up in Michigan" is "an important story in my work": "The book is supposed to be a definitive collection of all stories up to now. Without Up in Michigan it is not that" (*Letters*, 468). He repeated in a second letter the same day his hope that Perkins would not exclude the story from the collection, "I don't like to publish it without Up in Michigan" (*Letters*, 470).

Unfortunately, critics have not shared Hemingway's enthusiasm for "Up in Michigan." The simplicity of the plot has sidetracked critics from the story's stylistic complexity. There are only a handful of commentaries on this work, and most of them do little more than recount the plot, the least interesting aspect of the story: the romantic young girl, Liz, becomes infatuated with Jim Gilmore, Hortons Bay blacksmith. He seduces her on a dock by the lake and drunkenly passes out.[3] Even the most recent study of the story promises "A Long Look at Hemingway's 'Up in Michigan'" but delivers instead an investigation of the plot not only as it is, but also as it could be, asking, "after what we have seen of Jim's character, is there any chance that the future will put things right? What if Liz becomes pregnant? Could she confide in Mrs. Smith . . . ?"[4]

Ironically, the 1920s short story is characterized by a movement away from a focus on conventional, go-ahead plot. Writing about this phenomenon, William Peden explains that the Lost Generation writers were only comfortable with the short story genre when it was "freed from the 'tyranny of plot.'" They substituted in its place "the immediate, the instant, the *now-ness* of life and art, in a manner supportive of Pound's concept of the Image."[5] By focusing on action, rather than on aesthetics, we divert attention away from the moods, attitudes, and characterizations that are the fundamental elements of the story.

Perhaps the writer who did the most to change attitudes about plot was Hemingway's contemporary, James Joyce. Joyce and Hemingway first met in the early spring of 1922, a time when Hemingway was revising "Up in Michigan."[6] The two, of course, were famous literary drinking buddies; one anecdote describes Joyce starting fights only to cower behind Hemingway, saying, "Deal with him, Hemingway! Deal with him!"[7] But their relationship was more than social. Frank O'Connor, one of the few critics to analyze in any detail Joyce's influence on Hemingway, does not overstate the case when he claims that Hemingway "must have been one of the first of Joyce's disciples. Certainly, so far as I can ascertain, he was the only writer of his time to study what Joyce was attempting to do in the prose of *Dubliners* and *A Portrait of the Artist as a Young Man* and work out a method of applying it."[8] In a letter to Arthur Mizener, Hemingway acknowledged his devotion to Joyce: "Jim Joyce was the only alive writer that I ever respected. He had his problems but he could write better than anyone I knew. Ezra was nice and kind and friendly and a beautiful poet and critic. G. Stein was nice until she had the menopause. But who I respected was Mr. Joyce and not from his clippings" (*Letters*, 696). Morley Callaghan quotes Hemingway as saying, "James Joyce is the greatest writer in the world."[9] Carlos Baker recounts Hemingway's claim that for a poet "born in this century or in the last ten years of the preceding century" to deny the influence of Pound, "is as if a prose writer born in that time should not have learned from or been influenced by James Joyce."[10] According to Willard Potts, Joyce read and critiqued Hemingway's manuscripts, "something he apparently did for no one else."[11] Morley Callaghan also recorded seeing Hemingway with the proofs of *The Sun Also Rises* under his arm, headed for a conference with Joyce.[12]

Joyce reportedly proclaimed that "There is much more behind Hemingway's form than people know."[13] Joyce should know—there is much more of Joyce behind Hemingway's form (in the writings, not in the barroom brawls) than people know. To render the attitudes and moods that distinguish a scene, Hemingway uses some of the same stylistic techniques found in James Joyce's early works. Particularly, in "Up in Michigan," he puts into practice what Joyceans affectionately refer to as the "Uncle Charles Principle." Hugh Kenner explains that in Joyce's work, especially in *Dubliners*, the narrative voice may appear to be third-person, omniscient, but actually the narrative voice reflects, through diction and sometimes syntax, the character in closest proximity. As Kenner describes it

[Joyce's] words are in such delicate equilibrium . . . that they detect the gravitational field of the nearest person. One reason the quiet stories of *Dubliners* continue to fascinate is that the narrative point of view unobtrusively fluctuates. The illusion of dispassionate portrayal seems to be attended by an iridescence difficult to account for until we notice one person's sense of things inconspicuously giving place to another's. The grammar of twelve of the stories is that of the third person narrative, imparting a deceptive look of impersonal truth. The diction frequently tells a different tale.[14]

Kenner cites many specific examples of the principle in Joyce's early fiction. When the narrator of "The Dead" says, "Lily, the caretaker's daughter, was literally run off her feet," the idiomatic "literally run off her feet" is characteristic of what the poorly educated servant would say. The phrase would not be used by a detached narrator. The same narrator sounds very much like we would expect Freddy Malins to sound and focuses on Malins's concerns: "He had been told that celery was a capital thing for the blood." A similar example occurs when the narrator of *A Portrait of the Artist as a Young Man* describes Uncle Charles's morning routine: "Every morning, therefore, Uncle Charles repaired to his outhouse." "Repaired" is a word that Uncle Charles, with his "notions of semantic elegance," would use. Kenner explains that these word choices might be said to carry with them "silent quotation marks"; he describes this fictional novelty as "the normally neutral narrative vocabulary pervaded by a little cloud of idioms which a character might use if he were managing the narrative."[15]

From his very first short stories, Hemingway experimented with new and intriguing ways to apply the third-person narrator. John Atkins writes that Hemingway told him:

> The first person gives you great intimacy in attempting to give a complete sense of experience to the reader. It is limited however and in the third person the novelist can work in other people's heads and in other people's country. His range is greatly extended and so are his obligations. I prepared myself for writing in the third person by the discipline of writing *Death in the Afternoon;* the short stories and especially the long short stories of "The Short Happy Life of Francis Macomber" and the "Snows of Kilimanjaro."[16]

By experimenting with a third-person narrative voice that takes on the speech characteristics of various characters, Hemingway was able to combine the intimacy of the first person with the extended range of the third person.

By speech characteristics I mean more than just diction. Because all of the characters to a large extent share the same idiomatic English, diction alone will not reveal whose point of view is affecting the narrative voice. Like Joyce, Hemingway used a narrative voice that adopts not just the idiomatic phrases, but also the speech rhythms, syntax, and attitudes representative of the characters in "Up in Michigan." From the beginning of the story we get details that would more appropriately come from the consciousness of one of the town's residents: "Jim Gilmore came to Hortons Bay from

Canada. He bought the blacksmith shop from old man Horton. Jim was short and dark with big mustaches and big hands" (81).[17] Only someone familiar with the area would speak of "old man Horton." The same voice describes the town, noting that "Up the road a ways was the Methodist church" (82). The colloquial "up the road a ways" again reflects the speech of a native, not of a conventional narrator.

As soon as Liz is mentioned, the narrative voice shifts, taking on elements first of Mrs. Smith's character and then of Liz's character. Mrs. Smith, described as a "large clean woman," sees in Liz someone who "had good legs" and who "always wore clean gingham aprons" (81), traits Mrs. Smith, a clean woman herself, would find desirable in a waitress.

Liz would be especially interested in Jim's appearance, his build, hands, and mustache. Most important, though, the rhythm of the sentences is one that comes to be associated with the young girl: "Liz liked Jim very much. She liked it the way he walked over from the shop and often went to the kitchen door to watch for him to start down the road. She liked it about his mustache. She liked it about how white his teeth were when he smiled" (81). These stylistic effects, diction and syntax, are directly tied to characterization. The lines reflect the excessive romanticism of a girl who watches to see the object of her fantasies so that she "could take the way he looked up to bed with her" (84). The rhythm of the sentences emphasizes her dreaminess, and the simple diction ("she liked it about") realistically reflects the way she would talk. A seemingly inconsequential detail like the repetition of the commonplace "liked" says a great deal about Liz. The naive young girl has neither the education nor the imagination to render her emotions effectively through language. Sheldon Norman Grebstein sees in this passage the Stein-Anderson influence: "Anderson in the naïveté of attitude, simple diction and the emphasis on the characters' emotions; Stein in the heavy repetitions." He singles out the point of view, however, as being Hemingway's unique "effort to produce the effect of a subjective voice without actually using an I-narrator." Grebstein concludes that by connoting "the simplicity, the one-thing-at-a-time quality, yet also the obsessiveness of Liz's perceptions," Hemingway has created a narrative voice that reflects the "attitude" of the character.[18]

In the fourth paragraph, the style associated with Liz is replaced by the more objective, informative tone of the Hortons Bay native: "Hortons Bay, the town, was only five houses on the main road between Boyne City and Charlevoix" (81). But again colloquialisms intercede in a passage that seems to be impartial truth: the phrase "Up the road a ways" reminds the reader that this is not a conventional, third-person, omniscient narrator.

The narrator tells us that after dinner "Liz cleaned off with Mrs. Smith" (84). Again, the narrator assumes the vocabulary of the characters; we would

more likely expect to hear Liz or Mrs. Smith use these words to explain
that they cleared the table and did the dishes. Liz's timidness about asking
for special permission to bake for Jim is reflected in the structure of the
sentences that describe her fear: "Liz wanted to make something special for
Jim to take but she didn't finally because she was afraid to ask Mrs. Smith
for the eggs and flour and afraid if she bought them Mrs. Smith would catch
her cooking. It would have been all right with Mrs. Smith but Liz was
afraid." Here the repetition of the word "afraid" three times, as well as the
pace of the sentences achieved through a long series of conjunctions, reinforces the subject of the passage. Joyce did a similar trick in "The Boarding
House," where Mary and Polly Mooney have an awkward exchange: "She
had been made awkward by her not wishing to receive the news in too
cavalier a fashion or to seem to have connived and Polly had been made
awkward not merely because allusions of that kind always made her awkward but also because she did not wish it to be thought that in her wise
innocence she had divined the intention behind her mother's tolerance."[19]
Notice the repetition of "awkward" three times, and the stacked preposi-
tions that affect the pace of the sentence.

The narrative voice continues with descriptions of Liz's behavior that
seem to come from Liz herself: "The night before they were to come back
she didn't sleep at all, that is she didn't think she slept because it was all
mixed up in a dream about not sleeping and really not sleeping." The
narrator tells us that when Liz "saw the wagon coming down the road she
felt weak and sort of sick inside." Liz's emotional state is reflected by the
tentative and confused nature of the sentences' diction and syntax. Through
the form of the sentences the reader sees that Liz does not understand what
is happening to her. She is not exactly sick, but her feelings of infatuation
are "sort of" like being sick. Her emotional turmoil is related in a sentence
about dreaming and waking, the romantic confusion of illusion and reality—
a sentence that is itself so confusing as to be virtually indecipherable. The
narrator captures Liz's excited anticipation when the men return, "Liz
hadn't known just what would happen when Jim got back but she was sure
it would be something," but, in contrast, the chopped rhythm of the subsequent sentences shows Liz's disappointment, her dashed hopes: "Nothing
had happened. The men were just home, that was all" (83). Just as the
rhythm of the sentences captures the deflation of Liz's feelings, sentence
structure similarly responds to the sudden boost she feels when Jim appears
unexpectedly: "She was thinking about him hard and then Jim came out" (84).

In the dinner scene the narrator further shows his versatility—he very
much becomes one of the boys. When the men return from the hunting trip,
the narrator assumes traits of their speech. For instance we are told that
"That night Charlie Wyman stayed to supper at Smith's" (83). "Stayed to

supper" is a colloquialism appropriate for this particular crowd. When Jim returns from having "fetched in the jug of whiskey," the narrator relates the details: "It was a four-gallon jug and there was quite a little slopped back and forth in the bottom. Jim took a long pull on his way back to the house" (83). The narrator echoes what the characters would be likely to say when he uses the words "Quite a little," "slopped back and forth," and Jim's "pull" (83).

As befits the "strong, silent type," Jim himself is defined more by what he does and what he sees than by what he thinks or what he feels. His emotions are restricted to pride over his kill, "Yeah aint it a beauty?" (83), and his coldness reverberates through his curt command to Liz, "Come on for a walk" (84). Jim's personality is reflected in the narrative voice's matter-of-fact listing of his activities:

> He talked about the shop to D.J. Smith and about the Republican Party and about James G. Blaine. In the evenings he read *The Toledo Blade* and the Grand Rapids paper by the lamp in the front room or went out spearing fish in the bay with a jacklight with D.J. Smith. In the fall he and Smith and Charley Wyman took a wagon and tent, grub, axes, their rifles and two dogs and went on a trip to the pine plains beyond Vanderbilt hunting. (82)

The verbs in these sentences emphasize action, more specifically, a series of completed actions. More often for Liz, the past progressive tense is used, implying more passivity and the continuing action of seemingly endless waiting ("Liz was sitting," "She was thinking," "she was frightened"). Sentences describing Jim also reflect his coarseness, emphasizing the physical appetite: "Jim began to feel great. He loved the taste and the feel of whiskey. He was glad to be back to a comfortable bed and warm food and the shop. He had another drink" (84). Whereas sentences describing Liz are often long, repetitive, abstract, and inner-directed, those describing Jim are short, clipped, action-packed, and outer-directed.

This mediation between the subjective and objective is present in almost every detail the narrator provides. Throughout the story, the most straightforward, objective "facts" take on subjective nuances. Jim's "big hands" mentioned in the first few lines of the story appear later, "the hand that felt so big in her lap went away and was on her leg" (85). One of Jim's favorite activities, "spearing fish in the bay with a jacklight" (82), takes on added significance when we consider his activity on the dock this particular night. As James Spenko notes, the stiffness of the deer the men shot is a detail later echoed in the description of Liz submitting to Jim's embrace. "She held herself stiff because she was so frightened" (84).[20]

Even the scenic descriptions the narrator provides reflect, at first, Liz's excessive romanticism, and then later, her dashed hopes. In the beginning the bay is pictured in all its idyllic serenity:

> A steep sandy road ran down the hill to the bay through the timber. From Smith's back door you could look out across the woods that ran down to the lake and across the bay. It was very beautiful in the spring and summer, the bay blue and bright and usually whitecaps on the lake out beyond the point from the breeze blowing from Charlevoix and Lake Michigan.

We see the lake from a different perspective when Liz is confronted with the harsh reality of her relationship with Jim. The romantic, dreamlike scene becomes cold and dark: "There was no moon and they walked ankle-deep in the sandy road through the trees down to the dock and the warehouse on the bay. The water was lapping in the piles and the point was dark across the bay. It was cold" (85). The summer breeze and the whitecaps give way to a pervading mist: "Liz started to cry. She walked over to the dock and looked down to the water. There was a mist coming up from the bay. She was cold and miserable and everything felt gone" (85).

Even the title itself suggests that Hemingway is manipulating the subjective and objective dimensions of the story. The "up" in the title refers to an objective, geographical designation; however it also alludes to Liz's emotions, which are nothing but "up" in the beginning and anything but "up" in the end (a further, bawdier, pun pertaining to Jim's condition is undoubtedly also implied).

Gertrude Stein told Hemingway that "Up in Michigan" was *inaccrochable*, "unhangable, she explained; like a picture that a painter paints and can't exhibit because of its moral offensiveness."[21] The topic is indeed an intimate one, and Hemingway needed a way to handle this intimacy with delicacy. Since the narrative voice alternately reflects various characters, Hemingway can mediate between intimacy and distance. In a 1924 letter to Edmund Wilson, Hemingway described his method in *In Our Time* as an attempt "to give the picture of the whole between examining it in detail. Like looking with your eyes at something, say a passing coast line, and then looking at it with 15x binoculars. Or rather, maybe, looking at it and then going in and living in it—and then coming out and looking at it again" (*Letters*, 128). His technique can also be compared to the focusing of a camera. At first we have close-up views of Liz, the town, and then the group of men, especially Jim. Later, however, as the act is consummated on the dock, the camera pulls back, leaving us with the feeling of coldness, the feeling of detachment, and the "cold mist coming up through the woods from the bay" (86).

Consider how different the story would be if it were told in the first person with either Liz or Jim as narrator. In the case of Liz as narrator, the intensely emotional story would almost certainly lapse into pathos; with Jim as narrator, it would have been very difficult for Hemingway to communicate the emotion involved, and we would lose the sympathetic portrayal of Liz. With his experimental, third-person narrative voice (or voices would be more accurate), Hemingway is able to maintain distance and yet not sacrifice this sense of immediacy.

The Uncle Charles Principle, the integration of the subjective and objective elements of a narrative, is Hemingway's way of depicting a scene that reverberates with emotion. The vividness of the story does not depend on action but results from Hemingway's aesthetic innovations to contrast subtly Liz's idealism, naiveté, and vulnerability with Jim's coldness, coarseness, and cruelty.

John Atkins admonishes Hemingway for such an unorthodox approach: "An artist must focus, must distinguish between foreground and background (unless he is an abstract painter)"[22]—or an experimental prose stylist rendering the subtle shadings of emotion.

Notes

The author wishes to thank Professor Harvey Sessler and Professor Susan Beegel for their helpful suggestions.

1. Kenneth Lynn, *Hemingway* (New York: Simon and Schuster, 1987) 208.

2. *Ernest Hemingway, Selected Letters: 1917–1961*, ed. Carlos Baker (New York: Charles Scribner's Sons, 1981) 246. Subsequent references cited parenthetically in the text. Since 1938, "Up in Michigan" has appeared in all of Scribner's collections of Hemingway's works and it was translated into Portuguese in 1970 (Mário Pontes, trans., "Aconteceu em Michigan," *êla ela* [March 1970]: 99–105).

3. In addition to the sources cited below, see the following works where "Up in Michigan" is mentioned briefly: John Atkins, *The Art of Ernest Hemingway: His Work and Personality* (London: Spring, 1964) 221; Carlos Baker, *Hemingway: The Writer as Artist* (Princeton: Princeton UP, 1952) 135; Joseph DeFalco, *The Hero in Hemingway's Short Stories* (Pittsburgh: U of Pittsburgh P, 1963) 55; Richard B. Hovey, *Hemingway: The Inward Terrain* (Seattle: U of Washington P, 1968) 8; Robert W. Lewis, Jr., *Hemingway on Love* (Austin: U of Texas P, 1965) 4–5; Paul Smith, "Hemingway's Apprentice Fiction: 1919–1921," *American Literature* 58.4 (December 1986): 586–87; Arthur Waldhorn, *A Reader's Guide to Ernest Hemingway* (New York: Farrar, Straus and Giroux, 1972) 43–44; Philip Young, *Ernest Hemingway: A Reconsideration* (University Park: Pennsylvania State UP, 1966) 179–80. Constance Cappel Montgomery gives the story more attention, but from a biographical, rather than a critical perspective; see *Hemingway in Michigan* (New York: Fleet, 1966) 119–27. Jackson J. Benson finds the story interesting as an early example showing "the transition of a style and the interplay of stylistic influences," particularly those of Stein and Anderson; see "Ernest Hemingway as Short Story Writer," in *Hemingway*, ed. Horst Weber (Darmstadt: Wissenschaftliche Buchgesellschaft, 1980) 357–58.

Charles A. Fenton and Sheldon Norman Grebstein make similar observations; see *The Apprenticeship of Ernest Hemingway: The Early Years* (New York: Viking, 1954) 152–54 and *Hemingway's Craft* (Carbondale: Southern Illinois UP, 1973) 79–80.

4. James Leo Spenko, "A Long Look at Hemingway's 'Up in Michigan,'" *Arizona Quarterly* 39.2 (Summer 1983): 118.

5. William Peden,"The American Short Story in the Twenties," *Studies in Short Fiction* 10 (Fall 1975): 368.

6. Richard Ellmann mistakenly notes that the two met in the spring of 1921, but Hemingway did not arrive in Paris until late December of 1921. Hemingway's biographers agree that the two writers met in the early spring of 1922. Kenneth Lynn states that "the first version of 'Up in Michigan' was written in Chicago in the late summer of 1921, just before Hemingway's marriage to Hadley Richardson on September 3; the second and final version was written in Paris five months later" (Lynn, 109). For more information on dates for the five "Up in Michigan" items in the Ernest Hemingway Collection at the John Fitzgerald Kennedy Library, please see "Three Versions of 'Up in Michigan,' 1921–1930," by Paul Smith, *Resources for American Literary Study* 15.2 (Autumn 1985): 163–77.

7. "The American Storyteller," *Time* (13 December 1954): 75, recounted in Richard Ellmann, *James Joyce*, rev. edn. (New York: Oxford UP, 1982) 695.

8. Frank O'Connor, *The Lonely Voice* (New York: Harper & Row, 1963) 156.

9. Morley Callaghan, *That Summer in Paris* (New York: Penguin, 1963) 28. For more on the Joycean influence on Hemingway, see Robert E. Gajdusek, *Hemingway and Joyce: A Study in Debt and Payment* (Corte Madera: Square Circle P, 1984) and James Schroeter, "Hemingway via Joyce," *Sewanee Review* 10.1 (January 1974): 95–114. Both writers emphasize the influence of Joycean wordplay, particularly on Hemingway's later work.

10. Carlos Baker, *Ernest Hemingway: A Life Story* (New York: Charles Scribner's Sons, 1969) 236.

11. Willard Potts in a footnote to Nino Frank's "The Shadow That Had Lost Its Man" in *Portraits of the Artist in Exile,* ed. Willard Potts (Seattle: U of Washington P, 1979) 79.

12. Callaghan, 107.

13. Ellmann, 695.

14. Hugh Kenner, *Joyce's Voices* (Berkeley: U of California P, 1978) 16.

15. Kenner, 15–17.

16. John Atkins, *The Art of Ernest Hemingway: His Work and Personality* (London: Spring 1964) 72–73.

17. Ernest Hemingway, "Up in Michigan," *The Short Stories of Ernest Hemingway* (New York: Charles Scribner's Sons, 1966) 81–86. All further references cited parenthetically in the text.

18. Grebstein, 79–80.

19. James Joyce, *Dubliners,* 1914 (New York: Penguin, 1967) 64.

20. Spenko, 116.

21. Lynn, 170.
22. Atkins, 77.

3

Ethical Narration in "My Old Man"

Phillip Sipiora

*Composed during the summer and fall of 1922, "My Old Man" follows hard
on the heels of "Up in Michigan" and shares that story's importance as one
of the earliest works reflecting Hemingway's maturing artistic judgment and
the benefits of his literary apprenticeship. Yet, as Phillip Sipiora's essay
points out, "My Old Man" has been neglected precisely because of its status
as apprentice fiction, repeatedly dismissed as a slavish imitation of Sherwood Anderson's "I Want to Know Why." Such critical neglect is particularly surprising as there is little agreement on what this ironic story intends
to reveal about the jockey Butler's ambiguous morality. Sipiora offers a
systematic explanation of the mode of narration in "My Old Man," outlining
the way it deliberately shapes our response to the story's characters and
their values. His tools are unusual—theories of rhetoric elucidated by Aristotle and Quintilian—but they provide, for the first time, the formal principles of narrative exposition necessary for a truly analytic response to "My
Old Man." Sipiora's treatment reveals a more complex story than previous
critics have observed in "My Old Man" and enlarges our comprehension of
the shared understanding Hemingway has created between teller and
reader.*

Die Geschichte steht für den Mann

"My Old Man," one of the earliest prose fiction works of Ernest Hemingway, originally appeared in Hemingway's first book-length publication,
Three Stories and Ten Poems (1923). This complex narrative, which details
the developing relationship between a father and son as told from the point
of view of the 12-year-old narrator and son, Joe Butler, has generated con-

siderable attention since its publication, having been frequently anthologized in a variety of publications as representative of various genres and methods of narrative exposition.[1] Yet despite the popular reception of "My Old Man," there has been a relative paucity of critical attention devoted to this important early work. What criticism there is generally focuses on one or more of the following three areas of inquiry: (1) the influence of Sherwood Anderson on Hemingway; (2) the morality or immorality of Butler; or (3) patterns of narrative revelation. Although some of these explanations are relatively persuasive as far as they go, none offers a systematic examination of Hemingway's mode of narration, which is instrumental in shaping our response to character—and therefore values—in the narrative. Joe's *method* of exposition is integrally connected to the credibility of narration, and what I attempt to do in this essay is to explore the techniques of Joe's exposition— his "ethics of narration"—and try to demonstrate the means by which these strategies establish his credibility, a credibility that in turn manipulates reader response in a fundamental way. Before attempting to detail certain principles underlying this kind of narration, I will briefly summarize the major criticism of "My Old Man."

The Critical Reception

One of the earliest accounts linking Hemingway to Anderson was Herschel Brickell's 1925 review of *In Our Time*, which suggested that "My Old Man" had been influenced by several of Anderson's tales of horse racing.[2] Subsequent accounts of Hemingway's indebtedness to Anderson abound. Earl Rovit, for example, suggests that there are thematic and tonal similarities between Anderson and Hemingway: "'Up in Michigan' and 'My Old Man' are very Andersonian in texture and in feeling."[3] Kenji Nakajima insists that "My Old Man" was written "under the influence of Sherwood Anderson and his story, 'I Want to Know Why.'"[4] In analyzing "Up in Michigan" and "My Old Man," Charles Fenton asserts that they "can be fairly described as Andersonian."[5] Joseph Flora considers "My Old Man" to be Hemingway's most derivative short fiction: "More than any other story Hemingway wrote, it shows the influence of Sherwood Anderson."[6] In comparing Anderson to other modern American writers, including Hemingway, Christian Messinger argues that "Anderson sensed both the longing for success that gripped track people and the disorder that accompanied overidentification with horses and racing."[7] Messinger concludes that "Hemingway's boy narrator echoes the Anderson-like melting feeling about race horses."[8] Yet perhaps the most aggressive assertion of Anderson's influence on Hemingway comes from Philip Young:

The clearest direct obligation of the *Three Stories* is to Sherwood Anderson. "My Old Man," a good piece in its own right, is Hemingway's version of one of Anderson's best efforts, the widely reprinted "I Want to Know Why," which had appeared two years earlier. Both stories are about horse racing, and are told by boys in their own vernacular. In each case the boy has to confront mature problems while undergoing a painful disillusionment with an older man he had been strongly attached to. It doesn't look like coincidence.[9]

The extent to which Hemingway's themes and techniques of composition were influenced by Sherwood Anderson is, of course difficult to demonstrate. What is important, however, is that so many fine critics have limited their interpretations of this important work by assuming that "My Old Man" is explicitly imitative of Anderson's themes and techniques, often without much substantive textual support.

The second general category of criticism comprises evaluations of Butler's ethics as sportsman and father. Those critics who view Butler as a benevolent father generally advance the argument that he is fundamentally good because he demonstrates affection and concern for Joe, and does not actively participate in fixing horse races in the present time of the story. Sydney Krause, for example, suggests that "the story sufficiently establishes Butler's virtue" and concludes that Butler is "militantly honorable."[10] Nakajima arrives at the conclusion that Butler's nature *and* behavior are exemplary: "We can assume that the old man is so good-natured. . . . [P]robably we can assume that after all he is rather good as man, too."[11] Ray Lanford insists that Butler sacrifices himself for honor by refusing to hold Gilford back in the final race, and surmises, therefore, that "Mr. Butler is not a son of a bitch."[12] Lanford goes on to suggest that Butler has redeemed himself, and the critic expresses concern that the reader cannot enter the narrative and "set Joe straight" about his father: "We wish we could reach into the story and tell the boy what we know; if only we could let him know that his old man was in fact a father of whom he could be proud."[13] Yet there are equally articulate discussions that argue that Butler is fundamentally dishonorable. In his analysis of love in "My Old Man," Robert Lewis states that Joe "is trying desperately to love his crooked father" and is "[f]orced to face the fact of his father's crookedness."[14] Angel Capellán reads the tale as "a child's shocking discovery of the corruptness of his deeply loved father."[15] B. A. Hauger argues that Joe learns about evil from two basic sources, Butler and the world of horse racing: he says the work is "a story of a young boy's discovery of evil in the two things he loves most in the world, his father and horse racing."[16] Leo Gurko locates a theme of discovery in the story: "The boy in 'My Old Man' discovers that his idolized father, a jockey, was a crook."[17] Joseph DeFalco argues that the narrative reflects Butler's "stage-by-stage moral disintegration."[18] Some readers, however, equivocate over Butler's character and behavior. Sheridan Baker, for example, describes Butler as "pathetically good as father and bad as man."[19] And Larry Grimes concludes that Butler is a problematic figure: "The old man is an example of the silent, vital hero, although it is difficult to determine whether he is a dumb ox or a stoic tutor to be admired and imitated."[20] According to Grimes, Joe's narration is necessarily ambiguous: "It is possible, according to the narrator's design, to interpret the story as a testimony to the father's integrity. It is also possible to show that while Butler is a man of principle, he is not principled in all things."[21]

The third class of criticism, narrative revelation, is given cursory treatment by many of these same critics. Nakajima argues that there is an explicit duality to Joe's narration that distinguishes between "what he feels and what he perceives."[22] Peter Nicolaisen cites Joe's youthful vocabulary as indicative of naïveté, and concludes that Joe perceives no logical connections among the separate events in the story.[23] And Grimes places Joe's narration under the general rubric of play:

> The narrator is neither a dreamer nor an ethical character. He is a storyteller. Storytelling is one form of human activity designated by the word "play." The storyteller enters into a world beyond the ordinary. His world, unlike the day-to-day world, is a complete world. . . . The story bears its own design, or rules, and is deliberately set apart from duration. The story is no accident; the teller must will it since all play is voluntary.[24]

In what is probably the most detailed discussion of narrative technique in "My Old Man," Hauger analyzes the relationship between first-person perspective and theme. She argues that the story reveals a theme of disillusionment through the subjective revelations of the narrator. Hauger then advances the argument that there is an ironic discrepancy between opposing dimensions of Joe's perceptions and narrative presentation: "Joe is trying to be like the ideal father he pictures instead of the real Butler he indirectly presents to the reader. Further irony develops from the contrast between Joe's naive, romantic interpretation and description of events and the reader's actual perception of them."[25] Yet there are some major problems with Hauger's distinction between split perception and narrative revelation. Joe is our only source of representation; perceptions (and receptions) can be reflected *only* through his act of narrating. Conceptions cannot travel unfiltered from narrator to reader. Hauger's reading is questionable when she asserts that father and son necessarily experience different, and often opposing, perspectives, attitudes, and emotions. At the St. Cloud event, for example, Butler cheers for Kircubbin for economic reasons and Joe roots for Kzar for emotional and aesthetic reasons, yet Joe is not totally unaware of the "other" reality of this predetermined event. Joe clearly overhears Butler soliciting the name of the winning horse from George Gardner, who has committed himself to throwing the race:

> "He [Kzar] won't win," George says very low, leaning over and buttoning the bottoms of his paints.
> "Who will?" my old man says, leaning over close so nobody can hear.
> "Kircubbin," George says, "and if he does, save me a couple of tickets."[26]

Hauger is incorrect, however, in arguing (along with many others) that Joe has been "idealizing his father throughout the story,"[27] and that, consequently, he experiences bitter disillusionment when the conclusion "reveals" Butler's "true"—that is, nefarious—character. The reader, according to Hauger, presumably experiences interpretative paralysis if he or she is not "astute enough to view Butler from a realistic standpoint instead of accepting Joe's narrative at face value."[28] What is meant by a "realistic standpoint"? How does a reader recognize narration at face value, even assuming that there can be determinate, semantic constructions representing "reality" at "face value"? The relationship among teller, tale, and audience is necessarily complex, as Scholes and Kellogg suggest: "In the relationship between the teller and the tale, and that other relationship between the teller and the audience, lies the essence of the narrative art."[29] Narrative interpretation is particularly problematic when narrative revelation is not subjected to formal, systematic examination.

I am not attempting to suggest that Hauger and others have necessarily arrived at erroneous interpretations; I suggest instead that they offer less complete readings than the complexity of the story warrants. Any critical reading is necessarily incomplete; indeed, most disciplines involved in hermeneutics have long recognized fundamental limitations of interpretation. Yet Hauger's emphasis on narrative technique does offer an important beginning, and an exploration of her approach might provisionally provide the ground for at least a tentative explanation of the means by which narrative technique shapes our response to specific thematic conclusions.

Formal principles of narrative exposition are essential interpretative tools because they are the only means by which readers can attempt to respond analytically to any narrative's values, implicit, explicit, or both implicit and explicit. That is why any reading of Butler—honorific, pejorative, or mixed—is *produced by* and, simultaneously, *complicated by* Hemingway's mode of narration. Butler may indeed be a composite of contradictory ethical stances; he does represent multiple values—crooked at times, honorable on other occasions, and sometimes right and wrong at the same time, depending upon the context of the situation. However, we must be aware that these values come to us filtered through a voice of indeterminate maturation. Does Joe's narration take place in late adolescence, late twenties, thirties, or forties? Is there any method of separating the *time of narration* (Joe's maturity) from the *narration of time* (Joe's adolescence)? Gérard Genette argues that there is no method to separate them, on the ground that time of narration is always indeterminate: "[Narrative] analysis can look at the narrating instance only as it is given in the final state of the text, as a single moment without duration."[30] How many temporal perspectives are there in "My Old Man"? The text gives no clue, other than to suggest that the present tense of narration is one of relative maturity looking back at childhood experience. We can only be sure, according to Grimes, that there is at least a double temporality in the narrative: "An older initiated Joe Butler is telling his own story—the story of an initiation into the world of time and memory called forth by the death of his father."[31] However, perhaps the time of narration is not of critical significance if the reader considers the revelation of present-time plot activity more important than a determination of insight gained by a receding consideration of distant experience.[32] This issue is significant because literary narrative, according to Genette, represents a unique combination of elements that cannot be understood without a specific kind of distillation: "A narrating situation is, like any other, a complex whole within which analysis, or simply description, cannot *differentiate* except by ripping apart a tight web of connections among the narrating act, its protagonists, its spatio-temporal determinations, its relationship to the other narrating situations involved in the same narrative."[33] Indeed, it might be argued that "My Old Man" contains multiple narratives. Larry Grimes echoes this sentiment in suggesting that Joe's attitude toward time and reminiscence interferes with authorial narration: "Hemingway's point of view for the story complicates the perspective of the narrator-agent because of the attitude the narrator adopts toward the world of memory."[34]

The following reading attempts to offer one possible explanation of the mode by which Joe establishes credibility as narrator—that is, ethical narration. We have seen a polysemy of responses to "My Old Man," many of which are routinely documented by what some critics refer to as an "objective reality" within the narrative—which is often taken to be markedly distinct from Joe's perception of that reality. Yet narrator perceptions, unless demonstrably unreliable (as in some of Ford Madox Ford's work, for example), derive from a privileged epistemology. As David Carr argues, "Narrative requires narration; and this activity is not just a recounting of events but a recounting informed by a certain kind of *superior knowledge* (emphasis added).[35] Carr goes on to suggest that the process of narration involves a unique *heuresis:* "narration constitutes something, creates meaning rather than just reflecting or imitating something that exists independently of it."[36] I would suggest that any reading of "My Old Man" is undermined if it does not consider the narrative vehicle that enables readers to make critical judgments. One method of examining narrative interpretation involves a synthesis of rhetorical and literary approaches to narrative in antiquity, which I will briefly outline and then apply to narrative technique in "My Old Man."

Rhetorical and Literary Narration

It is common knowledge that literary criticism, theoretical and practical, has been concerned with narration since at least the fourth century B.C.,[37] although it is not commonly known that narration has been a fundamental area of investigation in the rhetorical arts for approximately the same length of time. There have always been reciprocal connections between literary and rhetorical arts, and Quintilian argues that literary studies provide the foundation for rhetorical studies: "Unless the foundations of oratory are well and truly laid by the teaching of literature, the superstructure will collapse."[38] Narration is the most consistent link between these disciplines forming the superstructure of effective discourse. As John O'Banion points out, literature and rhetoric are inextricably intertwined in Quintilian's approach to classical *paideia:* "It is hard to overstate the importance of literature in Quintilian's pedagogical theory. Similarly, it is hard to overstate the importance of the art of narration, the primary benefit to be acquired from such study."[39] Quintilian considers narration to be *the* basic rhetorical process. He gives narration prominent attention in his monumental 12-volume treatise on education, *Institutio Oratoria,* which examines narration and proof as complementary techniques in all liberal arts, while emphasizing the literary arts.

Classical *narratio* involved both a sequence of events (change over time) and a resultant proof or logical result of a specific sequence of narrated events (cause and effect). For Quintilian narration is also epistemological: "Short stories [*Narratiunculas*] from the poets should in my opinion be handled not with a view to style but as a means of increasing knowledge" (1.9.6). In following the educational ideal of Isocrates (arguably the most influential philosopher and rhetorician in antiquity), Quintilian emphasizes moral duty, which may be said to constitute an ethics of narration serving rhetoric and literature: "it is but a step from this [rhetorical exercise of evaluation] to practice in the comparisons of the respective merits of two characters" (2.4.21). Quintilian understands the process of narration to be the essence of literary discourse: "Narrating involved the connections of characters and plot, of persons, motives, and the web of events in which lives are lived."[40]

Quintilian argues that the function of rhetorical narrative is one that provides the linear sequence of plot development with the logical conclusion or proof that persuades a particular audience within the context of the particular circumstances of the situation. Literary narrative sequentially reveals the development of action and language, leading to an assessment or evaluation at the conclusion of the narrative. Yet narration is far more than a literary or rhetorical chain of events; it depends heavily upon the specific context of the rhetorical or literary situation. The Greek term for this specific kind of context is *kairos* (due measure, right timing, or spatial proportionality), whereas the Latin term is decorum (proportionality, propriety, or appropriateness).

Quintilian is quite specific in defining the characteristics of narration, which are plausibility, lucidity, and brevity. Plausibility, or probability, is particularly important—even more important than the "truth" of the narration. Quintilian advises orators to be particularly concerned with plausibility because auditors will not necessarily know the truth, and will be influenced to believe what is probable. Quintilian states, "There are many things which are true, but scarcely credible, just as there are many things which are plausible though false" (4.2.34). An effective narrative, then, must contain those elements that make for persuasive probability. These elements of effective narration are particularly important to Aristotle's concept of ethical persuasion.

Lucidity and brevity are also fundamental to persuasive narration. Quintilian defines lucidity, or clearness, as language that is not "unusual" (a concern Aristotle shared), free from ambiguity, and explicitly related to the subject matter. The narrator achieves lucidity by "setting forth our story in words which are appropriate, significant and free from any taint of meanness, but not on the other hand farfetched or unusual" (4.2.36). A lucid narrative must be proportionate to its subject matter, and "appropriateness" is "the key to lucidity."[41] Appropriateness might be defined as "fitting," "contextual," or "of proper measure."[42] Brevity is the third characteristic of persuasive narration, and Quintilian states that the narrator should always begin at the appropriate place, "avoid irrelevance, and finally cut out everything the removal of which neither hampers . . . nor harms" (4.2.40). Quintilian's view of narrative in rhetoric and literature is complemented by Aristotle's presentation of the ethical proof, as presented in *The "Art" of Rhetoric*. Aristotle does not advance the interconnections between rhetoric and poetics in the *Rhetoric*,[43] but his detailed presentation of ethical argumentation illustrates, I believe, the establishment of credibility in literary as well as rhetorical narratives.

In his *Rhetoric*, Aristotle formulates three fundamental rhetorical appeals or proofs *(pisteis)* by which a speaker or writer achieves his or her persuasive purpose: the ethical appeal, the pathetic appeal, and the logical appeal. Although these are devices intended to serve the purpose of rhetorical persuasion, they are equally applicable to literary persuasion. All of these appeals play a role in narrative (and narrator) credibility, yet, I would argue, it is the ethical appeal that most shapes reader response to first-person narration.

The ethical argument is derived from ethos, which means character, yet not necessarily good character as in the usual sense of ethical.[44] Aristotle considered the ethical appeal to be the most important element of persuasion: "Moral character, so to say, constitutes the most effective means of proof" (1.2.4–5). There are three components to the ethical appeal: (1) Good sense *(phronesis)*; (2) good character *(aretê)*; and (3) good will *(eunoia)*. Edward Cope summarizes the ethical argument as one "which consists in conveying to the audience a favorable impression of *your own character,* in making them believe . . . that you are an honest man and incapable of misrepresenting the facts of the case, intelligent enough to thoroughly understand them, and well disposed to your hearers and their interests."[45] In this definition, Cope alludes to the most important elements in the establishment of credibility. Good sense means the ability to demonstrate practical judgment; in literary narrative it involves the ability to reveal dialogue, thought, and action that are credible and plausible. In Wayne Booth's taxonomy of narrators, the narrator with good sense is consistently "reliable."[46] Good will means the ability to relate the events, words, and thoughts of the story with sincerity and empathy for the reader. The orator or narrator must share some of the reader's basic assumptions, what Kenneth Burke calls identification.[47] Good moral character carries the unspecialized meaning of ethical; a narrator demonstrates goodness through his or her narrative by demonstrating a trustworthiness in narrator revelation. The reader must believe that the narrator would not consciously deceive him or her. In first-person narratives where the narrator directly addresses the reader, such as "My Old Man," the ethics of the narrator are particularly important because of the intimacy of the relationship between narrator and reader. Yet this relationship is a reciprocal one. As David Carr states, "we [as readers] are constantly striving, with more or less success, to occupy the storyteller's position with respect to our own actions."[48] In the following analysis, I attempt to show how this relationship between narrator and reader develops, through the creation of a special bond between teller and audience that is based upon principles of ethical proof and narrative probability. The collective components of ethical narration shape reader response to character and, therefore, to meaning in the story. Joe's narration, taken as both sequential process and persuasive discourse, controls the process of interpretation.

Ethical Narration

The diverse interpretations of "My Old Man" cited above suggest that there
is little agreement among professional readers about what values the narrative represents, as we have seen, for example, in opposing views of Butler's
ethics. I suggest, however, that Butler is both good and evil and that the
ways in which we response to his morality are shaped by Joe's narration.
We are manipulated by the narrator because Joe's ethical narration secures
a relationship with us that confers credibility and legitimacy on him *as
narrator*. Joe begins the process of establishing his veracious persona in his
introductory address: "I guess looking at it, now, my old man was cut out
for a fat guy, one of those regular little roly fat guys you see around, but he
sure never got that way, except a little toward the last, and then it wasn't
his fault, he was riding over the jumps only and he could afford to carry
plenty of weight then" (151). The tone and attitude of Joe's introduction
clearly reveal the boy's devotion to his father, yet by commencing the
narrative with the uncertain perspective, "I guess," Joe signals a problematic understanding of his father that narrator and reader must face together. The uncertainty in Joe's voice registers a certainty of affection for
his father and what his father has become—a disciplined athlete facing the
ultimately undefeatable foe: mortality of the flesh. However, the reader
cannot distance himself or herself from the intimacy established by the
honesty of Joe's presentation. As Genette argues, the reader is not an inert
receptacle but actively participates in the process and epistemology of the
narrative act: "speculative imperialism, such certainty of truth, could lead
one to think that the receiver's role here is purely passive, that he is limited
to receiving a message he must take or leave and to 'consuming' after the
event a work that was completed far from him and without him. Nothing
would be more contrary."[49] Joe's initial diffidence indicates that he really
does not know how to judge Butler, who has been both good and bad
father—good in the sense that his words and paternal actions demonstrate
a real affection for his son and bad in his involvement in corrupt horse
racing. Joe's introduction is also representative of his willingness to accept
his father's shortcomings, as long as they do not transgress the inner life of
their relationship as father and son. In stating that Butler's weight gain
"wasn't his fault," Joe foreshadows his own indisposition to judge his father's
"outer" life of turpitude (fixing races and betting on fixed races) *and* recti-
tude (thwarting fixed races). Joe's introduction, then, reveals a double (and
not necessarily contradictory) vision of Butler.

The reader cannot avoid being drawn into the narrative from the very
beginning, a process that serves to establish a bond among Joe, Butler, and
audience. In describing Butler's training exercises, Joe implores *us* to share

his own sense of devotion to his father: "Say, it was a treat to see my old man skip rope, too. . . . Say, you ought to have seen wops look at us sometimes. . . . They sure looked as though they thought the old man was nuts" (152). This passage exemplifies the well-known Hemingway opposition of "us" against "them," yet what is significant about the opposition in "My Old Man" is the reader's explicit inclusion in the "us." Joe's direct entreaty to us as readers forces the reader to take sides in the developing conflicts Joe and his father face. The developing relationship between narrator and reader capitalizes on the *eunoia* and *aretê* established in the introductory passage, and both ethical modes intensify a progressing rapport between teller and listener.

Critics such as Nicolaisen suggest that Joe is naive at best and imperceptive at worst, yet the text does not support this conclusion. Joe consistently reveals his *phronesis* in performing as a perceptive, credible narrator. Early in the story, Joe demonstrates his knowledge *and* understanding of the intense physical and mental preparation Butler must go through in order to remain competitive. After describing his father's training routine, Joe remarks: "That's the way it was keeping down to weight. . . . Most jocks can ride off all they want to. A jock loses about a kilo every time he rides, but my old man was sort of dried out and he couldn't keep down his kilos without all that running" (153). Joe consistently shares the agony of his father's battle to remain physically competitive, yet it is a bond that can only be held together by a symbiosis of mutual understanding. Butler's treatment of Joe is neither atypical nor unexpected, given the intimacy of their relationship. Joe's realization (and articulation) of his father's struggle, however, is representative of Joe's uncanny ability to perceive inner suffering.

Butler's constant struggle to support himself and Joe forces them into a peripatetic existence, moving back and forth from France to Italy—the setting for two of the narrative's three major conflicts. It is in San Siro that Butler becomes agitated upon seeing Regoli, whose presence probably reminds Butler of a past fixed race. What is important about this scene, however, is not Joe's instinctive response to defend his father's reaction to Regoli, but rather Joe's subsequent narration that reflects the tightening of the bond between father and son. Their experiences are now collective and unified: "Well, it would have been all right, maybe, if *we'd* stayed in Milan" (emphasis added) (154). However, things do not remain "all right" for very long. Shortly after Butler's encounter with Regoli, one of the most important incidents in the story occurs: Butler wins the Premio Commercio. It is Butler's *specific performance* in this race—by "shooting her out of the field the last hundred meters" (155)—that precipitates his encounter with "Holbrook and a fat wop." Holbrook contemptuously calls Butler a son of a bitch because Butler apparently reneged on an agreement to throw the Premio Commercio by holding his horse back. In fact, he does the exact opposite by driving his horse to win. Any horse-racing novice knows that races can be fixed in only one way—by restraining predetermined horses, usually heavy favorites. It is precisely because he has dishonored his agreement with Holbrook that Butler is forced to accept the abuse of being called a son of a bitch in front of his only son who loves him dearly. Joe immediately recognizes that "something went wrong," but perceptively understands that there is an honorable justification for Butler's passive reaction to the insult. Joe tells us, "I was scared and felt sick because I knew something had happened and I didn't see how anybody could call my old man a son of a bitch and get away with it" (156). Joe does not understand the reason for the epithet because he is unaware (as is the reader) of any unethical act by his father—as jockey—in the present time of the narrative.

Three days after the Holbrook incident, Joe and his father return to the tranquility of France. Joe's description of their return is technically similar to his introductory description of his father. He draws the reader into his impressions and judgments through empathetic, direct address, which presumes common assumptions between narrator and reader: "I got to like it [Paris] though, part of it, anyway, and say it's got the best race courses in the world. Seems as though that were the thing that keeps it all going. . . . I guess that's one of the busiest parts of the town [Café de la Paix]. But, say, it is funny that a big town like Paris wouldn't have a Galleria, isn't it?" (157). Joe, like his father, has learned to rely upon horse racing to "keep things going," yet there is angst in his rhetorical question. Joe's narration is beginning to reveal an understanding of the dark side of life that all Hemingway heroes come to know. It is at this point that "My Old Man" can properly be defined as *Entwicklungsgeschichte*—a work in which a novitiate achieves insight.

The narrator's awareness of the darker dimensions of reality is emphasized by his phronetic understanding of the pragmatics of "getting through life," more specifically the only professional life he knows—horse racing. Joe's detailed chronicle of a jockey's professional code reveals a new maturity in the narrator-reader relationship. Joe begins to explain, with patronizing expertise, the rules of the sport: "If a jock's riding for somebody too, he can't go boozing around because the trainer has an eye on him if he's a kid and if he ain't a kid he's always got an eye on himself" (159). This explanation is ironic, of course, in that Butler clearly does not keep an eye on himself, but that does not lessen Joe's perception. In fact, it emphasizes Joe's sentience by revealing his ability to see beyond his father's violations of the code, and it signals the emergence of Joe's code of conduct.

The race at St. Cloud, the second major incident of the story, is significant in revealing Joe's reaction to and perception of his father's involvement
in a different kind of corruption. Joe begins his description of the setting of
the race with emphatic attention to physical detail, and his narration is
characterized by a youthful awe conjoined with a mature sense of the "realities" of horse racing. This adolescent exuberance—"you never saw such
horses. This Kzar is a great big yellow horse that looks like just nothing but
run" (160)—does not interfere with his sophisticated understanding of the
pervasive presence of corruption. Indeed, he tells us that he can readily
identify horses "with a shot of dope in them" (160). Joe also tells us that he
is aware that "something big was up" (161) after overhearing Butler's conversation with George Gardner, Kzar's jockey. Joe clearly knows that Gardner is going to hold back the five-for-ten favorite, yet nonetheless allows
himself to become overcome with emotion during the race, "temporarily"
forgetting that his father has wagered heavily on Kircubbin. Because Joe
knows the race is illegitimate he cannot hide his apprehension from the
reader; his *aretê* compels an honest description of his reaction to the race.
One indication of his compulsion to report the event truthfully is his frequent use of the term "funny," which for Joe usually means unprincipled
("funny" characterizes corrupt jockeys, con artists, and prostitutes [165–
66]). As the horses approach the stretch, Joe notes that "Everybody was
looking funny and saying 'Kzar' in a sort of sick way" (164). When Joe
realizes that Kircubbin has won he says that "I felt all trembly and funny
inside" (164). Joe feels "funny" inside because he realizes that by knowing
Kzar was going to lose he himself became an active accomplice in corruption, and no degree of rationalization can erase that knowledge.

Has Joe, then, become unethical to the reader? I would argue that he
has not, on the ground that his *relationship* with the reader has never been
violated: Joe's *eunoia* has not been compromised. In fact, his overt concern
for narrative integrity enhances his good will toward the reader. After ad-
mitting that he "felt funny," Joe implores the reader to believe that his own
"displaced loyalty" was unintentional: "Honest, watching the race I'd forgot
how much my old man had bet on Kircubbin. . . . But now that it was all
over it was swell to know we had the winner" (164). By what code of
morality can Joe be indicted for placing loyalty to his father above allegiance
to a blatantly and thoroughly corrupt enterprise? Joe knows that fixed races
are wrong, but *at this point* they are not as wrong as disloyalty to his father.
Joe pays a significant price for attempting to reconcile these opposed loyalties—he loses his innocence: "Of course I knew it was funny all the time.
But my old man saying that [Gardner is a great jockey for holding Kzar back]
right out like that sure took the kick all out of it for me and I didn't get the
real kick back again ever" (165). Reflecting upon his now-compromised

values, Joe decides that the correct ethical choice was his instinctive response: "I wish I were a jockey and could have rode him instead of that son of a bitch" (165). By this admission, Joe, once again, reinforces his narrative *ethos*. He is *now* prepared to replace his father's values with his own. The price he has paid—his loss of innocence—is not unregenerative. The experience of participation in corruption sparks Joe's desire to reverse the outcome of the race, signaling an ethical maturity.

Any examination of narrative technique in "My Old Man" would necessarily be incomplete without a consideration of the events surrounding the climactic Prix du Marat. Joe begins his description by telling us that Butler has obtained his racing permit and purchased Gilford, a steeplechase racehorse. Relations are exceptionally good between father and son. Joe tells us that he is particularly proud of his father after his recent success as an owner-jockey: "I felt as proud of him as though it was the first race he'd ever placed in. You see, when a guy ain't been riding for a long time, you can't make yourself believe that he has ever rode" (169). We have seen gushing filial admiration through much of the story, yet in the conclusion the admiration is intensified by Joe's entreaty to the reader to share a growing, more mature love and respect for Butler. These latter emotions are based upon the integrity of Butler's physical and emotional "comeback" more than on anything else. In fact, Butler is now made anonymous, just "a guy," a common fellow. Yet the "you" in Joe's description includes narrator *and* reader. The narrator universalizes Butler by making him anonymous, yet at the same time the reader is drawn into a shared understanding of the obstacles Butler must face in having to prove himself all over again.

Butler does not remain "just a guy" for long, however. His days of fixing races are long behind him, as suggested by Joe's summation of his relationship with his father: "I was proud of everything" (169), which presumably includes Butler's decision to "stay straight." No other inference seems probable after Joe has stated quite clearly how important honest horse racing is to him. It would be hypocritical for him to state that he is proud of everything if there were any question of Butler's active involvement in corruption. A second sign of Butler's reformation is the fact that he has received his permit, which precludes any recent major offense. The third (and most important) indication of Butler's integrity is the fact that he incurs the wrath of crooked gamblers in San Siro, Milan, and Auteuil, which strongly implies that he no longer fixes races and, therefore, cannot be counted on as "one of them." This evidence builds a formidable case for Butler's rehabilitation, which is symbolically represented in the colors he chooses for his death ride—a black jacket and hat representing his former reprobacy, contrasted with a white cross delineating his redemption.

Butler's last ride exemplifies his renewed vigor and fidelity to the sport of racing. Joe synecdochically recounts the beginning of the race with optimistic expectation: after the turn the horses "came out with the old black jacket going third" (170). As they enter the stretch, Joe creates the appearance that Butler will win the race: "I saw them coming and hollered at my old man as he went by, and he was leading by about a length and riding way out" (171). Butler loses both the race and his life, but maintains Joe's respect, in spite of what the conclusion superficially implies in the exchange between two insiders, who apparently lost money because of Butler's accident:

> "Well, Butler got his all right."
> The other guy said, "I don't give a goddam if he did, the crook. He had it coming to him on the stuff he's pulled."
> "I'll say he had," said the other guy, and tore the bunch of tickets in two.
> And George looked at me to see if I'd heard and I had all right and he said, "Don't you listen to what those bums said, Joe. Your old man was one swell guy."
> But I don't know. Seems like when they get started they don't leave a guy nothing.
> (173)

This final act of narration is not a rejection of the evaluation that Butler was a swell guy but, on the contrary, reflects a probable conclusion to the sequence of events leading up to it. The action and language of "My Old Man" reveal Butler to be, essentially, a loving and good father, in spite of his uncertain past and willingness to bet on a fixed race. Joe knows that his father is not untainted, and Joe's concluding words embrace his concern for Butler's reputation and the legacy it leaves to his son. Joe's concern for the reader's sensibility is reflected in his use of the conditional "seems." Joe, as narrator, resists the conclusion that his father's death is justified, as implied by the remarks of the disgruntled gamblers. Their sentiments are mere popular opinion, representative of only what *may* shape reader judgment. Joe's final words draw upon the strength of the relationship between narrator and reader and, in so doing, create the circumstances under which the reader, rather than crooked sportsmen (including Gardner), judges Butler. "They" never leave a Hemingway protagonist anything. It is the shared experience of teller and reader, based upon an ethics of understanding, that is the affirmative residue of this tale.

Notes

1. "My Old Man" appears in at least six Hemingway anthologies, dozens of general readers, various collections of sports fiction, and at least two manuals examining the art of narration. It is often included in high school anthologies, and at least one textbook on the pedagogy of literature examines "proper" approaches to the work.

2. Herschell Brickell, *New York Evening Post,* 17 October 1925: 3.

3. Earl Rovit, *Ernest Hemingway* (Boston: Twayne, 1963) 43.

4. Kenji Nakajima, *"Lacrimae Rerum* in 'My Old Man,'" *Kyushu American Literature* 22 (1981): 18.

5. Charles A. Fenton, *The Apprenticeship of Ernest Hemingway: The Early Years,* 1954 (New York: Octagon, 1975) 149.

6. Joseph M. Flora, *Hemingway's Nick Adams* (Baton Rouge: Louisiana State UP, 1982) 146.

7. Christian K. Messinger, *Sport and the Spirit of Play in American Fiction: Hawthorne to Faulkner* (New York: Columbia UP, 1981) 278.

8. Messinger, 355.

9. Philip Young, *Ernest Hemingway* (New York: Rinehart, 1952) 177.

10. Sydney J. Krause, "Hemingway's 'My Old Man,'" *Explicator* 20 (1962): item 39.

11. Nakajima, 20.

12. Ray Lanford, "Hemingway's 'My Old Man,'" *Linguistics in Literature* 1 (1976): 18.

13. Lanford, 19.

14. Robert W. Lewis, Jr., *Hemingway on Love* (Austin: U of Texas P, 1965) 13.

15. Angel Capellán, *Hemingway and the Hispanic World* (Ann Arbor: UMI Research P, 1985) 2.

16. B. A. Hauger, "First Person Perspective in Four Hemingway Stories," *Rendezvous* 6 (1971): 29.

17. Leo Gurko, *Ernest Hemingway and the Pursuit of Heroism* (New York: Crowell, 1968) 176.

18. Joseph DeFalco, *The Hero in Hemingway's Short Stories* (Pittsburgh: U of Pittsburgh P, 1963) 57.

19. Sheridan Baker, *Ernest Hemingway: An Introduction and Interpretation* (New York: Rinehart, 1976) 26.

20. Larry E. Grimes, *The Religious Design of Hemingway's Early Fiction* (Ann Arbor: UMI Research P, 1985) 29.

21. Grimes, 33.

22. Nakajima, 18.

23. Quoted in Wayne E. Kvam, *Hemingway in Germany* (Athens: Ohio UP, 1973) 176–77.

24. Grimes, 33.

25. Hauger, 30.

26. Ernest Hemingway, *In Our Time,* 1925 (New York: Charles Scribner's Sons, 1955). All subsequent references are to this edition.

27. Hauger, 30.

28. Hauger, 30–31.

29. Robert Scholes and Robert Kellogg, *The Nature of Narrative*, 1966 (London: Oxford UP, 1976) 240.

30. Gérard Genette, *Narrative Discourse: An Essay in Method* (Ithaca: Cornell UP, 1980) 225.

31. Grimes, 30.

32. Genette argues that narrative time is a more important consideration than narrative space:

    > I can very well tell a story without specifying the place where it happens, and whether this place is more or less distant from the place where I am telling it; nevertheless, it is almost impossible for me not to locate the story in time with respect to my narrating act, since I must necessarily tell the story in a present, past, or future tense. This is perhaps why the temporal determinations of the narrating instance are manifestly more important than its spatial determinations. (215)

33. Genette, 215.

34. Grimes, 30.

35. David Carr, *Time, Narrative, and History* (Bloomington: Indiana UP, 1986) 59.

36. Carr, 62.

37. In *The "Art" of Rhetoric*, trans. J. H. Freese, 1926 (Cambridge: Harvard UP, 1975), Aristotle observes that the study of language and style had only recently made much progress. (III.i.5).

38. Quintilian, *The Institutio Oratoria of Quintilian*, trans. H. E. Butler, 4 vols. (Cambridge: Harvard UP, 1958). All subsequent references are to this edition.

39. John D. O'Banion, "Narration and Argumentation: Quintilian on *Narratio* as the Heart of Rhetorical Thinking," *Rhetorica* 5 (1987): 333.

40. O'Banion, 335.

41. O'Banion, 336.

42. The Roman concept of appropriateness, "decorum," was closely related to and derivative from the Greek concept of *kairos*, meaning the "right time" or "due measure." The concept of *kairos* has a rich tradition in Greek philosophy, rhetoric, and poetics.

43. Although many literary critics are now beginning to explore relationships between rhetorical and literary theory, the connection has never been traced to Aristotle, at least to my knowledge. One bridge connecting rhetoric to poetics occurs in chapter 19 of the *Poetics*, the subject matter of which is thought and diction. Aristotle consigns thought *(dianoia)* to the domain of rhetoric; actions or incidents *(pragmasin)* are to be considered under the same rubric as dramatic speeches, that is, as rhetorical forms of discourse.

44. Most translations of Aristotle's *Rhetoric* are in general agreement that "good character" *must* be revealed exclusively by the discourse, and not by any preconceived idea of the speaker's character.

45. Edward M. Cope, *An Introduction to Aristotle's Rhetoric with Analysis Notes and Appendices* (London: Macmillan, 1867) 109.

46. See Wayne Booth, *The Rhetoric of Fiction* (Chicago: U of Chicago P, 1961) 158–61.

47. Identification is a complex relationship between narrator and encoder and involves a reader's response to many elements of the narrative. As Booth points out: "What we call 'involvement' or 'sympathy' or 'identification' is usually made up of many reactions to authors, narrators, observers, and other characters" (158).

48. Carr, 61.

49. Genette, 259.

4

"Out of Season" and Hemingway's Neglected Discovery: Ordinary Actuality

James Steinke

"Out of Season" marks a special place in the development of Hemingway's career as a short story writer. Composed in April 1923, after "Up in Michigan" and "My Old Man," "Out of Season" is the latest of three stories included in the author's first minor book, Three Stories and Ten Poems, *and the earliest of the four "marriage group" stories of his first major book, the Boni & Liveright* In Our Time. *Hemingway himself seemed to think that "Out of Season" marked his transition from apprentice to professional, recalling in* A Moveable Feast *that the story was the first he had been able to write after the now-legendary loss of all but two of his early manuscripts, and that it was the first to use his now-famous "iceberg" theory—"that you could omit anything if you knew that you omitted and the omitted part would strengthen the story and make people feel something more than they understood." Yet despite these compelling reasons to look closely at "Out of Season," criticism, with one important exception, has done little more than repeat Hemingway's published remarks about this short story—that "Out of Season" is merely "an almost literal transcription" of a row between the author and his first wife (presumably about her desire to continue a pregnancy he did not welcome), and that the "real end" of the story was that "the old man hanged himself." The exception is a ground-breaking 1983 article by Paul Smith, "Some Misconceptions of 'Out of Season,'" which uses a careful analysis of the story's heavily revised manuscripts to call these assumptions (and Hemingway's veracity) into question and to challenge scholars to reconsider this important work.*

Here James Steinke attains a fresh view of "Out of Season" by discounting psychobiographical theory-of-omission readings entirely. He does not equate the young man and his wife with Hemingway and Hadley or assume that their quarrel outside the frame of the story has been about anything so marriage-wrenching as abortion. Nor does Steinke find any evidence within the story to suggest that its real end is Peduzzi's suicide. For this critic, "Out of Season" is a comedy of everyday errors, a fine story of "ordinary actuality."

Hemingway is . . . the most significant of living poets . . . so far as the subject of EXTRAORDINARY ACTUALITY is concerned.
> —Wallace Stevens, 1942

Consider that perhaps "Out of Season" is not about the collapse of a couple's marriage. Perhaps this early story is also not a disguised autobiographical projection of the young Hemingway's alleged obsession over not wanting Hadley to have their first baby. Was it really written from feelings of guilt for his apparently dismayed reactions to her pregnancy (incidentally first publicized unsympathetically—and distorted?—by Gertrude Stein in *The Autobiography of Alice B. Toklas*) and therefore veiled in an implicit style?[1]

Perhaps instead, the story is about a married couple who, having had an argument, try on the husband's initiative to go on a fishing trip before the season is legally open—the husband unknowingly having hired a guide who is not really a guide but a drunk—and whose day then goes haywire, quite untragically turning into a series of little mishaps. Perhaps the experience in "Out of Season" is in fact comic, though not especially to the characters themselves at the time. Perhaps the function and effect of the comedy are, remarkably, not to reduce the drunk Peduzzi to a farcical human being, and the story became the young Hemingway's chance for a dramatic, undismissive study of the man. Perhaps, after he lost all but a few of his manuscripts in 1923, Hemingway was using his ear for voice to discover a new subject—ordinary actuality.

The subject of Hemingway's most celebrated fiction, which Wallace Stevens defined succinctly in the 1940s as "extraordinary actuality," has led us to neglect lighter, less grave stories and sections in the novels. In compensation—though more, I suspect, out of puzzlement, as with "Out of Season" and other stories[2]—critics have located portents in the biography and psyche of the writer, claiming these are what must be implied by certain stretches of the dialogue and sometimes by the action and structure as well.[3]

With "Out of Season," Hemingway complicated the matter with some of his own statements.[4] In *A Moveable Feast* he said he was putting into practice in this story "a new theory that you could omit anything if you knew that you omitted and the omitted part would strengthen the story and make people feel something more than they understood."[5] The omitted "real end" of the story "was that the old man hanged himself." Yet if Hemingway had not mentioned this omitted hanging, the reader could not derive it from "Out of Season." Peduzzi's excited delusions in the closing moments about wanting to go fishing the next day with the young couple are too energetic to suggest he will kill himself. There is critical consensus that it is not possible to derive or infer a suicide from Peduzzi's behavior; nevertheless, Hemingway's claim that the real end was the guide's hanging has encouraged readers to find "what is omitted" from the actual events, by turning to their sense of Hemingway's own life story.

The few interpretations of "Out of Season" have never broken loose from the psychobiographical notion that the couple's conflict is a presentation of the collapse of a marriage. By itself, the story supports an entirely different notion; yet as a result of the marriage-on-the-rocks idea a basic failure of focus has also been claimed, since Hemingway *emphasized* the guide in saying the real end was omitted: "Is it the story of a marriage collapsing or is it Peduzzi's story? Is it both stories or neither? Where, in fact, is its center?" In this view "Out of Season" has a "peculiarly fuzzy focus."[6] Moreover, in reference to Hemingway's theory of omission and the omitted suicide, Carlos Baker has said "the theory worked badly in the case of 'Out of Season.' Peduzzi came through as an oaf but not as a potential suicide."[7] Yet while it is true that Peduzzi does not come through as a potential suicide, it may be not that the theory worked badly with this story, but only that it worked in another way—to balance the reader's view of Peduzzi with an understanding and sympathy for the couple, particularly the wife. The focus sharpens when we realize what the story's subject is and that the story is not tragic but comic: sober in tone, but not heavy, and occasionally very funny.

The title suggests the subject. For the "young gentleman" everything goes wrong. In fact, things go wrong for each main character in "Out of Season," though not seriously so. Many things are out of season; this is a story about "one of those days."[8]

We are set right by realizing the story is about all three characters—the husband, the wife, and Peduzzi—and by seeing how the theory of omission actually works here. What is left out is not the real end but, more important, the beginning of the story—the quarrel that precedes the opening, about which it is futile to seek details as they are not given. Because of this unpresented quarrel certain definite feelings keep affecting each character. That event prior to the story's opening—the quarrel at lunch—is really the strengthening part, easily missed the first time one reads the story's *first page*, yet clearly inferable from the couple's later conversation. Awareness of that event gives the reader the advantage of understanding the wife's feelings so that the opening details have a greater force beneath them, though we only eventually know why.

If we imagine the lunch already ruined by some argument, the wife reluctant to go on the outing but persuaded to, and having consented to, we realize her state of feelings is bad enough. But then, as the story opens, we see that among other things, she must follow behind with the fishing rods as a ridiculous precaution against arrest for fishing out of season (as if *her* carrying the rods would deceive a gamekeeper!), led by a guide who is not only drunk but whose notions about what he is doing are being frantically improvised. The omitted quarrel has consequences for the wife and for the husband as well, and recognition of those consequences will keep us from too narrow and unsympathetic a view.[9]

Carlos Baker points out that "although one might classify 'Out of Season' as a fishing story, the point of the story is that nothing (including fishing) is done."[10] As a general statement this seems accurate enough. But while the characters are not doing what they would like to be doing, there is nevertheless a great deal going on. To say that the point is that nothing is done, and to skip the couple's experience by stating that the "strength of the story is in the portrayal of the officious guide, Peduzzi, a fine characterization,"[11] offers a misleading, partial view, easily corrected by a summary of the action, which brings us to the story's chief concerns.

This fishing trip, the title tells us, is taking place before the season has opened. The young husband and wife are now at odds with each other from their quarrel at lunch, yet both leave to go with the Italian guide whom the husband earlier has found to take them to a good spot. But Peduzzi is not really a guide. He is the town drunk, and before the outing he has characteristically gotten very drunk. He parades his prizes through the town. The husband and wife, unaware of what all this means to Peduzzi and preoccupied with the feelings from their argument, try unsuccessfully to resolve their disagreement while stopping at an inn to buy Peduzzi the marsala he has requested. Later, when they reach the river and the guide claims they are only a half hour's walk from the fishing spot, the wife turns back. The river is rain-swollen and muddy, hence not so fishable, but Peduzzi quickly changes his advice: "It is good here, too," he says.[12] The husband halfheartedly follows Peduzzi's example in getting the rods ready right at that spot, whereupon it is discovered Peduzzi has no lead for sinkers. The expedition must be abandoned. Peduzzi has failed as a guide. His "day was going to pieces before his eyes" (178). The story ends with the husband's turning down, evasively, Peduzzi's energetic and desperate proposal that they all go fishing the next day.

We get an important glimpse, during the couple's conversation at the inn, of their earlier quarrel. One consequence for the husband of being preoccupied by the disagreement with his wife is that his usual vigilance is gone—a vigilance that only returns slowly toward the end of the story. At the story's opening, the young gentleman is half willful, half vague, and lets Peduzzi push him along while the young lady is openly unwilling. The husband and wife continue together through an oddly occurring series of events, no two of which combine well on this chilly, windy, rainy afternoon. To their further irritation, the husband and wife seem to promote chain reactions of these unfortunate events simply by their own proximity to each other and by their feelings. Simultaneous with this presentation and extending beyond it is a study, not without sympathy, of how inured the alcoholic Peduzzi is to illusion. The chain reaction of little things going wrong and a study of the drunken guide are integrated with each other by the objective narration that seems to move leisurely and as if without plan. However, as one learns to read it, the story goes from one unfortunate moment to the next, each bizarrely arising from the mistake or misunderstanding before it. Read this way, the story reveals itself as comprising many events densely packed—a catalogue of plausible little catastrophes all flowing into one another, and at some moments ventilated by a comic incident that only the reader can savor.

Early in the story we are told that it is "a wonderful day for trout fishing" (173), though this assessment is from Peduzzi's special point of view, expressing his elation over having a new job as guide. Actually it is windy and a little rainy: a "windy day with the sun coming out from behind the clouds and then going under in sprinkles of rain" (173).

But the first minor catastrophe of the "wonderful day for trout fishing" (173) is not even presented in the story—as we discover later when the young gentleman tries to reopen the subject of the quarrel on a conciliatory note. The substance of the couple's argument is not stated; it is not as important as the feelings that become clear now:

> "I'm sorry you feel so rotten, Tiny," he said. "I'm sorry I talked the way I did at lunch. We were both getting at the same thing from different angles."
> "It doesn't make any difference," she said. "None of it makes any difference." (175)

The wife's last remark, however, makes all the difference both to the two of them and to the reader. Without it the wife would have been answering his attempted conciliation with something like agreeableness, but by saying "*None of it* makes any difference" (emphasis added) she tells the husband (and the reader) unmistakably that a gulf has opened between them. What she is saying here is that she does not have the energy for this conflict and that it is not resolvable on his terms, so now, talking is useless. That is how she feels at the moment.

None of the incidents in the story so far has helped bring the wife and husband any closer; quite the opposite is the case, in fact, as in this passage:

> Everyone they met walking through the main street of town Peduzzi greeted elaborately. *Buon dì*, Arturo! Tipping his hat. The bank clerk stared at him from the door of the Fascist café. Groups of three and four people standing in front of the shops stared at the three. The workmen in their stone-powdered jackets working on the foundations of the new hotel looked up as they passed. Nobody spoke or gave any sign to them except the town beggar, lean and old, with a spittle-thickened beard, who lifted his hat as they passed. (174)

Yet the couple are hardly aware of the comic part they are playing in this silent little drama. Peduzzi is playing a new role, conspicuous to everyone (including the reader), except to the husband and wife. They are being treated as his clients in a new career, releasing in him a new confidence, a buoyant feeling based on the illusion that he has now achieved new status in the community. The husband is off guard enough not to feel as uncomfortable as his wife does.

But it is clearly evident to her that the guide is not trustworthy. Peduzzi seems to perceive vaguely the wife's feeling through his own insistent expansiveness, so he plays up to her. But she does not play along:

> Peduzzi stopped in front of a store with the window full of bottles and brought his empty grappa bottle from an inside pocket of his old military coat. "A little to drink, some marsala for the Signora, something, something to drink." He gestured with the bottle. It was a wonderful day. "Marsala, you like marsala, Signorina? A little marsala?"
>
> The wife stood sullenly. "You'll have to play up to this," she said. "I can't understand a word he says. He's drunk isn't he?" (174)

The wife is quicker than the husband at seeing through Peduzzi's manner, and she is less patient with it. She, at least, senses that something is distinctly amiss in all this.

Everything the husband and wife say to each other expresses how on edge they are. Moreover, they are accompanied by the excitable and effusive Peduzzi, whose manner does more to advertise his unreliability and even desperation than it does to help ease relations. It takes the husband longer than the wife to notice that they are being hustled along.

While the couple are having their lunch, Peduzzi, already drunk, gets "three more grappas" under his belt: "At the cantina near the bridge they trusted him for three more grappas because he was so confident and mysterious about his job for the afternoon" (173). So Peduzzi is good and drunk.

The husband, preoccupied as he is with the recent unpleasantness, does not notice: "The young gentleman came out of the hotel and asked him about the rods. Should his wife come behind with the rods?" (173). For a while, though, the focus is still on Peduzzi and on what he sees—his wish to accommodate the young man, which means having the signorina walk behind them—and on his wish to effect their evasive strategy:

> "Yes," said Peduzzi, "let her follow us." The young gentleman went back into the hotel and spoke to his wife. He and Peduzzi started down the road. The young gentleman had a musette over his shoulder. Peduzzi saw the wife, who looked as young as the gentleman, and was wearing mountain boots and a blue beret, start out to follow them down the road, carrying the fishing rods, unjointed, one in each hand. Peduzzi didn't like her to be way back there. "Signorina," he called, winking at the young gentleman, "come up here and walk with us, Signora, come up here. Let us all walk together." Peduzzi wanted them all three to walk down the street of Cortina together. (173)

Here, at the beginning of the story only a slight mention tells us what the wife's feelings are: "The wife stayed behind, following rather sullenly" (173). She is reluctantly participating in her husband's plan to evade the authorities. Even more noticeable is Peduzzi's wanting to make this his show. Feelings build, particularly hers. The reader shares the wife's perspective to a certain extent but can watch all this with no vested interest in going fishing or leading tourists, free of her irritation and anxiety.

Given her feelings, it must be all the more uncomfortable that Peduzzi is so much in the foreground. We see that Peduzzi is not exactly an "oaf" as Baker has called him.[13] That word is too simply dismissive. Hemingway's attitude includes a perception of the rather awful pathos of Peduzzi's condition presented through Peduzzi's eyes—we follow his feelings more than, or as much as, those of the couple. In this attention Hemingway pays, there emerge some rather complicated feelings for old Peduzzi, and they include a wry compassion.

The story, perceived this way, reveals a whole series of moments in which the reader and, gradually, fitfully, the husband and wife, see the distance between reality and Peduzzi's view of it. In one such moment, Peduzzi attempts to right everything with a flourish and offers to carry the fishing rods. He is trying to cancel by a kind of gallantry the useless, evasive strategy of having the wife follow some distance behind with the rods. Later, to inspire confidence, he says: "I know them at the municipio. I have been a soldier. Everybody in this town likes me. I sell frogs . . ." (176).

The way Peduzzi is both energetic toward the couple and pursuing his illusions makes him increasingly desperate to seem reliable. He goes up the steps of "the Specialty of Domestic and Foreign Wines Shop" and not only finds it locked—he has not gone there much—but "'It is closed until two,' someone passing in the street said scornfully. Peduzzi came down the steps. He felt hurt. 'Never mind,' he said, 'we can get it at the Concordia'" (174). He is embarrassed at the Concordia because they probably know him there (and perhaps would even refuse to serve him) and sure enough, the girl whom the young gentleman asks to pour one more drink "for a *vecchio*" (175), laughs, amused at these foreigners' being taking in by Peduzzi, who is striding around outside. On their way again, he assures them extravagantly, "I sell frogs. What if it is forbidden to fish? Not a thing. Nothing. No trouble. Big trout, I tell you. Lots of them" (176). Peduzzi a little later says:

> "There," . . . pointing to a girl in the doorway of a house they passed. "My daughter."
> "His doctor," the wife said, "has he got to show us his doctor?"
> "He said his daughter," said the young gentleman.
> The girl went into the house as Peduzzi pointed. (176)

Focused on so momentarily, amid the wife's irritation, the language barrier, and Peduzzi's pride as a parent, that quiet, little rejection by the daughter who went into the house "as Peduzzi pointed" is both comic and pathetic. For the first day at a big, new job as a guide, things are going wrong left and right for Peduzzi, yet with "much winking and knowingness" he pursues his role in "d'Ampezzo dialect and sometimes in Tyroler German dialect" (176). "He could not make out which the young gentleman and his wife understood the best so he was being bilingual. But as the young gentleman said, *Ja, Ja*, Peduzzi decided to talk altogether in Tyroler. The young gentleman and the wife understood nothing" (176). Still another mishap. And this leads to the genuinely pathetic, comic, and forlorn moment when Peduzzi, "his coat blowing in the wind" (176), has finally brought them to the promised river: "It was brown and muddy. Off on the right there was a dump heap" (176).

As they approach the river the young couple have another conversation. It reveals again that the subcurrent of feelings between the husband and the wife is changing, very interesting to follow, and not static or portentous as critics have stated. They begin to talk with a new reasonableness which is, in its way, endearing given their earlier feelings at the Concordia. The way the wife is responding here is better than silence, and in some sense it is an answer to the husband's effort of conciliation back there. These facts establish the way the story concerns itself with a particular afternoon, and not "with everything going wrong with a marraige."[14] There is no indication in the story that the marriage is coming to an end because of this problem in communication. Marriages survive arguments and days like this.

The husband and wife have not been talking, however, with Peduzzi who "talked rapidly with much winking and knowingness"; they walk "down the hill across the fields" and turn to follow the river bank. The husband makes an attempt to see things clearly: "Everybody in town saw us going through with these rods. We're probably being followed by the game police now. I wish we weren't in on this damn thing. This damned old fool is so drunk, too" (176). It is an effort to reach his wife after their quarrel, as was his less persuasive effort at the Concordia (upon reflection, an ironic place name). He finally begins to wish they were not going fishing. He has good reasons, ones that his wife surely shares, and now he is including her— "We're probably being followed. . . ."

Nevertheless, there is still a clash of wills; they have both been taking opposite sides of an argument. Despite the husband's good reasons to turn back, the wife knows he will not do so, and knowing this, she replies angrily: "Of course you haven't got the guts to just go back," said the wife. "Of course you have to go on" (176). He replies with irritation, which he then moderates: "Why don't you go back? Go on back, Tiny." She responds to the slight improvement in his tone by not escalating the quarrel: "I'm going to stay with you. If you go to jail we might as well both go" (176). The tension is certainly evident, produced by their opposing wills, yet so are the efforts they make to react in a balanced way. However, all sorts of little incidents and perceptions, particularly in regard to their guide, have been increasing the tension so that their efforts are not equal to it. The husband's concern for her is genuine, but his suggestion that she go back conveys also that he has not changed his mind. He ignores the issues he has just brought up—the illegality of the whole thing, his own regrets, Peduzzi's drunken condition. Yet in a sense, this ignoring is understandable from him, since his wanting to go fishing initially meant he was underplaying these things from the beginning, before the story started. His attitude that they should be going fishing on this day is part of the story's iceberg, though the image should not be applied to the couple's relationship. The conflict between the two in "Out of Season," carefully and even delicately rendered, does not loom; it ends like a branch snapping, which does not mean that the whole tree is going to break. It ends when the wife decides to leave without fanfare or unpleasant flourishes:

> "He says it's at least a half hour more. Go on back, Tiny. You're cold in this wind anyway. It's a rotten day and we aren't going to have any fun, anyway."
> "All right," she said, and climbed up the grassy bank. (177)

The husband is finally starting to see things as they are.

Another part of the story's iceberg, and an almost entirely visible one, that does have to do with a kind of hopeless psychological disarray, is the presentation of Peduzzi's reactions to the conflict between the husband and wife. Peduzzi is too caught up in playing the guide, gesturing at the river and so on, to observe with any quickness or accuracy what the feelings are between the husband and wife. His reactions are too slow, too much behind the events we see, as with the wife's climbing the grassy bank to go back, for him to grasp what happens. He reacts not to what the reader sees but to a slightly later event which then speeds up his response in compensation. We know why the wife leaves and so Hemingway's shift to Peduzzi, to his delayed awareness, is sad and funny:

> Peduzzi was down at the river and did not notice her till she was almost out of sight over the crest. "Frau!" he shouted. "Frau! Fräulein! You're not going."
> She went on over the crest of the hill.
> "She's gone!" said Peduzzi. It shocked him. (177)

Every action is a compensation now. He is not aware that he is obsessed by his role of guide, and the husband still seems dazed enough to be taken in by this driven improvising:

> He took off the rubber bands that held the rod segments together and commenced to joint up one of the rods.
> "But you said it was half an hour further."
> "Oh, yes. It is good half an hour down. It is good here, too."
> "Really?"
> "Of course. It is good here and good there, too."
> The young gentleman sat down on the bank and jointed up a rod, put on the reel and threaded the line through the guides. (177)

But he has not yet seen the whole of how things are, or he would not be doing this.

Peduzzi, upon discovering that he has no sinkers, then becomes excited and desperate: "You must have *piombo. Piombo*" (177). He sifts "through the cloth dirt in the linings of his inside military pockets" (177). His reply to the proposition they will get some *piombo* and fish tomorrow perfectly registers his emphasis and suspicion: "At what hour of the morning? Tell me that" (178). All these details express the sense of an effusive energy out of proportion to the occasion and to the missing object—the "*piombo.*" We can see, as does the young gentleman finally, that the energy and the disarrayed reactions, now desperate, now full of hope, even pleasure, have their source here:

. . . [Peduzzi's] eyes fixed on the end of the narrow brown bottle. He drank it all. The
sun shone while he drank. It was wonderful. This was a great day, after all. A wonderful
day. (178)

There are feelings in that energy: gladness, crazy hope, and all the time a
discontinuity with reality—that is, illusion. We notice the jump forward in
Peduzzi's thinking a moment later: "Days like this stretched out ahead. It
would begin at seven in the morning" (178).

Peduzzi, eyes glistening, calling his benefactor *"caro"* (178), is a daunt-
less actor doing everything to make his illusion more elaborate. Boldly he
asks for five lire "for a favor" (178), which instantly becomes a sum enabling
him to provide "everything for tomorrow. *Pane, salami, formaggio . . .* bait
for fishing, minnows, not worms only" (178–79), a list concluded by the
giveaway, "Perhaps I can get some marsala" (179). When he successfully
cadges four lire from the young gentleman, Peduzzi's sense of style for his
new status returns: "'Thank you, *caro*. Thank you,' said Peduzzi, in the
tone of one member of the Carleton Club accepting the *Morning Post* from
another" (179).[15] He feels wonderful. The depiction of these feelings carries
with it a sense that Hemingway's view is a compassionate one—Peduzzi is
a man in such energetic pursuit of his delusion: "This was living. He was
through with the hotel garden, breaking up frozen manure with a dung fork.
Life was opening out" (179).

But the story and the final subtle tone do not end here. Hemingway's
feeling for Peduzzi continues to come through in the presentation of the
closing details: "'Until seven o'clock then, *caro*,' he said, slapping the young
gentleman on the back. 'Promptly at seven'" (179). The young man, "putting his purse back in his pocket," says that he may not be going. "'What'
said Peduzzi, 'I will have minnows, Signor. Salami, everything. You and I
and the Signora. The three of us'" (179). But the young man, finally seeing
what kind of a day it has been, is able to resist another fiasco with Peduzzi
along and tells him he may not be going, "very probably not. I'll leave word
with the padrone at the hotel office" (179).

Peduzzi is a sad case all right, but he does not know it, and so we see
him slapping the husband on the back and protesting as the story ends.
Peduzzi's undaunted alcoholism, his mistaken notions of the future, his good
will, thrown together with the couple's being at odds, the quarrel at lunch,
the husband's lapse of vigilance, illegal fishing, more little mishaps at the
inn, a fishing spot next to a dump heap on a brown, muddy river: the
unstated subject is apparent all the way through "Out of Season"—things
going wrong and somehow comically snowballing against the background of
Peduzzi's life. Things go wrong for the couple and for the guide, but they
are little things, quite within the range of ordinary actuality.

Notes

1. For the most recent psychoanalytic and biographical interpretations see Kenneth S. Lynn, *Hemingway* (New York: Simon and Schuster, 1987) 201–4, and Jeffrey Meyers, *Hemingway: A Biography* (New York: Harper & Row, 1985) 154. See also Gertrude Stein, *The Autobiography of Alice B. Toklas* (New York: Harcourt Brace, 1933).

2. See my "Hemingway's 'Cat in the Rain,'" *Spectrum* 25 (1983): 36–44, and "The Two Shortest Stories of *In Our Time*," in *Critical Essays on* In Our Time, ed. Michael S. Reynolds (Boston: G. K. Hall, 1983) 216–26.

3. Kenneth G. Johnston, "Hemingway's 'Out of Season' and the Psychology of Errors" *Literature and Psychology* 21 (1 November 1971): 46. As Johnston states it, "the woman is in the early stages of pregnancy and the man is openly opposed; the story takes place in the aftermath of a bitter quarrel on the subject." Where does Johnston find the husband opposing the wife's desire to have a child? Such a conflict, as well as Johnston's evidence for it, are critical inventions, but their underlying assumption is a common one: in the biography you can find the omitted part, which can be regrafted into the story.

   Johnston also groups four quite different stories—"Cat in the Rain," "Hills Like White Elephants," "Cross-Country Snow," and "Out of Season"—around an event supposedly omitted from all of them: Hemingway's dismayed reaction to Hadley's pregnancy. Johnston writes, "all four were either written, or begun, or conceived in the spring of 1923 during Hadley's pregnancy" (46). How does a critic determine when a story was "conceived"? "Hills Like White Elephants," for example, was written at least four years later in Le Grau-du-Roi.

4. For a valuable discussion of this issue and the story's structure see Paul Smith, "Some Misconceptions of 'Out of Season'," in *Critical Essays on* In Our Time, ed. Michael S. Reynolds (Boston: G. K. Hall, 1983) 235–51.

5. Ernest Hemingway, *A Moveable Feast* (New York: Charles Scribner's Sons, 1964) 75.

6. Paul R. Jackson, "Hemingway's 'Out of Season,'" *The Hemingway Review* 1.1 (Fall 1981): 16–17. Jackson's note on the critical history of the story is useful: "A casual glance at twenty-six studies of Hemingway's fiction shows that twelve either do not mention the story or refer to it only in passing. In many of the remaining, the story is often treated in cursory fashion. It fares no better in individual articles. Kenneth G. Johnston's "Hemingway's 'Out of Season' and the Psychology of Errors" stands quite alone. See also Paul Smith, "Some Misconceptions of 'Out of Season,'" cited above, note 4.

7. Carlos Baker, *Ernest Hemingway: A Life Story* (New York: Charles Scribner's Sons, 1969): 109.

8. My approach here differs in that I will be treating "Out of Season" as a separate work of art—distinct from others, more than fictionalized personal history, a comic not a tragic story—and paying particular attention to the configuration of feelings and to relationships as revealed by dialogue and action. For a study of the story's places see: Dix McComas, "The Geography of Ernest Hemingway's 'Out of Season,'" *The Hemingway Review* 3.2 (Spring 1984): 46–49.

   To see the story itself afresh, for crucially longer passages of the text, I will be intent on raising to explicit statements certain high-probability inferences in a sustained way. This kind of meditative process seems to me invited by Hemingway's implicit style—its challenge and pleasure.

9. As in Arthur Waldhorn's attack on the wife: "That ur-bitch character seems to have ample reserves of sallies like the one she launches when her husband lamely continues their illegal fishing expedition, 'Of course you haven't got the guts to just go back.'" *A Reader's Guide to Ernest Hemingway* (New York: Farrar, Straus and Giroux, 1972) 45. See also Richard Hovey's view that this is "another story of marital dissatisfaction . . . we have to conclude that wives do spoil the fun of men who want to go fishing." *Hemingway: The Inward Terrain* (Seattle: U of Washington P, 1968) 10.

10. *Hemingway: The Writer as Artist*, 4th edn. (Princeton: Princeton UP, 1972) 121.

11. Baker, *Writer as Artist*, 121.

12. *The Short Stories of Ernest Hemingway* (New York: Charles Scribner's Sons, 1966) 177. All further quotations from this edition are cited by page in my text.

13. Baker, *Life*, 109.

14. Hovey, 10.

15. Concerning the Max Beerbohm and Carleton Club references, Paul Smith believes the narrative point of view could be critical of the young gentleman, in which case "Hemingway's early experiment with selective omniscience got out of hand—a not unlikely possibility." Smith allows, however, that a "more neutral reading of the references . . . would argue that neither is intended pejoratively" (Smith, 245). I favor the more neutral reading that "He was thinking, what in hell makes him say marsala? That's what Max Beerbohm drinks" (174), is meant to suggest further the husband's somewhat abstracted state, and the Carleton Club reference is comically descriptive of Peduzzi, given the context—next to a muddy river in northern Italy.

5

Hemingway's Italian *Waste Land:*
The Complex Unity of "Out of Season"

Bickford Sylvester

Bickford Sylvester offers a sharply contrasting vision of "Out of Season."
For this critic, the story is heavily indebted to Eliot for its treatment of
spiritual alienation in the modern world. Sylvester perceives "Out of Sea-
son" as "an ironic twentieth century version of the corrupted Fisher King's
encounter with the young knight who is to restore his vitality" and a key to
understanding Waste Land *parallels in* In Our Time. *Sylvester's "Out of*
Season" is therefore weightier and more tragic than Steinke's. Readers will
have to choose sides in this argument or resolve for themselves "Out of
Season's" resonant ambiguities. Either course suggests a future of vital
controversy for this unjustly neglected short story.

Sixty-five years after the initial publication of "Out of Season" in *Three
Stories and Ten Poems,* scholars continue to glance at one aspect or another
of the story, uncomfortably assuming that it lacks the focusing purpose
usually accounting for every detail in a Hemingway narrative. None has
provided a full analysis of what I shall suggest is a complex artistic structure,
as consummately organized as anything Hemingway subsequently composed.[1] Carlos Baker's brief commentary remains one of the most trenchant,
recognizing the story's importance to literary history as Hemingway's first
use (after the debacle of his lost manuscripts) of the new style and the
narrative technique of omission that were to make him famous. Baker particularly notices the device of developing "two intrinsically-related truths
simultaneously" (the couple's marriage and the fishing are both out of season), and so creating a "metaphorical confluence of emotional atmospheres"

that gives the story "its considerable distinction."[2] But I want to explicate a more fundamental "confluence of emotional atmospheres" in the story and attribute it to a more comprehensive binary pattern in the narrative. Both Peduzzi and the young American are lost guides, each seeking in the other guidance the other cannot give. Furthermore, especially when the story is read as a part of *In Our Time*, this futile contretemps (in which *"vecchio"* expects "young gentleman" to restore some sense of purpose in his day and vice versa) can be recognized as an ironic twentieth-century version of the corrupted Fisher King's encounter with the young knight who is to restore his vitality.

Hemingway had read Pound's copy of *The Waste Land* in early February of 1923, only two months before writing this story. Just after reading the poem he went on an extended walking tour with Pound, who was not only Hemingway's mentor but the collaborating editor of that widely acclaimed work of the previous year by Eliot—a writer with whom Hemingway felt considerable rivalry. He composed "Out of Season" in mid-April, within weeks of separating from Pound and continuing on to Cortina, the setting for the story.[3] And exactly as does Eliot in *The Waste Land*, Hemingway uses the Fisher King legend to draw "a continuous parallel between antiquity and modernity,"[4] exposing the degradation of the modern from the ancient precedent to which it is compared. Thus the "emotional atmospheres" flowing together at the story's deepest level are those of a mythless present and of early periods of belief. What is out of season, at bottom, is emotional fulfillment in our time, in a twentieth century out of step with fundamental human needs.

This deprivation is the source of the story's tangled motives and tangled relationships (between husband and wife and between men of different generations), in accord with the theme of *The Waste Land* that metaphysical uncertainty leads to emotional paralysis impairing social, sexual, and ultimately physical life in the human community. Accordingly, we will presently see, Hemingway's story is structured around three parallel abortive quests: the two men's attempts to find temporary psychological escape (searches ironically compared to failed quests for spiritual life through rituals of wine and water), and the wife's attempt to find the emotional security she needs to bear a child, a quest to perpetuate physical life doomed by the spiritual alienation of the modern world.

The evidence of this dimension is unobtrusive, as decades of unresponsive readers attest. Composition of this story was what Baker calls "the gateway" to Hemingway's best writing;[5] and in this early experiment with his celebrated obliquity, Hemingway was possibly overly subtle.[6] Be that as it may, it was apparently the experience of composing "Out of Season" that released the "explosion" of stories following within the next year and one-half—nine of the *In Our Time* stories in one seven-month period after the Canadian exile for Bumby's birth.[7] And since we can see a *Waste Land* pattern running through all of this ensuing material, it is consistent and worthwhile for us to consider that pattern as the likely catalyst and examine its presence in the precipitating story. In fact, the *Waste Land* presence in "Out of Season" will be most readily apparent to us if we approach the story as part of the collection, and if we also closely examine the neglected literal details of the narrative, before tracing their mythic implications.[8]

In *"Waste Land* Parallels Unifying *In Our Time,"* I have shown at length that both the male and the female protagonists in the various stories and interchapters of the collection are parts of an intended composite character, like the many-voiced, double-sexed narrator of Eliot's poem.[9] This composite is a child who grows to young adulthood disappointed by every expected source of leadership and support in the older generation—from biological parents through representatives of the spectrum of social and religious institutions identified by the entire "Evening Prayer," of which Hemingway's title is an allusive "fragment" like those employed by Eliot. These older people fail their dependents because, unlike those in the prayer, twentieth-century functionaries are not "saved" by belief in a purpose beyond themselves. Without a commonly accepted myth, the supposed leaders of the community are turned in upon themselves by Prufrockian anxiety over the "overwhelming question" of apparently purposeless human endeavor and are of no use to their dependents.

Locked "in the prison of their own egos," as Kimon Friar puts it,[10] Eliot's emotionally paralyzed lovers introduce us to the modern wasteland and leave us there. It is as the ultimate recipient of just such a legacy that the recently shattered Nick Adams of "Big Two-Hearted River"—accepting at last that he is utterly on his own—sets forth to learn how to feel without having his feelings spin into madness. In his earlier personae throughout the collection, he has repeatedly sought in others the guidance he needs, as a human being, as an American and European romantic idealist, and as a twentieth-century man set up and let down by the Western tradition. This son of Dr. and Mrs. Adams has had his trust betrayed by many expected sources of guidance; chief among them has been an array of father figures who have made him (in his male personae) as inadequate a lover, husband, and father as they. Thus we have the egocentric husbands of the stories in the "marriage group," including "Out of Season," shunning the adult emotional demands of the unfortunate women who look to them for guidance and security. In the work as a whole, these role models range from the two literal fathers (neatly bracketing the protagonist's quest for external guidance from "Indian Camp" through "My Old Man") to the concluding vignette's parody of a king, that ultimate human father figure of the book's titular prayer and of the myth informing Eliot's poem.

"Oh that king," Hemingway wrote to Pound in August 1923,[11] for the king is central to both the 1924 and the 1925 versions of the material. As impotent a functionary as the wounded Fisher King of legend, the Greek king of "L'Envoi" has never acted as a connection between his people and those natural mysteries symbolized by an answering tug of vitality deep in opaque waters. Nor has he ever been "saved" by a sense of divine mission, like the British kings of earlier times evoked by Hemingway's title. The crowning father figure of Hemingway's collection has never held the power to keep and transmit rejuvenating order and therefore can neither lose it nor seek to regain it. The drab ordinariness of this king's materialistic vision of a new life in America is what the mythical king's yearning for restored spiritual service to his community has descended to. This king (a mocking reminder of the glory that was Greece) is the final devastating comment on the failure of the Western tradition in this century, "L'Envoi" sending Hemingway's book on its way.

Now this closing condemnation of external guides immediately follows the final pair of stories making the same point. In "Big Two-Hearted River, I and II" the protagonist, as Nick Adams, accepts the necessity in our time for every man to become his own Fisher King, which for Nick means overcoming betrayal by even his own emotions, overwhelmed as they have been by successive disillusionments. In the final story Nick hooks, feels, and loses a giant fish, in symbolic enactment of man's longing for, and loss of, connection to natural and divine order. (The fish is described in language used in *The Waste Land* for a missing vision of vitalized or presently tenable divinity.) In mastering the shock of this fundamental deprivation (the root of all others), Nick begins to learn an age-old emotional discipline that came automatically to men in times of belief: the discipline of self-control, one of the three disciplines from the *Upanishad* ("give, sympathize, control") that Eliot selected as emotional capacities universal to historical periods of shared belief. According to Friar, the resolution of *The Waste Land* urges those living in the twentieth century to develop by rote practice these emotional strengths of people living in times of consubstantial myth.[12] That is what Nick is on the way to accomplishing with the last and most essential of Eliot's three disciplines. Thus he will eventually be able "to fish the swamp"—to live feelingly, if without supporting faith, in the spiritual morass of this century. And with that control will come the freedom to give and to sympathize, which would have made his failed fathers accessible to him, so that he could have learned how to be accessible to those seeking his guidance.

Enter the "young gentleman" of "Out of Season," then, the protagonist in one of his earlier adult personae. He is in the middle of his quest for order, before harsh experience has entirely weaned him from his reliance on mentors and intermediaries.[13] So it is appropriate within the context of the collection, as well as psychologically convincing within the story, that Peduzzi, the aging town drunk seeking drinking money from a more pleasant source than his job as a manure shoveler (135), find a willing mark in this young American tourist with clean new tackle (133), whose projected purpose for coming to Cortina has been frustrated by the spring ban on fishing. Thus (to continue, now, reading through the story as psychological realism), the two conspire secretly to fish despite the ban. Peduzzi parleys his day's new job into drinking credit and attention, while the tourist and his wife have lunch. Then the two men set off through town for the river with the wife, at her husband's suggestion, walking several steps behind them with the rods, so that onlookers will not realize that the men are going to fish (125–26). Yet as critics as far apart in time and method as Carlos Baker and Kenneth Lynn have failed to see,[14] Peduzzi has a more imperative emotional agenda than his quest for a liquor supply or even for a comfortable, respectable occupation, and the disruption of that agenda does make him desperate enough for us to anticipate emotional extremity, although not necessarily or specifically the suicide Hemingway later claimed he left out of the story.[15]

To restore the regard he has lost in his town by drinking, this member of the older generation seeks not merely status but genuine approval. Thus his raffishness is borne of desperation as he risks arrest by cajoling the young man's wife to "walk down the street of Cortina together" with the men (126), "three abreast" (127). As Jackson points out, Peduzzi wants to be seen as the village's representative in escorting these visitors from a wealthy land.[16] He also wants true camaraderie with the couple—to refer to a married woman as "Signorina" as well as "Signora" (126) is to straddle a fine line between disrespect and flattery. Its acceptance as flattery by the husband would be proof of a certain equality or even intimacy between the men.[17] The same rather desperate gamble must be recognized in Peduzzi's winks, nudges, and repeated use later of the familiar *"caro"* (134). Fundamental to Peduzzi's motives in bringing the young wife forward, though, is his need to show the villagers that he is a fit associate for a decent and proper young matron. His own daughter's retreat, as he points to her further down the road (130), shows the reputation for indelicacy that he wishes to amend by marching abreast with the innocent young couple—on equal terms with a family, in a position befitting a parent, elder, and former military defender of his community.

In fact, a pathetic aspiration to respectability qualifies his crass motives in all of his attempts to display and sustain his relationship with the young couple. When he needs more liquor and suggests that they buy marsala instead of the grappa he has been drinking, we think at first that he does so because a request for sweet wine is less likely to be rejected by these innocents than a request for harsh common brandy. The immediately ensuing incidents prove his motives more complex. It is one thing to have won the small victory (125) of being trusted for more grappa at the cantina (the word means "basement" and such shops are ground-level, open ends of storage cellars, frequented by working-class males). But it would be something else to walk "*up* the steps" (127, italics mine) to the "Specialty of Domestic and Foreign Wines Shop" (whose closing hours he does not know, not because he is drunk but because he is seldom a patron) and to present himself with ten lire in his hand (127).

The scorn of the village passerby hurts him (127) because it acknowledges the impropriety of his attempt. But rather than retreat to the cantina, he is driven to an even greater display of temerity; he envisions himself escorting his splendid charges into the Concordia Hotel and paying with the ten-lira note, as their apparent host. That is why he is genuinely shaken, and so humiliated as to be uncharacteristically inarticulate, when the young American stops him outside the door by asking: "*Was wollen Sie?*" This gesture of exclusion by a youthful newcomer who has never seen him before (127) confirms for Peduzzi the folly of his pretension to gentility, a folly already signaled by the cold stares of his townsmen (126) and the passerby's scornful remark at the wine shop (127). He reluctantly yields the possessively folded note.

The Concordia represents the very nexus of those values and attitudes motivating Peduzzi throughout the trio's journey. It is where families go, where there are pastries rather than the rough snacks of cantinas, where wine rather than grappa is served, out of glasses rather than cups and bottles. Moreover, it is where men drink sitting at tables with women and where one reads newspapers. To a man of the working class, it is a bastion of middle-class respectability. Peduzzi's aspiration to that status accounts for his choice of marsala in the first instance. Although it is an alcoholic's choice because it is fortified, this wine is also the parlor drink of Italy, served on special occasions in small glasses, just as Max Beerbohm had served it in 1922 to the group of journalists Hemingway accompanied at Rapallo.[18] The young man's question to himself about why an Italian peasant and a personification of British Edwardian elegance choose the same wine (127), clearly invites the reader to think about Peduzzi as seeking more than intoxication.

But "the door of the Concordia shut on the young gentleman and the wife" (128); Peduzzi is excluded, as he has been before, we assume from the waitress's amusement when "a *vecchio*" is mentioned (128). Peduzzi will not have the satisfaction of impressing her with his ten-lira note and proving his right to be in such an establishment. It says a great deal for his depth of feeling that he does not wait at the door, like a tramp or servant, and that when the rattled young man carries a glass outside for him, he has removed himself to the other end of the building, "out of the wind" (129) which in this story stands for far more cutting adversities than those of the elements, as it will so often in Hemingway's subsequent fiction. Reminded by his wife that he is to buy wine to go rather than the three glasses he has ordered, the distracted American orders a quarter liter (128). Thus Peduzzi's portion of the wine is relegated to a bottle later tilted crudely in the field (133) in the company of the other man. Ironically alienated from her husband, even within this domestic setting, the wife remains at her table; her glassful of wine is not poured into the quarter-liter measure with the two men's (128), an omission that also figures in the mythic implications we will presently observe in this scene. And as the party leaves the Concordia the waitress, another young female, remains inaccessible within, "amused" at Peduzzi's presumption—as unresponsive as the wife and Peduzzi's daughter to any dimension in the veteran beyond his embarrassing, alcoholic surface.

His hurt pride forces him to even greater risks to assert his dignity. He will carry the phallic "rods" himself, muttering of fancied status at the *municipio* as a military veteran (129) and attempting unsuccessfully in two languages to make some human connection that will give the couple faith in his guidance and thus sustain the relationship he needs, not only for money but for his stubborn vestige of self-respect.

Peduzzi suffers a penultimate frustration of both of these needs when the wife turns back, pierced by a cold wind in her marriage that Peduzzi has been as oblivious to as she has been to his deprivation. This is the last in the series of feminine exclusions, leaving him with only the other man. Peduzzi is more than hurt. It has "shocked him" (131) to realize that this supposedly innocent "young gentleman" from a better world can share a domestic disorder he knows all too well. Things will not be what he had expected, but he must not lose the man too. Thus he instantly sets up to fish where they are, rather than further down the river as he had intended (131).

But what is left of his day begins "going to pieces before his eyes" (133) as soon as the two men are alone. The spot Peduzzi has been forced into is visible from the town, and the already nervous young man is in fact "relieved" when the lack of lead sinkers makes fishing futile. Despite assurances to the contrary by Kenneth Johnston and Lynn, there is no need to look to the young man's guilt over the pregnancy of wife and trout for an explanation of his "radical change" at the riverside,[19] and there is nothing radical about his decision. Once actually at the river, hardly any experienced fisherman with the feel of big trout on his mind could be dissuaded by the ethics of a saint or the most gravid of wives from at least trying to *play* a fish or two, regardless of the season—if he felt removed from any reasonable chance of being observed, and if there were any hope at all of getting a strike. But the likelihood of a surface strike in muddy water like that in the story is negligible, as this young man admits he knows (133). And once reminded of that he would have no incentive to take the slightest risk of arrest to cast into such water, without lead to carry his bait to the bottom where it might possibly happen to pass immediately before a trout holding by a rock.

But why does the young man have to be reminded, too late, of water conditions and a tackle requirement any fisherman of his admitted experience would have foreseen? The actual focus of the scene is on the young man's reasons for neglecting this potential impasse while still in Cortina, where he could have bought the lead that was his only hope of connecting with a fish. As the story indirectly but pointedly reveals, he had more than enough opportunity to do so. No fisherman having the rudimentary prior understanding of spring runoff from the mountains that this young man sheepishly acknowledges (133) would have failed to inquire about the likelihood of muddy conditions, and consequently have the subject of sinkers explicitly mentioned, either by his guide or himself, in Cortina when (we now learn) Peduzzi had expressly asked about tackle (133).[20] No experienced fisherman would have been so oblivious, that is, if he had been focusing on actually playing fish. A chief point of the episode is that this young man therefore has not been at all focused on his ostensible and advertent wish to play trout but has had a different primary motive in going fishing, a motive we must assume to be the need for diversion from his unfulfilled personal life.

Further evidence is his ambivalent reaction to the danger of arrest, a reaction revealing an apparently habitual conflict between his conscious and unconscious goals that would account for the distraction and irresolution he displays throughout the story. A psychologically integrated sportsman, accepting his share of the obsessiveness overtaking fishermen, would have made a clean-cut choice beforehand about the legal consequences of fishing out of season. He might have decided against entering into a situation where the anticipation of joy (which *is* fishing) would be canceled out by fear of arrest, and yet turning back would be impossible for him. (This is precisely the young man's dilemma. "Of course you have to go on," says his all-too-experienced wife [130].) Or a mature sportsman might have decided that the pleasure was worth the risk and accepted at the start his responsibility for any penalties and disgrace. Either way, he would not have allowed himself to drift uncommitted into an ambivalent half-life of mixed sensations as this young American has done, both on this fishing trip and in his marriage.[21] However, this as-yet very "young" man can hardly deal beforehand with these practical, emotional consequences of his trip, when his primary motive in fishing is an unacknowledged need to escape the overwhelming responsibilities of adulthood and marriage and has little to do with fishing. That is why he is not disappointed when he has no way to get down to the fish. His dilemma has been resolved; indeed, we wonder if in his extraordinary inattention to his tackle he has, in fact, been unconsciously setting up a passive way out of the conflict between his fear of disgrace and his fantasy of diversionary fulfillment.

Furthermore, this conflict between advertent and inadvertent motives relates the episode at the river not only to the rest of the story but to the book as well. Within this larger context, the young man fails to think ahead about the practical requirements of fishing and is also habitually indecisive. In Hemingway's already-ordered imagination this American suffers from the same emotional syndrome that distracts others of his generation in the ensuing material collected for *In Our Time*. In the character structure of that book the composite protagonist's first "father," Doctor Adams, does not face beforehand the practicalities of an obviously likely Caesarean in "Indian Camp"[22] or think ahead of the baby's father, precisely because he is distracted from his conscious purpose by a primary need for sexual, racial, and professional validation that his unrealistic Victorian morality will not allow him to acknowledge until too late. And in "Out of Season" (as we have seen) his "son" seeks, in the familiar absorption of fishing, not fish but temporary respite from his fear of dividing himself with an adult female. It is "not exactly" hell for members of his anxiously self-absorbed generation of males to think of this dilemma, as Nick says in "Cross-Country Snow," the story eventually placed immediately after this one (146). But it is close to that; and it is easier for the young gentleman to think of the remembered magic of fishing (as Nick dwells on the satisfying sensations of skiing) when adulthood turns out not to be the unmixed "fun" (read "fulfillment") missing in modern life.

As for Peduzzi's part in overlooking the lead, he also can only have been distracted from his advertent purpose. Alcohol did not make him forget to ask about tackle generally, and he has clearly been sincere in his plan to provide the young man with a chance to fish. It is Peduzzi who mentions the lead now, with genuine consternation (132), when he could very well keep silent and let the boy flog the water at least as long as there is wine in the bottle. Many a legitimate fishing guide would do just that. But he has some honor in this, as in bearing his terrible need to drink, in the next incident (133), until the man who bought the wine has had a modicum. Only then does Peduzzi drain the bottle, as he knows he must once he starts. In this he is pointedly more forthright in dealing with his emotions than is the American. But he has overlooked the key to connection between man and fish, because he, too, has been distracted, by his inadvertent primary interest in social acceptance.

At the psychological level, therefore, the *piombo* buck passing dazzlingly symbolizes the failure of each man to immerse himself in life's real but limited tasks at hand, because each seeks compensation for, and evasion of, a feeling that life is fundamentally overwhelming and disappointing. Without his conscious and unconscious purposes acknowledged and coordinated, neither man can display that emotional "purity of line through the maximum of exposure" (articulated in *The Sun Also Rises*)[23] that is the ultimate mark of adulthood—and particularly of masculinity, not only in *In Our Time* but of course in all of Hemingway's works. The two "leaders" in this story are indeed both "tangled" within (132), as are the fishing leaders in the young man's "leader box."

Hence follows the psychological relationship between the young man's indecisiveness and the sexual implications sometimes observed in the *piombo*.[24] The young man has "no lead" to make up for Peduzzi's equally empty "pockets" because he lacks that unity of purpose essential to the substance and authority of leadership. Consequently, the young man vacillates to the very end between disgust with the whole enterprise and a tantalizing, unexpressed fantasy that with some sinkers he might possibly hook a fish the following day. That is why he cannot even let Peduzzi down cleanly by declining, now, either to go or not to go.

It is ironic that in his own reluctance definitely to rule out another day of attempted respite from his own threatening desperation, the young man allows Peduzzi to hope for another clean, well-ordered day against his alcoholic's eternity of emptiness. In supplying the four lire he knows will not cover the proposed supplies (and so will be used for drink), the young "gentleman" is actually paying to avoid mentioning Peduzzi's self-deception, in order not to verbalize his own.[25] This youth from a supposedly carefree new world, whose simplicity Peduzzi has sought to exploit, exists in the same complex half-life as he, and has exploited him with a passive inadvertency exceeding his own. That realization, when Peduzzi stumbles to the padrone the next morning to learn that he has been rejected even by the young man (despite the cruel advance payment), will make another yawning day seem all the longer to him; he even dares to hope to the end that all three of them will be together again (135).

For us to feel Peduzzi's impending despair, therefore, there was in fact no need for Hemingway to "put in" anything about Peduzzi's being discharged or killing himself, if that really was an option Hemingway initially considered.[26] Nor does it matter—when Hemingway did add these events later on, in what amount to footnotes to his text—whether the details in letter and reminiscence were fiction or fact. Our search for a historical Peduzzi is as irrelevant to our interpretation of the narrative itself as it may be important to our understanding of Hemingway's attitude toward his reader's psychology.[27] Within the story Peduzzi's longing for respect and escape is palpable and demonstrable, making us sympathize with him, despite his self-deception, at least as much as we sympathize with the equally anxious and self-deceiving young man.

We have in this first story of the fresh *In Our Time* material, then, an essential situation that reverberates in the final vignette. Although the Italian peasant is significantly more admirable than the Greek king, in each case the old-world authority figure met in a garden by a younger questor from the new world[28] is in fact on a self-centered and mundane quest of his own. The members of this generation of "leaders" have had no psychological or spiritual secret of living to impart to the younger generation of questors, as I have remarked, so that both generations find only mirrors of their own confusion and emptiness. Moreover, this association of fishing guide and king in ironic tandem makes us think of fishermen and kings together, especially in the way that they are collapsed in *The Waste Land*. When we consider story and poem further, we notice that both present pairs of emotionally estranged lovers touring the Alps in the spring. (Hemingway's story was also *composed*, we remember, in "the cruellest month" of Eliot's opening line.)[29] In both works, too, this emotionally sterile human sexuality reflects ironic reversals of expected joy in nature at its most fecund season, because contemporary figures of the Fisher King fail to provide fruitful connections between man and water—in scenes whose similarities include images of intrusive urban blight: Eliot's working-class Englishman (explicitly related to a king) is reduced to fishing in a "dull canal . . . round behind the gashouse" (11. 189–90); and Hemingway's Italian peasant is forced to guide his charge to a "brown and muddy" river by "a dump heap" (131).[30]

In this parallel between poem and story we can find a rationale for many otherwise puzzling details of the narrative, beyond those I have explicated in the literal plot. When this elderly and impaired fishing guide meets a "young gentleman coming down the path," speaks to him "mysteriously," and is "mysterious" again at the cantina about his job (125), this insistent and rather unusual language calls attention to itself.[31] In the first place, it establishes Peduzzi's dominance in the story as a provocative, gnomic figure, a would-be imparter of concealed wisdom (he later is described as talking "rapidly with much winking and knowingness" and nudging the wife in the ribs [130]). We can see, in this opening emphasis on the mysterious, suggestions of an "alternate realm"[32] in which an impure, older man awaits a young nobleman and discusses some common interest in a secret mission having to do with fishing. Since in such a realm the mystery is of the highest spiritual significance, we are prepared to look for further evocations of traditional mysticism. We find the next in three references to the mystical number three describing the harmonious relationship Peduzzi seeks by having the wife come forward so that they can "all three . . . walk together" as "the three," "three abreast" (126–27).[33] Thus Peduzzi's concern for social appearance is thrown into ironic relief by its association with man's longing for an order beyond human community.

That association is enforced and intensified when it is the "Concordia" that they approach "three abreast" (127). The name of this hotel (cited three times) suggests harmony and order in any context. Within this building the detailed events I have discussed for their psychological and social importance to Peduzzi are also arranged as an ironic inversion of Christian communion. The marsala Peduzzi chooses (and about which the young gentleman's question so pointedly nudges the reader) is not only considered socially elegant; it is also one of the general types of wine (fortified and thus stable in air) often used sacramentally in Italy (although marsala itself is unacceptably "muddy" [128]).

Moreover, within this building barred to Peduzzi (and as a result of the young man's distraction), the wine is poured in glasses, as though to be shared by the three in a social ritual made vaguely religious by repeated references to the number three. ("'Three marsalas.' . . . 'Two, you mean?' . . . 'No, . . . one for a *vecchio'*" [128].) But only the wife takes a table, and the wine is not consumed by either man, and possibly not by the wife. Instead, the young man, reminded of what he is doing, says, "Put these *two* in, *too*" (128, italics mine), as he orders the measurement of wine to take out. His language calls our attention to a departure from the pattern of mystical threes to a distinctly utilitarian pattern of fours and fives in the text, as the girl measures out a quarter liter of the wine. But in addition to that, his characteristic change of plans aborts entirely even the pale and secularized ritual at first suggested. What takes place as a result is that the wine is returned from drinking vessels through a *quartino* (this measuring cup looks like a large cruet, the vessel holding wine for the chalice), and thence into "a very small slim brown bottle" as far as possible in color and shape from any sacramental vessel and, in fact, the sort of container in which wine comes from cellar to church. Then the "narrow brown bottle" is finally carried to the fields (where its shape and color are again specified [133]), and its contents are consumed there. As a result, the progress of communion wine (from growth through bottle and cruet to cups for three concelebrant priests performing solemn mass in the early and medieval church) is traced, approximately but clearly—in reverse.[34] Thus the most ancient pattern of communion is at once evoked and, in effect, cancelled.

We see, therefore, the purpose of the apparently gratuitous reference to the *bianco* (128). The girl's offer of this inexpensive wine, another type used sacramentally, has at once strengthened the religious implications of the drinking details and pointed up Peduzzi's spiritual disqualification. For the marsala, elegant and costly in the worldly terms of interest to Peduzzi, is less appropriate to the religious significance of the drinking scene than is the clear, white *bianco*, humble yet pure.

At the same time, as we think of the bottle at the end of the mass-in-reverse, we see that the phallic significance suggested by the description of the bottle is equally mocked. In the medieval version of the Fisher King legend, as Eliot saw that legend unifying sexuality and spirituality in man's imagination, the young knight's purity of purpose transfers potency to the spiritually corrupt and therefore powerless former keeper of the mysteries symbolized by the grail. But here what is transferred in the field (in an awkward ritual of secular conviviality that itself is forced and false) is the stuff of oblivion. Appropriately, as Peduzzi drains the bottle the sun appears, an irrelevant coincidence marking Peduzzi's alcoholic delusion of fulfillment rather than his actual attunement to natural order.[35]

It is the secularization of all this wine ritual, however, that registers most deeply, particularly in the Concordia incidents. In that community gathering place—a tellingly modern substitute for church, or Chapel Perilous of grail legend—the ritual is social rather than spiritual, and the communion (even had wine been consumed) would have been between men rather than with the mysteries of the universe. This discrepancy between Peduzzi's mundane preoccupation with social restoration and the desired spiritual restoration of his legendary predecessors is almost as awful as his spiritual alienation itself.[36]

Now the use of wine in Christian communion represents the fundamental unity between natural and divine realms and affirms man's ability to partake of both realms at once. Thus, in this allusion to the Christian communion, Hemingway is not digressing from the Fisher King legend. That legend, particularly as it is alluded to in both its preliterate and medieval variations in *The Waste Land*, proves the common preoccupation of pagan and Christian with nature, and especially with water, as a source of ultimate mysteries.[37] The canceled communion at the Concordia thus symbolizes modern man's exclusion from all forms of transcendent belief common in earlier human experience—atavistic or religious. This exclusion therefore embraces and parallels the subsequent failure of guide and novice at the riverside to effect contact with natural vitality. Accordingly, as I remarked at the outset, the story portrays failed secular searches (ironically compared to mythic quests for spiritual renewal through wine and water), two misdirected efforts accounting for the sterile emotional life of all three protagonists, and thus ultimately for the loss of any possible physical renewal through a child. The ancient connection between spiritual, emotional, and physical disease, affirmed by *The Waste Land,* is reaffirmed.

The mythical implication of the missing lead at the river is that neither self-absorbed—and therefore shallow—prospective communicant has the gravity (the double meaning of this word is revealing) to plumb the depths of the water for its hidden life. Each has lost the external perspective that allowed primitive man and religious man to identify their discovery of fish with their apprehension of a separate realm—concealed yet there and therefore mysterious. There is the mystical as well as the psychosexual importance of depth in the legend informing the story.

This failure of Peduzzi's generation to fathom the depths of nature and pass on to the next generation some viable translation of nature's secrets accounts at the level of myth for the confusion of languages as the *vecchio* tries without success in both Italian and German dialects to reach the young couple, who understand "nothing" (130), in more ways than one. His polyglot attempts reminds us, of course, of Eliot's many-tongued speakers. But Eliot uses his fragments of different languages positively, as part of a synthesis "shored against" the modern chaos. Hemingway's negative allusion to the faithless builders of the Tower of Babel is his invention, therefore. With it he manages to allude to his direct model, the poem, yet display an original variation on Eliot's method in that work—as he also does, obviously, with the highly original reversal of the communion we have noticed.

The opacity of Peduzzi's language is associated, furthermore, with the opacity of the marsala as well as of the river water; Peduzzi's wine of secular status and the water he presides over are *both* "muddy" (128, 130). Since these media for man's understanding of divinity and of nature are unclear, Peduzzi's inability to communicate with the young Americans is fitting enough. As a Fisher King figure with nothing to pass on to their generation, he incurs their resentment, as he has also provoked the mistrust and resentment of other younger people in his village, both middle and lower class. "The bank clerk stared at him from the door of the Fascist café. . . . The workmen in their stone-powdered jackets . . . looked up. . . . Nobody spoke or gave any sign to them except the town beggar, lean and *old*" (126, italics mine). This cold silence, when added to the anger of Peduzzi's daughter and the contempt shown by the girl at the Concordia, suggests more than the social scorn we have already discussed. It suggests that frustration and resentment that a cross-section of his community might well feel toward the generation of villagers who fought the war to end all wars yet left those who came after them a world with no clear sense of direction. The reference to fascism suggests the hunger in postwar Italy for some clear and absolute structure. It was a hunger intensified, I would assume, by the confused loyalties of a border town governed by Austria until annexed by Italy at the war's end, as Dix McComas notes.[38] The desperation that led to such extremes as fascism is a reasonable, objective correlative for the excess of feeling demonstrated against this personally harmless veteran. Some of his ostracism can be accounted for as social realism, if we think of Peduzzi as a misfit scapegoat. But the tension in the village also suggests the civic unrest of communities in all rebirth legends, communities whose leaders have failed in their annual missions. Something is definitely rotten in the town of Cortina, quite apart from the "rotten" feelings and marriage of the young Americans (128, 131); and whatever it is clearly focuses on Peduzzi.

The role of Tiny, the young wife, is Hemingway's original variation on the theme of feminine despair in *The Waste Land*. Unlike Eliot's neurasthenic women, Tiny is not an accomplice to the emotional sterility of her marriage, a sterility also threatening her physical procreativity. "Tiny" is a victim; her husband's pet name for her implies his unconscious resistance to her adult stature and needs.[39] Although during the action of the story she is generally irritable and is insensitive to Peduzzi, her husband's habitual lack of direction would try any wife; and by denying her the security and continuity she desires as a potential mother, he threatens her identity as a woman. Thus when Tiny states hopelessly, "It doesn't make any difference. . . . None of it makes any difference" (129), she expresses more than the ennui of Eliot's distracted female (1. 131): "What shall I do now? What shall I do?" She speaks as the voice of fertility, realizing that she will never, ever, be able to communicate with her sexually arrested husband, whose emotional inadequacy stems from the metaphysical inadequacy of his fathers.[40] But the fundamental despair in the voices of both women has the same root cause, and the cold wind that cuts through Tiny's "three sweaters" (129) is the wind that blows under the woman's door in *The Waste Land*. It is that legacy of spiritual emptiness, inherited by the twentieth century, that Hemingway—following Eliot—was later to call "*nada*": "'What is the wind doing?' / Nothing again nothing" (11. 119–20).[41]

In the concluding paragraphs of the story, Peduzzi's interests are again associated with the number three, now joined by seven. These are numbers resonant of religious mysticism in Hemingway's later narratives, and they here complete the connection of Peduzzi with the "mysterious." Seven is the hour of meeting for the next day set by the young man, in a spasm of chagrin, to atone for his carelessness about the tackle. The hour is hopefully incanted by the *vecchio*—in a sequence of three (134–35), and his last plea is: "The three of us" (135).[42]

In directing our sympathy throughout *In Our Time* toward the plight of the failed Fisher King figure, albeit degraded, and in stressing the poignancy of this king's futile wish to be restored by a youth who can only return his spiritual impotence, Hemingway strikes out on his own in a brilliant interpretation, both of Eliot's thematic myth and of the ills of this century. It is an interpretation that leads to his young, composite protagonist's ultimately accepting his generation's responsibility for its own restoration, in the concluding story of *In Our Time*, as we have seen. It thus provides a healthy counterbalance to the dominant emphasis in that book on the failure of fathers.

Lest we be concerned about the looseness of the parallels I have traced (the presence of unmatched details in the comparison of story, myth, and poem), we should remember that the modernist method of Eliot and Pound is not to construct the one-to-one equations of allegory but to assemble mosaics of allusion that in their cumulative effect make the reader *feel* a coherent parallel between narrative and myth, between present disorder and past order—and between the present work and earlier works alluded to. This was Hemingway's métier, a method he had not exploited systematically by the winter of 1922–23, but to which his imagination was particularly adapted. And when he was forced, by a fortuitous theft, to begin writing anew just as Eliot and Pound were producing, in *The Waste Land*, a mosaic organized around the one myth Hemingway could best comprehend—*that* was a moveable feast, not only for Hemingway but for modern literature.[43] Thus "Out of Season" assumes an importance in literary history beyond that cited by Baker. It is a document of the process of appropriative accretion central to the modernist method, practiced at the very highest level, where genius ignites genius and the tradition shaping the individual talent is in turn reshaped and renewed.

Yet what it tells of borrowings and beginnings is only part of this story's importance (in addition to its intrinsic merit). We can find in their germinal state in this narrative more than I have explicated of the essential patterns shaping Hemingway's canon. In reflecting upon the Fisher King legend as interpreted in the story and collection, we are reminded not only of the legend's similarly ironic role in *The Sun Also Rises* immediately following[44] but also of that legend's positive extension as the Hemingway hero matures, discovering powers that can be passed on and reciprocated. It is because Santiago fishes far out beyond all people (while these two remain in sight of the community) and because he lowers his bait deeper into the mile-deep sea than any other fisherman, that the old man as successful Fisher King has imparted purity of purpose to the youthful Manolin. And that is why the boy is a true "young gentleman," a budding champion who can return this later *vecchio*'s resolution when it flags near the end of his journey. The same is true of Colonel Cantwell's renewal by Renata—his son, daughter, and alter ego. Something close to this reciprocation is performed for Thomas Hudson by the strange young warrior Willie, and (temporarily) for David Bourne by the even stranger Marita. But such further considerations are for another chapter in our reestimation of the story.

Now that Hemingway studies are accepting Hemingway as a conscious, literate artist fully in the modernist tradition, we are ready to appreciate his creative appropriations of the works of others and of fragments of past cultures. Perhaps the essence of his genius was that by quintessential allusion he could evoke the power of the most traditional and intellectually complex material and could do so throughout his career without distorting the naturalistic surfaces of his narratives. Indeed, had he left more conspicuous evidence of the alternate worlds empowering his surfaces, readers might have appreciated during his lifetime the extent of his accomplishment. But it is more likely that the fault has not been in the oversubtlety of Hemingway's texts, but in our unwillingness before the last decade to think of him as a creative assimilator of ideas as well as of sensations, or to accept the dominant role of mysticism in his works. Now that we are increasingly recognizing both of these dimensions in his fiction, we would do well to look to the beginning of it all, in the delicately balanced, organic compression of "Out of Season."

Notes

1. Only three commentators have suggested coherence in the story as a whole: Joseph DeFalco, *The Hero in Hemingway's Short Stories* (Pittsburgh: U of Pittsburgh P, 1963) 163–68; Paul R. Jackson, "Hemingway's 'Out of Season.'" *The Hemingway Review* 1.1 (Fall 1981): 11–17; and Paul Smith, "Some Misconceptions of 'Out of Season,'" in *Critical Essays on* In Our Time, ed. Michael S. Reynolds (Boston: G. K. Hall, 1983) 243–51. Only DeFalco and Smith have seen the story as successful.

2. Carlos Baker, *Ernest Hemingway: A Life Story* (New York: Charles Scribner's Sons, 1969) 109.

3. Baker, 107–9. Michael Reynolds (interviewed in Boston, August 1988) has not been able to date the story's composition more precisely in preparing his forthcoming *Hemingway: The Paris Years* (London and New York: Basil Blackwell, 1989).

4. The words are Eliot's, describing Joyce's method (and his own) in his celebrated essay, "Ulysses, Order, and Myth," *Dial* 75 (November 1923): 483; this was an article Hemingway surely read, with satisfaction, while composing some of the later *In Our Time* material.

5. Baker, 109.

6. In *A Moveable Feast* (New York: Charles Scribner's Sons, 1964), he remembers having concealed meaning from his early readers and having thought ruefully that "it would not be bad if they caught up a little" (75). As George Dekker and Joseph Harris observe,

"One of Hemingway's major tactical problems in his early fiction is to make [cultural] allusions count—and thus place his characters and actions in a timeless perspective—without ruffling the quotidian vernacular surface of his narrative. Sometimes he exercises so much tact or indirection that he nearly defeats his own complex purpose": "Supernaturalism and the Vernacular Style in *A Farewell to Arms*," *PMLA* 94 (March 1979): 311. This subtlety is a feature—in Hemingway's fiction of all periods, I would add—placing extreme demands on his readers.

7. Baker, 132.

8. Many of the surface events that will prove to have mythic significance have never been discussed at any level. Furthermore, Hemingway's method of communicating meaning in this story reflects an aspect of his work only recently commonly acknowledged (upon our access to his manuscripts and reading material and our consequent attention to his consistent use of cultural and literary allusion). Indeed, for many readers the full interpretative approach required by Hemingway's allusive texts is still relatively novel. The following discussion is, therefore, of necessity three essays in one: an outline of the *Waste Land* parallels (not yet widely recognized in *In Our Time*) that provide a metaphorical context for "Out of Season" as part of an artistically unified collection; an explication of the literal narrative of the story as psychological realism (pointing out a rationale for its many hitherto puzzling details); and a concluding examination of the mythical dimensions of those details, as they are conveyed by allusions to the Fisher King legend and to Eliot's treatment of that legend.

   The pioneering demonstration of Hemingway's highly literate approach to his craft is Richard P. Adams, "Sunrise Out of the Wasteland," *Tulane Studies in English* 9 (1959): 119–31. See also Charles R. Anderson, "Hemingway's Other Style," *Modern Language Notes* 76 (May 1961): 434–42. An able later explication is Dekker and Harris's (see note 6 above). Representative recent studies in this vein are the important, if sometimes adventurously fanciful, monograph by Robert E. Gajdusek, *Hemingway and Joyce: A Study in Debt and Payment* (Corte Madera, Calif.: Square Circle P, 1984); Allen Josephs, "*Toreo*: The Moral Axis of *The Sun Also Rises*," *The Hemingway Review* 6 (Fall 1986): 88–99; and H. R. Stoneback, "From the rue Saint-Jacques to the Pass of Roland to the 'Unfinished Church on the Edge of the Cliff,'" *The Hemingway Review* 6 (Fall 1986): 2–29.

9. Bickford Sylvester, "*Waste Land* Parallels Unifying *In Our Time*: Hemingway's Confirmation as a Modernist," *Up in Michigan: Proceedings of the First National Conference of the Hemingway Society*, eds. Joseph Waldmeir and Joseph Marsh (Traverse City: The Hemingway Society, 1983): 12. See pp. 11–16 for a fuller explication of this and the other parallels between poem and story outlined below, but excluding comment on "Out of Season," which I discuss for the first time in the present essay.

10. Kimon Friar, "Notes," *Modern Poetry: American and British*, eds. Kimon Friar and John Malcolm Brinnin (New York: Appleton-Century-Crofts, 1951) 493. Friar's notes to *The Waste Land*, 472–97, make up one of the most useful analyses of the poem yet published.

11. *Ernest Hemingway: Selected Letters, 1917–1961*, ed. Carlos Baker (New York: Charles Scribner's Sons, 1981) 92.

12. Friar, 492–93.

13. Although fully grown and married, he still responds as a youth when an older stranger echoes the paternal overture of the brakeman in "The Battler"—"Come here, kid, I got something for you": Ernest Hemingway, *In Our Time* (New York: Charles Scribner's

Sons, 1955) 65. In accord with my approach in this essay, all references to "Out of Season" and its companion stories are to this book, in its most accessible "uniform" edition, and will be included in parentheses in my text.

14. Baker, 109; Kenneth S. Lynn, *Hemingway* (New York: Simon and Schuster, 1987) 202.

15. For Hemingway's oft-cited remarks on the biographical origin of the story, and on having left out the real-life Peduzzi's suicide so as to have "a tragic story *without* violence," see his letter to Fitzgerald of December 1925, in which he claims to have complained to the padrone, whereupon the gardener lost his job at the hotel and hanged himself in the stable (*Letters*, 180–81). See also *A Moveable Feast*, 75. Not even the latest researcher, Michael Reynolds (see note 3 above), could find any record of such a man. Nor could Kenneth Lynn, who searched local records for suicides by likely models for Peduzzi, although Lynn did not attempt the very difficult, but perhaps possible, task of finding remaining memories of a colorful reprobate Hemingway might have encountered (interview, Washington, D.C., September 1988). I will comment on Hemingway's claim later in my text and more fully in notes 26 and 27 below.

16. Jackson, 14. Jackson, 13–14, is the first commentator to notice in any way the vulnerability, the disappointed need for social status, and the final frustration that I expose at length below in discussing Peduzzi's role at the story's literal level. Unfortunately, in my opinion, Jackson is distracted from a fuller explication of Peduzzi's characterization by his misguided criticism of the narrative's shifting focus, first on Peduzzi's perceptions, then on the American's. Actually, this alternating focus seems to me artistically appropriate and effective, given the parallel and reciprocative positions of the two characters.

17. For this and subsequent observations about Italian village life in the story, I am indebted to my former colleague Professor Carlo Chiarenza, Director, Commissione per gli scambi culturali fra l'Italia e gli Stati Uniti, Rome.

18. Baker, 89.

19. Kenneth G. Johnston, "Hemingway's 'Out of Season' and the Psychology of Errors," *Literature and Psychology* 21 (November 1971): 45: Lynn, 204. Cf. note 40 below.

20. Had the subject never come up, we could believe that the young man had simply assumed (unwisely) that a local guide would supply local necessities. But when we learn that the guide had asked *him* if he had everything he needed, and that the young man had answered with perfunctory assurance (in a mountainous region, in April), we know we are being given something further to think about.

21. Looking back to the stage in a modern young man's development portrayed in "Out of Season," a more mature Nick Adams of "Big Two-Hearted River" remembers having habitually locked himself into the same emotional (and ultimately moral) mixture of sensations. In Nick's case it had been with the hot fried bananas he could formerly neither enjoy nor stop eating. This little-noticed passage defines the protagonist's developing adjustment to the restricted satisfactions of this century. For Nick can now face his emotional limits beforehand, forcing himself to wait until hot food has cooled enough to be tasted without pain (188)—and postponing precisely the same cancellation of joy by pain that he must eventually experience in fishing the swamp. He will wait to fish the swamp until he has enough control to bear inevitable loss and still retain his ability to function—and can thus achieve the severely restrictive victory accompanying full adult consciousness in the modern world.

22. From the deleted portion published posthumously as "Three Shots" (*The Nick Adams Stories* [New York: Charles Scribner's Sons, 1972] 13–15) we know that in a manuscript version the doctor has been summoned unexpectedly from a temporary campsite in the woods across the lake. But the narrative Hemingway chose to publish allows us to assume that the Indians have rowed to the beach at the lakeside cottage described in the next story (25), a summer residence where the doctor surely keeps his medical kit with ether, scalpel, and sutures.

23. Ernest Hemingway, *The Sun Also Rises* (New York: Charles Scribner's Sons, 1926) 168.

24. DeFalco, 167.

25. Peduzzi gets drunk on four lire in the first line of the story. When his request for five at the end is adjusted to the same four, there can be no other point than the suggestion to the reader that this four will be spent as were the first. The American cannot know this. But he does know that the marsala at the Concordia cost him more than five lire by itself, so that Peduzzi could not for that amount begin to pay for his proposed supplies and must, obviously, want the money now to sustain the effect of the marsala. This cannot suggest to the American or to us that the desperately sincere Peduzzi intends not to appear the next morning, but only that he needs immediate drinking money, finds an excuse for asking (the food and bait) that will also make the next day attractive to his client, does not dare ask for a realistic amount for fear that would put the young man off, and is as distracted as always from future practicalities. He will show up in the morning unprepared; the padrone, as befits his title, will have the *piombo* to tell him the young man is not coming; and Peduzzi's cruelly prolonged dream of escape, dignity, and camaraderie will be shattered. These are the events the reader can be expected to predict from the evidence included in the story, and they establish Peduzzi's plight as poignant, indeed.

26. Hemingway told Fitzgerald that when he wrote "Out of Season" he did not "put in the hanging" because he did not "think the story needed it" (*Letters*, 181). I obviously agree; careful readers should predict the next morning's misery and find that moving enough, without needing further dramatization of Peduzzi's emotional extremity. But the fact is that readers have not been careful in their response to this particular story. Thus Hemingway must have felt when writing to Fitzgerald, and felt even more strongly 30-odd years later when composing *A Moveable Feast*, that his readers manifestly *did* need some such dramatic physical act "put in" in order for them to notice Peduzzi's extreme vulnerability. It was clear that the old man's complex characterization had not registered in all that time, perhaps because (as critical responses continue to demonstrate) his brash surfaces made readers leap to the conclusion that he was a flat character—exactly as, within the story, his townsmen and the young couple fail to look beyond Peduzzi's embarrassing manner. Hemingway's "revelation" of eventual suicide does correct precisely this distortion. Although no such specific outcome is implied in the narrative that I can see, thinking of suicide prompts the reader to view Peduzzi as serious, sensitive, and somehow a victim, and thus to become alert to the various subtleties of characterization I have explicated.

   Hemingway's comments, then, can be taken as I shall label them, as belated footnotes withheld until critical confusion or neglect proved them necessary, to be accepted for their artistically appropriate effect on their audience, regardless of their literal substance. (That is their functional relationship to the narrative, after all, however much they have been misread and whatever our speculation as to Hemingway's rationale for offering them.)

27. An advantage of viewing Hemingway's comments as creative adjuncts to his text is that, like my reading of the story, it does not require our awkward blanket dismissal of an author's stated intention. It assumes, on the contrary, that if Hemingway lied about details, he did so to illuminate, rather than to conceal the true focus of his work—to promote a truth beyond mere fact, the truth of fiction. Cf. Smith, 238, and Lynn, 202. My reading therefore accepts and extends the *implications* of a real-life model's suicide, but it can do so solely because those implications sensitize us to suffering and cruelty objectively present in the story.

   There remains the question of Hemingway's motive in maintaining such obliquity—in adding fiction to fiction—even while attempting, let us assume, to steer us in the right direction. Hemingway's practice of "leaking" invented autobiographical incidents as the supposed bases for his works is a subject I have addressed elsewhere in exploring his calculated use of fictionalized autobiography as an artistic device, generally—as an extension of exactly the kind of dialogue Hemingway the artist has with his readers through the narratives themselves ("Public Faces, Private Fictions: The Hemingway *roman à clef*," a paper delivered at the 1988 meeting of the Modern Language Association). But all that is relevant here is that in this case the secondary fiction promotes our response to what is already there in the primary fiction, and that only by allowing Peduzzi's desperation to register can we recognize the balanced binary structure of the plot and therefore grasp the story's essential themes. (Witness Lynn, on his way to a reductive reading that diminishes both author and story: his first step is to dismiss Peduzzi as "the bold and devilish guide" and nothing more, 202.)

28. That all Greeks want to go to America is an American perspective, suggesting an American narrator; it is also likely that the subject has come up because of the interviewer's nationality. As for his age, the visitor's worldly tone perhaps associates him with the several older narrators in the stories and interchapters. But after the stories' constant focus on an expanding youthful consciousness, the reader imagines this interviewer to be a later persona of the composite protagonist, at about Nick's stage in "Cross-Country Snow." Thematically, the American abroad encountering emptiness where wisdom had been expected evokes familiar Jamesian ironies. These are reinforced in "L'Envoi" by a title repeating Pound's ironic echo of Chaucer and the French tradition in "Hugh Selwyn Mauberley," a poem excoriating exactly the decline, in England, from Apollonian idealism to tawdry expediency that Hemingway's king reflects.

29. T. S. Eliot, *The Waste Land*, in *The Complete Poems and Plays: 1909–1950* (New York: Harcourt Brace, 1950) 37: 1.1. Subsequent line references are in parentheses in my text.

30. See Larry E. Grimes, *The Religious Design of Hemingway's Early Fiction* (Ann Arbor: UMI Research P, 1985) 27.

31. Smith notes, 243, that "the adverb *mysteriously* was an initial addition" to this passage in Hemingway's typescript of the story, "and the adjective *mysterious* a final one." I have noticed, in the Hemingway manuscripts generally, that such initial and subsequent additions customarily serve to supply and/or progressively reinforce the *thematic* significance of an emended passage, exactly as do these all-important introductory indicators of Peduzzi's mythic role. The similarly thematic detail of Peduzzi's gnomic "winking and knowingness" that I have cited is also an addition (Smith, 241). See also the other accretions Smith has listed, 240–41 et passim, which include the *Waste Land* imagery of muddy water, muddy wine, and dump heap I cite.

32. For this term applied to other Hemingway plots, see Robert M. Hogge, "Twentieth-Century Medievalism in Hemingway," *Up in Michigan* (see note 9 above) 120.

33. For Hemingway's similar use of this number elsewhere, see Rosemary Stephens, "'In Another Country': Three as Symbol," *University of Mississippi Studies in English* 7 (1966): 87–96.

34. I stress an approximation because for an absolute parallel to the mass there would have to be some reference to water mixed with the wine. The drinking vessels, glasses, would have to be described as cuplike in some way to represent the chalice, and there would preferably be only one glass, passed around. In fact, at the time of the story only one priest would actually sip the wine from the chalice; the other priests would not do so except in the ancient and medieval ceremony I have mentioned. However, in the earliest masses multiple chalices were used: A. Cornides, "Concelebration," *New Catholic Encylopedia* (Washington, D.C.: Catholic U of America, 1987) 103. But all this is to put too fine a point on detail. As it is, the scene suggests the abortive reversal I have described, with an added irony that the supposed leader and primary celebrant of the aborted ceremony at the hotel is excluded as unworthy, forced to have his communion cup offered to him outside the building, as would a leper in the medieval church. The woman, whom we will presently see as the spirit of fertility, does not take part in the ritual, even in its reverse form.

35. Equally irrelevant appearances of sunshine at the conclusions of *The Red Badge Of Courage* and *Billy Budd* are illustrative antecedents in American naturalism.

36. As for related ironies, the discrepancy between alcoholic and religious uses of wine is at once humorous and awful, as is that between a selfish, illicit venture and a quest associated in myth with the salvation of community.

37. In the sacramental mixture of wine and water, symbolizing the blood and water flowing from Christ's side, the wine represents the divine in Christ, the water the mortal. (In partaking, man celebrates Christ's willingness to descend so that man might ascend.) But in the ritual of baptism, immersion in water itself represents a commitment to the spiritual. Christ was a fisher of men, and the fish is a symbol of Christ. It is this immemorial association of water with the mysteries that the Fisher King myth reflects.

38. Dix McComas, "The Geography of Ernest Hemingway's 'Out of Season,'" *The Hemingway Review* 3.2 (Spring 1984): 48, 49.

39. The fact that Hemingway and Hadley sometimes used this term for each other, no doubt with affection as well as irony, should not distract us from its negative use by a fictional character.

40. By a concatenation of Freudian associations, Johnston and Lynn (see note 19 above) argue that Tiny is pregnant and that the couple's disagreement at lunch ("Out of Season" [129]) has been over her husband's wish that she have an abortion. However, pregnancy and abortion are not explicitly referred to, as they are, respectively, in the later stories cited as comparative evidence by these scholars. What is clearly implied by the narrative as a whole, though, is that Tiny is chilled by her husband's need for satisfactions outside their relationship, resents his inability to compromise with her conflicting interests, and accepts at last that a man whose one gesture of consideration is to turn back a woman who wants to "stay with" him (131), must continue on the longer journey of their life together without ever sharing her desire to share. This desire—the necessary emotional precondition for nurturing and parenthood, and thus the very *spirit* of fertility—is what is being killed off

within Tiny, whether she is presently with child or not. She will be rendered in fact a perpetual Signorina, Signora in name only, if she does "stay with" a husband addicted to the same peripatetic evasion of commitment we see pursued by the boy-men of "Cat in the Rain" and "Hills Like White Elephants." The scene with Peduzzi is an instance of this evasive pattern's menacing Tiny's womanhood. It is psychologically plausible as well as structurally consistent, therefore, for the couple's argument at lunch to have been, not over abortion (an iceberg with no visible tip in the story), but over the illicit tryst we witness the husband arranging immediately before lunch—the one subject we know he had to discuss during the meal, to inform Tiny of her totally unexpected departure less than "forty minutes or an hour" away (125). We are prompted to bring to the surface this knowledge we have of things untold when we realize that both meeting (125) and argument (129) are disclosed only in connection with lunch and that lunch is mentioned nowhere else, so that meeting and argument are linked by "three-cushion shot."

In the most likely scenario, I think, what the young man later apologizes for is having berated Tiny when she failed to support his defensive enthusiasm as he announced that he had unilaterally committed the rest of their day to yet another last-minute diversionary scheme. Thus tongue-lashed, she has been forced to tag along and even to carry the phallic instruments of what for her cannot be the "fun" her husband has fantasized (131), but rather an experience subverting her feminine needs and fraught with risks that are pointless to her. Accordingly, her position "lagging behind" in the procession is at once symbolism and body language, as she "sullenly" resists stepping forward to join the men (126).

Indeed, the male libido's displacement from nest to quest in this story (represented by the fishing rods Tiny so reluctantly holds) is the first instance of a difference in the sexes seen finally in Hemingway as innate rather than neurotic. What begins here as "different angles" of vision (129) created by the alienation of a twentieth-century male becomes that paradox of nature's design touched upon in Robert E. Gajdusek's discussion of "An Alpine Idyll" in chapter 12 of this volume, and by Oliver Evans in "'The Snows of Kilimanjaro': A Revaluation," *PMLA* 76 (December 1961): 601–7. Also see my "Winner Take Nothing: Development as Dilemma for the Hemingway Heroine," *Pacific Coast Philology* 31 (November 1986): 73–80, which considers most of the major works.

41. See Grimes, 27–28. The emptiness of Tiny's life is most dramatically revealed, as Smith stresses, in the futile exchange with her husband at the Concordia (129) cited above. In demonstrating the structural centrality of "discord at the Concordia" (Smith, 247–48) and in suggesting the scene's connection to the river episodes, Smith's impressive analysis of the manuscripts squares with my reading of the story, it seems to me, despite his dismissal of Peduzzi's central role. At the mythic level, the ironic ceremony at the hotel is the focal point of all three abortive quests for spiritual life, as I have shown. And at the literal level, the human alienation both inside and outside the door of the hotel identifies the parallel flights that unite youth and *vecchio*, giving the story exactly the comprehensive symmetry that Smith rejects, unnecessarily, I think, by denying the twin plights of the two men. Then, too, Smith has labeled both the opening and closing scenes "Peduzzi and the young gentleman," 242–43, in my view suggesting twin billing. See also note 31 above.

42. Although he is himself aware, at most, only of yearning for a surrogate daughter and for some reassuring semblance of domestic order, Peduzzi's plea sounds through much of Hemingway's canon. The sense that life can never be "opening up" completely (135), no day be truly "wonderful" (133), for men without women, no matter how intense (in later narratives) the exclusively male moments of harmony with the rest of nature: this is the shadow falling always just beyond experiences of masculine camaraderie in Hemingway,

darkening yet deepening the vision of life portrayed on other rivers, other seas, from the mountains above Burguete to the islands east of Havana.

43. Hemingway's ability to approach the Fisher King legend as experience rather than as research (to feel the sensations that *prompted* the legend Eliot used) allowed him the unexplored territory an artist's ego requires. Consequently, his powers were both identified and released, as the artistic results demonstrate in story and collection.

44. For a discussion of the novel as thematically a sequel to the collection in this regard, see Sylvester, "*Waste Land* Parallels," 16–18.

6

"A Very Short Story" as Therapy

Scott Donaldson

With one or two notable exceptions, "A Very Short Story," composed in June and July of 1923, has received very little criticism. Here Scott Donaldson postulates that critics have neglected this short story because of its brevity ("A Very Short Story" occupies only two scant pages in The First Forty-nine*) and because of "its relative lack of merit when measured against the best Hemingway short fiction." According to Donaldson, that lack of merit is the result of Hemingway's failure to distance himself from the story's autobiographical material, his 1919 jilting by nurse Agnes von Kurowsky, who had cared for his war wounds in Italy. This study of "A Very Short Story's" composition shows Hemingway attempting to cauterize the memory of Agnes as he moves, through three successive drafts of the story, toward a more impersonal yet more bitter vision of their relationship. For Donaldson, "A Very Short Story" takes on a special importance as therapy, therapy that would later allow Hemingway to approach a love affair between a wounded ambulance driver and his nurse with the artistic detachment necessary to achieve the classic novel,* A Farewell to Arms.

Other than a 1971 linguistic analysis and Robert Scholes's fine discussion in *Semiotics and Interpretation*, "A Very Short Story" has been largely ignored in Hemingway scholarship.[1] One reason is its relative lack of merit when measured against the best Hemingway short fiction, for reasons that are analyzed below. Yet as a study in the process of composition, "A Very Short Story" well repays close scrutiny.

Ernest Hemingway met Agnes von Kurowsky in the Red Cross hospital in Milan, where he had been taken to recuperate from his July 1918 wounding on the Austrian front. She was 26, a Red Cross nurse, very attractive, and not without experience in affairs of the heart. He was barely 19, good-looking, charming in his eagerness to confront life, and innocent in the ways of courtship. Despite the difference in their ages, they fell in love. When he sailed for the States from Genoa in early January, it was understood that he would get a job, she would follow, and they would be married. That did not happen, however. Agnes soon transferred her affections to an Italian officer, and wrote Ernest the bad news less than two months after his departure from Italy.

When the letter arrived at Oak Park in mid-March 1919, young Hemingway was devastated. If, as he wrote his friend Howell Jenkins, he then attempted to cauterize her memory "with a course of booze and other women,"[2] the therapy was not entirely successful. A residue of pain filled the hollow place that had housed his love for the Red Cross nurse and would not go away until he could write about it. "You'll lose it if you talk about it,"[3] Jake Barnes warned, and the obverse of the maxim was that you could get rid of it by talking or writing about it. When Ernest left Hadley Hemingway, it took him only two months to put the tale into fictional form in "A Canary for One."[4] When Agnes von Kurowsky rejected him, it took him four years to write a story about it.

Actually the story went through at least three versions: the pencil draft headed "Personal" or "Love" (version A), Chapter 10 of *in our time* (1924) (version B), and "A Very Short Story" of *In Our Time* (1925) and the collected stories (version C).[5] Most of the changes Hemingway made between the first draft and final copy worked to render the account at once more impersonal and more bitter. In the two-page, handwritten draft (version A), the love affair is depicted tenderly, and little blame is directed at Agnes. In this version she is called "Ag," the narrator is unambiguously "I," and the two of them are often "we," as in the straightforward "We loved each other very much." Those six little words do not appear in either subsequent version, nor does the following account of letter writing inside the hospital: "Daytimes I slept and wrote letters for her to read downstairs when she got up. She used to send letters up to me by the charwoman."

Using the first person pronoun and the name "Ag," together with placing the story in Milan, conformed to the practice Hemingway often followed in his early career: beginning with names drawn from experience but later changing the names as the experience became transformed from reportage to fiction. There were legal as well as artistic reasons for such changes. The female character here remained "Ag" in Chapter 10 of *in our time*, but became "Luz" in *In Our Time* upper case. That was the way it should stay, Hemingway instructed Max Perkins when *The First Forty-nine Stories* were in preparation in 1938: "Ag is libelous. Short for Agnes."[6] But version A's accuracy in the matter of names may also have reflected

Hemingway's attempt to indicate how he felt about the broken affair. The subject was love, after all, and the tone of the piece in the first draft is unmistakably romantic.

Version A was originally headed "Personal" and began "There were flocks of chimney swifts in the sky. The searchlights were out and they carried me. . . ." Then this broke off, and was crossed out in favor of the new heading "Love" and the remainder of the story. Since Chapter 10 of *in our time* (version B) is also called "Love" in early typescripts, the presumption is strong that version A functioned as a preliminary draft for the *in our time* chapter published in 1924. Apparently he was trying during the interim to find the right way to approach the subject of lost love. In version A he even penciled in one sexually suggestive passage—

> "I said, 'I love you, Ag,' and pulled her over hard against me. And she said, 'I know it, Kid,' and kissed me and got all the way up onto the bed."

But this was deleted.

The most significant difference between version A and the two that followed was that the first draft did not censure Agnes in its closing section, either overtly or through the sarcasm that pervades the later versions. Ag had not kept the faith, of course, but in version A Hemingway provided her with an excuse for this failure. After the armistice, he wrote, "I went home to get a job so we could get married and Ag went up to Torre di Mosto to run some sort of a show. It was lonely there, and there was a battalion of Arditi quartered in the town. When the letter came saying ours had been only a kid affair I got awfully drunk. The major never married her, and I got a dose of clap from a girl in Chicago riding in a Yellow Taxi." The loneliness made her do it, and Ag got her due punishment when "the major" failed to marry her. These extenuating circumstances persist (and are even adumbrated on) in versions B and C, but they are outweighed there by a sardonic resentment of Ag's faithlessness.

Each version begins with the wounded protagonist on the roof with Ag (or Luz) beside him on the bed, "cool and fresh in the hot night." (Remember how Daisy Buchanan told Gatsby she loved him: "You look so cool.") In each version, too, the nurse "stayed on night duty for three months" and the patient, once on crutches, took the temperatures so that she would not have to "get up from the bed"—his bed. All three versions have the lovers praying together in the Duomo, along with the declaration that they wanted to get married. But the particulars of these scenes changed substantially from version A to versions B and C. What Hemingway chose to change had considerable effect on the story that resulted.

Most of the revisions involve additions rather than deletions, a pattern, as Paul Smith has demonstrated, that is often characteristic of Hemingway's working method. The only important omissions are "We loved each other very much," the business about writing letters to each other during Ag's three months of night duty, and the confessional "I got awfully drunk." In the way of substitutions, Milan becomes Padova in version B and is Anglicized to Padua in "A Very Short Story" itself, where Ag is changed to Luz. More important, the "I" of the first draft gives way to the seemingly more objective third person "he" in versions B and C (in no case is the protagonist given a name). This objectivity is more apparent than real, as Robert Scholes demonstrates in "Decoding Papa: 'A Very Short Story' as Word and Text."[7] The sketch reads perfectly, Scholes points out, if the "he" of the text is transposed to "I" and makes no sense if the "she" is converted to the first person. In other words, the "I" voice continues to speak from behind the facade of the "he." Moreover, most of the other changes Hemingway made are in the form of addenda designed to sharpen awareness that the "he" of the story has been done wrong. The deck has been stacked against Luz.

Version A contains only four paragraphs. Versions B and C—the story as it appeared in *in our time* and *In Our Time*—run to seven paragraphs and about twice as many words as the first draft. The first three versions of version A are substantially transferred to subsequent versions, and the first paragraph itself (other than the change in pronouns and place name) remains fixed throughout. In paragraphs two and three, however, Hemingway makes some important additions. Paragraph two of version A deals with Ag on night duty, her preparing him for his operation, the joke about "friend or enema," and his taking temperatures so she could stay in his bed. The same paragraph in the printed story contains four additional sentences that strongly imply a sexual bond between them. After the friend or enema joke, for instance, versions B and C have "He went under the anaesthetic holding tight onto himself so he would not blab about anything during the silly, talky time." Not in front of the doctors and other nurses, that is, for as the other added sentences reveal, their affair was not a secret to his fellow patients. After the sentence about taking temperatures, versions B and C go on to reveal that "There were only a few patients, and they all knew about it. They all liked Ag. As we walked back along the halls he thought of Ag in his bed." These thoughts, in the context of the patients' all knowing about it, were presumably carnal. This was no casual nurse-patient infatuation, the story is insisting.

Paragraph three, about praying in the Duomo before he returns to the front and about their wanting to get married, is fleshed out by the addition of one clause and one full sentence. The clause places other people in the Duomo, and so tends to dispel the romantic aura of the two wartime lovers alone in the great cathedral. The sentence expands on their desire to get married. "They felt as though they were married, but they wanted every one to know about it, and to make it so they could not lose it." Once they were really married, they could tell the world—doctors, nurses, her Red Cross superiors, his parents, everyone—about their love. Marriage would not only validate their love but fix it in concrete, "make it so they could not lose it." Again Hemingway's revisions stress the seriousness of their affair, but now he foreshadows the danger that what they have together might be lost.

Such foreshadowing is more appropriate in a short story than in a sketch, and in the process of composition Hemingway was uncertain which of the two he was creating. The corrected proofs of *in our time* use the heading "Chapter 10," crossed out but restored by an authorial "Stet." Beneath that another title, "A Short Story," is crossed out but not restored. So the piece appeared as yet another "chapter" or sketch among those collected in the 1924 *in our time*. The following year, however, he converted the piece from sketch to full status as "A Very Short Story" among the much larger ones of *In Our Time*. In its earliest version even that diminutive title would have claimed too much. Hemingway must have sensed that he had broken off version A too abruptly and without sufficient directions to guide his readers, for from the fourth paragraph on almost everything in "Chapter 10" and "A Very Short Story" (versions B and C) is new.

The fourth paragraph of versions B and C takes up the love letter motif, but in revision it is as if only Ag is writing them, hence giving him every reason to expect her undying love:

> Ag wrote him many letters that he never got until after the armistice. Fifteen came in a bunch and he sorted them by the dates and read them all straight through. They were about the hospital, and how much she loved him and how it was impossible to get along without him and how terrible it was missing him at night.

The fifth paragraph is concerned with their parting in Italy, and the understanding they reached at that time. They "agreed he should go home," and she "would not come until he had a good job and could come to New York to meet her," but on this latter point they were in anything but agreement. "On the train from Padova to Milan they quarreled about her not being willing to come home at once. When they had to say good-bye in the station . . . they kissed good-bye, but were not finished with the quarrel. He felt sick about saying good-bye like that." Still, the unnamed narrator—perhaps by this time we can call him Ernie, as Ag did—was willing to accept this condition and any other she imposed. "It was understood he would not drink, and he did not want to see his friends or any one in the States." What was understood between them, in other words, was that he should give up all vices and entertainments, including friendship, and not get involved with anyone else. No such conditions were exacted of her.

The sixth paragraph, after presenting expository details about his going back to America and Ag's opening a hospital in Torre di Mosto, proceeds to develop at length two topics barely touched on in version A: Ag's seduction by the Italian major and the contents of her good-bye letter. In versions B and C, it was not only lonely for Ag, but lonely "and rainy" as well:

> Living in the muddy, rainy town in the winter, the major of the battalion made love to Ag, and she had never known Italians before, and finally wrote a letter to the States that theirs had been only a boy and girl affair. She was sorry, and she knew he would probably not be able to understand, but might someday forgive her, and be grateful to her, and she expected, absolutely unexpectedly, to be married in the spring. She loved him as always, but she realized now it was only a boy and girl love. She hoped he would have a great career, and believed in him absolutely. She knew it was for the best.

This long addition traces a curious emotional course. In the beginning it provides Agnes with still more valid excuses for her inconstancy. She had only succumbed after the rain and mud and the loneliness and the wiles of the Italian major conspired to diminish her resistance. Again this emphasizes the seriousness of the love between the narrator/protagonist and his nurse: she did not easily break the faith.

Once the paragraph switches to what she wrote in her final letter, however, the tone changes abruptly. The trigger to this charge seems to be the phrase "boy and girl affair," later repeated as "boy and girl love." Following this phrase, the story launches into that long periodic sentence about how sorry she was and so on that ends with the sarcastic revelation that "she expected, absolutely unexpectedly, to be married in the spring." Here the full weight of her perfidy, built up previously by her love letters and the conditions she'd insisted on before they could be married, is expressed by the snide "expected, absolutely unexpectedly."

In the final paragraph, version B omits mention of his getting drunk on receipt of the letter about theirs having been a "kid affair," but otherwise elaborates on the consequence of the breakup. The major "did not marry her in the spring," the story reads, and then rather nastily adds, "or any other time." Nor did the narrator demean himself by replying to the letter she wrote him about *her* jilting by the major. He did not get drunk, either. Instead he followed a foolish and costly course of male assertiveness. "A short time after he contracted gonorrhea [changed from "got a dose of the clap" in the typescript for "Chapter 10"] from a salesgirl from the Fair riding in a taxicab through Lincoln Park."

The few alterations Hemingway made in version B, "Chapter 10," to version C, "A Very Short Story," are of minor significance. Most are made to suggest the fictitiousness of people and places. Milan is Padua, Torre di Mosto is Pordonone *[sic]*, "The Fair" becomes "a loop department store," and Ag becomes Luz. The most important revision inserts three words in the fourth paragraph. Fifteen of Luz's letters came in a bunch, Hemingway wrote, "to the front." Those words conjure up a picture of a harried soldier perusing the letters from his loved one during a respite from combat. In fact, it was Agnes who went off to various "fronts" on behalf of the Red Cross, while Hemingway was recovering in hospital, first from his wounds and then—after a very brief visit, not on duty, to the front—from jaundice. The attempt here is obviously to arouse sympathy for the male narrator, and nearly all the revisions from version A on aim for a similar result. In effect, that is what is wrong with "A Very Short Story." The narrator is too good, too noble, too unfairly wronged. He is too close to Hemingway himself, or at least to that Hemingway who—four years later—was still bitterly resentful of his rejection by Agnes von Kurowsky.

"A Very Short Story" ranks as one of Hemingway's least effective stories. Behind a pretense of objectivity, it excoriates the faithless Agnes. Even four years after the jilting, he was too close to his subject matter to achieve the requisite artistic distance. But he does seem to have dissipated his bitterness against her in the process. Twice again—in "Along with Youth," his 1925 beginning-of-a-novel, and in *A Farewell to Arms* (1929)—he explored the subject of love between a wounded soldier and his nurse, but in both cases the rancor is gone. In "A Very Short Story," apparently, Hemingway did manage to get rid of it by writing about it.

Notes

1. Emile Benveniste, *Problems in General Linguistics*, trans. Mary Elizabeth Meek (Coral Gables: U of Miami P, 1971) 223–30; Robert Scholes, "Decoding Papa: 'A Very Short Story' as Word and Text," *Semiotics and Interpretation* (New Haven: Yale UP, 1981) 110–26.

2. Ernest Hemingway to Howell G. Jenkins, 16 June 1919, *Ernest Hemingway: Selected Letters, 1917–1961*, ed. Carlos Baker (New York: Charles Scribner's Sons, 1981) 25.

3. Ernest Hemingway, *The Sun Also Rises* (New York: Charles Scribner's Sons, 1926) 245.

4. See Scott Donaldson, "Preparing for the End: Hemingway's Revisions of 'A Canary for One,'" *Studies in American Fiction* 6 (Autumn 1978): 203–11.

5. The three versions of the story are located in folders 633, 94, and 94A at the Kennedy library: *Catalog of the Ernest Hemingway Collection at the John F. Kennedy Library* (Boston G. K. Hall, 1982) 13, 102.

6. Ernest Hemingway to Maxwell Perkins, 12 July 1938, *Letters*, 469.

7. Scholes, 110–26.

7

The Bullfight Story and Critical Theory

Bruce Henricksen

Bruce Henricksen deals with other "very short stories" composed during the summer of 1923 and neglected because of their brevity—the six bull-fighting vignettes dispersed as interchapters between the longer short stories of In Our Time. *Henricksen's unique strategy is to treat these six vignettes as a single short story showing both a logical, linear development of the narrative voice and sequentially arranged elements of plot, while at the same time investigating the many ways this "story" resists the formalist strategy of seeking unity and harmony. Henricksen subjects Hemingway's bullfighting story to a Bakhtinean analysis, describing how this polyphonic text gives full expression to the dialogic nature of the self. In the process, he reaches some startling and provocative conclusions about the ideological content of the bullfighting interchapters. Henricksen makes creative and exemplary use of postmodern critical methods, formulated for coping with the fragmented world of* The Waste Land, *to illuminate some of Hemingway's most bafflingly experimental fiction, itself a response to the "broken images" and "stony rubbish" of our time.*

Perhaps the most neglected of Hemingway's short stories is the one many readers have failed to discern at all. I am referring to the bullfight story that comes into being as the reader reassembles the six bullfighting fragments (chapters 9 through 14) dispersed as interludes between the longer, conventionally unified stories of *In Our Time*. Clinton S. Burhans, Jr., in "The Complex Unity of *In Our Time*," pointed to some common themes within the bullfighting interludes and also noticed that the larger sequence of interludes running throughout the volume inscribes bullfighting at the center of a widening and symmetrical gyre of violence. Reading through the volume sequentially, one encounters in the 16 interludes the topics of war, crime, bullfighting, and war.[1] E. R. Hagemann supplemented Burhans by dividing the bullfight interchapters into three subgroups and relating this tripartite structure to the structure of the bullring itself. More compelling was Hagemann's observation that, although the earliest interchapter was written in 1914, all the bullfight pieces were written in the summer of 1923 in Spain.[2] Burhans and Hagemann wrote under the influence of the New Critical paradigm, and the formalist's desire to find unity in the literary text prompted them to read beyond the apparently fragmentary nature of Hemingway's practice.[3]

The discovery, or as Roland Barthes might say the "writing," of the bullfight story reached a higher level of sophistication with Robert Scholes's discussion in *Textual Power* in 1985. Scholes found in the story such recurrent thematic oppositions as courage and cowardice, grace and clumsiness, success and failure, and life and death. And the final two interludes, Scholes pointed out, can be read as causally linked events of the same day. But the strongest argument for the unity of the six interludes—and we should note that Scholes's reading, too, is influenced by the desire to find unity—is the apparently logical, linear development of the narrative voice. At first the narrator, with expressions such as "wham" and "couldn't hardly," sounds like an American teenager describing his first bullfight. In the second and third interludes he begins self-consciously to employ the jargon of the bullfight. Later he is in a restaurant speaking with a matador, and finally he is behind the scenes as Maera dies.[4] Perhaps one could even locate the traditional elements of plot in this sequence—exposition, complication, climax, falling action, and denouement. The point is not to force the vignettes into a Procrustean bed in the effort to see "a" story, but to examine the inevitably problematic relationship between the individual text and our theoretical constructs.

Scholes's reading is suggestive precisely because it intends to reveal this problematic relationship—thus his hesitancy to impose more unity upon "the story" than it can bear. He is aware, for instance, of an objectivity in the tone of the second interlude that is not easily reconcilable with the enthusiasm of the first. While there is a movement from an outsider's point of view to an insider's that lends structure to the sequence of six, it is difficult to believe that the young American teenager of the first interlude has actually become the confidant of the matador Maera in the fifth. The attempt to find a unified, albeit maturing, narrative voice is further complicated by the suggestion in 13 that the narrator is now himself a matador:

> Yes, Maera said, and who will kill his bulls when he gets a *cogida*?
> We, I suppose, I said.

Therefore, as useful and as unavoidable as the formalist strategy of seeking unity and harmony is to our particular community of interpreters, it may be wise also to seek meaning in the ways a text resists this strategy. Wolfgang Iser speaks of those aspects of a text that resist our totalizing efforts as "latent disturbances."[5] These disturbances account for the defamiliarizing effect of the text while providing occasions for further interpretive acts. In what follows I will explore how the disturbances Scholes helps us see in the bullfight story lead to further inquiry concerning the act of reading. This act will be discussed under three categories with highly permeable boundaries.

Point of View and the Decentered Subject

One question Scholes directs us toward, then, concerns not simply point of view but also the ontological nature of the narrating subject. The traditional concept of the subject as a permanent, stable, and unique psychological entity that transcends and structures experience has been disputed by recent developments in the human sciences. For Jacques Lacan, for instance, the subject is always inhabited by alien discourses—in his famous phrase, the unconscious is the discourse of the Other.[6] For Emile Benveniste the first person pronoun is discursively necessary but representationally problematic.[7] And when, at the end of *The Order of Things,* Michel Foucault speaks of the disappearance of "man," he has in mind the exhaustion of a certain classical conception of the individual subject.[8] High modernism, with its nostalgia for wholeness but its preoccupation with fragmentation— fragments shored against my ruins, as someone in "The Waste Land" says— exists on the boundary between the classical and the postmodern thinking about human subjectivity.[9]

Mikhail Bakhtin, developing his theories in Russia during the years of Hemingway's own development as a writer, rejected a model of the self as a totalized, centered, monological entity. To Bakhtin, the subject is always constituted in part by "the other." Each of us is a particular arrangement of the various social or ideological voices available in our culture. "I" am always already a "we." Readers who assume that narrative point of view must reflect a single, unified consciousness will have difficulty with what Bakhtin calls "polyphonic" texts—texts that give full expression to the "dialogic" nature of the self.[10] Conversely, aesthetic principles that insist on monologic narrators are in fact politically freighted in that they seek to control or structure the narrative voice by denying its natural speech diversity. If ideology is that system of beliefs that seeks to define and construct individual subjects, then a Bakhtinean analysis of narrative voice is an attempt to reveal this process and to understand the relationship between subjectivity and the voices of the other.

Hemingway's bullfighting story offers a brief but interesting glimpse of this process. The distinctly American voice of the first interlude is also the voice of the innocent but enthusiastic outsider. In the second interlude the voice is more objective, and the first two interludes together show us two versions of the uninitiated subject. In the third interlude the narrator emerges as an "I," a self-aware subject, and that emergence seems to coincide with a further move away from the youthful, American voice of the first interlude (now the narrator speaks with drunken bullfighters in their cafés). As Lacan says, the subject "I" is always constituted as a loss—"It is necessary to find the subject as a lost object."[11] The next interlude focuses on Villalta, the consummate artist, and the narrative voice is appropriately less obtrusive. In the last two interludes the narrator seems to have lost both his youth and his Americanness almost entirely, perhaps now a bullfighter himself but in any case able to enter the point of view of the dying Maera.

Thus in the total story a voice or a subjectivity is being born and launched out of a diversity of voices sequenced as a movement away from the mother country and toward identity with a cultural "other." Speech diversity is not only heard in the different narrative voices of the separate interludes, but is also figured in the crowd noises, which recede as one progresses through the sequence and are only a distant backdrop to Maera's death. This final interlude is a subtle interweaving of points of view—a narrator's, momentarily the doctor's, in the far distance the crowd's, and of course Maera's. The bullfight story ends by reestablishing a kind of polyphony, as though to say that the story is never the property or product of a single subjectivity. But at the same time the story, functioning as a power discourse, has managed the exclusion of the opening voice.

The reader traces a shift in the identity of the narrator and, under the influence of the generic laws of the *bildungsroman,* is prompted to interpret this shift positively—as growth or maturation or the gaining of experience. The ideological message (the power discourse) thus conveyed is that authenticity involves separation from the values of the larger and original community, represented by the spectators, and identification with the values of a select, tightly codified, and largely alienated subculture. It is no accident that this newly born subjectivity becomes one with the dying Maera, since the birth of this ideologically preferred self has also been the death of a previous cultural identity.

John W. Meyer suggests the social significance of the question of how the literary text constructs a version of the individual subject:

Only in individualist societies is it so important to control what individuals are and how they behave and think. There it is understood that the society's success or failure, its integration or breakdown, is ultimately determined by the competence and conformity of the individual. As a result much of the effort of modern society goes into constructing appropriate individuals. [12]

In the bullfight story point of view is handled not to reveal the continuous development of a single, unified consciousness but, rather, to posit specific, disjunctive subjectivities arranged to constitute something like an ideological proposition. The story illustrates a relationship between point of view and ideology, a relationship that becomes clear when one brackets the New Critical versions of structural and discursive unity and abandons the traditional, bourgeois notion of the unified or monologic self. In such a reading one must also abandon the New Critical myth of the autonomous text and instead read the text in its context of social discourses. In this way the formal features of the text can still be studied, but in relation to questions that transcend the literary.

Hemingway's bullfight story, then, is a place where the reader can enact an encounter between traditional formalist aesthetics and more contemporary theoretical problems. No reader in today's interpretive community can or should entirely escape the pressure of the formalist assumptions that give shape and coherence to the story. But neither should the reader fail to hear the elaborate free play of voices and codes, a play implicit in Barthes's question of *who speaks*. [13] Furthermore, the story seems to illustrate the meaning of Lacan's question, "Where is the subject?" and of his refusal to accept a model of a unified consciousness. He writes that "the mind is not a totality in itself" and that "the idea of a unifying unity of the human condition has always had on me the effect of a scandalous lie." [14] Thus the response of many contemporary theorists to formalism rests on a belief in the interdisciplinary nature of literary studies; more specifically, such theorists argue that a theory of narrative voice or point of view must rest on assumptions at once psychoanalytic, philosophical, and social.

The Laws of Genre

Despite Aristotle's privileging of plot over character in tragedy, the bourgeois novel has seen things differently. As Barthes observes, "in *War and Peace* Nikolay Rostov is from the start a good fellow, loyal, courageous and passionate, Prince Andrey a disillusioned individual of noble birth, etc. What happens illustrates them, it does not form them." [15] The bourgeois novel, then, is a vehicle for the ideology of individualism. It tacitly devalues history, even when history is ostensibly its theme, by positing the transcendental sanctity and stability of the subject, and it tacitly supports the many social arrangements, such as private ownership, that depend on individualism.

Such propositions, I think, are valid on a high level of generality and have heuristic value when applied to the individual text. If the bullfight story has offered a preferred version of the subject as disengaged from his original community, then one can see a similar and consistently oppositional ideology implied in the relation of this "story" to the laws of genre. That is, the text breaks the laws, formulated in the community it rejects, that require a story to be about "the" individual and to answer comfortably to the traditional reader's need to experience a continuous subjectivity on the page. The most obvious sign of this transgression is the splitting of the story into fragments dispersed among more conventional stories, creating a sort of dialogue between traditional form and outlaw form.[16] The reader, in the bullfight story, is forced to abandon the old laws of her community of interpretation in order to read properly a story that is discontinuous with those interpretive norms and with the bourgeois world of the masses of outsiders who are left behind in the latter sections.

Thus the bullfight story replicates in miniature the ideological conflict or dialogue represented in the volume as a whole, where the reader finds a repressed or broken *bildungsroman*. In this case, the various Nick Adams stories, arranged to show Nick's development from early childhood to his return from the war, obey the law of the novel of growth and therefore posit the human subject in a familiar way. History—or "our time"—is the stage upon which Nick moves and grows. The "novel's" focus on his subjectivity (and the bourgeois reader's confidence in the reality and importance of this focus) precludes too close an analysis of the social and historical causes of society's failure. On the other hand, the volume as a whole questions this focus and the ideology of the *bildungsroman* by including stories that cannot be read under the law of this genre and that decenter Nick and his subjectivity upon the stage of his time.

In *The Postmodern Condition* Jean-François Lyotard describes postmodern thought as a challenge to traditional "master narratives" or paradigms which have provided grounding or legitimation for knowledge. If one can think of the postmodern not precisely as a historical period but as a tendency that is potential or latent in any period, then I have been suggesting that *In Our Time* can be read on one level as a dialogue between the modern and the postmodern—between master narratives (both social and literary) and "little narratives" or *petits récits*.[17] Indeed, the individual interlude or "chapter" in Hemingway's volume might be an excellent if somewhat literal example of Lyotard's notion of the *petit récit* that posits itself independently of traditional master narratives or discursive forms we call "stories."

Literature, Ideology, and Belief

One of the major articles of faith of New Critical theory concerned the separation of literature and belief. Art, according to Immanuel Kant and, later, Matthew Arnold, was "disinterested," a notion that became central to the theoretical enterprise of the modernist period. A well-known formulation of this notion was I. A. Richards's "Doctrine in Poetry," chapter 7 of *Practical Criticism*.[18] But this separation of poetry from belief has been criticized by recent theorists, especially by Terry Eagleton and Tony Bennett, as being anything but disinterested—as being in fact heavily invested in a political conservativism that would not have literature, or literary criticism, rock the boat.[19]

To read in opposition to this conservative tradition requires bracketing the New Critical notion of the autonomous object, instead connecting the "single" story to the larger canon of the author and to the even broader range of social texts that constitute the author's environment. This is the strategy of criticisms such as feminism and Marxism, which are oriented (in opposition to Richards) in a clearly defined system of beliefs and interests.

The most fruitful attempts to correct this isolation of the literary text have engaged in analyses not so much of the author's consciously or intentionally stated beliefs as of his or her ideological subtext or "political unconscious." Often the author's unstated investments can be glimpsed precisely at those points where critic Wolfgang Iser's ruptures or "disturbances" appear to worry the reading we have been producing under the rule of bourgeois culture's dominant belief in "the literary" as a depoliticized, aesthetic, and subjective discourse. Scholes names the subtext that can be glimpsed in the bullfight story, calling it a "deeply reactionary level of thought" which is present even "in Hemingway's most progressive or socially conscious moments."[20]

Chapter 12, the passage celebrating Villalta's exquisitely artistic kill, is the disturbance in the bullfight story that alerts us to a subterranean ideological pressure. In the previous interlude, chapter 11, a narrator, less clearly young and American than the narrator of the first interlude, has identified himself as "I," and an "I" narrator also steps forward in chapter 13. But the continuity is disturbed by chapter 12, the Villalta description, which in fact is told in the second person ("you could see . . ."). Despite the effacement of the narrator, this passage has often been admired as one of Hemingway's own most artistic descriptions, and Scholes therefore reads the bullfight story as an allegory of the growth of the artist.[21] At the very moment when Villalta "became one with the bull," Hemingway the artist became one with his subject matter in an act of narrative self-effacement.

The notion that the artist should withhold himself in his work, should vanish like a god behind his creation, is another piece of modernist dogma— art should "show" dramatically, not merely "tell," as Wayne Booth describes the issue in *The Rhetoric of Fiction*.[22] But the literary code (practiced by both author and reader), which would foreground the aesthetic in the Villalta passage, functions as an alibi for the violence that is being celebrated. The supposedly objective showing (Booth's third chapter deals with the belief that authors should be objective) is also a telling, and the message demands a value-oriented, not merely an aesthetic, response. The same can be said of Hemingway's insistence, in *Death in the Afternoon* and elsewhere, on seeing bullfighting as tragedy. To inscribe killing within "the literary" is an attempt to remove it from moral scrutiny, since, as Richards says, "most readers, and nearly all good readers, are very little disturbed by even a direct opposition between their own beliefs and the beliefs of the poet."[23] Hemingway is selling violence, and "the literary," particularly under depoliticizing modernist assumptions such as those of Richards, is the ideal package in which to wrap this subtextual product.[24]

Scholes parallels the reader's cheering of Hemingway's performance in the Villalta passage with the crowd's cheering of Villalta himself. But he might have specified that this is a reader conditioned by the literary ideology described above to utter *O altitudos* in the presence of the aesthetic (Villalta's very name has altitude—*alta*—inscribed within it). How much less impressive is this statement from a nonfictional context such as the following from *Death in the Afternoon:* "A great killer must love to kill. . . . Killing cleanly and in a way which gives you aesthetic pleasure and pride has always been one of the greatest enjoyments of the human race."[25] Max Eastman was right, in the 7 June 1933 *New Republic,* to ridicule such nonsense under the title "Bull in the Afternoon." The emptiness of words like "great" and "cleanly," the pseudo-anthropology, and the unashamed coupling of the aesthetic and the hedonistic are clear to us here simply because our responses are not confused by a discourse that seeks to pass under the banner of the aesthetic.

Readers who have tried to find a positive significance in Hemingway's glorification of the bullring have viewed it as meaningful reconciliation of the violence of his time with a personal need for order and a code of conduct. Typical of such readings is that of David J. Leigh, S.J.:

> [T]he interchapters portray the narrow world of the bullring, where ritual preserves a minimum of purpose and achievement and a control of violence. This ring contrasts with

the lost world of the expatriate, where the smoke of dead ideals blinds all to any hope of achievement or self-realization.[26]

It is beyond the scope of a short paper to attempt to account for the ideological unconscious of much modernist literature and criticism. But it should give us pause to hear an author considered so central to our national tradition speaking on the eve of the Holocaust of the pleasures of killing. And it is only slightly less pleasant to find a Jesuit critic so equally charmed by "ritual" slaughter. Such criticism shows how traditional assumptions about the literary have concealed and disseminated the bull.

That the reactionary subtext in Hemingway should exist in opposition to other of his stated social attitudes is a problem only to readers who cling to Lacan's "scandalous lie"[27] about the centered, self-identical subject. Hemingway supported the Loyalist cause in the Spanish Civil War, opposed the Nazis in World War II, and later gained the attention of Joseph Mc-Carthy for supporting Fidel Castro. His politics were anything *but* reactionary. In other words, on the level of ideological and moral critique of the literary text we also discover discontinuities and oppositions consistent with our earlier observations concerning the dialogic and fragmented nature of the text and the subject. The unconscious text stands in opposition to the conscious text, the discourse of an Other.

Klaus Theweleit's *Male Fantasies* can be read as a gloss on this unconscious reactionary voice in Hemingway's text—this "other" self.[28] Hemingway is mentioned only once in this book, in the context of a discussion of "one of the most pervasive male fantasies in our society," which "concerns sexual relations with nurses," a fantasy Hemingway pretends is only "A Very Short Story" in *In Our Time*.[29] Theweleit, focusing on the years between World War I and the rise of Hitler, studies German popular literature and the journals and letters of men who became part of the Nazi military machine. He explores the projection upon history of a transpersonal, unconscious discourse, a fictional world view designed to ensure the survival of fascism. The fantasies of fascists, he claims, "share a strong family resemblance; following a set of paradigm [*sic*], they are in many cases almost identical."[30]

I do not mean to equate Hemingway's fictional world with the crude versions of fascist mythology Theweleit describes. But as the narrative voice of the bullfight story grows increasingly alienated from its original identity and community (mirroring Nick's "progress" in the total *bildungsroman* we assemble about him), the values implied in the subtext have disturbing affinities with fascist fantasies.[31]

These fantasies depicted a patriarchal, "masculine" organization of life. They are the production of what Deleuze and Guattari have called a desiring

machine, and what is desired are blood and death.[32] Politics, human relationships, sexuality, literary taste, and entertainment are all organized and
encoded by this desire. In addition to the nurse, Theweleit deals with such
figures as the mother, the whore, and the sister in ways that are suggestive
for the reader of Hemingway in view of many of Hemingway's private
experiences. Particularly important is Hemingway's hatred of his mother.[33]
Indeed, some of the fascists' journals reveal an interest in bullfighting, and
one Bogislaw von Selchow described a bullfight in which a *female* matador
is gored, much to his pleasure.[34]

Kenneth S. Lynn, with possibly a rather heavy hand, tries in his biography of Hemingway to offer sexual readings of Hemingway's bullfight scenes,
particularly the description of Maera's death in our story.[35] Certainly the
themes of frustrated sexuality in the stories surrounding and interpene-
trating the bullfight story of *In Our Time* make for interesting counterpoint—one would commence this larger, contrapuntal text with Mr. and
Mrs. Elliot's "trying" to have a baby, proceed to Nick's cool reaction to
Helen's pregnancy (two have "become one") in "Cross-Country Snow," and
end it with the womanless and self-sufficient Nick catching trout.[36] In between bulls, matadors, and spectators conduct their exchanges.

The bullfight story reads as a fantasized alternative to the more everyday world of the stories that surround it, a world in which men and women
at least try to procreate.[37] Discussing the binary relationship between the
everyday life of fascists and their fantasies, Theweleit says,

> They want to wade in blood; they want an intoxicant that will "cause both sight and
> hearing to fade away." They want a contact with the opposite sex—or perhaps simply
> access to sexuality itself—which cannot be *named*, a contact in which they can dissolve
> themselves while forcibly dissolving the other sex. They want to penetrate into its life, its
> warmth, its blood.[38]

This sounds remarkably like becoming one with the bull, and Theweleit's
section called "Sexual Murder: Killing for Pleasure" might be read alongside *Death in the Afternoon*.[39] Certainly there was nothing to contain these
male fantasies within specific national or geographic boundaries or to limit
them to a specific political organization, and they seem to have constituted
a large portion of the symbolic realm Hemingway entered in the process of
becoming a subject. They were an alien discourse to Hemingway and one
that, to his credit, did not override his consciously held political positions.
But in terms of Lacanean theory alien discourses are an aspect of what we
are. The "I," once again, is always a "we."

Hemingway's texts, in the Villalta description and elsewhere, wed killing (not always unconsciously) to aesthetics and creativity. Such a conjunc-

tion is characterized, almost as though Hemingway is the primary target, when Theweleit says of fascists:

> Human productions as a rule invest their objects with life. It is the living labor of the artisan that allows a table to be created from a tree, the worker's living labor that forges a tool out of raw metal; the mother's living labor that enables a newborn infant to become a person. The production of our men acts conversely. It divests social products, both people and things, of the life that has entered into them, especially in war. Their mode of production is the transformation of life into death. . . . [40]

Hemingway stated as a structural principle his belief that all stories, if followed to their logical conclusion, end in death. It is the narrative "labor" of "Mr. and Mrs. Elliot" to leave the couple childless and figuratively to castrate Mr. Elliot, just as the crowd cuts off the pigtail of the failed matador in the third section of the bullfight story. It is the narrative labor of this story to kill Maera, and "dead" is the story's last word. As a male fantasy, *A Farewell to Arms* is a narrative engine producing Catherine's death—and she, too, becomes aestheticised in the process, a "statue." This novel, like "A Very Short Story," takes revenge on the nurse who in reality left Hemingway.[41] *For Whom the Bell Tolls* produces the heroic death of the male fighter, and as the record makes clear, Hemingway's life was an extended production of his own death.

It might be argued that the preceding paragraph depicts Hemingway at his worst and is a highly selective characterization. But I have attempted here to speak only of a single voice among the diverse voices constituting Hemingway's texts. Yet the voice I have described is a strong one; it is the narrative voice that seems to emerge in a privileged way as the earlier, more innocent and domesticated voice recedes in the bullfight story. It does not enter into a dialogue with the earlier voice, and this reveals what Bakhtin calls a monologic tendency.

Bakhtin writes of the "polyphony" of a Dostoevsky novel in terms of the relative autonomy the characters seem to have—they seem to escape the control of the narrator and to live independently. The opposite of Dostoevsky's practice (Bakhtin takes Tolstoy as an example) is the monologic one that "finalizes" each character. To finalize characters, or people we know in our actual lives, is to withhold from them a certain level of respect and empathy, to treat them as objects or finished products incapable of change or free agency. Concerning this monologic, finalizing tendency Bakhtin writes, "This faith in the self-sufficiency of a single consciousness in all spheres of ideological life is not a theory created by some specific thinker; no, it is a profound structural characteristic of the creative ideological activity of modern times, determining all its external and internal forms."[42]

Hemingway would seem to be such a modernist, more like Tolstoy than Dostoevsky, since his characters are often entirely dominated by the will of the narrative.[43] Scholes's discussion of "A Very Short Story," noted above, offers an excellent example of how point of view functions as an instrument of male power, vilifying, if not literally killing, the woman in question. She is dismissed as frivolous and manipulative, and the story ends by violating the logic of point of view in order to claim that the major would never in the future marry her. Here, with a quite real vengeance, is the need to finalize and dominate a character. This urge to finalize is a literary practice that harmonizes with the sort of fantasies Theweleit documents, and Bakhtin himself suggests that finalization results from the failure to embrace fully the life process.

In Our Time, by virtue of its structure and its fragmentation, its continuities and discontinuities, may be Hemingway's most polyphonic text. But even here certain voices, like the indirectly quoted letters of the nurse in "A Very Short Story," are heard only so a dominant sensibility can ridicule or dismiss them. Other examples would be the way Mr. Elliot's subjectivity is presented only to be laughed off the stage, or more subtly the way the innocent narrator of the first bullfight interlude is abandoned. The bullfight story reveals in microcosm the movement away from the voice of the innocent and the outsider and toward an identity with a masculine elite that has separated itself from everyday values and dedicated itself to a theater of death.

Scholes, in both *Semiotics and Literature* and *Textual Power,* demonstrated how a brief text of problematical status can raise essential questions concerning fictional form and the creative labor of reading. With his observations as our base, we have seen how the bullfight story can further direct us toward a confrontation between traditional aesthetic and literary assumptions on the one hand and some of the significant departures of contemporary theory on the other. The contemporary reader's willingness to deprivilege, if not to ignore entirely, the formalist's desire for unity, together with her willingness to see a relationship between discontinuities in the text and discontinuities in the human subject, can lead to an understanding of the connection of both text and subject to the larger discourses or fantasies of the society surrounding them.

The results of this analysis have not seemed complimentary to the author. But speculations about the unconscious are not supposed to be flattering, and it is to Hemingway's credit that the subtext we have glimpsed here remained repressed in his consciously formulated politics. These speculations have theoretical value, however, because they question basic attitudes toward "the literary" with which so many of us have been indoctrinated and because they no longer conceal criticism's grounding in beliefs and interests. The danger is that such analyses may seem merely the work of disgruntled academics interested mainly in bashing (or goring) our literary lions. This danger is a small price to pay for a corrective to the stale notions that literature has no moral or political force, that literary texts do not have ideological subtexts, and that the bard is always to be idolized.

Notes

1. Clinton S. Burhans, Jr., "The Complex Unity of *In Our Time*," in *Critical Essays on Ernest Hemingway's* In Our Time, ed. Michael S. Reynolds (Boston: G. K. Hall, 1983) 91–93.

2. E. R. Hagemann, "'Only Let the Story End as Soon as Possible': Time-and-History in Ernest Hemingway's *In Our Time*," in Reynolds, 56, 59.

3. The best collection of articles on *In Our Time* is Michael S. Reynolds's 1983 anthology. In addition to Burhans and Hagemann, other writers collected in this volume who touch upon the question of the structural coherence of the interchapters are Robert M. Slabey, Jackson J. Benson, Linda W. Wagner, and David J. Leigh, S.J.

4. Robert Scholes, *Textual Power: Literary Theory and the Teaching of English* (New Haven: Yale UP, 1985) 62–73. Here Scholes is developing an observation made by Robert M. Slabey in his 1965 essay, "The Structure of *In Our Time*," reprinted in Reynolds, 76–87.

5. Wolfgang Iser, *The Implied Reader: Patterns of Communication in Prose Fiction from Bunyan to Beckett* (Baltimore: Johns Hopkins UP, 1974) 286.

6. Jacques Lacan, "Of Structure as an Inmixing of Otherness Prerequisite to Any Subject Whatever," in *The Structuralist Controversy*, ed. Richard Macksey and Eugenio Donato (Baltimore: Johns Hopkins UP, 1972) 186–95.

7. Emile Benveniste, *Problems in General Linguistics*, trans. Mary Elizabeth Meek (Coral Gables: U of Miami P, 1971) 223–30.

8. Michel Foucault, *The Order of Things* (New York: Vintage, 1973) 386–87.

9. "The Waste Land" is another modernist work in which point of view and the identity of the subject are problematical.

10. See Mikhail Bakhtin's analysis of "Discourse in the Novel," in *The Dialogic Imagination*, ed. Michael Holquist (Austin: U of Texas P, 1981) 259–422.

11. Lacan, 186–95.

12. John M. Meyer, "Myths of Socialization and Personality," in *Reconstructing Individualism: Autonomy, Individuality, and the Self in Western Thought*, ed. Thomas C. Heller, Morton Sosna, and David E. Wellbery (Stanford: Stanford UP, 1986) 212.

13. Roland Barthes, *Image, Music, Text*, trans. Stephen Heath (New York: Hill and Wang, 1977) 111, 142.

14. Lacan, 289–90.

15. Barthes, 104n.

16. Hemingway knew John Dos Passos in Paris in the 1920s, and Hemingway's interchapters, like Dos Passos's "newsreel" and "camera eye" fragments, show a desire to rewrite the generic code of realism by incorporating material from supposedly nonliterary genres such as journalism.

17. Jean-François Lyotard, *The Postmodern Condition: A Report on Knowledge*, trans. Geoff Bennington and Brian Massumi (Minneapolis: U of Minnesota P, 1984) 31–60.

18. I. A. Richards, *Practical Criticism: A Study of Literary Judgment* (New York: Harcourt, Brace, and World, 1929).

19. See Terry Eagleton's discussion of the interests that constituted literary knowledge during the nineteenth and early twentieth centuries in England in *Literary Theory: An Introduction* (Minneapolis: U of Minnesota P, 1983) 1–53. For Tony Bennett's discussion of the concept of "the literary" as a vehicle for the transmission of bourgeois interests, see especially chapters 5 through 9 of his *Formalism and Marxism* (London and New York: Methuen, 1979).

20. Scholes, 72.

21. This interpretation is supported by the fact that *Death in the Afternoon* (New York: Charles Scribner's Sons, 1932) often shifts topic abruptly from bullfighting to writing—see for instance pages 189 through 192.

22. Wayne Booth, *The Rhetoric of Fiction*, 1961 (Chicago: U of Chicago P, 1983) 3–20, 67–85.

23. Richards, 255.

24. I use the word "Ideal" to suggest how the concept of literature functions as an "idealization" in Marxist terms, that is, as an abstraction that represses the material and historical origins of textual production.

25. *Death in the Afternoon*, 232.

26. David J. Leigh, S.J., "*In Our Time:* The Interchapters as Structural Guide to a Psychological Pattern," in Reynolds, 132.

27. Lacan, 290.

28. I am grateful to Marcus Smith for alerting me to the importance of Theweleit's study.

29. Klaus Theweleit, *Male Fantasies* 1, trans. Stephen Conway (Minneapolis: U of Minneapolis P, 1987) 126.

30. Theweleit, 88.

31. The propositionally stated or rationalized beliefs and policies of fascists or Nazis are another matter and do not directly concern me here. Hemingway, of course, opposed such beliefs and policies.

32. *In Our Time* begins with "On the Quai at Smyrna," In this story the narrator is clearly haunted by images of dead animals and babies. In the next story, "Indian Camp," the young Nick confronts childbirth and death. The "work" of the volume as a whole, if one can apply something like Freud's notion of a dreamwork, is to arrive at a kind of symbolic accommodation with these originary, traumatic experiences. Horror is overcome by learning to love it. This movement is encoded in miniature in the bullfight interludes.

33. These relationships are dealt with at length in Kenneth S. Lynn's biography, *Hemingway* (New York: Simon and Schuster, 1987).

34. Theweleit, 63–64.

35. Lynn, 212–13. See also comments on sexual imagery in the bullfight pieces by Jackson J. Benson, "Patterns of Connection and Their Development in *In Our Time*," in Reynolds, 116–17.

36. To assemble a *bildungsroman* about Nick, in the same way that the bullfight interludes might be assembled into a short story, one must invent the repressed chapter that would tell us what happened to Helen, since she is nowhere in view in "Big Two-Hearted River." The "novel" has gotten rid of her, but how? The structural device of fragmenting the novel into separate (and separated) stories represses this question.

37. Jackson J. Benson (in Reynolds, 104) and Robert M. Slabey (in Reynolds, 83) briefly raise questions concerning the connections between the stories and the chapters.

38. Theweleit, 36.

39. Theweleit, 183ff.

40. Theweleit, 216.

41. See Scholes's feminist reading of this story in *Semiotics and Interpretation* (New Haven: Yale UP, 1981) 110–26.

42. Mikhail Bakhtin, *Problems of Dostoevsky's Poetics*, trans. Caryl Emerson (Minneapolis: U of Minnesota P, 1984) 82.

43. On the American scene, an opposition between Faulkner and Hemingway might reveal some of what Bakhtin seeks to clarify with his comparison of Dostoevsky and Tolstoy. Texts such as *Absalom, Absalom!*, *The Sound and the Fury*, and *As I Lay Dying*, each with its particular juxtapositions of various points of view, suggest Bakhtin's polyphony, whereas most of Hemingway's works are dominated by a single, monologic viewpoint or subjectivity.

8

From the Waste Land to the Garden with the Elliots

Paul Smith

*Written in the cruelest month of 1924, Hemingway's cruelest short story,
"Mr. and Mrs. Elliot," has long embarrassed many critics into silence, while
others, shuddering with distaste, have dismissed it as an incomprehensibly
aggressive assault on a comparatively inoffensive target—the very minor
expatriate poet, Chard Powers Smith. Here, for the first time, critic Paul
Smith provides compelling textual, biographical, and literary reasons to
believe that this story is far more complex and well worth a second look.
Smith argues persuasively that in "Mr. and Mrs. Elliot" Hemingway, as
was his wont, was attempting to combat the powerful literary influence of
T. S. Eliot with sexual and artistic insults, with a satirical punch below the
belt. Smith's essay views the story as a sophisticated satire not only of the
Chard Powers Smiths and the Tom Eliots, but of the social and literary
pretensions of well-heeled expatriates. It further underscores "Mr. and
Mrs. Elliot's" significance as Hemingway's earliest exploration of the tortuous relationship between an artist's sexual and creative impulses, and as an
almost uncanny prediction of the sexual triangle that would destroy the
author's first marriage and echo in the despairing pages of his posthumously
published novel,* The Garden of Eden.

"Mr. and Mrs. Elliot" has been both more *and* less neglected than it deserves to be. One might wish that those biographers who found in it yet
another instance of Hemingway's bad taste, callous contempt, and occasional stylistic infelicity had neglected the story altogether; one might also
wish for a larger company of critics who thought of it as, possibly, a short
story. Never a story to attract much critical notice, once the object of its

satire was revealed, there was little more to say except to regret its triviality.[1]

Now, of course, everyone knows that it was originally titled "Mr. and Mrs. Smith," that Hemingway had Chard Powers Smith in his sights, and that the two exchanged angry and characteristic letters in 1927, two years after the story's publication. Smith called Hemingway "a worm who attempted a cad's trick, [and] a contemptible shadow"; Hemingway, of course, threatened to knock him down.[2]

Most biographers have followed Carlos Baker in dismissing the satire as a "malicious gossip-story" ridiculing the Smiths' "alleged sexual ineptitudes."[3] We are not told who, other than Hemingway, made that allegation, or with what evidence if it was not common knowledge. But for Hemingway, Chard Powers Smith was an easy mark and natural enemy, several times over: he was independently wealthy; he had degrees from both Harvard and Yale; he lingered in Latin Quarter cafés, rented chateaux along the Loire, and wrote poetry in perfect classical meters with perfect Petrarchan emotions; and Yale published his first volume in 1925.

By the spring of 1924 Hemingway was writing at an astounding pace, nearly half his titles had been published and *re*published—six poems, six *in our time* chapters, and "My Old Man"—and he turned again to Edward O'Brien. He wrote that he had "quit newspaper work," was "about broke," and needed an agent to "peddle" the ten stories he had written. He enclosed three, one of which he was sure would not sell but which O'Brien could keep "as a souvenir." This story was titled "Mr. and Mrs. Smith."[4]

I suspect that Hemingway sent the story partly as an appreciative memento to the publisher who first accepted "My Old Man" and partly to pass on literary gossip—but not to be published, for soon after that he sent a typescript of the same story to Jane Heap for publication in the *Little Review*'s winter issue of 1924–25 with the name Smith crossed out and Elliot inserted.

Hemingway's motive for changing the name from Smith to Elliot might have arisen from his inordinate fear of a libel suit. Or perhaps, sometime in the late spring of 1924, his original satiric intent was deflected by the news that Mr. and Mrs. Smith's "alleged sexual ineptitudes" had been overcome, tragically, for Mrs. Smith died in childbirth in Naples on 11 March 1924, a month before Hemingway wrote his story and sent it to O'Brien as a souvenir. Perhaps, finally, submitting the story to the very literary *Little Review*, Hemingway decided to direct his satire against another poet, one with more fame than Chard Powers Smith: T. S. Eliot, who had been published in that journal since 1917 and was by Hemingway's lights even more deserving of contempt.

Why Eliot? Consider the ways in which Hubert Elliot's career in the story is similar to the poet Hemingway most envied and whose success he could not abide. Like Hubie—in the annals of history or gossip—T. S. Eliot came from Boston, was a graduate student at Harvard, wrote long poems, was a virgin, was enticed (in the polite phrase) by his wife on the dance floor, and by all biographers' accounts, suffered through a loveless marriage of "sexual ineptitude."[5]

Hemingway was always and in several ways one step behind Eliot. He arrived in Paris in December 1921 at about the time that Eliot returned from his six-week stay in a sanatorium above Vevey in Switzerland, retrieved his wife from another sanatorium near Paris, gave Ezra Pound some 1,000 lines of the draft of *The Waste Land,* and returned to London. In their month in Paris the Hemingways set up digs on the rue Cardinal Lemoine and then departed for two weeks of skiing at Chamby, above Montreux, only a few miles from the sanatorium Eliot had left.[6]

When Hemingway returned to Paris and belatedly presented his letter of introduction to Ezra Pound, the poet might well have shown him "The Waste Land" manuscripts he was editing, if only to impress this young, arriviste writer with his editorial authority. And Pound, as given to gossip as Hemingway, must have passed on the tales of the Eliots' troubled marriage of which, by several accounts, "everyone within miles of it was aware."[7] Vivien Eliot's marginal note on the typescript of the "Game of Chess" section of the poem—she wrote "Wonderful"—may be no more than innocent literary praise,[8] but rumor overcame that benign notion to whisper that, of course, she recognized herself as the harried and neurotic woman in those lines. So did Hemingway when he crossed out Smith's name, wrote first "Eliot," then "Elliott," then finally dropped the last *t*—leaving, as in all his occasional satires, a clue to identify his victim.

So one returns to the now-delightful exchange of letters between Chard Powers Smith and Hemingway in January 1927. Smith noted, with good reason, that the story "suggests my wife at no point" and delicately implied that neither he nor his wife was sterile. But he went on to charge that Hemingway still had to learn the difference between writing like a "reporter" from motives of "petty malice" and writing like a true artist. That must have stung Hemingway to respond with his typical barroom invitation to step outside, but buried in his response are a backhanded apology and explanation. Hemingway wrote that he recalled the contempt he had for Smith, but he admitted that it was a "very cheap emotion and one very bad for literary production."[9] Hemingway did not contradict Smith's assertion that the story had nothing to do with his wife—by 1927 he could not—but he could, lamely, imply he had a larger literary object in mind, namely (as it were) T.S. Eliot.

One of the more persuasive arguments for Eliot as the object of this satire is Hemingway's deep indebtedness to the older and more famous poet—a paradox in any other writer than Hemingway. "Mr. and Mrs. Elliot" is one of Hemingway's three early responses to either the manuscripts of Eliot's poem he saw in Paris in March 1922 or the published version Pound showed him in Rapallo in February 1923. The two other stories completed before this one reflect the poem: "Out of Season" of April 1923, with its setting by a turbid river by a dump heap and other testimony of sterility; and "Cat in the Rain" of March 1924, with its frenetic dialogue and the direct allusions to Sweeney and Mrs. Porter in its preliminary notes.[10]

Hubert and Cornelia Elliot of Hemingway's story are so like the deracinated figures of Eliot's poems that they would have been unnoticed along the shores of the Starnbergersee or chatting in the Hofgarten with those who "read, much of the night, and go south in the winter."[11] And, like the neurotic and sickly women and their indifferent companions in the poem, the Elliots' union is as barren and rootless as the landscape through which they aimlessly drift. These evident literary origins lift the story above the merely occasional: it is to Eliot's "Burial of the Dead" what "Cat in the Rain" is to Eliot's "Game of Chess."

There are inviting bits of biography that tempt us to return to the personal experiences behind the story. Nothing in the lives of the Smiths or the Eliots quite fully accounts for some of the story's details, and so we might add a third couple to this composite portrait: Mr. and Mrs. Hemingway. Like Hubert and Cornelia Elliot, the Hemingways sailed to Europe soon after their marriage (not so the Tom Eliots); for all Hemingway's claims of poverty, he was living well on Hadley's not insubstantial trust fund. Ernest, like Hubert, was 25 in 1924; and, although he was no virgin, he had married an older woman. And consider this passage on the Elliots' arrival in Paris, added to the 1925 version of the story: "Paris was quite disappointing and very rainy. . . . [E]ven though someone had pointed out Ezra Pound to them in a café and they had watched James Joyce eating in the Trianon and almost been introduced to Leo Stein . . . , they decided to go to Dijon."[12] The Hemingways arrived in a rain-swept Paris, may have seen but did not meet Pound and Joyce, and left three weeks later. Or consider this passage on the Parisian cafés: "So they all sat around the Café du Dome, avoiding the Rotonde across the street because it is always so full of foreigners, . . . and then the Elliots rented a chateau in Touraine."[13] One of Hemingway's earliest *Toronto Star* articles of 1922 similarly condemns the Rotonde as a "showplace for tourists in search of atmosphere."[14] While the Elliots fled to a chateau on the Loire, the Hemingways left for a chalet in Chamby.

If the story reflected this much of the three years before it was written, it was uncannily prophetic of the next three. It was in the Loire valley of Touraine in the spring of 1926 that Hadley, motoring with Pauline and Jinny Pfeiffer, first recognized her competition. By June, Ernest and Hadley and Pauline were at a hotel in Juan-les-Pins, where, in Carlos Baker's nice phrase, "there were three of everything."[15] Hemingway's story had ended:

> Elliot had taken to drinking white wine and lived apart in his own room. He wrote a great deal of poetry during the night and in the morning looked very exhausted. Mrs. Elliot and the girl friend now slept together in the big mediaeval bed. They had many a good cry together. In the evening they all sat at dinner together in the garden under a plane tree and the hot evening wind blew and Elliot drank white wine and Mrs. Elliot and the girl friend made conversation and they were all three quite happy.[16]

David Bourne in *The Garden of Eden* did his writing in the mornings, of course, for he was otherwise engaged at night, although the regimen of his threesome was as exhausting as Hubert's. The dinner in the garden, the white wine, the hot evening wind, and the bisexual arrangement sketched in the story all find interminable variations in that late, bruised, and windfallen novel. Perhaps even the conflict between Catherine Bourne's jealousy and Marita's admiration of David's writing is suggested in Cornelia and her girlfriend's typing: with the touch system, Mrs. Elliot "found that while it increased her speed it made more mistakes. The girl friend was now typing practically all of the manuscripts. She was very neat and efficient and seemed to enjoy it."[17]

With the longer view of Hemingway's career and the literary history of his times, "Mr. and Mrs. Elliot" deserves another reading. I would argue that it is one of his best and most sophisticated satires, better than anything in *The Torrents of Spring*, as good as the satiric passages in *The Sun Also Rises*, and a satire that transcends its seminal gossip to reveal the social and literary pretensions among the elite expatriates who knew enough to frequent the Café du Dome rather than the Rotonde, but not much more.

Certainly the story should be read again for its importance in the Hemingway canon: it is his first portrait, if not a self-portrait, of the artist; it begins his long and sometimes querulous consideration of the relationship between the artist's sexual and creative impulses; and it should take its place, first with the "marriage tales" of the 1920s and then with the last, so far, of his posthumously published novels.

Finally, the story confirms the depth of Hemingway's indebtedness to T. S. Eliot. Sometime in late 1927 Hemingway listed on the back of an envelope his literary borrowings. The first was to "everybody" for his early imitations, and the second was to Elliot (note the spelling) with the phrase "watered the waste land and made it bloom like a rose."[18]

I am certain Hemingway recognized some similarity between the Chard Powers Smiths, the Eliots, and the figures in "The Waste Land." At least one other in that cast of the living and the literary did—Mrs. Smith. In a holograph dedication to the volume of poems Chard Powers Smith wrote as a memorial to his dead wife, he described her death: "Olive Cary Macdonald died in childbirth in Naples on March 11, 1924. 'Good-night, ladies, good-night, good-night,' she whispered."[19] To which one can only reply: "Goodnight Tom. Goonight Chard. Goonight Ernest. Ta ta. Goodnight, sweet ladies, good night, good night."

Notes

I am indebted to Professor Bruce Stark (University of Wisconsin/Milwaukee) and to Stanley I. Mallach and Allan S. Kovan of that university's library for a photocopy of the Hemingway typescript of "Mr. and Mrs. Elliot" published in the *Little Review* 10 (Autumn-Winter 1924–25): 9–12. I am also indebted to Professor Michael S. Reynolds (North Carolina State University) for sharing his discovery of the holograph "Dedication to OCM" at the Bancroft Library, University of California/Berkeley, intended for Chard Powers Smith's *Along the Wind.*

1. Carlos Baker and Charles A. Fenton are typical of those who dismiss the story; Joseph DeFalco is the only critic who has analyzed it at some length. See Baker, *Ernest Hemingway: A Life Story* (New York: Charles Scribner's Sons, 1969); Fenton, *The Apprenticeship of Ernest Hemingway* (New York: Farrar, Straus, Young, 1954); and DeFalco, *The Hero in Hemingway's Short Stories* (Pittsburgh: U of Pittsburgh P, 1963).

2. Chard Powers Smith to Ernest Hemingway, 2 January 1927, John F. Kennedy Library and Hemingway to Smith, ca. 21 January 1927, in *Ernest Hemingway: Selected Letters, 1917–1961,* ed. Carlos Baker (New York: Charles Scribner's Sons, 1981) 242.

3. Baker, *Life,* 133.

4. Hemingway to Edward O'Brien, 2 May 1924, *Letters,* 117.

5. See Eliot's biographers—Peter Ackroyd, *T. S. Eliot* (London: Hamish Hamilton, 1984); Caroline Behr, *T. S. Eliot: A Chronology of His Life and Works* (New York: St. Martin's P, 1983); Lyndall Gordon, *Eliot's Early Years* (Oxford: Oxford UP, 1977); and T. S. Matthews, *Great Tom: Notes towards the Definition of T. S. Eliot* (New York: Harper, 1974).

6. Baker, *Life,* 84–85.

7. Matthews, 45.

8. Ackroyd, 115.

9. Hemingway to Smith, 21 January 1927, *Letters,* 242.

10. Items 670–74, John F. Kennedy Library.

11. T. S. Eliot, "The Waste Land," in *The Waste Land and Other Poems* (New York: Harcourt, 1934) 29.

12. Hemingway, "Mr. and Mrs. Elliot," *In Our Time* (New York: Boni & Liveright, 1925) 112.

13. Hemingway, "Mr. and Mrs. Elliot," in *The Short Stories of Ernest Hemingway* (New York: Charles Scribner's Sons, 1938) 163.

14. Hemingway, "American Bohemians in Paris," in *Dateline: Toronto, Hemingway's Complete* Toronto Star *Dispatches, 1920–1924,* ed. William White (New York: Charles Scribner's Sons, 1985) 114.

15. Baker, *Life,* 168, 171.

16. Hemingway, "Mr. and Mrs. Elliot," *In Our Time,* 115.

17. Hemingway, "Mr. and Mrs. Elliot," *Short Stories,* 164.

18. Item 489, John F. Kennedy Library.

19. Chard Powers Smith, holograph "Dedication to OCM," Bancroft Library, U California/Berkeley. Intended for *Along the Wind* (New Haven: Yale UP, 1925).

9

Hemingway's "On Writing":
A Portrait of the Artist as Nick Adams

Lawrence Broer

A fragment omitted from Hemingway's summer 1924 masterpiece, "Big Two-Hearted River," "On Writing" remained unpublished until 1972, when Philip Young included it in the posthumous anthology The Nick Adams Stories. *"On Writing" contains Nick's reflections about the literary life as he fishes for trout, reflections undisguisedly Hemingway's own as Nick muses about what he has learned from James Joyce, Ezra Pound, Gertrude Stein, Theodore Dreiser, Sherwood Anderson, Ring Lardner, Donald Stewart, Nathan Asch, e.e. cummings, Archibald MacLeish, bullfighting, and Cézanne landscapes. Critics have probably neglected the "story" for the same reason that Hemingway wisely omitted it from "Big Two-Hearted River"—"On Writing" commits the identical sin of which it accuses James Joyce: "That was the weakness of Joyce. Daedalus in* Ulysses *was Joyce himself, so he was terrible. Joyce was so damned romantic and intellectual about him." Yet in Lawrence Broer's opinion, "the weakness of Joyce" is the strength of "On Writing." Because Hemingway uses Nick in "On Writing" as Joyce used Daedalus in* Portrait of the Artist as a Young Man, *the "story" becomes an illumination of the generic artist's formative process and an intriguing comment not only on "Big Two-Hearted River" but on other Nick Adams stories as well.*

Critics have praised Hemingway's "objectivity" as if the author's precise presentation of concrete detail were his major accomplishment. In landmark discussions of Hemingway's craft, Mark Schorer cites "insistence on the objective and unreflective, on the directness and the brevity of syntactical constructions"[1] as the style that made Hemingway famous, and E. M. Halliday argues that the clarity and sharpness of Hemingway's objective projection of reality are two of Hemingway's most "celebrated virtues."[2] Unlike Joyce, Halliday says, Hemingway leaves no confusion as to where the subjective (the labyrinth of the hero's mind) ceases, and the objective (the material world) begins.[3] Harry Levin notes that in Hemingway's quest for "immediacy," the writing seems so intent upon the "actual" that his readers become "beholders."[4] Finally, John Graham observes that "the testimony of the participant's senses can be accepted as objective, if limited, fact."[5] Graham recognizes that Hemingway's typical narrator is no mere receiving instrument, but reflects that the relationship between subject and object may be so direct and simple that no challenge is offered to the reader demanding extended mental activity, subtle or otherwise.[6]

Few writers have been as successful as Hemingway at projecting felt experience—what *feels* or *seems* actual—with such vitality and immediacy. The view of Hemingway as a literalist or objectivist was of course encouraged by Hemingway's axiom that a writer should only write about what he has personally experienced, by correspondences between Hemingway and his protagonists, and by the author's frequent use of aesthetic absolutes to describe his artistic goals, his quest for the "true," the "pure," and the "real." In a famous passage in *Green Hills of Africa* (1935), he said that "A writer's problem does not change. . . . It is always how to write truly and having found what is true, to project it in such a way that it becomes part of the experience of the person who reads it."[7] Oft quoted is Hemingway's declaration in *Death in the Afternoon* (1932) to write—"knowing *truly* what you really felt, rather than what you were supposed to feel," and to put down "what *really* happened in action . . . the *real* thing, the sequence of motion and fact which made the emotion. . . ."[8] In a letter to his father, Hemingway declared that he could achieve a third or even a fourth dimension in prose—"the feeling of actual life"—so that "when you have read something by me you actually experience the thing."[9] Hemingway's forte was to evoke poignantly the good things life offers—the earth's sensual rhythms and tactile delights—but praise of verisimilitude in Hemingway's work has too often steered critical interest to the character of Hemingway rather than to the nature and quality of his art. The view of Hemingway's fiction as therapeutic process—Cowley's or Young's readings of the work as exorcism or ritualistic expiation[10]—suggests even a kind of creative helplessness in which the author was not in control of his art. Hemingway, Cowley said, is a novelist who wrote not as he should or would but as he must, subject to personal demons.[11] Or the author comes across as a kind of master recorder—a writer capable of the most lucid modern prose—but somehow more artistically simple-minded and straightforward than his more praised contemporaries, Joyce and Faulkner.

In *The Garden of Eden* (1986) and the posthumous Nick Adams story called "On Writing,"[12] Hemingway shows that his use of personal experience, his approach to "truth," was far from simple or direct. Rather his relationship to his material was intricate, complex, and profoundly subjective.[13] "Above all else," the aspiring writer declares in "On Writing," "you had to do it from inside yourself" (239). "Nick in the stories was never himself," he explains, rather you had to "create your own people" (238), to reconstitute reality in the crucible of imagination.

Hemingway had said it before—prose was architecture, not interior decoration.[14] In *A Moveable Feast*, he wrote, "I was learning something from the painting of Cézanne that made writing simple true sentences far from enough to make the stories have the dimensions that I was trying to put in them. . . ."[15] The "real thing," that which produced beauty and great emotion, was not the simple reproduction of people and events, the "objective data of experience,"[16] but that which the artist makes in rearranging conventional ways of seeing the world. This is exactly what David Bourne does in *The Garden of Eden*. The novel's numerous references to "invention" and to things "made up" indicate Hemingway's interest in the postmodern theme of subjective reality—reality as artifice—which he employs here in an ambitious and ingenious way. Through David's preoccupation with "imperfect memory,"[17] and through the interweaving of the fictions David writes with the one he is in, Hemingway portrays fiction and reality as indistinguishable—suggesting that it is not literal truth that matters, which is always shifting and elusive, but the symbolic or personal truths that we ourselves create through "imperfect remembering" and subjective coloration. David Bourne's creations are humanistic and vital; Catherine's are perverse and self-destructive. With the blocking of life-directed, creative energies, Catherine's tormented mind turns to dangerous, exotic forms of invention which intensify to disaster by the story's close.

As with David Bourne, writing is the chief passion in life for the protagonist of "On Writing." When discussed at all, "On Writing" is viewed as a fragment of or alternative ending to "Big Two-Hearted River."[18] As we shall see, the similarity of setting and character does make for informative intertextual study. Nick in "On Writing" is still exorcising some nameless anxiety typical of the shell-shocked hero of "Big Two-Hearted River"—anxiety related to the mutilations of war, the end of human relationships, the death of love. Nick remembers experiences we know from "The End of Something," "The Three Day Blow," "Cross-Country Snow," "My Old Man," "Indian Camp," and "Big Two-Hearted River." But "On Writing" is no mere appendage or missing portion of the iceberg of the more famous story. Like *The Garden of Eden,* "On Writing" is intriguing metafiction that comments not only upon other Nick Adams stories but upon the entire corpus of Hemingway's fiction. Its exuberant tone and fluid imagery project a far more hopeful and healthy character, one aware of the power of art to shape human destiny and less afraid of complexity.

Hemingway uses Nick in "On Writing" precisely as Joyce uses Stephen Daedalus in *Portrait of the Artist as a Young Man*—to illuminate the formative process of the generic artist while using art to exorcise personal demons and to reshape a world of failed traditional values. Like Stephen, Nick exults in creativity as his greatest pleasure and raison d'être. Nick "felt almost holy about it" (239). But Nick chides Joyce for working too close to life, for using Stephen Daedalus as a too-literal representation of himself in *Ulysses.* Nick's joy of invention comes from personal discipline and from learning to transform discontent into creative energy. He always worked best, Nick reflects, when Helen was unwell: "Just that much discontent and friction" (238). But most of all his pleasure comes from learning to reconstruct rather than copy reality, which makes writing "more fun than anything" (238). As with Cézanne, Nick's major artistic inspiration, his fidelity is not to external experience but to the reality inside himself. He remembers that at one point, his "whole inner life had been bullfights" (236). Writing about "anything actual" was in fact a mistake. "The *only* writing that was any good was what you made up, what you imagined. That *made* everything come true" (237). Everything he had done well "he'd made up," like "My Old Man": "he'd never seen a jockey killed and the next week Georges Parfrement was killed at that very jump and that was the way it looked. . . . None of it had ever happened" (237). Nick says his family could not understand that. They assumed it was all personal experience. He had, for instance, "never seen an Indian woman having a baby. *That* was what made it good" (238). Later he reflects, "If it sounded good they took your word for it" (240).

We would today call the subject of this story postmodern—exploring the connections between audience and art, and the interrelatedness of life and art as fictional constructs. As with Stephen Daedalus and David Bourne, Nick's salvation lies in learning to approach life as an open-ended text in which he can write his own life story. Far from being an orthodox tale about the problems of Nick's war trauma and postwar emotional readjustment, "On Writing" transforms itself into a provocative story about ways of perceiving reality, about the impossibility of determining truth in absolute terms, about the way perception arises from the relative roles we play, and about the way the nature of the perceiver determines what is perceived. It is the text's nonclosure, its plurality of meaning, its presentation of character through multiple perspectives, and its rejuvenated system of language (the use of new "signifieds" for old "signifiers") that hold center stage.[19]

Nick consciously disputes surface objectivity, blurring the distinction between art and the actual by describing himself walking across the stream in a Cézanne painting. When Nick writes that he steps into water that was "cold and actual" (240), it is simultaneously Cézanne's conception as well as the real stream that Nick wades. As with David Bourne, the narrator lives half in the world of invention and imperfect memory and half in the present. Fantasy and reality merge as Nick reconstructs bullfights, fishing trips, and complex relationships with old friends: "sometimes he had it that way in dreams" (236).

Central to Nick's fluid epistemology is that nothing stands still. Events are recounted as a kaleidoscopic blur of shifting, elusive emotional associations, "storms on the lake . . . climbing up, sliding down, the wave following behind . . . the mail and the Chicago paper under a tarpaulin . . . the wind in the hemlocks . . ." (236). Truth is always situational, determined by mood, a weather change, for instance, variables of time or place, others' perceptions, or entrenched prejudice. Subjects such as fishing or bullfighting, love or poetry were tragic or comical, fake or real, because people "thought" they were so; people treated you this way or that because you were Spanish or French, English or American (234). Nick's imperfect remembering consists of surmise, hearsay, images from movies, phrases from newspapers, so that he can only "guess" why he has lost certain girls, why he first liked bullfights, or who the great writers are. Your values come from "this fake ideal planted in you" and "you lived your life to it" (235). Struggling to understand his love of bullfighting, he reflects, "That must have been Maera" (237). What Nick remembers about his "horror" of people getting married "*probably* [my italics] resulted from his association with older . . . non-marrying people" (235). He knows that whether fishing was more important than marrying was something "he had built . . . up" (234). Evaluating writers, he muses that "Young Asch had something but *you couldn't tell*" [my italics] (239). So did Ring Lardner—"maybe" (239). Ironically, only the greatest impressionist of them all, Gertrude Stein, would know if he, Nick, ever got things right (239).

Nick dislocates fixed perceptions by introducing a simultaneity of conflicting points of view in the manner of a Picasso collage, what Patricia Waugh calls an "interpretation of frames."[20] As those impenetrable, problematical currents and shadows and blinding glare pile up on Nick to complicate his musing about the "truths" of fishing, hunting, bullfighting, art, and love, he, along with the reader, must sort out contradictory explanations of "the way it was" from multiple perspectives provided by Helen, Bill, Bill's dentist, Kate, Odgar, and others whose realities are as personal and ambiguous as his own. Helen is remembered a certain way because Nick's friends did not like her, which also distorts her feelings about them

(235). Nick, Don, Chink differ on bullfighting because they view it with varying degrees of *afición* (237). Perceptions of reality, of value, are as self-reflexive as the river's "mirror" that symbolizes the swirling currents and shadowy depths of Nick's own mind (233).

Nick's awareness of reality as an open, dynamic text informs his efforts to construct a more durable, authentic self. His playful use of language foregrounds his narrative as artifice, connecting linguistic systems to the formation of the "actual" or "real." "Once Bill meant Bill Smith," he muses. "Now it means Bill Bird. Bill Bird lives in Paris now" (234). Nick knows that sentimental language and the duplicitous moral abstractions of movies or romantic novels make the world "unreal" (233, 237) and that short of avoiding language altogether, he must challenge the traditional signification of words that have turned into clichés by inventing new language conventions. Nick resists the outworn language and traditional wisdom of "all the books" (233) and seeks more inventive or "true" systems of significa-tion that will overturn the "fake" language, fake ideals, of his cultural inheri-tance.

The aesthetic perspective of "On Writing" shows that Hemingway's quest for "the real thing" was a matter of simulation rather than recalling and simply reproducing what he had seen or felt. Such a view obligates us to examine Hemingway's characters as complex, independent creations rather than simple projections of Hemingway. It challenges the view of the code hero as a static or inflexible individual closed to new ideas. Finally the story's postmodern formulations remind us that Hemingway is a writer for all times whose resources of imagination and invention are too seldom em-phasized. It illustrates the problematical richness of fiction whose meanings vary and which possesses multiple dimensions—physical, psychological, lit-erary, social, and metaphysical. In *Critical Practice*, Catherine Belsey ex-plains why a story such as "On Writing" excites our interpretive imagination and why its reader must be an active participant in the creation of meaning rather than a "beholder" of direct or simple truths: "Composed of contradic-tions, the text is no longer restricted to a simple, harmonious and authorita-tive reading. Instead it becomes plural, open to rereading, no longer an object for passive consumption but an object of work by the reader to produce meaning."[21]

We can only guess what it is that Nick holds "in his head" at the end of his narrative (241), as Nick can only guess what has happened to the dazed rabbit he helps on the trail. He no doubt identifies with its hurt as he picks the animal up, pulls ticks from its head, and places it under a sweet fern bush beside the trail. Just moments before, Nick had freed trout from his sack back into the stream, rationalizing that they were too big to eat. These life-affirming actions conclude a portrait of a young artist who was gentle, compassionate, and vulnerable, and for whom self-discipline and artistic ingenuity made life worthwhile.

In their treatments of "Big Two-Hearted River," to which "On Writing" was originally appended, Philip Young and Sheridan Baker appear impressed more with the usual correspondences between Nick and Hemingway than with the aesthetic implications of "On Writing" for the larger story. Young stresses the interchangeableness of author and protagonist; for example "the river narrowed" may be a direct reference to the river at Fossalta.[22] Baker highlights events Hemingway recorded directly rather than those he made up. What Hemingway counts as fiction, Baker says, contains a "high saturation of actuality."[23]

To foreground the story's verisimilitude rather than its artifice again compromises the author's remarkable inventive skill and obscures the story's epistemology. Like the streams Nick makes up in "Now I Lay Me" ("Some nights I made up streams . . . it was like being awake and dreaming"), it is the symbolic stream Nick fishes, his psychic experience, that matters in this tale. Baker himself notes Hemingway's breach with journalistic accuracy. The river is not the Two-Hearted River, it is the Fox. Its color comes from swampy vegetation, not, as Hemingway seemingly reports, from pebbles on the bottom. Projecting figurative rather than literal meanings, Hemingway changes the time of the burning of the town of Seney, increases its devastation, and defies fact by blackening his grasshoppers. He puts the flat site of Seney on a hillside to make Nick's climb an allegorical one and to foreground impressionistic effects.[24]

The therapeutic aspect of Nick's fishing trip has been much discussed.[25] Just as the trout hold themselves "steady in the current,"[26] Nick seeks to distance himself from the painful memories of war and to calm his nerves by occupying himself with the simple, elemental challenge of making a good camp. Nick can manage tasks that are direct and physical, but allowing his mind to work will invite feelings of vulnerability and helplessness associated with the war. The only memory Nick allows himself ("his mind was starting to work" [218]) is of a friendship with Hopkins, the loss of which troubles Nick. The physical therapy is effective; he welcomes the earth against his back, the smell of canvas and sweet fern, the taste of hot beans and coffee; the ailing Fisher King is on the mend, his "now living rod" (224) resurrected amid the primitive rhythms of wood and stream. Nick feels stable as long as he avoids philosophical abstractions or moral complexity, those parabolic shadows and swampy tangles that prevent him from fishing the stream's darker, faster water until a later time. Suggesting psychic exploration for which Nick is not yet prepared, such fishing would be "a tragic adventure" (231), facing hidden depths and unpredictable currents where the water suddenly piled up on you (229), and vision was obscured by "the half light" (231) and overhanging trees.

Ironically, Nick feels he has left such thinking behind, with the concomitant need to write (210), whereas it is only when he fords the deeper stream, the stream of consciousness as well as the stream of life itself, bringing repressed experience to consciousness, that he will complete his return to health. Herein lies the essential difference between the wounded exsoldier in "Big Two-Hearted River," who can let out his mental line only so far before the strain becomes unbearable and he becomes sick and shaky (226), and the aspiring writer in "On Writing," who has acquired the courage to confront traumatic past experience and the necessary knowledge of self and craft to transmute such experience into art and thus create a more stable and durable identity. In short, the Nick of "Big Two-Hearted River" is not sufficiently ready to practice what Nick in "On Writing" has learned from Cézanne—that people and events restructured in the imagination will produce greater satisfaction than anything he has ever known. Conversely, as Philip Young observes, "On Writing" recalls the "very moment when the mature career began." Nick is "off to start the story that Hemingway writes in 'Big Two-Hearted River.'"[27]

In "Big Two-Hearted River," then, Hemingway has superbly mastered the artistic and epistemological intricacies with which his protagonist must come to grips. While Nick resists the exertions of mind, Hemingway's mind and artistic conscience operate brilliantly, exemplified by the creation of an imperfect and morally uncertain, parabolic world whose meanings defy closure and in which truth is personal and self-created. Nick's best efforts to steady or fix or simplify life are contradicted by a world of flux, perpetual motion, and moral uncertainty. Nick's vision during his climb through the fire-burned countryside is blurred by aching muscles, by the dark, fragmentary pine trees (211) which he "could hardly see" in the heat-light ("If he looked too steadily they were gone. But if he only half-looked they were there . . ." [211]), by the unsettled dust, frequent rises and descents (212), rising mist (216), and dark vegetation (229). Later, his efforts to hold himself steady in the stream are met by uncooperative currents, varying shallows and deep pools, and tortuous bends. The elusive trout change "their positions by quick angles" (209); the glassy convex surface of the pool distorts their shapes, and the larger trout disappear completely in the "varying mist of gravel and sand raised . . . by the current" (209). It is only "the shadow of the Kingfisher" that he perceives moving up the stream to become lost in the sun and swift current.

Nick's epistemological dilemma is further complicated by contradictions in his own soul—the tendency to gentleness and compassion versus the impulse to cruelty. The same grasshoppers with which he empathizes he later uses for bait, crushing or slamming them with his hat (222), "threading the hook under his chin, down through his thorax and into the last segments of his abdomen." Nick's schizophrenic sensibility, half primitive, half civilized, allows him to feel happy about the trout he releases into the stream, whose pain Nick has caused.

It is both Nick's inability to know reality for sure, as he can only "wonder" about the fire-scarred town of Seney, the sooty grasshoppers that whirl up in front of him, or the long-range implications of his own psychic wound, and his willful flight from such realities that Nick must confront to progress beyond the emotional holding pattern of "Big Two-Hearted River." The inner equilibrium Nick seeks awaits not in distancing himself from the emotional baggage he has left home from his trip, baggage the reader will bring to the reading, the conjunctive experience alongside the reader's own intrapersonal river, but by eliciting the moral courage and imaginative presence of the maturing artist in "On Writing."

Notes

1. Mark Schorer, "The Background of a Style," *Ernest Hemingway: Critiques of Four Major Novels*, ed. Carlos Baker (New York: Charles Scribner's Sons, 1962) 88.

2. E. M. Halliday, "Hemingway's Narrative Perspective," in *Critiques of Four Major Novels*, 175.

3. Halliday, 177.

4. Harry Levin, "The Style of Hemingway," in *Hemingway and His Critics*, ed. Carlos Baker (New York: Hill & Wang, 1961) 111, 113.

5. John Graham, "Ernest Hemingway: The Meaning of Style," in *Critiques of Four Major Novels*, 184.

6. Graham's observation that the subject is "aware of his act of perception" is a major tenet of postmodern fiction (184).

7. Ernest Hemingway, *Green Hills of Africa* (New York: Charles Scribner's Sons, 1935) 37.

8. Ernest Hemingway, *Death in the Afternoon* (New York: Charles Scribner's Sons, 1932) 2.

9. Cited in *Ernest Hemingway: On Writing*, ed. Larry Phillips (New York: Charles Scribner's Sons, 1984) 153.

10. See Malcolm Cowley, "Nightmare and Ritual in Hemingway," in *Hemingway: A Collection of Critical Essays*, ed. Robert P. Weeks (Englewood Cliffs: Prentice Hall, 1962) 40–52, and Philip Young, *Ernest Hemingway*, Pamphlets on American Writers 1 (Minneapolis: U of Minnesota P, 1959).

11. Cowley, 51. Studies as recent as those by Jeffrey Meyers and Kenneth Lynn stress the writing as the product more of private hurts than of artistic ingenuity.

12. Ernest Hemingway, "On Writing," in *The Nick Adams Stories,* ed. Philip Young (New York: Charles Scribner's Sons, 1972) 233–41. All further references to "On Writing" are to this edition.

13. James Nagel points out that while little understood by modern scholars, Hemingway's mode was basically impressionistic as early as 1920. Impressionism was a movement Hemingway could hardly have avoided. Nagel discusses the "epistemological distortions" that keep Nick's perceptions in a constant state of flux. The alleged objective narrator must continuously struggle with problems of truth and illusion, and finally the reader must rely on his *own* perception and sensitivity to reveal the psychic drama. See "Literary Impressionism and *In Our Time,*" *The Hemingway Review* (Spring 1987): 17–26. For other commentary on epistemological complexity in Hemingway's work, see Emily Stipes Watts, *Ernest Hemingway and the Arts* (Urbana: U of Illinois P, 1971); Richard Peterson, *Hemingway: Direct and Oblique* (Paris: Norton, 1969); Raymond Nelson, *Hemingway: Expressionist Artist* (Ames: Iowa State UP, 1979); Sheldon Norman Grebstein, *Hemingway's Craft* (Carbondale: Southern Illinois UP, 1973).

14. *Death in the Afternoon,* 191.

15. Ernest Hemingway, *A Moveable Feast* (New York: Charles Scribner's Sons, 1964) 13.

16. Mario Praz, "Hemingway in Italy," in *Hemingway and His Critics,* 118.

17. Ernest Hemingway, *The Garden of Eden* (New York: Charles Scribner's Sons, 1986) 174, 211. As early as *Death in the Afternoon,* Hemingway remarks that the only reality is what one remembers, and "Memory, of course, is never true" (100).

18. See Joseph M. Flora, *Hemingway's Nick Adams Stories* (Baton Rouge: Louisiana State UP, 1982).

19. I am indebted to Constance Pedoto for her insights into Hemingway's postmodern tendencies. See her dissertation, *"Il Gioco del Nulla:* Ernest Hemingway and Italo Calvino's Construction of Nothingness" (U of South Florida, 1988).

20. Patricia Waugh, *Metafiction: The Theory and Practice of Self-Conscious Fiction* (London and New York: Methuen, 1980) 8.

21. Catherine Belsey, *Critical Practice* (London and New York: Methuen, 1980) 104.

22. Philip Young, "Big World Out There: The Nick Adams Stories," in *The Short Stories of Ernest Hemingway: Critical Essays,* ed. Jackson J. Benson (Durham: Duke UP, 1975) 39.

23. Sheridan Baker, "Hemingway's Two-Hearted River," in Benson, 158.

24. Baker, 151, 157.

25. See the aforementioned essays by Cowley, Young, and Baker.

26. *The Short Stories of Ernest Hemingway* (New York: Charles Scribner's Sons, 1966) 209. All further references to "Big Two-Hearted River" are to this edition.

27. Young, "Big World Out There," 42.

The Writer on Vocation: Hemingway's "Banal Story"

George Monteiro

With George Monteiro's consideration of "Banal Story," we move out of In Our Time *and into the contents of Hemingway's second major collection of short fiction*—Men Without Women. *Written during the winter of 1925, "Banal Story" has been neglected because it depends on readers' understanding numerous allusions to* The Forum—*an American monthly magazine well known in the 1920s but now long forgotten. Monteiro makes this short story accessible by sharing his researches into back numbers of* The Forum, *describing the actual targets of Hemingway's satire in "Banal Story." This source study reveals a complex work that not only assaults the banality of a particular magazine's literary aims, but also the smug complacency of any author who, immured in his study, presumes to write about an unexperienced life beyond the walls. According to Monteiro, this satire, in its turn, is parodied by "Banal Story's" graphic vignette of Maera's death from pneumonia and the matador's reduction by the popular press to a colored picture that can be rolled up and put in a pocket. Although he expresses reservations about the quality of the "smart alecky" and dated narrative told in the first part of "Banal Story," Monteiro's analysis emphasizes that this seldom-discussed short story is, like "On Writing" before it, an early experiment in art that self-consciously reflects upon its own artifice.*

During the winter of 1925, which he spent in Schruns in the Austrian Vorarlberg with his first wife Hadley and his young son Bumby, Hemingway wrote "Banal Story." He confirmed as much in a letter to his editor Maxwell Perkins in 1938 when they were deep in the problems surrounding the contents and their arrangement in the book that would soon appear as *The*

Fifth Column and the First Forty-nine Stories.[1] Topical references in the story date the writing of at least the first draft of "Banal Story" as no earlier than late January of 1925.[2] Whether or not Hemingway knew it at the start, this experimental narrative was destined for publication in some small magazine. No large-circulation journal of the day would have tolerated the seemingly cavalier shift both in thematic viewpoint and in narrative point of view, with no attempt whatsoever at providing the reader with a transition, that Hemingway effects in "Banal Story." As it turned out, Hemingway's story appeared in the Spring/Summer 1926 issue of the *Little Review*. The next year Hemingway included it in *Men Without Women* (1927), his second collection of short stories and one in which, as he described it, in all the stories, "almost, the softening feminine influence through training, discipline, death or other causes," was "absent."[3]

"Banal Story" melds two contrasting parts, unequal in length, linked by the voice of an implied narrator. The first part, which runs three times as long as the second part, focuses on a writer (much like Hemingway in his middle twenties) and his reactions to what he is reading at the moment, first, one infers, in an unidentified newspaper, and then, at greater length, in a promotional flier for the well-established American monthly magazine, *The Forum*.[4] Eating an orange and moving around in his cold room—from his chair at his writing table to a seat on the electric stove that seems to give off little or no heat—this writer, who (again like Hemingway) is probably an American living at the moment away from his home in Paris, concludes that "Here, at last, was life."[5] He reads about newsworthy events in distant places. There is fresh snow—21 feet of it—in Mesopotamia and a prizefight in Paris. On the night of 27 January 1925, "far away in Paris," Edouard Mascart, the French featherweight champion of Europe, had knocked out an Englishman, Danny Frush. He knocked him "cuckoo" at one minute and 20 seconds of the second round. The Associated Press reported: "No count by the referee was necessary. Frush was out for several minutes."[6] In Australia the English cricketers are "sharpening up their wickets" and end up losing all three matches to the Aussies, a defeat that upsets "all London."[7] This, Hemingway's young writer decides, is "Romance."

He then turns to the promotional flier for *The Forum*. During 1925 *The Forum* promises to bring its readers "prize short-stories"—"warm, homespun, American tales, bits of real life on the open ranch, in crowded tenement or comfortable home, and all with a healthy undercurrent of humor"— "will their authors write our best-sellers of to-morrow?" Like the Hemingway who was, we now know, on the verge of writing *The Sun Also Rises* but who was then fearful that he might never write a first novel, he must read those stories, the writer promises himself.

The flier has more. Momentous questions will be addressed: the growing world population, the threat scientific knowledge poses for believers, the gum-choppers in the Yucatan jungles. His attitude becomes more and more smart-alecky. It anticipates the pose Hemingway's implied author (with similar hints of self-directed irony) would adopt later in the same year when he turned to the writing of *The Torrents of Spring.* "Do we want big men—or do we want them cultured?" asks *The Forum.* "Take Joyce. Take President Coolidge. What star must our college students aim at? There is Jack Britton" (who had provided Hemingway with a subject for his boxing story "Fifty Grand"). I have not found any such flier promoting *The Forum* for 1925, but an examination of the contents of the magazine for that year shows that Hemingway has real targets in mind. The reference to James Joyce seems to have been his own idea, but on the other matters, see the article on the politics of the presidential election, "Coolidge Versus Davis," and look at the earnest piece written by "an observant student at Yale," "Big Men—or Cultured?" which "voices a protest against the spirit of 'be a big man or bust'" that its author believes works against the university's true purpose, which is to serve as a retreat where the student can acquire culture for its own sake and not for some practical purpose or ulterior reason.[8] The article ends on a note, incidentally, that would have touched the Princetonian Scott Fitzgerald more closely than it would Hemingway: "Indeed, no matter what his intended college [the author's example throughout has been Yale University], it can do no harm for a prospective undergraduate to consider whether he would rather be a Big Man at twenty-two, or a well-rounded, possibly a great man at forty."[9] It was Nick Carraway, it will be recalled, who wrote about himself in *The Great Gatsby:* "I was rather literary in college—one year I wrote a series of very solemn and obvious editorials for the Yale News—and now I was going to bring back all such things into my life and become again that most limited of all specialists, the 'well-rounded man.'"[10]

Hemingway's unnamed reader continues: "And what of our daughters who must make their own Soundings. Nancy Hawthorne is obliged to make her own Soundings in the sea of life. Bravely and sensibly she faces the problems which come to every girl of eighteen." The target here is the motherless English heroine of Arthur Hamilton Gibbs's *Soundings,* a novel serialized in seven installments in *The Forum* beginning in the October 1924 issue and running through April 1925, with a nod in the direction of Hemingway's own young heroine in "Up in Michigan," a story that would have been unpublishable in *The Forum* (or anywhere else for that matter, as Hemingway had discovered). The first installment of Gibbs's now deservedly forgotten piece of fiction had carried an epigraph: "Life is an uncharted ocean. The cautious mariner must needs take many soundings 'ere he conduct his barque to port in safety."[11]

"Are modern paintings—and poetry—Art?" asks Hemingway. "Yes and No. Take Picasso." In June 1925 *The Forum* did just that. In a debate on the question "Is Cubism Pure Art?" the two sides are argued: "Picasso's Achievement" and "Picasso's 'Failure.'"[12] And how about "civilization"? See the multipart series "What Is Civilization?" beginning in the January 1925 issue and running until October of the same year. Then there are the tramps. "Have tramps codes of conduct? Send your mind adventuring," writes Hemingway, who in "The Battler" examined the conduct of Ad Francis and his companion Bugs on the road. His target here, however, is an article entitled "Tramps and Hoboes," which a preliminary note describes: "Living and moving among us, in this settled and civilized era, is a nomadic population of over a hundred thousand men and boys,—our tramps and hoboes. Their faults and their virtues,—for they have virtues, even if their behavior is essentially anti-social,—and their picturesque language and habits are depicted in this article by a sympathetic observer."[13] And in the course of his reading Hemingway's writer refers to pieces on other topics and personalities such as George Bernard Shaw ("Ulysses and Einstein: A Dialogue between George Bernard Shaw and Archibald Henderson"), who seems not to recognize the names of any of the contemporary American writers mentioned to him, boasting "I never read any books,—at least hardly any; but I have no prejudice against American books,"[14] and Joan of Arc, who is featured in a full-page advertisement plugging Mark Twain's book on the subject.[15] Incidentally, it might be instructive or at least amusing, to tick off the 12 stories, one per issue, that Hemingway's writer would have read in 1925, had he kept his promise to himself: "Interval" by Kate Mullen, "Poor Man's Inn" by Richard Hughes, "Too Good to Be True" by James Aton, "Old Mossy Face" by Anthony Richardson, "Aunt Jane's Sofa" by Francis B. Biddle, "Maternal" by Ethel Cook Eliot, "Will Turner's Wife" by Ursula Trainor Williams, "Crown's Bess" by Du Bose Heyward, "An Apostle of Thunder" by, again, James Aton, "Palmleaf Gambling Hells" by Robert Dean Frisbie, "Mr. Rooster Rebels" by Dorothy Canfield, and, at last, in December, "Justice" by Louis Bromfield.[16] "*Forum* writers talk to the point, are possessed of humor and wit," promises the flier; but unlike the self-parodying author of the first part of "Banal Story" itself, "they do not try to be smart and are never long-winded."

The second part of "Banal Story" is something else. It appears to differ radically from the first part, both in subject matter and tone. The sarcasm that runs through the first portion of the story disappears, giving way to a pervasive irony. This part is shorter than the account of the writer reading *The Forum*'s flier, running only to a single paragraph comprising six sentences of short to moderate length. It is not written in Hemingway's breezy, sniping, *Torrents of Spring* style, but more in the style of the vignettes he published in Paris in the Three Mountains Press edition of *in our time* (1924) and then reprinted, with some changes, in the Liveright volume, his first collection of stories, *In Our Time* (1925). Rather than exuding sarcasm, this part works through irony. While the unnamed writer reads the booklet advertising *The Forum* and exhorting its potential readers to "Live the full life of the mind, exhilarated by new ideas, intoxicated by the Romance of the Unusual," the great Spanish bullfighter Manuel García Maera lies dying of pneumonia. Here, too, in faroff Spain, is life. Contrast the scene of the American writer collecting heat by seating himself on the electric stove ("How good it felt! Here, at last, was life.") with that of Maera, "a tube in each lung, drowning with the pneumonia."

In the writer's part, the word "life" appears four times; in the bull-fighter's, not once. Yet in the time of Maera's death there is the life that infuses Hemingway's sensitively ironic style. No matter that the "men and boys bought full-length colored pictures" of Maera "to remember him by, and lost," sad to say, "the picture they had of him in their memories by looking at the lithographs" and then rolling them up and putting them away in their pockets, thereby burying the reproductions even as they had attended to the burial of the bullfighter himself. Intended to memorialize Maera the bullfighter, whose glory lay in his actions in the bullring, the colored pictures show him at full length, static, inert, impersonating what a photographer would take to be *the bullfighter as celebrated public figure.* No wonder the "bull fighters were very relieved he was dead, because he did always in the bull-ring the things they could only do sometimes." Yet the fact is that 147 bullfighters showed sufficient respect for Maera to follow him out to the cemetery where he was placed in the tomb next to that of Joselito, universally considered to be the greatest bullfighter modern Spain has known.

Elsewhere Hemingway would insist that only the bullfighter lives his life all the way up. And even the stark naturalism of Maera's death cannot diminish the quality of his life. In *Death in the Afternoon* (1932) Hemingway would pay his final tribute to Maera:

> He was generous, humorous, proud, bitter, foul-mouthed and a great drinker. He neither sucked after intellectuals nor married money. He loved to kill bulls and lived with such passion and enjoyment although the last six months of his life he was very bitter. He knew he had tuberculosis and took absolutely no care of himself; having no fear of death he preferred to burn out, not as an act of bravado, but from choice.[17]

In the final year of his life Maera had "hoped for death in the ring," writes Hemingway admiringly, "but he would not cheat by looking for it."[18] As a matter of fact, Hemingway had himself already given Maera the very death he wanted. In the sixteenth vignette of *in our time*, published in the spring of 1924[19] (and therefore well before Maera's death in Seville in December 1924), Hemingway had imagined the death in the bullring that would elude Maera:

> Maera lay still, his head on his arms, his face in the sand. He felt warm and sticky from the bleeding. Each time he felt the horn coming. Sometimes the bull only bumped him with his head. Once the horn went all the way through him and he felt it go into the sand. Someone had the bull by the tail. They were swearing at him and flopping the cape in his face. Then the bull was gone. Some men picked Maera up and started to run with him toward the barriers through the gate out the passage way around under the grandstand to the infirmary. They laid Maera down on a cot and one of the men went out for the doctor. The others stood around. The doctor came running from the corral where he had been sewing up picador horses. He had to stop and wash his hands. There was a great shouting going on in the grandstand overhead. Maera wanted to say something and found he could not talk. Maera felt everything getting larger and larger and then smaller and smaller. Then it got larger and larger and larger and then smaller and smaller. Then everything commenced to run faster and faster as when they speed up a cinematograph film. Then he was dead.[20]

Surely this was a story that would not have appealed to the editors of *The Forum*. Neither, of course, would "Banal Story," which can hardly be described as "warm" or "homespun" or a bit of "real life on the open ranch." Its theme is banality, the banality of both the kind of story (fictional or otherwise) that *The Forum* promises and delivers to its readers and, in a deeper sense, the kind of smart-alecky narrative told in the first part of Hemingway's "Banal Story." The irony is that the self-parodying writer warming himself from the bottom up, with his pseudo-Menckenian facility for rather easy sarcasm, was never completely exorcised by the author who, in a different mood and at the top of his form, could write such deeply sensitive stories as "Indian Camp," "Hills Like White Elephants," and the two vignettes on Maera's death, imagined and actual.

Minor though it otherwise may be, "Banal Story" gathers considerable biographical significance when it is seen for the ironic gesture towards its author's own self-conscious need for exorcism that it was at least partly intended to be.

Notes

1. *Ernest Hemingway: Selected Letters, 1917–1961*, ed. Carlos Baker (New York: Charles Scribner's Sons, 1981) 470, and Carlos Baker, *Ernest Hemingway: A Life Story* (New York: Charles Scribner's Sons, 1969) 137.

2. Phillip R. Yannella, working from a manuscript in the *Little Review* files and a letter to Jane Heap, dates the composition of "Banal Story" as falling "between 28 January and 30 January [1925]" ("Notes on the Manuscript, Date, and Sources of Hemingway's 'Banal Story,'" *Fitzgerald/Hemingway Annual 1974*, ed. Matthew J. Bruccoli and C.E. Frazer Clark, Jr. [Englewood: Microcard, 1975] 176).

3. *Letters*, 245.

4. *The Forum* described itself, in the words of Henry Goddard Leach, its editor at the time: "A Non-Partisan Magazine of Free Discussion. What Is Praised in This Issue May Be Attacked in the Next. The Forum Aims to Interpret the New America That Is Attaining National Consciousness in the Decade in Which We Live" (74 [Aug. 1925]: 161).

5. "Banal Story," *Men Without Women* (New York: Charles Scribner's Sons, 1927) 214–17. Subsequent references to this story are to this edition.

6. "Frush Knocked Out by Mascart in 2D," *New York Times* (28 Jan. 1925): 11. Yannella says that Hemingway misspelled the fighter's name, the correct spelling being "Muscart." ("Notes on 'Banal Story'": 176). If so, so did the *New York Times*.

7. "Test Cricket Game Stirs All London," *New York Times* (23 Jan. 1925): 16.

8. *The Forum* 73 (Feb. 1925): 209.

9. *The Forum* 73 (Feb. 1925): 214.

10. *The Great Gatsby* (New York: Charles Scribner's Sons, 1925) 5.

11. *The Forum* 72 (Oct. 1924): 433.

12. *The Forum* 73 (June 1925): 769–83. The debate, with spirited reactions from, among others, Frank Jewett Mather, Jr. and John Sloan, continued in the letters columns of the issues for July (146–50) and August (296–98).

13. *The Forum* 74 (Aug. 1925): 227. The author is Towne Nylander. Incidentally, one also thinks of Robert Frost's poem "Two Tramps in Mud-Time" when the author observes that "many housewives are inconsiderate enough to suggest the wood-pile [to a tramp] as a preliminary to eating" (236).

14. *The Forum* 72 (Oct. 1924): 455.

15. *The Forum* 73 (Feb. 1925): preliminary pages, unnumbered.

16. For another look at the contents of *The Forum* in 1924–25, see Wayne E. Kvam, "Hemingway's 'Banal Story,'" *Fitzgerald/Hemingway Annual 1974*, 181–91.

17. *Death in the Afternoon* (New York: Charles Scribner's Sons, 1932) 82–83.

18. *Death in the Afternoon*, 82.

19. See Audre Hanneman, *Ernest Hemingway: A Comprehensive Bibliography* (Princeton: Princeton UP, 1967) 6.

20. *in our time* (Paris: Three Mountains Press, 1924) 27; facs. ed. Bloomfield Hills: Bruccoli Clark Books, 1977.

11

Hemingway and Turgenev: *The Torrents of Spring*

Robert Coltrane

Not long after completing "Banal Story," Hemingway undertook a more extended exercise in literary satire. The Torrents of Spring, a novella-length work of short fiction completed in November 1925. Unlike the enduring satire from which it draws its epigraph, Henry Fielding's Joseph Andrews, The Torrents of Spring remains largely unread today because its story makes little sense without knowledge of Hemingway's target, Sherwood Anderson's Dark Laughter, and because knowledge of Dark Laughter, a bestseller in 1925, is today restricted solely to the most conscientious scholars of American literature. Although several studies of The Torrents of Spring have examined its parody of Dark Laughter in detail, Hemingway's satire continues to suffer the fate of most jokes requiring explanation. Here Robert Coltrane provides a refreshingly different way of reading The Torrents of Spring, examining its relationship to the novella by Turgenev from which Hemingway took his title. Not satisfied with merely delineating the many parallels between these two stories of "springtime yearnings" and infidelity, Coltrane goes on to demonstrate how Hemingway used his allusions to Turgenev as a means of disguising his sexual and artistic frustrations, while attacking those who continued to misjudge the nature of his literary ambitions. The resulting informed vision of The Torrents of Spring may reopen this work to critical consideration.

Critical studies of Ernest Hemingway's *The Torrents of Spring* have generally been limited to an examination of the satirical elements, in particular the parody of Sherwood Anderson's *Dark Laughter*. While Hemingway's parody was aimed primarily at Anderson's writing style, the setting, plot, and two female characters were a combination of Hemingway's personal and literary experiences. Although a number of competent studies have been made of Hemingway's satirical technique and his biographical sources, no one has examined the relationship between Hemingway's *Torrents* and the novella by Turgenev from which Hemingway took his title.[1] The primary purpose of *Torrents* was to provide amusement, but it also provided Hemingway a means of fictionalizing his personal frustrations and commenting indirectly on those who insisted on misjudging his literary aspirations. Hemingway is saying satirically that Turgenev's *The Torrents of Spring* is the work Anderson should have tried to emulate but was incapable of emulating. Therefore, Hemingway's only choice was to hold Anderson's work up to ridicule by parodying its stylistic excesses, while pointing to Turgenev —by means of the title—as the proper way to tell the story about springtime yearnings that lead to infidelity. I propose to examine how Turgenev's *Torrents* served as a source for Hemingway's *Torrents*, how these two works are concerned with Hemingway's personal and professional relationships of the mid-1920s, and how they are related to Hemingway's other fiction of that period.[2]

The Motivation to Produce a Satire

According to Carlos Baker, Hemingway wrote *The Torrents of Spring* in "seven to ten days at the end of November," or approximately from 23 to 30 November 1925. He had likely been sent a copy of *Dark Laughter* by Liveright around the beginning of September and, according to Baker, had finished the first draft of *The Sun Also Rises* by 21 September.[3] Since he did not write *Torrents* until some two months later, one might ask what happened in November to inspire his sudden and rapidly produced parody of Anderson. Many studies suggest that Hemingway's only motivation was to produce a work which would allow him to break his contract with Liveright, so that *The Sun Also Rises* could be published by a more prestigious firm, preferably Scribner's. While this motive no doubt accounts in part for Hemingway's insistence that Liveright publish *Torrents*, Hemingway had other reasons, just as compelling, for writing a satire at this time. I suggest that Hemingway's reading of Constance Garnett's translation of Turgenev's *The Torrents of Spring* sometime between 25 October and 16 November served as the catalyst that fused into a concentrated satirical outburst all the professional and personal frustrations that had been accumulating in him during the latter part of 1925.[4]

For example, the publication of *In Our Time* by Boni & Liveright on 5 October 1925 brought numerous reminders by reviewers of Hemingway's artistic association with Sherwood Anderson. In the omitted preface of *Torrents*, Hemingway sarcastically noted that he had decided from then on to write exclusively like Sherwood Anderson since so many critics had said the only value of *In Our Time* was its resemblance to Anderson's writing.[5] The reviewers did not recognize that Hemingway's study of Turgenev's *Fathers and Sons* and *A Sportsman's Sketches* in the Garnett translations had enabled him by this time to surpass Anderson in craftsmanship.[6] It was from Turgenev rather than Anderson that Hemingway had learned economy of style, especially the revealing of a character's inner turmoil through carefully selected landscape details and description of action. An example from the work under consideration here, Turgenev's *Torrents of Spring,* will serve to demonstrate the effect Hemingway had mastered. When the central character, Sanin, is waiting to risk his life in a duel, Turgenev conveys his agitated mental state both directly and indirectly:

> He walked up and down the path, listened to the birds singing, watched the dragonflies in their flight, and like the majority of Russians in similar circumstances, tried not to think. He only once dropped into reflection; he came across a young lime-tree, broken down, in all probability by the squall of the previous night. It was unmistakably dying . . . all the leaves on it were dead. "What is it? an omen?" was the thought that flashed across his mind; but he promptly began whistling, leaped over the very tree, and paced up and down the path.[7]

Hemingway's ability to use physical details and minimum authorial interpretation like Turgenev to convey mental turmoil is already evident in the stories included in *In Our Time,* the best example being "Big Two-Hearted River":

> Ahead the river narrowed and went into a swamp. The river became smooth and deep and the swamp looked solid with cedar trees, their trunks close together, their branches solid. It would not be possible to walk through a swamp like that. The branches grew so low. You would have to keep almost level with the ground to move at all. You could not crash through the branches. That must be why the animals that lived in swamps were built the way they were, Nick thought. . . . Nick did not want to go in there now. He felt a reaction against deep wading with the water deepening up under his armpits, to hook big trout in places impossible to land them. . . . In the swamp fishing was a tragic adventure. Nick did not want it. He did not want to go down the stream any further today.[8]

Therefore, while many of the reviews would only have been annoying, one very likely to have aroused Hemingway's wrath was the review published by the *New York Sun* on 17 October 1925.[9] The reviewer not only noted Hemingway's stylistic debt to Anderson and to Gertrude Stein but also concluded that Hemingway's work did not have "the big movement, the rich content of such a book as *Dark Laughter,*" a work Hemingway later described in *A Moveable Feast* as "terribly bad, silly and affected."[10] After returning Turgenev's *Torrents of Spring* to Sylvia Beach's bookstore on 16

November, Hemingway borrowed Donald Ogden Stewart's *A Parody Outline of History* on 23 November, the date Baker suggests for the start of *Torrents*. The sequence probably occurred as follows: after reading Anderson's *Dark Laughter* and finding it a disappointing failure, Hemingway turned to one of his favorite authors, Turgenev; while reading Turgenev's *Torrents*, he began to consider writing a satire to relieve the emotional strain imposed by the discipline of completing his first major novel ("I wrote it after I had finished the first draft of *The Sun Also Rises*, to cool out").[11] Several days later he consulted Stewart's book for guidance on the appropriate length for a parody. *A Parody Outline of History* is subtitled "a curiously irreverent treatment of American historical events, imagining them as they would be narrated by America's most characteristic contemporary authors"; for example, chapter 4 offers "The Courtship of Miles Standish In the Manner of F. Scott Fitzgerald." In letters to Horace Liveright and Scott Fitzgerald, Hemingway anticipated objections to the shortness of *Torrents* by suggesting the length was ideal for a humorous work and pointing out that it was five thousand words longer than Stewart's book.[12] He may also have derived from Stewart the idea of using puns on literary works as his chapter titles.

With his primary target, Anderson, already designated by the reviewers, Hemingway chose for his setting the same Northern Michigan area that he had earlier used in a number of the stories published in *In Our Time*. Having read Anderson's *Dark Laughter* and then Turgenev's *Torrents* around the same time, Hemingway would have noticed the similarities in the character relationships but would have been annoyed by the differences in writing style. Where Turgenev used a precise choice of words that involve the reader in the scene while also advancing the plot with economy—a technique Hemingway sought to emulate—Anderson's attempts at impressionism and stream-of-consciousness produced monotonous repetition, awkward fragments, and a ponderously slow pace.

Chapter 10 of *Dark Laughter* attempts to convey Bruce Dudley's impressions upon his arrival in New Orleans:

> Consciousness of brown men, brown women, coming more and more into American life—by that token coming into him too.
>
> More willing to come, more avid to come than any Jew, German, Pole, Italian. Standing laughing—coming by the back door—with shuffling feet, a laugh—a dance in the body.
>
> Facts established would have to be recognized sometime—by individuals—when they were on an intellectual jag perhaps—as Bruce was then.[13]

Compared to the precision of Turgenev, Anderson's writing is badly flawed. Given Hemingway's pride of craftsmanship, his reaction to being unfavorably compared with Anderson is not surprising: a parody of the "big move-ment" and "rich content" of *Dark Laughter*. He also satirized a number of other targets, including his personal relationships in Paris which had served as the emotional basis for several of the stories in *In Our Time*.

Source Material in Turgenev's *Torrents*

Hemingway found in Turgenev's novella more than a title. While Heming-way's two male characters, Scripps O'Neil and Yogi Johnson, are parodies of Bruce Dudley and Sponge Martin in *Dark Laughter*, the source for the two waitresses, Diana and Mandy, is not found in Anderson. Their relation-ship to Scripps—two women competing for the love of the same man—is a variation on the situation depicted by Turgenev, and also a disguised repre-sentation of Hemingway's emotional entanglements in 1925 with his wife Hadley and Pauline Pfeiffer.[14] A brief summary of Turgenev's *Torrents* will demonstrate that the character relationships are similar to those found both in Hemingway's *Torrents* and in Hemingway's personal relations while he was writing his parody.

In Turgenev's story, the young Sanin falls in love, while traveling in Germany, with a beautiful girl called Gemma, who works in a pastry shop. They are betrothed after Sanin rids Gemma of her unsavory fiancé, Herr Klueber. However, a wealthy woman named Maria Nikolaevna seduces Sanin while pretending an interest in purchasing his estate, which he wishes to sell so he can marry Gemma. Sanin becomes emotionally enslaved to Maria and abandons Gemma. We learn the affair was arranged by Maria's husband, Poloznov, merely as a challenge to Maria's ability as a seductress, a challenge made more interesting by Sanin's devotion to Gemma. Maria soon tires of Sanin and sends him away. Sanin has been the victim of an unscrupulous woman and has no one but himself to blame. Ironically, Gemma's happy marriage later to a merchant was made possible by Sanin's freeing her from Herr Klueber. Only the foolish Sanin loses. This tale of "the ultimate degradation of a man enslaved by his passion for a woman" is, according to Turgenev's biographer Leonard Schapiro, "possibly the most forceful statement by Turgenev of this recurrent theme in all his fiction."[15]

Given Hemingway's domineering attitude toward women, he would no doubt have viewed Sanin's submissiveness to Maria with contempt. However, since he was himself in a similar situation of being tempted by a wealthy, attractive woman to abandon an earlier commitment, the attitude of contempt one finds expressed in *Torrents* is directed by Hemingway as much toward his own deceitfulness as toward Sanin's. Turgenev's Sanin has committed himself to a woman he loves, only to be lured away from his commitment by an attractive, wealthy woman who pursues him relentlessly.

Similarly, in Hemingway's *Torrents*, no sooner does Scripps marry the elderly waitress Diana than he is attracted to the more vivacious and younger waitress Mandy. After trying unsuccessfully to save her marriage, Diana admits defeat and leaves Scripps to Mandy. This plot situation also reflects Hemingway's personal difficulties of the period: both Hadley and Pauline were trying to please him, a situation he found flattering but emotionally unacceptable. Diana's defeat by Mandy suggests that, subconsciously at least, Hemingway had already made his choice. Hemingway wrote out his frustrations by portraying both women, according to Kenneth S. Lynn, "as waitresses in the most degrading sense of the term," and suggested indirectly the faults that would cause him eventually to leave them both, "Hadley because she was too old, Pauline because she was too talkative."[16]

Hemingway had met Pauline Pfeiffer in March 1925, and by December she had become permanently involved in his life. Hemingway later recalled this period in the last chapter of *A Moveable Feast:* "An unmarried young woman becomes the temporary best friend of another young woman who is married, goes to live with the husband and wife and then unknowingly, innocently, and unrelentingly sets out to marry the husband."[17] The older, matronly Hadley was no match for the vivacious and wealthy Pauline, whose determined pursuit of Hemingway is reminiscent of Maria's seduction of Sanin.[18]

The Theme of Infidelity in the Sources

Infidelity permeates both Anderson's novel and Turgenev's novella. In *Dark Laughter*, Bruce Dudley escapes from his unsatisfactory marriage in Chicago by traveling to his boyhood home of Old Harbor, Indiana, where he goes to work for the Grey Wheel Company. Fred Grey, the owner of the company, is married to the sexually restless daughter of a wealthy banker, Aline, who finds Bruce attractive. When spring arrives, bringing emotional yearnings (hence the appropriateness of Hemingway's title), Aline Grey seduces Bruce. At the end of the novel, she deserts her husband and goes off with her lover. Hemingway parodies the Fred and Aline Grey relationship through the naked squaw who attracts Yogi Johnson at the end of *Torrents*. The squaw is married to a little Indian war hero who is a quadruple amputee and is thus equated with Fred Grey, also a war veteran. While playing pool, the squaw's husband admits he does "not shoot so good since the war" (65)—a satirical comment on Fred's virtually nonexistent sexual relations with Aline.

Similarities between Hemingway's two sources can be seen in the wealthy wives, Maria Nikolaevna and Aline Grey, both of whom deliberately pursue and seduce men they find attractive. In both stories the wife is having the extramarital relationship, while the ineffectual husband has no authority in the marriage. Turgenev's Poloznov is tolerated by Maria only as long as he is willing to find new young lovers for her. After long absence, Fred Grey is invited back into Aline's bed only when she discovers Bruce has made her pregnant. Hemingway's story, however, depicts the husband as being unfaithful to the wife, a disguised version of Hemingway's relationship with Hadley. By treating the characters in *Torrents* as a parody of Anderson's fiction, Hemingway obscured the personal relationships that provided the basis not only for this work but also for some of the short fiction he wrote during this period.

Similarities to the Shorter Fiction

Two of the best examples of Hemingway's use of indirection to disguise the story's intensely personal revelations can be found in "Cat in the Rain" and "Out of Season." Written during the 1923–24 period of Hadley's pregnancy and the birth of their son, these stories reflect Hemingway's discontent about the impending responsibilities of parenthood. They belong to the group Meyers says are concerned with "disintegrating relationships," which also includes two Petoskey stories, "The End of Something" and "The Three-Day Blow."[19] Both "Cat in the Rain" and "Out of Season" are sympathetic portrayals of the woman's point of view and depict the man's attitude unfavorably. Since Nick Adams, as Hemingway's most personalized alter ego, is always portrayed sympathetically, Hemingway presents the man as someone who is not Nick Adams. To promote reader sympathy for the woman, he calls the husband George in "Cat in the Rain" and refers to the man in "Out of Season" only as "the young gentleman." In a letter to Scott Fitzgerald, dated 24 December 1925, Hemingway further disguised the fact that these stories were based on his own marital experiences by giving misleading information to distract Fitzgerald from recognizing the stories' true emotional source, Hemingway's feelings of discontent about Hadley's pregnancy. He writes that "Cat in the Rain wasnt [*sic*] about Hadley" but about "a harvard kid and his wife that I'd met at Genoa." In the same letter he claims that the most important part of "Out of Season" is what he left out—the drunken guide supposedly hanged himself when he was fired because Hemingway had complained about his conduct. Hemingway tells Fitzgerald, "I meant it to be a tragic about the drunk of a guide."[20] The story, however, is not about the drunken guide, nor has any evidence been found that the man hanged himself.

A third story included in the disintegrating relationships group, "Mr. and Mrs. Elliot," has been considered critically only as a satirical attack on

Mr. and Mrs. Chard Powers Smith, due to Carlos Baker's claim that it was "a malicious gossip-story" that makes "fun of the alleged sexual ineptitudes" of the Smiths. Baker based his interpretation on the story's having been originally titled "Mr. and Mrs. Smith" and on an exchange of unfriendly letters between Smith and Hemingway.[21] "Mr. and Mrs. Elliot," also written in 1924, offers a variation on the antipaternity theme of "Cat in the Rain" and "Out of Season." It not only satirizes the Elliots' sexual ineptitudes but also ridicules their desire to have a baby, another disguised expression of Hemingway's discontent about Hadley's desire to become a mother. Much is made in the story of the fact that Mrs. Elliot, like Hadley, is older than her husband, who is the same age as Hemingway. Hemingway may well have been projecting his own feelings of helpless frustration about impending fatherhood into his creation of the Prufrock-like Mr. Elliot. When Mrs. Elliot's older girlfriend arrives to take over the running of their lives (besides being "very neat and efficient" she "was now typing practically all of the manuscripts"), we are reminded of the relationship between Gertrude Stein and her friend, Alice B. Toklas, which Hemingway was later to portray more viciously in *A Moveable Feast*. Mr. Elliot's sterility is a variation on the impotency motif recurrent in the fiction of this period, including *Torrents*.

The Petoskey Setting

More closely related to *Torrents* is the disguised presentation of Hemingway's marital difficulties with Hadley in two of the Petoskey stories written the previous year. They depict the breakup of Nick Adams's teenage romance, supposedly based on Hemingway's relationship in 1919 with a young girl named Marjorie Bump. According to Jeffrey Meyers, Hemingway's "unsatisfactory romance with Marjorie inspired two sour Nick Adams stories, 'The End of Something' and 'The Three-Day Blow,'" but they were written "when his love for his first wife was disintegrating" and are "more closely related to the fictional portrayals of the end of his marriage to Hadley . . . in 'Cat in the Rain' and 'Out of Season' than to his brief liaison with Marjorie."[22] In satirizing in *Torrents* his current emotional entanglements in Paris with two women, Hemingway returned once again to Petoskey where he had earlier been involved in a similar situation. He had apparently had sexual relations with an older waitress named Pauline Snow, the subject of a 1919 "Crossroads" sketch and the model for Liz Coates of "Up in Michigan," while at the same time he was attracted to the teenaged Marjorie Bump.[23]

"Up in Michigan," a Petoskey story written around 1921–22 when he was newly married, contains one of Hemingway's earliest attempts to conceal the use of personal experience through misdirection, even at the cost of offending family friends. He gave his characters the names of real Petoskey residents, Jim and Liz Dilworth, calling the man Jim Gilmore and the woman Liz Coates, and caused hard feelings at home according to his sister Marcelline.[24] His purpose was to disguise the real source for the story, his own sexual encounter with Pauline Snow.

Hemingway appropriately sets *Torrents* in Petoskey, the place where he himself first experienced the torrents of spring. Hemingway employed a number of devices found to be successful for the stories, such as the use of real people and actual locations. The Indians, the Blackmer Rotary Pump Factory, Braun's Restaurant (i.e., Brown's Beanery), and the scenic descriptions of the Petoskey area are all factual.[25] The amputee Indian war veteran is based on Billy Gilbert, a decorated hero whose marriage was destroyed by the war, described in another of Hemingway's "Crossroads" sketches.[26] He also used the previously developed technique of concealing the real-life situation by disguising it as something else. To obscure the fact that Mandy has Pauline's personality, Hemingway gives her Marjorie Bump's age and appearance, while the Hadley character, Diana, is presented as Liz Coates. Thus Hemingway is, in effect, presenting current autobiography in the guise of past autobiography.

Self-Ridicule in *Torrents*

The theme of physical and emotional impotence resulting from the war, which Hemingway had portrayed in his recently completed novel, *The Sun Also Rises,* also becomes a subject for ridicule in *Torrents* through the character of Yogi Johnson. Yogi has been made impotent through his experiences while a soldier in Europe, and his lack of sexual desire is reminiscent of Krebs, the veteran in another 1924 story, "Soldier's Home." Krebs likewise felt no desire for the young girls he saw when he got back home from the war. The source of Yogi's problem, however, is quite unlike that of Jake or Krebs, whose impotence results from their war experiences. In accounting for Yogi's impotence, Hemingway reveals that it was caused by disappointment in love. Hemingway satirizes Yogi's impotence by presenting the love affair as an anecdote derived from a dirty joke: a man discovers that his sexual encounter with a lovely lady has provided "peep-show" entertainment for the customers who pay to watch.[27] Yogi, however, never figures out that the beautiful woman who "seduced" him in Paris is a prostitute, and he is embittered because he believes the beautiful woman abandoned him for another man (78–79). Since the Negro women's laughing at the cuckolded Fred Grey is the only incident in Anderson's novel that remotely corresponds to Yogi's Paris story, we must once more look at Turgenev's

Torrents to determine what might have inspired Hemingway to include this anecdote.

Yogi's relationship with the prostitute recalls Sanin's relationship with Maria Nikolaevna. Like Sanin, Yogi meets a beautiful, wealthy woman who takes him to her "mansion" and, after seducing him, tells him she can never see him again. Although Maria is not a prostitute, she openly has affairs with a series of men whom she dismisses after tiring of them. Like Yogi, Sanin leads a life of apathy as a result of his encounter with Maria. Not until some thirty years later, when he decides to go to America to see his original beloved, Gemma, does he regain a sense of purpose in life. Yogi's manhood is restored through a character reminiscent of a girlfriend from Hemingway's youth, the American Indian girl Trudy (also called Prudie, for Prudence) whom Hemingway credits with initiating him into manhood. Hemingway had only hinted at their sexual relationship in a story written during the same period as *Torrents*, "Ten Indians," a story in which he emphasized Nick's feeling of betrayal by someone he thought cared for him.[28] Hemingway is here projecting into Nick's feelings of betrayal his own guilt about being unfaithful to Hadley. However, when Yogi's manhood is restored by the naked Indian squaw, we are reminded of the later story, "Fathers and Sons," in which Nick's earlier sexual relations with Trudy are described more explicitly, she being the one who, Nick says, "did first what no one has done better." This motif of sexual impotence, which is presented so strongly in *The Sun Also Rises* and then echoed in *The Torrents of Spring* through Yogi, is very likely a sublimated expression of the young Hemingway's own feelings of sexual frustration over his lack of personal freedom and artistic frustration over not having yet achieved the recognition he craved.

Not only did Hemingway project some of his own frustrations into the character of Yogi, but we also find hints of Hemingway in the portrayal of Yogi's friend Scripps. Scripps O'Neil has been described by critics as a parody on writers who cannot write, but he is also a satirically portrayed Hemingway alter ego—he has had two wives and at the end of the story takes up with a third, telling Mandy repeatedly "You are my woman now" (83). Through Scripps, Hemingway is satirizing some of the attitudes about marriage that he had earlier portrayed seriously in such stories as "Cat in the Rain" and "Out of Season."

Later, in *A Moveable Feast*, he would look back nostalgically on this formative period as a time in which he innocently allowed himself to be misled by others, especially Pauline, into betraying his ideals. Others were to blame for any mistaken decisions he had made. We can see from *Torrents*, however, that he was well aware of the consequences likely to result from the actions he planned to take. *Torrents* reveals to us that by means of a devastating parody he was willing to cut off his association with Sherwood Anderson, who had become an artistic embarrassment, no matter what others thought he might owe Anderson; that by creating this parody, he could be ruthless in his business dealings by placing Liveright in a position where he had no choice but to release Hemingway from his contract. And finally, though satirically disguised, his relationship with Hadley was finished, and he was aware that he was going to begin a new relationship with Pauline, a relationship he did not feel entirely comfortable about.

Torrents is as personal as any of Hemingway's other works, perhaps one of the best reasons why Hemingway insisted so strongly to both Liveright and Perkins that *Torrents* was a work worthy of publication.[29] It shows us a Hemingway we would not see again. Just as he abandoned Turgenev as a guide after learning all that master had to teach him, so did he abandon the use of parody after it had served its purposes. The techniques of disguise and misdirection that Hemingway employed in *Torrents* would become a standard literary device in subsequent works, but he would not again resort to the use of an extended satire as a means of relieving personal and professional frustrations.

Notes

1. John T. Flanagan in "Hemingway's Debt to Sherwood Anderson," *Journal of English and Germanic Philology* 54 (October 1955): 507–20, provides examples that demonstrate what Hemingway had satirized in Anderson's work; Richard B. Hovey in "*The Torrents of Spring*: Prefigurations in the Early Hemingway," *College English* 26 (March 1965): 460–64, provides typical humorous passages from *Torrents* and explains how they function as satire; Delbert E. Wylder in "*The Torrents of Spring*," *South Dakota Review* 5 (Winter 1967–68): 23–35, analyzes the characters and situations being parodied in *Torrents* through an extensive comparison with Anderson's *Dark Laughter* and *Many Marriages;* Paul P. Somers, Jr., in "The Mark of Sherwood Anderson on Hemingway: A Look at the Texts," *South Atlantic Quarterly* 73 (Autumn 1974): 487–503, provides a stylistic comparison of *Torrents* and *Dark Laughter*, illustrating the parody on Anderson's writing style. Constance Cappel Montgomery's *Hemingway in Michigan* (New York: Fleet, 1966) identifies the biographical sources.

2. The edition of *Torrents of Spring* cited in this study is found in *The Hemingway Reader* (New York: Charles Scribner's Sons, 1953) 25–86; references are cited parenthetically in the text.

3. Carlos Baker, *Ernest Hemingway: A Life Story* (New York: Charles Scribner's Sons, 1969) 155 and notes to section 22, 590. In a letter to Horace Liveright, dated 28 August 1925, Anderson requested a copy of *Dark Laughter* be sent to Hemingway; see *Letters of Sherwood Anderson*, ed. Howard Mumford Jones and Walter B. Rideout (Boston: Little, Brown, 1953) 146. With a maximum travel time by ship of about 10 days, the copy of *Dark Laughter* should have reached Hemingway before the end of September.

4. The dates Hemingway borrowed Turgenev's *Torrents of Spring* from Sylvia Beach's bookstore are cited by Noel Fitch in "Ernest Hemingway—c/o Shakespeare and Company," *Fitzgerald/Hemingway Annual 1977*, 175, as 25 October to 16 November 1925, based on

Hemingway's lending library cards in the Sylvia Beach Collection at Princeton University Library. Using the same source, Michael S. Reynolds gives the dates as 27 October to 16 November, in *Hemingway's Reading, 1910–1940* (Princeton: Princeton UP, 1981) 194.

5. Reprinted in *The Fitzgerald/Hemingway Annual 1977*, 112.

6. See Myler Wilkinson's *Hemingway and Turgenev: The Nature of Literary Influence* (Ann Arbor: UMI Research P, 1986) for an examination of the influence of Turgenev's *Fathers and Sons* and *A Sportsman's Sketches* on Hemingway's style.

7. Ivan Turgenev, *The Torrents of Spring*, trans. Constance Garnett (1916; rpt. Freeport, N.Y.: Books for Libraries, 1971) 86–87.

8. Ernest Hemingway, *The Short Stories of Ernest Hemingway* (New York: Charles Scribner's Sons, 1953) 231.

9. The review, by Herbert J. Seligman, is reprinted in *Critical Essays on Ernest Hemingway's* In Our Time, ed. Michael S. Reynolds (Boston: G. K. Hall, 1983) 15–16.

10. *A Moveable Feast* (New York: Charles Scribner's Sons, 1964) 28. Prior to the publication of *Torrents*, Hemingway had expressed his distaste for the sentimental writing and borrowed thinking of *Dark Laughter* in a letter to Edwin L. Peterson dated 30 March 1926, summarized by Ray Lewis White in "Hemingway's Private Explanation of *The Torrents of Spring*," *Modern Fiction Studies* 13 (Summer 1967): 262–63.

11. Ernest Hemingway, *The Hemingway Reader* (New York: Charles Scribner's Sons, 1953) 24.

12. *Ernest Hemingway: Selected Letters, 1917–1961*, ed. Carlos Baker (New York: Charles Scribner's Sons, 1981) 173, 185.

13. Sherwood Anderson, *Dark Laughter* (1925; rpt. Cleveland: World, 1942) 74.

14. See Kenneth S. Lynn, *Hemingway* (New York: Simon and Schuster, 1987) 303–4.

15. Leonard Schapiro, *Turgenev: His Life and Times* (New York: Random House, 1978) 250.

16. Lynn, 305.

17. *A Moveable Feast*, 209.

18. See Jeffrey Meyers, *Hemingway: A Biography* (New York: Harper & Row, 1985) 172–93, for Hemingway's relationship with Hadley and Pauline during 1925 and 1926.

19. Meyers, 152–53.

20. *Letters*, 180.

21. Baker, *Life*, 133; exchange of letters cited in notes, 585.

22. Meyers, 49.

23. Reynolds states that Bill Smith's letters suggest "Pauline Snow was the actual name of a Horton Bay waitress" who was the biographical source for Liz Coates; see *Critical Essays*, 5. Hemingway's sketch of Pauline Snow has been published in "Crossroads—An Anthology," in Peter Griffin's *Along with Youth: Hemingway, the Early Years* (New York: Oxford UP, 1985) 124.

24. Cited by Meyers (147), who suggests that the last names of the characters came from Oak Park residents, Frances Coates and a department store owner named Gilmore.

25. Montgomery, 167–69.

26. See Griffin, 126–27.

27. Daniel R. Barnes, "Traditional Narrative Sources for Hemingway's *The Torrents of Spring*," *Studies in Short Fiction* 19 (Spring 1982): 148–49.

28. "Ten Indians" was begun in 1925 and finished in May 1926 in Madrid; see Baker, *Life,* 169. The final revision was completed in May 1927 while on honeymoon with Pauline (Baker, 186).

29. In his letter to Liveright, dated 7 December 1925, Hemingway defends the literary merits of *Torrents;* see *Letters,* 172–74. In a letter to Perkins, 30 December 1925, Scott Fitzgerald states that one of Hemingway's conditions for giving *The Sun Also Rises* to Scribner's is that they publish *Torrents* first; see *The Letters of F. Scott Fitzgerald,* ed. Andrew Turnbull (New York: Charles Scribner's Sons 1963) 195–96.

12

"An Alpine Idyll": The Sun-Struck Mountain Vision and the Necessary Valley Journey

Robert E. Gajdusek

"An Alpine Idyll," completed in early May 1926, concerns itself with a different rite of spring, an Austrian peasant's journey down from the mountains to bury his wife in the newly thawed earth of a valley cemetery. The grotesquerie of this short story, whose interpretation centers on the peasant's motives for hanging a lantern from his wife's jaw during her corpse's long winter storage in the woodshed, has repelled many critics, who view "Alpine Idyll" as either "sick or morbid." Robert Gajdusek abandons this squeamish posture to examine the short story's almost mythological structure. He reads "Alpine Idyll" as a parable of "arrested cycles," a story about abstraction from the cycles of nature, from winter and spring, cold and warmth, darkness and light, death and birth, and most of all, of abstraction from the natural times to end something and to seek renewal. In doing so, Gajdusek himself brings to "An Alpine Idyll" the "new poetic attentiveness" and "healthy skepticism toward existing critical responses" he asks of its readers.

"An Alpine Idyll" is a neglected Hemingway short story.[1] In 1975, when Jackson Benson edited his seminal work, *The Short Stories of Ernest Hemingway: Critical Essays*, its comprehensive checklist listed only *one* essay on the story and less than a dozen commentators on it who had briefly made remarks in passing in otherwise focused major critical works. When such critical lack of attention is measured against the 43 (often extensive) entries listed for "Big Two-Hearted River" or the 63 for "The Snows of Kilimanjaro," a just sense of the story's obscurity emerges. As of this writing, there are less than a half dozen critical essays on the story in print. Were "An Alpine Idyll" truly an inept or a merely shocking failure, as it has been judged, there would be no need for this article or the few others that are now beginning to cry for the story's rescue. It is, in fact, an astonishingly intricate, well-told tale that exemplifies the best in Hemingway—it is Hemingway all the way, pure and classic in form. It has undoubtedly been overlooked because, more successfully than other tales, it has demonstrated the iceberg technique at its most exemplary: the visible tip has, by a most startling exposure kept the vast bulk hidden and unsuspected. Carlos Baker, speaking of Hemingway's short stories, said of them, "they are so readable as straight narratives that one is prepared to accept them at face value—to admire the sharp lines and clean curves of the eighth of the iceberg above the surface, and to ignore the real causes of the dignity or worth of the movement."[2] The problem is that when the eighth that is visible shocks or repels, there may be scant desire left to discover the "real causes." It is partly for this reason that some of the best and most subtle of Hemingway critics have been among those who have summarily dismissed "An Alpine Idyll."

Attention should be paid to this kind of oversight, for that it has existed as it has, luring the astute and the sensitive to remand the story to relative obscurity, is itself fascinating.[3] There are many who have judged "An Alpine Idyll" not worth the reader's time. One leading Hemingway critic ascribes to it "a detectable streak of morbidity" and asks, "How else can one explain 'An Alpine Idyll,' a relatively pointless tale?"[4] Another major critic describes it as "very close to what was called several years ago the sick joke" and relegates "the masculine bravado here" to "the level . . . of goldfish-eating."[5] To Richard Hovey it is a "grotesquerie,"[6] and Arthur Waldhorn joins others in judging it "a grotesque tale."[7] Many of the most extensive studies on Hemingway have utterly ignored it, and it exists in major commentary largely in remarks of dismissal. Yet, when Klaus Mann reacted to "An Alpine Idyll" and "A Simple Enquiry" in the *Neue Schweitzer Rundschau* in 1931, he said, "They are masterworks . . . extracts from life in which each word is loaded with destiny. The essence is bitter, but wonderfully strong." Hemingway's style, to Mann, was "Nothing other than a miracle."[8] Carlos Baker, recognizing Hemingway's metaphoric structure, suggested that one should read the story "with as much awareness, and as closely, as one would read a good modern poem,"[9] and surely he is right. It is Joseph Flora who has seen this most fully, recognizing that "An Alpine Idyll" is a story "about perceiving stories," and that, within the confines of the story, only one, like Hemingway, sensitive to what is being said, can interpret it, for "the narrator knows better than to accept conventional interpretation."[10] If Flora is right, and I think he is—his work on "An Alpine Idyll" is very perceptive—

Hemingway readers must bring new poetic attentiveness to this familiar tale and a healthy skepticism toward existing critical responses.

Among those who have lingered to study aspects of the tale, there has been an almost fastidious revulsion from its central image. The story was initially turned down by *Scribner's* magazine for being "too terrible"— Robert Bridges believed it would be "too hard a blow for the magazine"[11]— and Baker himself, despite his interest in the tale, spoke of the peasant's "inhuman lack of feeling for his wife" and indicated his belief that the tale itself grew out of a taste "for the macabre."[12] Richard Hovey speaks of the story's anaesthetization and dehumanization of love "through habit and routine."[13] Bern Oldsey speaks of "the peasant brutality and coarseness" of the tale.[14] Charles Fenton names it "a brutal short story,"[15] and Kenneth Lynn calls it "a particularly brutal and guilt-drenched story" and refers to Olz in it as "a bestial Austrian peasant" with "an oafish name."[16] Raymond S. Nelson describes Olz's "stolid imbecility" as "only a few cuts above Neanderthal man."[17] Such comments on what is read as the callousness of the peasant and his act, or on what is taken to be an immature desire to shock on Hemingway's part, accordingly account in part for the scant attention paid. As Joseph Flora said, "the story seemed to many too anecdotal, merely a study in the bizarre."[18]

Yet, Carlos Baker is among those who have seen more in "An Alpine Idyll." He readily recognizes that it is only "apparently" a "simple tale," and that it is Chekhov-like. Baker's deeper appreciation comes from his peripheral recognition of the iceberg: "the story is not 'about' the peasant."[19] The story's aspirations or literary pretensions seem to have been perceived most by those who read it fresh in the 1920s. The editors at *Scribner's* magazine recognized that it was "like certain stories by Chekhov and Gorky."[20] Ezra Pound, early in 1927, responding to this story that Hemingway had sent him for inclusion in *Exile*, after it had been turned down by *Scribner's*, commented, "this is a good story (Idyll) but a leetle litterary and Tennysonian. I wish you wd. keep your eye on the objek more, and be less Licherary."[21] How later Hemingway critics, who were censuring the story's brutality and coarseness, accommodated themselves to Pound's sense of its Tennysonian echoes is unknown, but Pound's comment reveals his ready recognition of the story's ambitions. Kenneth Lynn felt that Pound's criticism of "An Alpine Idyll," where he charged Hemingway with "following too closely 'in the wake of H.J. [Henry James],'" was suggesting that Hemingway "carried his Jamesian facility for talk too far and allowed his characters to indulge in more of it than was wise."[22] Still, such recognitions of the story's aesthetic aspirations are few, and even among those who have studied the story with some care, much more typical have been comments that dismiss it without really having come to terms with it. Edward

Hattam, who is listed in Jackson Benson's bibliography for the story[23] as having the single existing article on the story as of 1966,[24] treats the story of the peasant as a "tall-tale" told by the villagers to make fools of outsiders, while Fraser Sutherland finds the irony of the story "laid on so thick as to be slab-like."[25]

Undoubtedly its bizarre eccentricity of subject is partly responsible for this fate, but the passivity of its narrator and his friend, who seem in the story to be there merely as witnesses to the tale about another, who is only peripherally seen and not understood by anyone in the story, is also responsible for critical oversight. This is ironic for, in a way, the story is Hemingway's art carried to its perfection: the story's epiphany remains unstated, the story's meaning remains implicit, its point of view rests unemphasized, but all are carefully, elaborately established.

To enunciate the structure and significant imagery of the story, it will be necessary to retell it in part, stressing and citing details. The story seems another "Cross-Country Snow," but here Nick and, this time, his friend John have descended from the high Silvretta country where they have been skiing for a month.[26] Unlike the other story, which ends with the protagonists still up in the mountains and lamenting what they see as their necessary descent and only looking forward to further skiing at some time in the future, Nick and John have on this occasion been "up" too long, and are suffering from the effects of too much sun. In the high country they had not been able to get away from the sun, and it had finally spoiled the snow, creating "spring skiing," where the snow was only good in the early morning and again in the evening. This sun, in which they could not rest, has made them tired of skiing and, aware they have stayed too long, John declares, "You oughtn't to do anything too long," and Nick agrees, "No. We were up there too long." To this, John, seemingly unnecessarily continues, "Too damn long. . . . It's no good doing a thing too long."[27] Their repetitions, like their ski runs, have become almost unconscious and drain the vitality from statement as from experience: their style of expression begins to establish the meaning of the piece. They are, therefore, finally, unlike Nick and George of "Cross-Country Snow," glad to be down in the valley and glad that there are other things in life besides skiing. Nick admits that the high mountain spring seemed to him "unnatural" when measured against "this May morning in the valley." The "too much sun" up above has ruined things.

As the two companions come down into the valley, they pass a churchyard where a priest, departing from a burial service in the yard, bows to them but does not speak, a fact that John makes much of: "a priest never speaks to you. . . . They never answer." In the churchyard a sexton and a peasant are completing the burial of the peasant's wife, the peasant finally "spreading the earth evenly" on her grave, "as a man spreading manure in a garden." Later, drinking together with the innkeeper and the sexton in the taproom of the inn, the boys learn that the peasant's wife had died "last December" and has only now, in May, been brought down to the soft earth of the valley for burial. It has only been possible to bring the body down from on high for burial since the snow has melted and gone. There is no mystery about the wife's death—she died of heart trouble that everyone knew she had—but there is a mystery about the radical deformation of her features, and the sexton tells of the priest's demand that Olz, the peasant, reveal the cause. It is Olz's confession, however slight, that is at the heart of Hemingway's story; all other details of Nick and John's skiing and their drinking together in the inn are secondary to their reaction to this tale.

Olz tells how, after properly reporting his wife's death to the authorities, he had placed her body in his woodshed across the top of the big wood, but that when he started to use this wood, he had had to move her and then had placed her "up against the wall."[28] Her mouth was open, and when he came into the shed and had no place to hang the lantern, he "hung the lantern from it." The reader is the one, along with Nick and John, to imagine the gradual effect of this often-repeated process. The grotesque deformation of the woman's mouth is a result of her husband's need for light, which she, finally rigid and no longer supple, supports. Despite this "use" of his wife, Olz affirms that he "loved her fine." The innkeeper, who has elicited the story from the sexton, thrice declares such peasants to be "beasts" and tells Nick and John thrice that they "wouldn't believe" the story he is about to have revealed to them. Hemingway's story ends with John first interrupting the tale, "How about eating?" and then again, interrupting its conclusion, "Say . . . how about eating?" and Nick responding "All right."

Some of the readers of this seemingly perverse little tale have seen the point of it all as another stage in the gradual hardening of the boys to life's painful ironies and tragedies: "in our time," they affirm, one is gradually inured to the bizarre and horrible and gets on with the business of life in spite of it. Young has argued that "Nick is hardening a little. . . . A shell is growing over the wound to protect it a little,"[29] and Bhim Dahiya seconds Young on this.[30] Surely, John is shown throughout to be far less sensitive than Nick: he is largely concerned with sleeping and eating; he falls asleep with his head on his arms soon after they enter the inn, while Nick is apparently sensitively and meticulously noting the details of the room, the table, the people in the room, and the world beyond the room that can be seen through the window.[31] John does not awaken when the sexton and the peasant enter the room to drink or when the girl takes or brings orders or when the innkeeper comes to their table, but rather only when the girl brings the menu: "The girl brought the menu. John woke up." He has not bothered to learn much of the language of the country; he tunes out of the tale being told: "I can't understand it, anyway. . . . It goes too fast for me."

In radical contrast, the narrator has carefully noted the peasant's final *conscious* disregard of the sexton with whom he had earlier drunk a traditional drink—for which he insists on paying, *"Alles,"* before leaving for another inn, the Löwen[32]—and Nick has carefully studied the peasant's disregard of others and everything in the room. The peasant is described as ignoring the innkeeper and not seeming to see the waitress, though she stands beside him, and twice he is described as looking out the window. His attention and his respect seem pointedly to be located elsewhere. That they are placed beyond the room itself, in the landscape beyond the window where Nick's attention also has come to rest, suggests a genuine bond between peasant and Nick that goes unexamined and unstated. Hemingway has, on the other hand, with precision, in pointed contrast to the peasant's apparent unconsciousness, placed on display John's real unconsciousness.

In "An Alpine Idyll" we are asked to solve the riddle of the psychological source of the peasant's behavior with his wife's body and also his detachment in the inn, as well as the reason for the innkeeper's excess, and in every case, we are being taught by the writer that what seems is not what is. The black-bearded, high-booted, primitive peasant, who lives isolately alone far from others "on the other side" and who is throughout much of the year apparently totally cut off from contact with the world below, obviously has his own proud and emphatic code of values. Hemingway, who is careful about the meaning of such things, makes him the only one in the room to drink pure spirits; he orders schnapps while the others consume beer and wine. Intriguingly, the peasant is the only one associated with both love—"I loved her fine"—and war—"He wore his old army clothes." Nick has earlier noted how "evenly" Olz spread the earth upon his wife's grave. (Although Nick has returned to the valley to find "many letters" awaiting *him,* at no moment is the reader given any sense of the source of these—his human relations, except with John, remain a mystery.) The peasant is also the only one who is native to the area who is carefully defined as belonging both to the mountains and to the valley: "He lives on the other side of the Paznaun," we are told, "But he belongs to this parish." Seemingly coarse and crudely dressed, yet with patches on his elbows to suggest the care that he takes or that was taken with his person, he is nonetheless denounced as a "beast" by the innkeeper and condescended to by the sexton.

It is on the judgment of Olz that everything turns.[33] Certainly this point is the one that radically divides the critics. Most of them, as described, read him, as do the sexton and innkeeper, as bestial and crude. Even Carlos Baker, whose reading is often sensitive, tries in every way to make excuses for him. Baker urges that the reader recognize Olz "has lived too long in an unnatural situation," and that "his sense of human dignity and decency has temporarily atrophied." It must be Baker's need to absolve this man somehow of the terribleness of his deed that leads Baker to announce, "When he gets down into the valley, where it is spring and people are living naturally and wholesomely, he sees how far he has strayed from the natural and wholesome, and he is deeply ashamed of himself." There is certainly little natural and wholesome about either sexton or innkeeper, and there is no way to substantiate this deep shame that Baker infers. To support it, Baker regards Olz's exposure to the priest and sexton as a "coming to judgment" and describes the "unspoken shame of the peasant, who could not get away from the open staring eye of the 'natural' people who in a sense brought him to judgment."[34] I find small justification for this reading—just where do we see this sense of shame?—except perhaps the critic's wish to exonerate or cleanse the peasant of what is judged to be his terrible guilt.

In contrast to Baker, Myra Armistead urges in her essay on the tale that the reader note "the *valley people* (emphasis mine) have been telling and hearing [such] tales too long and have been insensitive to the feeling of their fellow men."[35] She perceptively points out the prejudice and lack of courtesy in the innkeeper, and she suggests that the attack on the peasant has its own covert motivations. John Atkins, also on the minority side, perceptively remarks, "There is a simplicity about the story and a dignity about the peasant which appeals ... to me. . . . It did not occur to the peasant that he was outraging his wife's body putting it to such obvious use." He refers to the peasant's love as "the crude, unsensational kind of love which exists among people who live hard, inarticulate lives."[36] This reading is given support by Hemingway's first wife, Hadley R. Mowrer, who in a letter of 11 February 1965 wrote, "The rough mountain peasants of these Alpine regions *would* joke about the frozen corpses awaiting springtime burial."[37]

J. Bakker argues that "Love has nothing to do with conventional morality, and this is probably the 'point' of the story."[38] He portrays the peasant as one bewildered by the priest's morality since, from his own set of values, he had not wronged his wife. Charles Fenton presupposes Hemingway's "revulsion at the peasant's callous treatment of his wife's corpse,"[39] but Joseph DeFalco writes that "The peasant's unawareness of having done something unnatural indicates his own absolute coming to terms with death. . . . The point is, he has accepted her death. Those who criticize him cannot accept naturally the knowledge of death; in fact for them outward form has all the importance in any situation."[40] Joseph Flora also tries to put reaction straight: "humor and disgust are not ... the only possible responses to the story Nick has heard." Flora acknowledges that "there have been moments in 'An Alpine Idyll' when Olz has appeared to invite more sympathy than curiosity. . . . Who is to say how another man might deal with grief?"[41]

Hemingway's portraits of innkeeper, sexton, John, and the priest are as carefully drawn as those of Chaucer's pilgrims, and they are meant to invite our moral judgment. The innkeeper is quickly revealed to be a rather noisy and intrusive busybody, who almost sneeringly takes delight in eliciting and spreading about the story of the tragedy. But the reader is expected to note additionally that the innkeeper insists on labeling the others as unbelievers before the tale, that he quickly, loosely generalizes—"All these peasants are beasts"—and that he bridles when corrected in his inaccuracies:

> "She died last November."
> "December," said the sexton.
> "That makes nothing. She died last December then . . ."

Economically, Hemingway has revealed something important about the imprecisions of the innkeeper and his edginess when contradicted, while he has also introduced a hovering sense of the language in which they speak: the awkward "that makes nothing" readily suggests the probable *"Mach's nichts"* or *"Das macht nichts"* of the actual exchange. When Nick asks what there is to eat the innkeeper replies, in what the reader should begin to see is his characteristic failure to relate reality and the mind's creations, "Anything you want. The girl will bring the eating-card."[42] The waitress when she arrives is shown to be almost too easily affable and also intrusive. The sexton, who is the only one in the room actually by role associated with the church, and who yet is familiarly addressed by his name, Franz, labels what the reader comes more and more to see as the pathetic encounter between Olz and the priest only as "very funny." When asked by Nick what he will drink, the sexton refuses, "Nothing," while shaking his finger; but when pressed, "Another quarter litre?," he immediately yields: "All right." Apparently neither his words nor his gestures mean much, and the turnabout is meant to seem appropriate for a man who has just drunk Olz's wine and is now about to share it with his enemy.

Early in the story John had noted that Nick's spoken greeting to the priest in the churchyard had been answered only by a bow: "It's funny a priest never speaks to you." The silent response of the priest is meant to be heard against the garrulity and intrusive affability in the inn. These details that Hemingway delicately places with these slightest of touches establish that the curious group in the inn, who laugh at the tragedy, who gain status by what they know of the tale, and who gossip almost leeringly over the sinister details, have no insight whatsoever into the peasant's psychology or values, as they also have none of his pride. John, on the other hand, who ignores the language he does not understand while remaining focused steadily on sleeping or eating, could far more readily be styled the "beast" of the piece. It is only the priest, the man of God in this valley village who apparently has the official role to deal with the problem of the events that have taken place high above in the unmelting snows, who is kept apart and by that separation made to seem of another order. Against the intrusive and eager desire to relay gossip on the part of the innkeeper and sexton, his initial reluctance to communicate with Nick and John comes to seem to define his integrity. As befitting a man of God, a keeper of the secrets of the confessional, his silences, like Olz's silences and like those high, cold, and removed heights from which Olz has come, speak of detachment from the world. If this detachment seems alienating and cold, it but reinforces Olz's own seeming distance from normal human sentiment.

The mouth of the woman is a finely focused metaphor, relating as it does to the process of eating as well as to the spoken, but notably not written, word. Throughout the story the spoken word is often found as gossip, as a calumnious means of inaccurately judging others. The two silent people of the story are the priest and Olz, neither of whom is related to food. The most gross and bestial of those pictured is John, who ends the story as he keeps urging Nick to accept food. The metaphors of the story tell that, pointedly, death suspends natural process. The mouth of the wife that dealt with words and food is at last stilled. This momentary arrest of process by death would normally be followed by decay and rot.[43] However, here it becomes unnatural suspension. In the story it really is nature itself, the seasonal return of spring, that urges that the cycles of life and death are unremitting, that death must find burial that out of it may come birth again: it is on an early spring morning that the boys watch the peasant spreading the earth over his wife's buried body "as a man spreading manure in the garden." There is a primal necessity for the end products of the eating process and for life itself to become at last the fertilizers of life. In the very end of the cycle the cycle is affirmed; death leads toward birth.

There seems to be a double meaning in the use to which the wife's mouth is put and what seems the almost deliberate deformation of that mouth by her husband who, although he "loved her fine," goes about his solitary business apparently unconscious of the effect upon her that his needs cause. The mouth of the wife is altered from an emblem of process into a seemingly dependable source of light, and it is by this means that Olz can carry out his lonely tasks. The transformation suggests a victory over process, albeit one achieved through censurable detachment. But it is just as much a victory of absolutism and immortality over mortality as the frozen wife at a great height, become at last a source of light, seems a victory of the spirit over the flesh. The real irony of "An Alpine Idyll" is that the seemingly callous and bestial Olz metaphorically participates in what seems a transcendent mastery of process. His repetitive movement of light rather than food to the mouth of his fixed wife metaphorically reads as a spiritualization of the physical. The dead woman, as undecaying, unchanging bearer of the light, has become in the poetics of the piece almost an icon of spiritual absolutism, of escape, however temporary, from the eternal wheel of existence. The reader should note how often such "spiritualizations" historically end in suspended death: eighteenth-century gardeners, reaching toward the "ideal" in the geometric patterns toward which they disciplined their plants, learned to replace aberrant life with fixed, colored gravel.

The delayed burial and Olz's retention and suspension of the dead woman, whom he keeps out of the processes of rot and decay at a great height, interrupt natural expectation and create an unnatural situation. But Olz unnaturally lives in an unnatural situation: he lives remote from mankind and without those connections and relations that might humanize his life. In that world of his, the unmelting snow is basically responsible. Hemingway has carefully established that there is complicity between nature and man, between the seasons and heights and snows and the alienation and estrangement from mankind inside man himself, as he has added to the priest's avoidances and silences and Olz's detachment and abandonment of the inn the setting of Austria that is also an actor in the drama. For a man to remain as Olz does for long at that high, skiing height, where the snows are unmelting, in itself is to exist in a bizarre state, and that elevation, keeping him "too long" away from those seasonal alterations and changes associated with natural process, seems a cause of monstrosity. If Olz lives in this unnatural world, the boys have been in it themselves "too long" and have equally suffered for their habitation of that world. In "Cross-Country Snow," Hemingway had let his readers recognize the unnaturalness of his protagonists' reluctance to give up their skiing: life "isn't worth while if you can't [ski]" rings strongly with an absurdity against the deferred responsibilities of fatherhood and life that await Nick below. Similarly, there is an absurd discrepancy sensed between Olz's "I loved her fine" and the actual use to which the body of the beloved wife was put.

In art, concrete detail serves thematic ends, and story is often parable. Olz has gone so far beyond his once well-loved wife that she merely at last serves to support his observation of other reality. Nick is meant to be led to reflection by the tale of Olz, as are we. Olz *seems* a common peasant who feels nothing as he uses his wife's inert body to hold his light, and *that* light seemingly serves no noble or abstract end, used as it is only that the brute man may keep himself warm. The terrible image of the deformed mouth is patently placed to shock, and the shock of horror is meant to be there, in part to tell us how quickly we forget, distort, and get beyond the source of our recognitions, how rapidly we put behind us the means to our transcendence. To take this to another level, we might reflect on how quickly experience becomes word becomes experience of the word and then neglect. Certainly Olz's silences and avoidances should not be taken for lack of feeling or guilt, nor should the image of the mouth merely elicit contempt and scorn against Olz. The loquacious ones in this story seem particularly unqualified to pronounce on feelings, and the wife's deformed mouth, if rather horrifying, is also poignant. Implicit in the peasant's act and in the deformed image is more than the transcendence of process, rather a victory akin to an artist's victory over matter; and also importantly implicit in it are a seeming loss of humanity and the desecration of the bond with the feminine—the cost of that victory. Olz is neither artist nor intellectual, but he may well paint a moral and teach a lesson to Nick, who has perhaps remained too long away from those who await him, or to any artist who may never have known fear of an artist's abstraction and the cost of it. "An Alpine Idyll" is fundamentally a story about the creative process and its human cost. The woman's deformed mouth as its central image is brilliant and unerringly right.

The artist's godlike creative function makes him or her precisely the one to sacrifice nature to personal ends: the greater such idealism and the more rarefied such vision, the more fantasy and imagination play fast and loose with nature and the greater the deformations nature suffers. The artist is ever the one who, in often serene detachment and necessary transcendence of materials can, like Whistler, paint a picture of his mother as merely "An Arrangement in Grey and Black," and can, like Hawthorne's and Poe's artists and scientists and imaginative adventurers, translate living flesh to a tone, a pigment, an area of color, a balance on a canvas, or a formal compositional problem. Hawthorne's Aylmer of "The Birthmark" and his Ethan Brand, and Poe's narrator of "Ligeia" and his artist of "The Oval Portrait," all sacrifice their women, however loved, to their absolutist fantasies of art or of high, cold abstract perfection. In the work of Edgar Allan Poe a host of Ligeias and women on rue Morgues are the cost of their or their narrators' broken ties with the real world and their unworldly desire to transcend the cycles of earthly process. Master of horror, Poe is also the writer who most fully explores the murderous cost of the imaginative creator's inhuman, creative vanity. Nathaniel Hawthorne's "Man in the Steeple" well knew that although he could gain a better and more accurate detached view of the world from his height, he *had* to descend finally and rejoin mankind in the streets below. Hemingway, who studied the problem, never doubted that the descent to the valley was the necessary balance for the mountain journey.

If I have argued for recognition of the aesthetic paradigm in the peasant's act, both Joseph Flora, in his pioneering study, and Ann Putnam, in her recent representation of Flora's arguments, [44] argue forcefully for reading Nick in "An Alpine Idyll" as the writer and artist who, in detachment and objective assessment of what he sees, is creating the materials out of which his stories will come. Joseph Flora contends that "An Alpine Idyll" is "an example of the artist's temperament—really the artist at work"—that it essentially is "the story of the coming into being of a story." He admits that, "By extension, the story asks how people can treat those they love in the frightful ways they sometimes do," and he acknowledges that "it is a major theme of the short stories," but, finally, he knows that the question we are left with at the end is "what to do with a story."[45] This is Nick's problem, and he has been observing it carefully, considering the framing and placing and structuring and disposition of the elements of the tale he is being given in every nuance and gesture that he has skeptically yet precisely observed.

Hemingway was not extolling those who manage to escape natural process any more than he was extolling the somewhat cowardly and selfish Nick and George of "Cross-Country Snow" or the vapid men of "Cat in the Rain" and "Hills Like White Elephants" for having held off the natural desires of their consorts. Hemingway always knew how necessary was the flight of his creator protagonists toward the high places apart, the tops of Kilimanjaros, where imaginative life, briefly separated from processes of rot and decay, or the disciplining and informing limitations of reality, might court its separatist dreams. He also knew that this way lay death and that too long and sustained a flight into rarefied ether—or simple expatriate rootlessness, as with Catherine and David on the Riviera in *The Garden of Eden*—could be unnatural and deadly. Eternity had to be bound to *now*, just as expatriate rootlessness finally needed authentic and native roots. Hemingway knew this as readily as Keats, who knew to "wreathe a flowery band" to bind him to the earth as he set out on his own celestial journey in *Endymion*. Only in death could Harry of "The Snows of Kilimanjaro" reach and remain at the sunstruck top of the Mountain of God in an extended and unbroken fantasy that would be the mountain's immortal equivalent.

There is a way in which "An Alpine Idyll" seems to be one of Hemingway's most poignant and most psychologically necessary statements, a work that at this point in his life he had to write. The deformed mouth of the woman arrested in natural process signals at once a violation she did not feel, being in her death beyond suffering, and a monstrosity in the husband who kept her there at that unnatural height, supporting his own needs and functions. That one emblem, the deformed mouth, speaks in "An Alpine Idyll" of the human and natural cost of an unnaturally prolonged victory over the cycles of nature. Bizarre and terrible as it is as an image, it affirms fully and directly, if metaphorically, Hemingway's aesthetic recognition of the human cost of his art. It is important, in an understanding of Olz and of Hemingway and of the artist behind the tale, to emphasize that Olz manipulates dead matter, that he deals with human but insentient materials, that his needs bring him to use human and emotionally bound materials, the mouth of his dead and beloved wife, toward abstract ends, those of illumination, and that such use implies distortion of them. Olz, however crude, stands in for the artist at work. Not as fastidious a statement, but one similar to Henry James's "Maude Evelyn," Hemingway's story allows his readers to fall into the banalities of the sexton and the innkeeper as it seemingly endorses their harsh judgments of Olz. Like "Cat in the Rain," however, "An Alpine Idyll" leads us to and through a series of revealing questions that could well apply to either story: Does the writer share the husband's callousness? Is the writer insensitive to the wife's plight? Could an insensitive man create such a structure? Is not one of the most interesting aspects the extent to which the story invites the pillorying of the character who seems biographically an extension of the author? In these stories, as in all his work, Hemingway is harder on himself and more rigorously moral than the vast majority of his readers. Such stories come out of the artist's careful, meticulous consideration of the relations between life and art and also out of guilt for his art's effect upon his life.

As the story is read back onto Hemingway, with that unavoidable and intrusive biographical interest so often unfortunately brought to his works, the critic wants to acknowledge the events surrounding its composition in the first days of May 1926. Immediately and inescapably the story seems a mea culpa for all the unnatural distortions of natural life that Hemingway's writer's life had brought to Hadley, and this is the way Kenneth Lynn would prefer to read the story. He writes, "Out of this troubling confrontation [with Hadley over his infidelity with Pauline] Hemingway produced, around the first of May, a particularly brutal and guilt-drenched story called 'An Alpine Idyll,' in which he symbolically dramatized both his callous treatment of Hadley as nothing more than a convenience to him during their months together in wintry Schruns and the effective burial of their marriage in springtime France."[46] Lynn is so enamored of his biographically manipulated reading that he repeats it at length in an April 1988 interview in *Johns Hopkins Magazine*.[47] However, Hemingway's emotional problems compounded with his aesthetic ones went far deeper than his guilt for infidelity or clandestine romance, as careful psychoanalytic readers can see in "Cat in the Rain," "Hills Like White Elephants," and "Out of Season." The artist's guilt, as he achieves abstract creativity at what seems the cost of the sterility of his biologically unreproductive wife in *The Garden of Eden*, is vividly to be seen in the holograph version of that work. And if Harry in "The Snows of Kilimanjaro" at last leaves Helen below together with his seemingly debrided, rotting, gangrened leg while he flies off in imaginative, deathlike fantasy to the sun-drenched top of the Mountain of God, the story as gesture seems a desperate acknowledgement of the lengths to which the artist may be driven to seize immortality in art out of otherwise wasted life. It is easy enough to speak of guilt for treatment of Pauline on safari, but that is not the whole of the story.

If the critic perhaps rightly refuses to be led from the work by biography, he or she nevertheless may see Nick—as the boy become man become that older man who leaves his skiing at last to descend and pick up those many letters that await him in the valley inn—as a man who has better things to do than ski, who has learned through trying too long that to extend a brief flight into an extended and then unnaturally extended time in the sun can have a genuine human cost, in the detachment and distance the human emotions may take from normal patterns of behavior. This more mature Nick may be able to acknowledge that he can unknowingly have become to others, in his detachment, monstrous.

What makes the story classic Hemingway is the extent to which it recapitulates or phrases patterns and metaphors that are present throughout the Hemingway canon. Two young men without women, rootless in a country not their own, have been enjoying themselves in the camaraderie of shared delight in techniques practiced with care and precision somewhere beyond civilized society, in nature. This describes the young skiers of "Cross-Country Snow" or the hunters of *Green Hills* or the fishermen of *The Sun Also Rises*, even as they epitomize the detachment and pride and satisfaction gained in such mastery and disengagement. Also in the story is a woman who has been taken out of process, removed from the usual terms of decay and rot that accompany life and death, and who in her rigidity and fixity within a medium of flow (water), held in a state of momentary suspension (snow), is inverted into being the basis and seeming source of light. Hemingway's works reveal this seemingly intricate pattern as recurring. At the end of *A Farewell to Arms*, Catherine, like her namesake who died on the wheel, is seemingly also martyred on the biological wheel she cannot escape. Turning toward her fulfillment within the seasons, she dies in time and in a falling rain that her wish for an immortality of "always" in love cannot control. Martyred on the cyclical, reproductive wheel to which she is tied, she nevertheless is last seen by Frederic as a statue, a woman of marble who, in his imagination, we are led to observe, has become the light which has led him to tell the tale the reader has just read. She in her achieved absoluteness remains in Frederic's mind to take him beyond the momentary, cyclical rain in which he walks away toward the abstract words he has finally fixed upon the novel's pages. Similarly, the peasant's wife remains in Nick's imagination, however John may impel him toward the absolving unreflectiveness of another momentary, cyclical meal. She also seems to remain in the mind of the peasant who has little to say to others and only looks out the window, like the Italian major in "In Another Country" whose wife has also died. With the melting of the snows of Les Avants above Montreux, the lovers in *A Farewell to Arms* are forced to descend from their unnatural sustained idyll to what will become again the turning, seasonal wheel of restored natural life in which Catherine will necessarily die, her abstract wishes for arrested time and immortal love destroyed by reality. Nick in "An Alpine Idyll" regards the high, alpine spring as "unnatural," and he and John descend from there to the fertile valley.

It is out of *arrested* cycles that the Hemingway hero again and again seizes his transcendent vision. Robert Jordan finds within a cycle of three days an eternity, and he realizes his "always" in the orgasmic "now" of love. Nick in "Indian Camp" takes from the fact of death in a place of birth a sense of immortality. Harry, in "The Snows of Kilimanjaro," realizes his imaginative visions and seizes his immortality only in a moment that is equivalent to his death. Such a moment can only be snatched from the jaws and claws of the hyenas and vultures, the predators who, in feasting on the dead, exemplify the eternally turning round of process in whose inescapable midst the dreamer contemplates the mountain. Stories like "Hills Like White Elephants" and "Cat in the Rain" have men who, in their detached existence or in dedication to abstract heights of imaginative speculation, try to take their women out of time by arresting their fecundity.

The holograph manuscript version of *The Garden of Eden* makes abundantly clear that Catherine's masculinization of herself, and her sun worship, are ways she tries to deal with David's inability to beget a child, and that they are ways that take her off the potentially fecund, feminine, biological Catherine wheel. David as artist is a man so given to his high, abstract speculations practiced in his abstracted expatriate life that he has effectively arrested natural process for Catherine. Catherine recognizes her fixity, her removal from the wheel of life, as the cost of his art, but as she tries to find compensation and a means of imitating David, she overly gives herself to the sun, and, like Nick and John of this story, who have also been up in the cruel sun too long, she has effectively sterilized her life relations. Brett in *The Sun Also Rises* leaves behind her a trail of ashes and the incantatory refrain, "rot," to remind the reader that this Circe indeed is the very wheel that Jake wants to get off or learn how to control.[48] Stopping the room from wheeling is part of that exercise for which his dephallused state has prepared him; it is also precisely what the peasant has managed to do as he has retained his frozen woman. Hemingway's title for his first novel names his mythic and desperate attempt to immerse the fixed, Apollonian sun in cycles that permit it the period of death and darkness that joins it with life. It is equivalent to the valley journey that must finally be added to the period of arrest at high, immortal heights.

"An Alpine Idyll" is an early exercise that carefully studies how the sun-given skiers must initially abandon the cycles of the valley world to explore an alternative world where indeed rot and process can be arrested, suspended and momentarily escaped. But they stay there too long. John reminds Nick that, to him, nothing is good sustained too long, and this avoidance of continued states labels John's fear of absolutes and his fundamental carnality. The supposedly beastly peasant, who remains above and beyond the snows through most of the year and who translates what would normally be the rotting body of his dead wife into a repetitive source of light, by that act seems one who successfully masters the earth's eternal cycles. The reader's instinctive revulsion from the image of the cost of this "success" and Hemingway's placement of horror at the center of such disregard for process tell us what we need to know. The plot reveals not expiation but the restoration of order in nature. A day in spring, pointedly a day in May—that begins with a day dedicated to revolution and to celebration of eternally renewing spring—amends December's seeming eternity of death maintained in a state like life. It does so as the husband spreads the "new earth" upon his wife's grave as though he were "spreading manure in a garden," as though he were bringing the products of natural process to nature to renew the reproductive cycle.

Throughout the story, with the slightest of touches, Hemingway has noted the need to balance abstract and physical worlds. As Nick sees the burial taking place on this beautiful spring day, he can "not imagine anyone being dead," but he immediately says to John, "Imagine being buried on a day like this." When John replies, "I wouldn't like it," Nick responds, "Well, . . . we don't have to *do* it." The shift he insists on noting is from imagining to doing. Later, John confesses that "Up in the hut I used to *think* about [beer] a lot," and Nick responds, "Well, we've *got* it now." Such suggestions of the distance between abstraction and reality, the speculative and the physical worlds, help underwrite the basic theme of abstraction from natural process.

This theme is augmented by the innkeeper's revealed distance between himself and fact and further augmented by Nick's minute observations through the window of the world beyond the inn. He sees the mill and the water wheel and the saw in the mill rising and falling, and he notes that the mill, like an inhuman process, seems to be operating with no one tending it. He also notes dust on the leaves and crows in the grass and sunlight passing through the empty glasses on the table inside the inn where he is sitting. This sight, which reconciles inside and outside, rising and falling, earth and sky, and which insists we note how birds descend and how dust rises, prefigures the fundamental religious and psychic meaning of the tale, the need for fixity in flow, eternity in time, and the transcendent spirit in the realm of the rotting flesh. Urging food on Nick as the story ends, John is calling for the burial of the image of the frozen lady just as emphatically as spring called for the physical burial of the real but suspended woman. The valley journey, metaphorically suggesting as it does the acceptance of and immersion in the feminine, certainly seems in Hemingway's psyche to be the necessary therapeutic balance to the sunstruck mountain vision of his men.

Notes

1. "An Alpine Idyll" was completed during the first days of May 1926. Already by the fifth of May Hemingway had dispatched it to Max Perkins for submission to *Scribner's* magazine for publication. When the story returned from them in June, rejected, Jeffrey Meyers tells us that Hemingway apparently sent it on to the Communist *New Masses*, which rejected it in turn in the fall of 1926. Undoubtedly, Hemingway then submitted it to Pound for inclusion in *Exile*, for we have Pound's letter of 21 December 1926, in which he discusses the too "licherary" story. Carlos Baker informs us that, at the publisher's request, on 21 January 1927, Hemingway sent his story on to Alfred Kreymborg, who took the story for his *American Caravan*, where it was first published. It was subsequently included by Hemingway in his *Men Without Women*, published on 14 October 1927. Baker ascribed the source of the tale to Hemingway's conversations in Schruns with Fräulein Gläser, who, according to Baker, had a taste for the macabre and had often talked to Hemingway about death and suicide.

2. Carlos Baker, *Hemingway: The Writer as Artist* (Princeton: Princeton UP , 1972) 119.

3. That such attention is now about to be paid was abundantly clear at the June 1988 Third International Hemingway Conference in Schruns, Austria, where the story was used as the centerpiece to focus the discussion of a heavily attended seminar on manuscripts and textual studies.

4. Scott Donaldson, *By Force of Will: The Life and Art of Ernest Hemingway* (New York: Penguin, 1978) 284.

5. Jackson J. Benson, *The Writer's Art of Self-Defense* (Minneapolis: U of Minnesota P, 1969) 54–55.

6. Richard B. Hovey, *Hemingway: The Inward Terrain* (Seattle: U of Washington P, 1968) 9.

7. Arthur Waldhorn, *A Reader's Guide to Ernest Hemingway* (New York: Farrar, Straus and Giroux, 1972) 37.

8. Quoted in Wayne E. Kvam, *Hemingway in Germany* (Athens: Ohio UP, 1973) 5–6

9. Baker, 121.

10. Joseph M. Flora, *Hemingway's Nick Adams* (Baton Rouge: Louisiana State UP, 1982) 208.

11. In Carlos Baker, *Ernest Hemingway: A Life Story* (New York: Charles Scribner's Sons, 1969) 171.

12. Baker, *Life*, 168.

13. Hovey, 9.

14. Bernard Oldsey, "The Snows of Ernest Hemingway," in *Ernest Hemingway: A Collection of Criticism*, ed. Arthur Waldhorn (New York: McGraw-Hill Paperbacks, 1973) 68.

15. Charles A. Fenton, *The Apprenticeship of Ernest Hemingway: The Early Years* (New York: Viking Press, 1954) 167.

16. Kenneth S. Lynn, *Hemingway* (New York: Simon and Schuster, 1987) 341–42.

17. Raymond S. Nelson, *Hemingway: Expressionist Artist* (Ames: Iowa State UP, 1979) 30.

18. Flora, 198.

19. Baker, *The Writer as Artist*, 119–20.

20. Baker, *Life*, 171.

21. Quoted in Jacqueline Tavernier-Courbin, "Ernest Hemingway and Ezra Pound," in *Ernest Hemingway: The Writer in Context*, ed. James Nagel (Madison: U of Wisconsin P, 1984) 183.

22. Lynn, 328.

23. Jackson J. Benson, *The Short Stories of Ernest Hemingway: Critical Essays* (Durham: Duke UP, 1975) 333.

24. Edward Hattam, "Hemingway's 'An Alpine Idyll,'" *Modern Fiction Studies* 12 (Summer 1966): 261–65.

25. Fraser Sutherland, *The Style of Innocence: A Study of Hemingway and Callaghan* (Toronto and Vancouver: Clark & Irwin, 1972) 42.

26. There is every reason why the unnamed narrator of the story should be regarded as being Nick, the somewhat older and more mature Nick of "Cross-Country Snow" and the other Nick Adams stories. Surely, it is not insignificant that he goes unnamed, and that fact should be stressed and interpreted, but there are many reasons why Hemingway meant the reader and critic to read into this narrator the history and sensibility of Nick Adams. Philip Young firmly declares of "An Alpine Idyll" and "The Killers," "The I of these stories is Nick Adams," and of the former he says, "the story is utterly without a 'point' if not seen in the context of the other [Nick Adams] stories." Young sees that the story's "focus . . . centers on the responses of the listeners. A change in their responses is the point" (Philip Young, *Ernest Hemingway: A Reconsideration* [University Park: Pennsylvania State U P, 1966] 59–60). His reading places the story in the corpus of Nick Adams stories and as a necessary and further stage in the development of Nick's awareness. Since Young judges that as its main function, for him it has no other "point" if not so seen. Joseph Flora seconds him, arguing, "On this point [Young] has been largely ignored, and that is unfortunate." Noting the great number of correspondences with "Cross-Country Snow," Flora cites these as the best evidence for considering "An Alpine Idyll" a Nick story, and he finally asks, "Who is the narrator if not Nick?" albeit "an older, more Europeanized Nick" (Flora, 199). Bernard Oldsey declares "An Alpine Idyll" "almost a continuation of 'Cross-Country Snow' or a slightly altered retelling" (Oldsey, 68). Flora

astutely continues his argument to identify the narrator as Nick by suggesting that "'An Alpine Idyll' gains as a story . . . by keeping Nick unnamed, which is not to say that Hemingway did not mean for his reader to recognize Nick Adams, or to relate the events of the story to Nick's life. The pursuit of the artist's personality may be a part of the challenge for the reader" (Flora, 211). Without joining in this argument now, I prefer to use Nick's name throughout interchangeably with the narrator of the tale.

27. Ernest Hemingway, "An Alpine Idyll," in *The Short Stories of Ernest Hemingway* (New York: Charles Scribner's Sons, 1966) 343–49. All quotations from the story refer to this edition.

28. The phrase "against the wall" is almost the incantatory refrain for the stories and vignettes of *In Our Time,* occurring insistently. It always carries with it a sense of desperation and extremity, as it identifies a position of retreat beyond which one may not go, where the implied fence radically separates two discrete worlds.

29. Young, 60.

30. Bhim Dahiya, *The Hero in Hemingway* (Atlantic Highlands, N.J.: Humanities, 1982) 43–44.

31. Those who look through the window, like Nick and the peasant, are obviously intent on what lies beyond, on the other side of possessed and given reality. The window suggests an invisible barrier between two discrete worlds and implies an abstract visual contact with what lies beyond. Others in the inn, who are intent only on wine or beer or sleep or one another, are suggested as materialistically held by their surroundings and as prisoners to them. It is important to note that Harry in "The Snows of Kilimanjaro" is finally, similarly intent on what lies above and beyond him and is associated with immortality, while Helen and the hyena and vultures are all intent upon food and life and death and the realities before them.

32. That the peasant goes to the Löwen—"the lions"—seems important. The lion is a solar beast and as such is associated with the world of fixity and light from which the peasant has descended.

33. There is a genuine mystery about the peasant's detachment that a Hemingway critic needs to explore. Is the detachment due to a fundamental alienation or to his inwardly turned grief; to a constitutional unperceptiveness or to his almost implacable and unsocial temperament? Is it a result of his sense of estrangement from others, caused by his being from "the other side" and a genuine outsider in this community? He is not a man of these high valleys nor one who intimately shares their customs or their garrulity and sociality—their ways are not his. Is this detachment perhaps a result of a focus of attention upon what are to him more important matters, the just-completed burial in the spring and his finally acknowledged severance from his wife who has companioned him, both living and dead, for so long? Olz has also come from a confrontation with the priest to a room where the judgments of those about him hover in this alien air. Has he absorbed something of the priest and sexton's earlier shocked reaction to his treatment of his wife's dead body, so that he now feels himself outsider among judgmental strangers? Or is there a pride that separates him from these strangers and almost-sniggering "others," so that he studiously ignores and refuses to acknowledge their presence about him and quickly disengages himself from them to go drink where he need not suffer their presence? That he is willing to drink in the Löwen seems to suggest that it is only from the innkeeper's inn and set of people that he separates himself. Is there then special meaning in the remarks of sexton

and innkeeper that come at the very end of the story: "'He didn't want to drink with me,' said the sexton. 'He didn't want to drink with me, after *he* knew about his wife,' said the innkeeper." [Note Hemingway's italics.] Is the sexton's knowledge of Olz's treatment of his wife a factor in the peasant's alienation or does it come from a disdain that has other sources? The sexton who sees the situation as "very funny with the priest" hardly seems to merit respect, but neither does the innkeeper, and for a dozen reasons. But what about the innkeeper's qualification, that it was only *after* "he" knew about "his" wife that the peasant refused to drink with the innkeeper? After who knew what? After he, the peasant, knew about his wife? But what was there additionally to know that he did not already know: that what he had done in perhaps innocence was wrong? Or is the innkeeper saying that the peasant chose not to drink with him after he, the *sexton*, knew about his, the peasant's wife—and knew what about his wife? Apparently the innkeeper is not in the room when the sexton comes into the inn with the peasant, but when they are there, the innkeeper goes over to the table and speaks in dialect to the sexton, who answers him while the peasant merely looks out of the window. It is immediately after the dialect speech, unrecounted, that the peasant stands and pays and leaves without drinking further, and while seemingly pointedly refusing to even acknowledge the sexton with whom he entered to drink. I think we may infer an insult that had been offered in the innkeeper's communication to the sexton, but the innkeeper seems to suggest that the refusal to remain was a result of the antecedent of "*he*" knowing "about his wife." We guess that the peasant must know that the sexton shares the priest's knowledge, but this suggests that what is known "about" the wife may be something the innkeeper has just transmitted to him. What is this "new" knowledge, whether new for sexton or peasant or both? Although little is known and everything remains ambiguous, a new and different suggestion begins to emerge of why the peasant may unconsciously have chosen to treat his wife as he did, and a second and metaphoric reason begins to be established why her undecaying suspension from rot is not only prescribed by weather but also a psychological and moral necessity for the peasant. His acts and her suspension are ways of artificially maintaining her as an absolute and away from and out of "the world's" corruption. The author has told us little, but much has been suggested. In "Indian Camp," as we remember that it was Uncle George who distributed cigars, we have a renewed interest in "other" causes of the Indian father's suicide. So here, we are similarly forced toward amplification of motivation and action.

Hemingway often deliberately creates riddles that need solution, knowing that "the heart of the matter" in a story may be the way in which signs are read or misread, observed or overlooked, and that frequently the meaning of a story may be the figure in the carpet, seen or unseen. One of his most spectacular devices is his use of ambiguous pronoun reference: he not infrequently excites several thematic levels of meaning in a story through deliberate obfuscation of reference. He seems to legitimize several antecedents for a particular pronoun, and he shifts antecedents bewilderingly, allowing them to become multiple and contradictory. In this way, by bringing in simultaneous, alternative possibilities, he studies the complexity of the mind as well as the complexity of situation. Most frequently, he deliberately blurs motivational information, so that the reader is left with something resembling life's riddles: Why does Nick in "Indian Camp" feel he will never die? Why does the Indian father in that story kill himself? "Where did Uncle George go?" Part of the greatness of Hemingway's style is its disdain for mere information, its contempt for glib answers, and its abdication of exposition. He forged a style that allowed the reader participation in the implementation and discovery of meaning.

34. Baker, *The Writer as Artist,* 120, 121.

35. Myra Armistead, "Hemingway's 'An Alpine Idyll,'" *Studies in Short Fiction* 14 (Summer 1977): 255–58.

36. John Atkins, *The Art of Ernest Hemingway* (London: Spring, 1964) 224.

37. Hattam, 261–65.

38. J. Bakker, *Ernest Hemingway: The Artist as Man of Action* (Assen, N.V.: Van Gorcum, 1972) 35–37.

39. Fenton, 167–68.

40. Joseph DeFalco, *The Hero in Hemingway's Short Stories* (Pittsburgh: U of Pittsburgh P, 1963) 216.

41. Flora, 207.

42. In Jack Clayton's film *The Pumpkin Eater,* script by Harold Pinter, there is a scene in which James Mason, in a café and about to order, suggests to Anne Bancroft that she can have "anything" she wants. He is summarily reproved by the waitress: "Anything on the menu."

43. Rot is one of Hemingway's major metaphors. It is Brett's favorite word, and as she moves through Paris and Pamplona, she leaves behind her a trail of ashes and rot. Her interjection "rot!" frequently disciplines the vanity of arbitrary absolutes. Cohn, who would think of her idolatrously as "absolutely fine and straight," obviously knows little about her. "The Snows of Kilimanjaro" vividly opposes the rot of gangrene to the top of the Mountain of God where the leopard lies undecaying. The contrast between the fixed or the eternal and the rotting or decaying is a constant of Hemingway's work. "An Alpine Idyll" is another of many works based fundamentally on this opposition.

44. Ann Putnam, "Dissemblings and Disclosures in Hemingway's 'An Alpine Idyll,'" *The Hemingway Review* (Spring 1987): 27–33.

45. Flora, 203–4, 209–11.

46. Lynn, 341–42.

47. Interview with Kenneth S. Lynn, "Hemingway Heretic," *Johns Hopkins Magazine* 30.2 (April 1988): 22–29.

48. The reader should remember how important getting off the wheel is as a Hemingway metaphor. In *For Whom the Bell Tolls,* Robert Jordan's very life depends on being able to get off Pablo's "merry-go-round." In *The Sun Also Rises,* Jake spends much time learning ways to stop the room from wheeling, to get beyond the feeling that he is going through something he has been through before. Indeed, the metaphor is at the heart of the meaning of "An Alpine Idyll" as it is at the heart of *The Garden of Eden.* After all, Eden is that garden, unlike the one for which the peasant seems to be spreading his manure, where reproduction and the cycles of generation do not exist; it is the prelapsarian world.

13

Waiting for the End in Hemingway's "A Pursuit Race"

Ann Putnam

Hemingway's "A Pursuit Race," begun in 1926 and concluded in 1927, presents another problem in "arrested cycles," the problem of William Campbell, who has quit the ceaseless, frenetic, pointless activity of his job as an advance man for a burlesque show to wait, shrouded in sheets, for death. Like a cyclist caught and passed in a pursuit race, he has simply gotten down off his bicycle and left the track. According to Ann Putnam, the few critics who have mentioned this short story seem to do so only to support interpretations of other, more "important" works. Putnam argues convincingly that such neglect is inexplicable. She reads "A Pursuit Race" as a story of "nada," blending humor and terror in the Gothic tradition of Poe, as "a masterpiece of compression and economy . . . as central to the Hemingway canon as 'A Clean, Well-Lighted Place' and 'The Killers.'"

"A Pursuit Race" is a fine little story hidden toward the back of Hemingway's collected stories. But on first reading it seems little more than a slight, slightly off-center story about burlesque shows, bicycle racing, and drug addiction, one of those quirky sketches Hemingway on occasion chose to write. Nothing more, perhaps, than a gloss on some notes leftover from Hemingway's days on the *Kansas City Star*, the story rarely gets so much as a critical nod. There is, for example, but a single entry in the *MLA Bibliography* that specifically mentions "A Pursuit Race."[1] However, there are a small number of book-length works that offer short analyses of the story, from a few lines to a few paragraphs, most often in terms of how the story reveals Hemingway's nihilism.[2] Thus although the story gets cursory mention here and there in critical reviews of Hemingway's short fiction, it is most often used to further some general point made first with other, seemingly more important works. Perhaps this comes of the story's position in *The Short Stories of Ernest Hemingway,* buried toward the end between equally disregarded works, or perhaps it is because the story was never published separately. More likely, because of the apparent poverty of the story's subject matter. Whatever the reasons, readers over the years have continued to ignore "A Pursuit Race."

The story was begun in 1926 while Hemingway lived in Paris, and then was published for the first time in the 1927 story collection, *Men Without Women.* Yet "A Pursuit Race" is a wonderfully subtle story, a masterpiece of compression and economy that is as central to the Hemingway canon as "A Clean Well-Lighted Place" and "The Killers," with which it shares striking similarities.

The gathering metaphor of the story comes from the bicycle races of Europe, which Hemingway followed avidly during the time he lived in Paris. It is a metaphor as potentially rich as that of the clean, well-lighted place with which it is allied.[3] As the narrator of the story explains:

> In a pursuit race, in bicycle racing, riders start at equal intervals to ride after one another. . . . [I]f they slow their riding another rider who maintains his pace will make up the space that separated them equally at the start. As soon as a rider is caught and passed he is out of the race and must get down from his bicycle and leave the track.[4]

The protagonist, William Campbell, has been in one such race, pursued by a burlesque show which has chased him from Pittsburgh to Kansas City where it has finally caught him. Employed as an "advance man," he is paid only so long as he can stay ahead of the show. But he cannot hold his "slight lead" over his pursuers and so in Kansas City, William Campbell gets down off his "bicycle" and crawls into bed. "You can't fire me because I've got down off my bicycle" (351), Campbell tells his boss, Mr. Turner, the story's only other character. Now William Campbell has not really been riding a bicycle; however, the metaphor he invents brilliantly describes his own desperate circumstances.

Here, as in many other stories, Hemingway uses a sporting event as the gathering metaphor for his tale.[5] It is one of the early and pervading misconceptions about Hemingway's fiction that his notorious "code" is really only an elevated sort of athleticism, which, though given in a brilliant style, and full of luminous surfaces, has little general significance. Truth to tell, Hemingway's stories are rarely *about* sports, although he often expresses his metaphysics in sports terms. In "A Pursuit Race," Hemingway has fashioned a striking metaphor from the world of cycling to portray humankind's position in a world that may "catch" one at any moment.[6]

To stay in the race, one must keep moving on a track that goes round and round, with no beginning and no sure end—an endless middle, endlessly repeated. Life becomes a repetitive circling that never seems to "lead toward any visible end." It becomes a "spectacle with unexplained horrors."[7] But the consequences of slowing down or stopping are defeat and ultimately death, here a living death for William Campbell, who in Kansas City got off his bicycle and pulled up the sheets. In this Hemingway world, life is one long pursuit race, an apt metaphor for the rat race of modern living which consists of pointless, meaningless activity that rarely if ever coheres into significant action.

In an earlier story, "My Old Man," the narrator had explained how "It's the pace you're going at that makes riding the jumps dangerous . . . it's the pace—not the jumps—that makes the trouble" ("My Old Man," 193).[8] When William Campbell can no longer "stand the pace," he drops out of the race and retreats to a peculiar kind of clean, well-lighted place, where time and its "remorselessness" have virtually stopped, marked only by the arrival of the "wolf" at the door, his reach for the whiskey bottle under the bed, and the tender mercies he finds at the end of a needle.

Out of these and a hotel room and a bed with a very peculiar top sheet, William Campbell fashions his own clean, well-lighted place. Here he waits, waiting out some drama that only death can end. Like many of Hemingway's stories, this, too, becomes a study in the art of waiting, the choreography of holding steady. It is a posture central to many of Hemingway's finest stories, stories in which the principal action is the activity of waiting as we see it in "Hills Like White Elephants," "A Day's Wait," "Now I Lay Me," "A Way You'll Never Be," "A Clean, Well-Lighted Place," "A Canary for One," and "The Killers," to name only a few.

These stories, which begin toward the end, take as their subject what one does while waiting for the end. They dramatize the failure of action to materialize in any paraphrasable form, portraying as they do a world where significant action is impossible. Characterized by their lack of surface narrative and coherence, they depict a world that is chaotic, brutal, and utterly capricious. "I can't stand to think about it. . . . I'm going to get out of this town," Nick says at the end of "The Killers" ("The Killers," 289). In a world such as this, the best one can do is to learn strategies for not running away—strategies for holding still with some dignity and pride. In these stories, each protagonist has fashioned a way to wait for the end. As Hemingway explains in the story "Get a Seeing-Eyed Dog," the best one may hope for is that he may eventually "get good" at the waiting, for often that is all there is. "Because I am not doing too well at this. That I can promise you. But what else can you do. Nothing, he thought. There's nothing you can do. But maybe as you go along you will get good at it."[9] Getting good at doing nothing, holding steady against fast water with some kind of style becomes the only measure of success available in a world of diminished possibilities and certain defeat. It is against this model that William Campbell's behavior can be measured and found wanting.[10]

In this we see the emergence of a complementary theme—the idea of the clean, well-lighted place where time can be made to hold still, at least temporarily, if one can learn strategies for holding steady against the remorseless rush of events always outside the control of the protagonist. In clean, well-lighted places of their own making, Hemingway protagonists, from the Nick Adams in "Big Two-Hearted River" to the Nick Adams of "Now I Lay Me," create certain rituals that enable them to hold steady against the fast current rushing all about them. William Campbell's ritual commences with the regular arrival of the "wolf" at the door and ends with the empty syringe—a ritual in sharp contrast to the dignity the old man in "A Clean, Well-Lighted Place" exhibits, as he takes care not to spill his drinks. Or the dignity of Ole Andreson, who has also quit the race, and who waits fully dressed for the inevitable coming of the killers, in the room that has become his own clean, well-lighted place.

Campbell's waiting, however, is characterized by a dangerous slackness, an obscene passivity, and a very costly soft focus which can, at certain times, be made to cover everything. Although the light bulb burns through the night, its intensity is softened by the sheet that covers Campbell's face. It is a perverse copy of Nick's camp in "Big Two-Hearted River," as Nick looks up at the sunlight coming through the canvas of his tent. For William Campbell, "It was warm and white and close under the covers" (351), but it is the whiteness of death, not the light of cleanliness and order. For this is no ordered place. Clothes are scattered about the room, a suitcase stands open on the floor, a bottle sits on a chair pulled up to the edge of the bed, and under the rumpled bedclothes lies a very disordered William Campbell, who has become little more than a talking corpse. Yet under the covers, and with the aid of a syringe and needle and a bottle within easy reach, Campbell has made himself a "good place." For it is "very cold in Kansas City" (350), and the magical white sheet can keep out a good deal more than the cold. Campbell's waiting, in contrast to Andreson's, is rude and silly, parodying his own defeat, his mind like the room where he stays, in chaos and disorder. There is no tension in the waiting, no graceful tautness, no decorum, and no manners.

In the story collections *Men Without Women* and *Winner Take Nothing*, we see the emergence of a recognizable *pair* of characters whose relationship determines the form and effect of the stories they inhabit. Again and again, Hemingway employs two characters to tell what is ultimately a single story. It is thus in "A Pursuit Race," which highlights the act of waiting, presenting it in a way that makes observation the story's principal action. Here and in other stories that employ this strategy, we get the uncanny sense that this strange *other* figure is in some sense the protagonist's double, an incarnation of some secret aspect of himself. Yet the two are peculiarly disconnected. Though they represent aspects of the same self, they remain forever split, forever alienated in the narrative.

This becomes apparent in the very structure of the story. On the narrative level, the two exhibit a curious lack of interaction. The presence of one does little or nothing to alter the circumstances of the other. The principal action is not confrontation or interaction, but a cautious, even secret, observation. One character sustains a blow while the other watches, sustaining a blow too, though from the side, as it were. Thus catastrophe strikes both characters, one directly and the other obliquely though no less profoundly. The crisis that is foregrounded, however, has special significance to the watchful character in the background, whose own drama often remains mysteriously obscured. "The Killers" works this way, for although the obvious casualty is Ole Andreson, the story reveals that the catastrophe is Nick's as well. "A Clean, Well-Lighted Place" works this way too, when the older waiter reveals his kinship with the old man who drinks late into the night of the clean, well-lighted café. And it is also thus in "The Battler," where the blow that is at once literal and symbolic has come to both Nick Adams and the prizefighter Ad Francis.

"A Pursuit Race" illustrates the tight unity of the two-protagonist story as clearly as any of the pairs stories. Here in particular, we get the strange sense that the two characters, William Campbell and his boss William Turner, are in some way parts of the same self. It is upon this sense that the story's resolution turns. At first it seems as though William Campbell the drug addict and Mr. Turner the burlesque show's busy manager—one disordered and slack, the other efficient and taut—are true antagonists. But they are both named William, and the frantic pace Mr. William Turner must keep seems on second glance to be only another version of the pursuit race William Campbell has run and now lost. "Mr. Turner stood beside the bed. He was a middle-aged man with a large stomach and a bald head and he had many things to do" (351). He has come to William Campbell's room because he feels in some fashion responsible for him and because he wants to help. But it is dangerous for him to stay too long. He is running his own pursuit race, and he dare not pause: "I got to go," he says. "I have to go. . . . I got a lot to do. . . . I better go" (354).

At the beginning of the story we expect the conflict to center upon a confrontation between William Campbell, the advance man who has quit his job, and William Turner, the man who had hired him. "You're a fool. . . . You're a drunken fool. When did you get into this town?" (351). But Mr. Turner is not Campbell's enemy; it is not Turner who has been pursuing him, nor is it Turner who has now finally "caught" him. It is not the "jumps," not the advance-man business itself, but the "pace," the business of living that is so utterly dangerous and for which there is all penalty and no cure for having failed. The point is important in appreciating how Hemingway often uses a pair of characters. Although Turner is "fond" of William Campbell, their relationship seems tangential at best, and their meeting here in a Kansas City hotel room seems almost as tangential. In terms of the story's structure and development, their meeting provides neither the source of the conflict nor its resolution. Rather, the meeting only illuminates what has already happened, none of which is dependent upon the meeting itself for realization. What action we have is the act of one character observing another. In the course of that observation, the reader becomes increasingly aware of the similarities between the observer, Mr. William Turner, and William Campbell, the one observed. It is a narrative strategy that draws us into the act as well; we come to stand beside Turner, who stares unashamedly at the figure under the sheet.

Beginning apart, the two characters are increasingly drawn together. Turner stands; Campbell lies on the bed, talking through the sheet. The initial contrast between the proper, upstanding Turner and the prone Campbell is the source of much of the story's humor.[11] "'When did you get into this town?' Turner demands (351). Campbell answers, then asks, 'Did you ever talk through a sheet? . . . I love it under a sheet. . . . You love me, don't you sheet?'" (351–52). Turner tries to reason with him. He sits down on the bed. "Be careful of my sheet," Campbell says (353). Then he discovers how he can "kiss this sheet and see right through it at the same time" (353). The contrast is funny, but it is also full of pathos, for we begin to see Campbell as Turner sees him, and this view reveals an increasing sympathy, even a tenderness of sorts. He is "fond of William Campbell; he did not wish to leave him. He was very sorry for him and he felt a cure might help. . . . But he had to go" (353). "Are you all right, Billy?" (354), he asks. Campbell himself knows very well the danger of staying and tells him, "Everybody's got to go. . . . I'm fine. You go along. I'll just lie here for a little while. Around noon I'll get up" (354). It is a line that strangely echoes what Ole Andreson says as he lies waiting, "After a while I'll make up my mind to go out" ("The Killers," 288). Then Turner turns to leave. Because he cannot risk being "caught," he must keep moving, must maintain his "slight lead" over his own pursuers.

But before he goes, he tells Campbell to take a cure for his alcoholism. However Campbell tells him, "I have a surprise for you. I'm not drunk. I'm hopped to the eyes" (352), and shows him the deadly configuration of blue marks on his right forearm. "They got a cure for that too," Turner says (353). But Campbell knows that "They haven't got a cure for anything." Yet Turner will not let it go. "You can't just quit like that, Billy, . . . I mean you got to fight it out" (353). But Campbell begins to feel the "nausea" which he knows will "increase steadily, without there ever being the relief of sickness, until something were done against it" (353).

Then Campbell explains the difference between them and why for him there can be no cure:

> Listen, Billy. . . . I want to tell you something. You're called "Sliding Billy." That's because you can slide. I'm called just Billy. That's because I never could slide at all. I can't slide, Billy. I can't slide. It just catches. Every time I try it, it catches. . . . It's awful when you can't slide. (353–54)

Because he can keep moving, "Sliding Billy" Turner can live in the "daily horror." He can stay in the pursuit race; he can keep the "pace" because he has learned how to "slide." That is, he can believe in the illusion that for the horrors of the race itself there are cures one can take. But despite his exhortations, Turner flees from the horror he sees in this Kansas City hotel room—a horror that would be his, too, if he ever lost his ability to "slide." Billy Turner can slide—can maintain the illusion that there are cures to be had—an illusion created against the darkness outside all lighted rooms. But when Billy Campbell tries to slide, the truth "catches," and he must get off his bicycle and quit the race.

William Turner returns, however, and in a flash of recognition we see that "Sliding Billy" Turner shares the very same "nausea" that is the real pursuer against which all must race.[12]

It is the story's epiphany, and the reader's discovery, as the two men are revealed to be brothers after all. Strangely, almost all readings of the story have focused on the existential dilemma illuminated by Campbell's darkly comic position under the white sheet and have completely ignored Turner's key function, upon which the story turns.[13] In the same way that we recognize the brotherhood of the older waiter and the old man who drinks his brandy long past closing hours, we learn that Turner is also of those who need a light for the night. Knowing this, Turner realizes that sleep is one of life's few invaluable offerings. When he returns to Campbell's room to find him sleeping, he does not wake him; he reveals himself to be a man who knows "what things in life were very valuable" (353). Whatever demons have pursued William Campbell, we realize now that William Turner knows them too.

"William Campbell's interview with Mr. Turner had been a little strange" (350). Indeed, seen from Campbell's perspective through the whiteness of the sheet, the scene takes on the feeling of a dream. In the dream, Turner appears next to the disordered man on the bed and becomes the relentless pursuer, the twin, the angel who would save him from his own devil. He is the other "William" who pursues Poe's "William Wilson." But the figure in the dream who stands by the bed and who would save the dreamer from the terror of his dreams finally must only let him sleep the deep sleep that is beyond dreaming.

So Turner looks down at the sleeping figure and sees a presentiment of things to come. Campbell sees in Turner an image of what he once was and now an image of his one last hope. Turner is Campbell's past; Campbell is Turner's future. Out of this doubling Hemingway has fit one story into the other. He has crafted a story with a unity of great subtlety and power and a redeeming humor strangely mixed with darkness. It is a mix Hemingway was to perfect in the story "The Gambler, the Nun, and the Radio," which also features cures and opiums, sliding and getting caught, purposeless, frenetic activity, and a dangerous slackness in the posture of waiting for the end.

"A Pursuit Race" is a true horror story, a story of "nada" whose sense of darkness blends humor and terror in a Gothic tradition worthy of Poe. We watch the disintegration of a man whose fate we might share but for our own ability to "slide." We become Billy Turner too, who, but for his hold on his illusions, would surely become "caught" by life's relentless pursuers. Hemingway ingeniously draws his readers into the scene, a narrative strategy by which we, too, become one of the silent, watchful others.

Notes

1. See Ernest Fontana's "Hemingway's 'A Pursuit Race'" in *The Explicator* 42.4 (Summer 1984): 43–45. This short article is a gloss on the term "wolf," which Fontana believes refers to Campbell's ostensible homosexual lover. Fontana's main point is that the story is really "an understated study of homosexual self-hatred." While Richard Hovey does not make an explicit connection between homosexuality and Campbell's anguish, he suggests that "A Pursuit Race" should perhaps be included in the "half dozen of stories [that] deal with homosexuality, a phenomenon [Hemingway] was drawn to in anxious, puzzled loathing." See Hovey, *Ernest Hemingway: The Inward Terrain* (Seattle: U of Washington P, 1968) 17. Both Fontana's and Hovey's interpretations seem to close up the story rather than to recognize the dilation and expansion that a more generalized reading of the story's despair offers.

2. See the following: Carlos Baker, *Ernest Hemingway: The Writer as Artist* (Princeton: Princeton UP, 1952) 123; J. Bakker, *Ernest Hemingway: The Artist as Man of Action* (Assen, N.V.: Van Gorcum, 1972) 85–86; Joseph DeFalco, *The Hero in Hemingway's Short Stories* (Pittsburgh: U of Pittsburgh P, 1963) 58–59; Charles A. Fenton, *The Ap-*

prenticeship of Ernest Hemingway: The Early Years (New York: Farrar, Straus, Young, 1954) 49; Fontana, 43–45; Sheldon Norman Grebstein, *Hemingway's Craft* (Carbondale: Southern Illinois UP, 1973) 186–88; Larry E. Grimes, *The Religious Design of Hemingway's Early Fiction* (Ann Arbor: UMI Research P, 1985) 75–77; Hovey, 17; John Killinger, *Hemingway and the Dead Gods: A Study in Existentialism* (Lexington: U of Kentucky P, 1960) 51–52; Tom Stoppard, "Reflections on Ernest Hemingway," in *Ernest Hemingway: The Writer in Context*, ed. James Nagel (Madison: U of Wisconsin P, 1984) 24; Arthur Waldhorn, *A Reader's Guide to Ernest Hemingway* (New York: Farrar, Straus and Giroux, 1972) 22; Edmund Wilson, "The Sportsman's Tragedy," *The New Republic* 53 (14 December 1927): 102–3.

3. In a wonderfully nostalgic essay, Tom Stoppard describes his enduring affection for Hemingway. "I will try to explain something of why I got bitten by Hemingway, and stayed bitten." He cites three passages that particularly illuminate Hemingway's ability to use the "associative power of words, rather than their 'meaning' [to make] prose work on its ultimate level." He chooses the fourteenth vignette in *In Our Time*, one from *The Sun Also Rises*, and the opening paragraph from "A Pursuit Race." He is particularly taken with Hemingway's use of the metaphor of the "pursuit race": "And what happens is that the burlesque show catches up with the metaphor and the metaphor has to get down from its bicycle and leave the page." See Stoppard, 19–27. For specific reference to "A Pursuit Race," see page 24.

4. Ernest Hemingway, "A Pursuit Race," *The Short Stories of Ernest Hemingway* (New York: Charles Scribner's Sons, 1966) 350. All future citations from the collected stories are to this edition and will be given in the text.

5. Edmund Wilson was one of the first readers to comment perceptively on Hemingway's use of sports metaphor as a method of indirection. He makes brief mention of "A Pursuit Race" in "The Sportsman's Tragedy," 102.

6. Hemingway's most famous use of sports metaphor is found in *A Farewell to Arms*, where he describes what happens when one is "caught off base." See *A Farewell to Arms* (New York: Charles Scribner's Sons, 1929) 327. Carlos Baker also sees the larger dimensions of the story, "a whole, widespread human predicament, deep in the grain of human affairs. . . ." See Baker, 123.

7. Ernest Hemingway, *The Sun Also Rises* (New York: Charles Scribner's Sons, 1926) 167.

8. See Joseph DeFalco, 58–59, for a reference to Hemingway's metaphoric use of the concept of keeping the "pace"—a term derived from the story "My Old Man."

9. Ernest Hemingway, "Get a Seeing-Eyed Dog," *Atlantic Monthly* 200 (November 1957): 68.

10. Baker compares Ole Andreson of "The Killers" with William Campbell in "A Pursuit Race." Perhaps the contrast is more revealing, for unlike Campbell, Andreson waits for the end with a certain degree of dignity which for Hemingway is often all that remains under the protagonist's control. See Baker, 123.

11. Sheldon Grebstein nicely analyzes the story's humor, albeit a dark humor, which is created through the juxtaposition of the postures of the two characters. See Grebstein, 186–87.

12. John Killinger uses the concept of "nausea" to indicate the existential condition of despair common to so many Hemingway protagonists. He sees Campbell's retreat to the bed as

a "realization of freedom." "He is nauseated, but he has decided to be free of the complicated pursuit race." See pp. 51–52. Campbell, however, seems more enslaved than ever, now that he has relinquished all control.

13. With a very few exceptions, most critics ignore Turner's function altogether. Sheldon Grebstein comments on Turner's role, but believes that he "pities Campbell and wants to help him but can not comprehend the sort of desperation that brought him to his breakdown." Larry Grimes suggests that, rather than being "brothers" as I have argued, Turner and Campbell "represent two contrasting voices. . . . Turner speaks for society (the show) and places great faith in its protective and restorative powers. Campbell, the lone advance man, has voted no confidence in society's way of making meaning." Grimes writes that, "according to the metaphor, the show is Campbell's opponent and his boss is the voice of that opponent." This interpretation fails to see that the story is as much about the quiet, watchful other as it is about the character who is foregrounded, that the story's point is wrapped up in this disclosure. Edmund Wilson, however, seems to be hinting at this when he states that the story "derives its whole significance from the last paragraph, in which the manager of the burlesque show, understanding what has happened and pitying his recreant advance man, refrains from waking him." See respectively, Grebstein, 186; Grimes, 76; Wilson, 102.

14

A Semiotic Inquiry into Hemingway's "A Simple Enquiry"

Gerry Brenner

Hemingway's "A Simple Enquiry," composed at roughly the same time as "A Pursuit Race," has proved anything but a simple inquiry for its handful of critics. Those few who have endeavored to interpret the story have been baffled by the not-so-simple inquiries it raises. Is Pinin a homosexual? Is the major who examines him a homosexual? Whatever the major's preferences, what are his motives for questioning Pinin? Is the adjutant in the outer office a homosexual? Why does he smile at Pinin's embarrassment? Hemingway's ironic title mocks the reader's attempts to understand the story, and here Gerry Brenner correctly groups "A Simple Enquiry" with "Hills Like White Elephants," "The Sea Change," and "The Mother of a Queen," puzzle stories whose interpretation pivots on an unarticulated word and on the sensitivity of readers' responses to sign-laden dialogue. Brenner goes on to conduct a thorough examination of "A Simple Enquiry's" ambiguous behavioral and linguistic signs, and concludes that this cryptic story deliberately defies interpretation. For Brenner, its "point" is the inscrutability of human nature (Pinin, the major, the adjutant—each may or may not conceal a secret) and the enigmatic nature of language. Brenner's semiotic approach reminds us that Hemingway was in many ways a more characteristically postmodern writer than his critics have allowed him to be, and exemplifies how postmodern critical methods can unfold for us the author's most experimental stories, too long ignored because they do not fulfill our antique expectation of a soluble interpretation.

Hemingway had a knack for reading signs that revealed character. Covering the Lausanne Conference of 1922 for the *Toronto Daily Star*, he derided

Italy's Fascist dictator: having received the press at Lausanne, Mussolini was absorbed in a book that held his rapt attention, ignoring the crowd of reporters. Hemingway, put off by what he regarded as political stagecraft, claims he "tip-toed over behind him to see what the book was he was reading with such avid interest. It was a French-English dictionary—held upside down." For the same dispatch Hemingway had been reading other signs as well, reporting that Turkey's leader, Ismet Pasha, "conceals his defective knowledge of French, which is a disgrace to an educated Turk . . . by pretending to be deaf."[1] Within a fortnight Hemingway was exposing Czarist diplomat and commissar for foreign affairs, Georgi Tchitcherin. Hemingway remarked the oddity of Tchitcherin always being photographed in military uniform, then poked around to find that the diplomat had never been a soldier but had, as a boy, been "kept in dresses until he was twelve years old" (69).

Hemingway's sign-reading talent partly explains his penchant for the phrase, "the true gen," what one hears redundantly called "the real low-down," "the true facts." "The gen," he wrote Malcolm Cowley in a 17 October 1945 letter, "Is RAF [Royal Air Force] slang for intelligence, the hand out at the briefing. The *true* gen is what they know but don't tell you. The true gen very hard to obtain [*sic*]."[2] Difficult to obtain or not, Hemingway's thirst for it never slaked, as evidenced even in his posthumous memoirs, *A Moveable Feast*—his "true gen" on the frauds, poseurs, and charlatans who passed for expatriated writers in Paris.[3]

Hemingway's need to read signs correctly—and the talent and compulsion to get "the true gen"—grew out of early experiences, for as a child he was perplexed by the conflicting bundles of signs that represented father, mother, and sister. Were other fathers respectably attired professionals one moment, outdoorsmen the next, apron-wearing cooks and home-canners the next? Was every infant-suckling, dress-wearing, high-toned mother also breadwinner, home architect, and domestic boss? And were all big sisters frocked and bobbed and held back from school so as to better mirror their "twin" little brothers?[4]

That Hemingway turned domestic sign-reading problems into a fictional forte is incontestable: getting "the true gen" on his characters' identities has perplexed generations of Hemingway's readers. Is Lady Brett an irredeemable bitch or does she undergo a moral transformation by the end of *The Sun Also Rises*? Is Jake Barnes pilgrim or pimp, an author of religious confession or of self-defensive, nasty slander? Is Frederic Henry a WWI survivor who narrates, through stiff upper lip, his experiences of a decade earlier so that readers will know what he learned? Or is he an AWOL soldier whose very recent love-loss compels him to tell his story—either as therapy (to keep from going crazy with his loss) or as testament (to explain why he will commit suicide as soon as his story is finished)? And Harry Morgan of *To Have and Have Not:* amoral tough or classically tragic hero?

Hemingway's habit of schooling himself in signs is further vouched for by his lifelong obsession with being an expert at everything he committed his attention to—bullfighting, topography, fishing, military history, big-game hunting, firearms, writing, and on and on. After all, the measure of the expert is his or her facility in reading signs and having the skill to know how to respond to them.[5] But some signs, Hemingway realized, lay beyond his ken, would not yield themselves up to his appetite for "the true gen," were too ambiguous for accurate reading. That's the nub of the problem that Hemingway's "little story about the war in Italy,"[6] "A Simple Enquiry," wraps itself around. A summary of the story and glance at what criticism has found in it will prime the narrativity behind my attention to the story's calculated particulars. For those particulars both invite reading the story's semiotic experimentation and allow the several ramifications I find in it.

A summary of the neglected story: While working away in a military hut at his desk on some papers, an Italian major delicately strokes oil from a saucer onto his sunburned and blistered face. He leaves to take a nap in an adjacent room, telling his adjutant, a non-com clerk, to finish their work, whereupon the clerk pulls a book from his coat, lights his pipe, and reads briefly, then closes the book because he has too much paperwork to do to enjoy the book. As the March sun slips behind a mountain, the major's orderly, Pinin, enters to stoke the stove with firewood, then exits into a room at the back of the hut. From his bunk room the major orders that Pinin be sent in to him. The clerk obeys, as does Pinin, shutting the door behind himself as ordered. From his bunk bed the major interrogates Pinin, asking his age, whether he's ever been in love with a girl, why he doesn't write the girl whom Pinin claims he loves, and, suddenly, if Pinin is corrupt. Pinin responds that he does not understand what the major's term means, eliciting the major's command that Pinin "needn't be superior." As Pinin steadfastly looks at the floor, the major studies him and, between pauses, asks, "And you don't really want—"; "That your great desire isn't really—." The narrator tells that the major reclines his head on his rucksack pillow and smiles: "He was really relieved: life in the army was too complicated." The major commends Pinin for being a "good boy" but cautions him again against being "superior" and to guard against the possibility of somebody else coming along and "taking" him. Pinin continuing to stand still beside the bunk, the major assures him that he need not be afraid, that he won't touch him, and then offers him the choice of returning to his platoon or staying on as the major's servant, where the chances that he might be killed are smaller. Permitted to return to whatever he had been doing, Pinin leaves the major's room, but not without drawing a smile from the clerk, who notices both that he was flushed and that his movements as he left the office were different than when he had carried in the firewood. Pinin enters with more wood for the stove. The major, hearing him walk across the floor, wonders if Pinin lied to him.

From this story we Hemingway critics have gleaned little. Of course we have snapped up its oblique homosexual bait.[7] For that surely is the gist of the major's questions, which he asks Pinin behind closed doors and which he interrupts only once, asking, "in the same tone of voice," if the clerk in the outside office can hear him. And the major's homosexuality surely accounts for his pauses, his unfinished sentences, and his admonition that Pinin guard against somebody "else" coming along and taking him. We Hemingway critics have also recognized in the story an artfully muted echo of Lawrence's "Prussian Officer."[8] But we have ignored the family resemblance between "A Simple Enquiry" and such stories as "Hills Like White Elephants," "The Sea Change," and "The Mother of a Queen." These latter three stories pivot upon a semantic crux, an unarticulated or ambiguous word—abortion, lesbian, and "queen" or homosexual. The semantic ambiguity upon which "A Simple Enquiry" pivots, of course, is the word "corrupt" or homosexual. Yes, we Hemingway critics long ago learned that the mystery of Jig's operation in "Hills" is but a red herring to distract readers from the story's major issue: how to *overhear* correctly the sign-laden dialog between Jig and the American man so as to *hear* her depth of character and his shallowness.[9] But we have not seen the pattern in this family of stories: they focus upon a foreground semantic riddle that simultaneously obscures and illumines the background network of signs that require discerning reading in order to resolve the textual conundrums of character and interpretation.

"A Simple Enquiry" is studiously minimal. A spare setting—a hut surrounded by snow above the windows; in one room a stove, two desks and chairs, and one map on a "pineboard wall"; in a second room a bunk and a nail from which hang the major's "cloth-covered helmet and his snowglasses." A stark and sketchy cast—three type characters: an officer, clerk, and orderly. Scarcely more than a breath of event—some paper shuffling, some stove feeding, some facial oiling, some entrances and exits, and two dozen lines of dialog. All in a quarter of an hour's time—if that.

It takes no semiotician to flag the numerable signs with which Hemingway punctuates such minimalist art, signs that convey unambiguous but not readily discernible information. The map on the pine-board wall, the room's only "decoration," signifies that *map-reading* is important to what the men in the hut engage in. The papers on which the major and his clerk work signify that *paper-reading* is also important—as is *book-reading* to the clerk, who momentarily sneaks some time to do it, until he finds himself too pressed by the work at hand to so indulge himself. When the major challenges Pinin's admission that he is in love with a girl by informing Pinin that he reads all the orderly's letters and knows that he does not write her, it becomes clear that *letter-reading* is also significant to the officer and to his clerk, who is left to finish up their paperwork while the major questions Pinin.

In addition to these sign-readings, Hemingway's narrator remarks still other signs to read, ones often ignored in the automatic but unreflective processes called into play in reading them. Outside the hut snow is banked above the windows. A trench, cut between the snow and the hut, has widened from the sun reflecting off the wall of the hut. These signs of nature's language require *weather-reading*, for they signify that the hut sits in some high alpine terrain. To nudge this decipherable conclusion the narrator remarks the date, late March, using an artificial sign system that requires *calendar-reading*: such snowbanks at this time of year need the altitude of alpine terrain. More significant than the sun's inscriptions on the snow are its legible signs on the major's face: blisters, tan, peeling skin, and sunburn. For these explain that the major's duties mandate spending much of his day in the sun. And from the signs around his eyes—"two white circles where his snow-glasses had protected his face from the sun on the snow"—it is unequivocal that part of the major's duties include reconnaissance work.

Some of the papers on which he and his clerk work, then, must be reports of information he has gathered, based on his reconnoitering and, perhaps, on what he has decoded from his observations in conjunction with that map on the pine-board wall of the hut. In brief, part of his job is that of a semiotician specializing in pragmatics: the reliability and accuracy of the knowledge he adduces from the signs he reads can affect whether the platoons, to which he offers to let Pinin return, will stand a greater or smaller chance of getting killed in combat. But the major's revelation to Pinin that he reads all of Pinin's letters signifies that the major's assignment entails yet other duties. A military intelligence officer, he is also his unit's censor. Neither snoop nor voyeur, his official capacity obligates him to read Pinin's and the other soldiers' mail, to determine if anyone sends or receives seditious or classified military information, however encoded. And by naming the non-com clerk an adjutant, Hemingway further stipulates the nature of the duties carried on in the office: by definition all adjutants assist their superior officers in administering and preserving correspondence and personnel records.

Notwithstanding either the major's professional sign-reading skills, or his access to private and personal documents, or his authority to interrogate a subordinate, Pinin confounds his attempt to discover, through the sign systems of behavior and language, the answer to whether Pinin is homosexual. Through none of several rhetorical strategies can the major pry from Pinin the knowledge he seeks, neither through semantic euphemism, asking him if he is "not corrupt"; nor through the intimidation of derisive condescension, telling him he "needn't be superior"; nor through the innuendo of unfinished but leading questions, asking "And you really don't want—" and "That your great desire isn't really—"; nor through the psychological pressure of timely pauses between those unfinished questions. To all of these maneuvers Pinin responds with a frozen gesture that the narrator thrice states, "Pinin looked at the floor," a decipherable but radically ambiguous sign. Although the major scrutinizes Pinin for some self-betraying sign, looking "at his brown face, down and up him, and at his hands," Pinin is ultimately illegible. True, the clerk smiles when he watches Pinin leave the major's room and walk out the door, for he reads discomfiture in Pinin's flushed face and awkward walk, Pinin's bodily movements differing from when he had earlier carried the firewood into the room and fed the fire. But the question of Pinin's sexual preference and identity remains more concealed than the terrain beneath the high-piled snowbank outside the hut.

Readers of Pinin's responses to the major's "simple enquiry" will certainly differ. Some will read the signs of his behavior as embarrassment, registering his dismay at having the door opened on his homosexuality, closeted or not. Others will read the signs of his behavior as mere taciturnity, manifesting his disillusionment at this invasion of personal matters by a respected superior. Yet others will read the signs of his behavior as awkward paralysis, recording his naive shock in discovering that such a world of corruption exists. And still others will cue upon the major's reproach that Pinin "needn't be superior," reading the signs of Pinin's behavior as shrewdness, revealing his mastery of the situation, adeptly stonewalling to thwart the major. Regardless of such readings, they are guesses in sign-reading.

So too are inferences about the clerk's smile when he watches Pinin leave the major's room. Does that smile signify his gloating and jealous pleasure that his own lover has been spurned by Pinin? Or is it an unfavored subordinate's smirk that at last a favored subordinate has suffered from a superior's rebuke? Or might it reveal the clerk's glee that the authoritarian officer has been defeated in a private skirmish with an unranked soldier? Like the major's question that ends the story, such questions go unresolved. Intellectual inquiry blunts against the riddling knot of a character's complex identity, a knot that can quickly drive readers outside the story to ask what signs the major had observed in the first place to have assigned them homosexual significance.

It were better if readers return to the text. For although the signs of the major's homosexual overture seem quite unequivocal, several considerations suggest that the certainty of such a reading may not stand up to closer scrutiny of the semantics and syntactics by which it has been inferred. Clearly the construction of the major's questions shows Hemingway's narrator affecting a transliteration of the syntax in Italian: "You are nineteen?" "You have ever been in love?" "You are in love with this girl now?" But this transliterated series of intonational interrogatives may also signal some obstruction or resistance in the major as he leads up to the central question of his simple enquiry. For within that series the narrator allows the major to switch to a declarative form: "I asked if you had been in love—with a girl." More, when the major finally issues his question about Pinin's corruptness, he does so in a highly complex sentence—"And that you are not corrupt?"—a sentence whose sense requires understanding the use of a consequential conjunction ("and" to mean "therefore"), an embedded but elided clause ("You are quite sure"), and a syntax whose negative subordinate clause ("that you are not corrupt") structurally depends for its force upon the positive construction of the ellipsis of its main clause ("You are quite sure"). The complete complex sentence would perhaps read, "And you are quite sure that you love a girl, and, therefore, are also quite sure that you are not corrupt?"

But a handful of other considerations may be more persuasive in casting doubt on the major's identity as homosexual. First, when the major admonishes or cautions Pinin to guard against being "taken" by somebody "else" who comes along, the "else" cannot refer to himself, for clearly he has failed to "take" Pinin, if such was his intent. The reference to someone else, then, may indicate that the major has detected in Pinin's correspondence some evidence that Pinin has already been "taken" by a homosexual. Second, when the major asks "in the same tone of voice" if the clerk in the outside office can hear him, his question may be an act of considerateness, not one of self-interested cautiousness. Both the major's desire to discover the truth behind his suspicions and the interference of his burdensome duties may have made it necessary for him to resort to an interview in his bunk room as the most private place for the delicate interrogation. Consequently, his "question" to the clerk in the main office may better show the major's sensitivity to Pinin's shame, were the clerk to hear and gossip about the camp or compound what he overhears. To conceal from the clerk the nature of the interrogation requires the major's careful vocal control and his judicious switch from a dyadic to a triadic conversational mode so as to keep the clerk from readily sensing the gist of the bunk room colloquy. Third, the major's incomplete queries ("And you don't really want—"; "That your great desire isn't really—") may be leading questions that seek only Pinin's denial or confirmation of the major's suspicions. Denial or confirmation would enable the major to know his orderly's sexual preference and to act accordingly in that knowledge, not enable him to exploit it. Fourth, the major's assurance that Pinin need have no fear, his pledge that he will not touch Pinin, and his offer to let Pinin return to his platoon all show the major to be unthreatening. As though he were an American jurist, the major's assurances are tantamount to a promise of no reprisals, for the lack of corroborating proof of Pinin's homosexual guilt finds him innocent. Fifth, when the major leans his head back on his rucksack and smiles, the narrator states, "He was really relieved: life in the army was too complicated." The narrator implies that the major is little interested in Pinin as a homosexual partner; his relief indicates both pleasure in finishing his task of questioning his orderly and gratification in suspending the suspicious habit of looking for complications that military life breeds.

By reexamining the major's alleged homosexual overture, I imply, of course, that an open reading of behavioral and linguistic signs finds him a complicated character. Indeed, the signs invite reading him as a professional soldier in the best sense. He works diligently at his job and jeopardizes his comfort and well-being by spending hours in the blinding and blistering sun. He fulfills his assigned duties, not shrinking from necessary invasions into his orderly's private life. And he conducts his interrogation with sensitivity and tact, sees to its privacy from scandal-mongering ears, and assures the interrogated orderly both that recriminations will not follow and that in the absence of incontrovertible evidence of guilt, his innocence will be honored.

More important, my reexamination reads the story's ambiguous signs permitting at least four identifications of the major. My reexamination finds him an exemplary professional figure. Most readers find him a despicably homosexual figure.[10] But his adjutant, whom the major commands in imperatives, may find him a stern authoritarian figure, one who tersely orders him to complete their work. And from his bunk he instructs the adjutant to send in Pinin to him. Finally, given the bunk room interrogation, Pinin may find the major an offensively effeminate figure. With unmanly delicacy he indirectly leads up to the question of Pinin's homosexuality. He considers the question he wishes to ask so offensive that he must gloss it with the euphemism, "corrupt." Or else his use of the term suggests his naïveté, so unfamiliar with erotic deviation that when the moment of trying to find the correct semantic term is upon him, he gropes for it and can come up with only a word that roughly approximates the label he has in mind. Either way, his response to Pinin's declaration, "I don't know what you mean, corrupt," elicits the mild reproof that he "needn't be superior." No brusque reprimand here, no "Don't be superior to me, private," no brutal correction or charge of sodomy. As the interrogation proceeds, the major's squeamishly incomplete questions, his twice-repeated commendations of Pinin as a "good boy," his soft admonitions and his gentle assurances all reveal an overrefined manner of conducting himself in an awkward situation. And they are all of a piece with the narrator's attention to the major's careful oiling of his painfully sunburned face, an oiling that stereotypically better befits womanish than manly behavior.

These four characterizations of the major may not congeal harmoniously for most readers. But within them are clustered signs that point at the irreducible core of the major's androgyny, a recurring feature of many of Hemingway's characters and an especially appropriate feature for a character in this 1927 volume of stories, *Men Without Women*.[11] More, these four characterizations vouch for Hemingway's careful manipulation of signs, showing his studied attempt to probe their radical ambiguity in this sparest of stories. Most, they not only reveal the story to be an "open work," one whose text guides but does not limit extensive interpretation,[12] but they also display the narrativity which actively constructs *stories* "from the fictional data provided by [the] narrative medium," a narrativity that manifests the role of any semiotic interpreter, "not free to *make* meaning but . . . free to *find* it by following the various semantic, syntactic, and pragmatic paths that lead away from the words of the text."[13]

Hemingway isolated his story's semiotic concerns in a war-time situation. But because the matters of war are so attenuated, I think it permissible to examine four ramifications in the small theater of Hemingway's not-so-simple "Enquiry." First, the scene of uniformed men in the hut transmits a hackneyed and didactic military message: in martial matters small or large, in behind-the-lines information office or on front-line battlefield, in encounters of psychological bullying or violent weaponry, knowledge is crucial to victory: the communication of incorrect, inconclusive, or ambiguous information jeopardizes the military objective of prevailing over an enemy. Second, the story's specifics illumine a psychological ramification, the universalities in the analogues of its reductive triangle.[14] I refer to the generic social and domestic triangle that underlies the story and may best explain its overlooked because subdued psychological resonance. That triangulated event—surely one that traumatized Hemingway as a child—addresses all persons, as major, clerk, or orderly, or as all three on different occasions. Simply, sooner or later all persons question (or imagine themselves questioning) a child or peer, subordinate or equal, to extract the information they deem important to their responsibilities or desires. So too have all persons been questioned by peer, parent, or superior from whom they wished or needed to keep secret or private or self-incriminating information. Likewise have all persons been the excluded observer of a riddling scene between two figures whose confrontation or colloquy signifies something more than can be fully known or correctly imagined. The psychological drama of such triangles surely whets curiosity and often propels simple and complex enquiries. *Enquiries?* That spelling invokes a third ramification: it suggests some intentional philosophical design in the story. Must it be accident that Hemingway, never a good speller, "misspelled" the noun in his story's title by using the letter "E," or sloppily inserted a variant spelling, one that Scribner's ever-slack copy editors paid no heed? Or can it have been deliberate that he chose to spell it with an "E," attempted in a minor semantic twist to call forth a philosophic tradition which seldom inquired, but customarily undertook enquiries, as did David Hume, for example, in his *Enquiry Concerning Human Understanding?*[15]

An interesting constellation of semiotic considerations points toward a final, an esthetic, ramification. In the story's triangle Hemingway has created a metafiction on readers' threefold semiotic roles.[16] As Hemingway's clerk, readers are *sign-receivers* who witness events in a sign-replete world. And so during the story the clerk reads papers, reads a book, reads papers again, and reads Pinin. A bystanding spectator, his perceptions enable him to receive signs which he decodes. Likewise has the major previously received signs that knowingly or unknowingly were sent by Pinin, signs he too has decoded. But the clerk and the major are also *sign-translators*, readers who go beyond a low-level sign-reception triad that requires them only to connect referent and signifier (*signifié* and *signifiant*). That is, the clerk and the major translate the signs they receive into concepts of a higher level of abstraction than mere decoding asks for. Consequently, the clerk's smile registers his translation of Pinin's behavior into a concept that amuses him, whatever that concept be. More clearly, the major's enquiry reflects his translation of the signs he received from Pinin into the concept of Pinin's "corruptness." Significantly, as sign-translators both the clerk and the major have formulated their conceptual conclusions partly on "absent" signs, either signs they have not perceived or signs they have perceived to be missing. The clerk, for example, has not witnessed the exchange in the major's bunk room; but that exclusion from perceiving signs has not prevented him from adducing *his* translation of the scene. (And clearly his wider knowledge of the daily events that circle about the hut inform his translated concept.) Similarly the major has inferred his concept of Pinin on the basis of some missing signs: there have been no letters from Pinin to a girl he claims to love. Little wonder that Hemingway found so attractive a "theory of omission" and tried to write his stories on the notion "that you could omit anything if you knew that you omitted [it,] and the omitted part would strengthen the story and make people feel something more than they understood."[17] After all, if readers are generically *sign-translators,* then signs left out may actually facilitate that translation habit.

As Hemingway's major, readers are also *sign-exchangers.* When denied the luxury of being passive readers, they attempt to express and communicate the meanings they have read to another respondent in what a semiotician would term a conjoined triadic exchange of signs.[18] And so the major's interrogation—whether exploitative or tendentious or considerate—replicates readers' attempts to convey through an exchange of signs with an audience the meaning and significance they have extrapolated from signs. (And if the image of the coercive major sits awkwardly in the reader's chair of your imagination, then imagine the clerk as sign-exchanger, telling his military cohorts after hours *his* version of the event that drew forth his smile.)

But what to do with Pinin the orderly? He is text, an orderly text at that. As well may he be the artist in the text. Either way, he fulfills the double role of artist-text: he is both *sign-utterer* and *sign-mute.* He has originated the signs that have elicited both the major's and the clerk's threefold responses. But while he provides his readers with many signs and has withheld yet others, he stands ultimately silent in the face of interrogation from his major reader, who represents interviewers, scholars, critics, pundits, and esthetes, all of whom, like the major, wish to know "the true gen" so as to be able to use it, erroneously believing that with it they will have knowledge that, because verifiable from an artist's confirmation, is valid. The artist, like Pinin, just may be totally at sea, ignorant of the signs he or she has sent that have been so misunderstood—as Hemingway might well be, were he to read this reading of his "simple" story. But even were he, unlike Pinin, forthcoming and responsive, his sign-reading would be of limited validity, autonomy being the destiny of every art object.

Artists whose work is truly significant must decline to answer our inquiries. They leave us as Hemingway leaves his major, perplexed, wondering if Pinin lied to him. Likewise, I end wondering, not knowing. I wonder if Hemingway wrote this story because what mattered to him were the epistemological riddles that his manipulation of the text's signs could provoke?[19] And I wonder if he was most pleased when his fiction, regardless of its countless signs, yielded irresolvable and conflicting concepts of his characters, left readers at the end of a narrative simply wondering, perhaps in perplexity at, perhaps in awe of, the signs they had received but were unable to satisfactorily and conclusively decode, translate, and exchange?

Notes

1. "Mussolini: Biggest Bluff in Europe," in *By-Line Ernest Hemingway: Selected Articles and Dispatches of Four Decades*, ed. William White (New York: Scribner's, 1967) 64.

2. *Ernest Hemingway: Selected Letters, 1917–1961*, ed. Carlos Baker (New York: Scribner's, 1981) 603.

3. See "A Self-Justifying Son: *A Moveable Feast*" in my *Concealments in Hemingway's Works* (Columbus: Ohio State UP, 1983) 218–31.

4. While these conflicting sign-bundles have often been attended to, the best documentation of the domestic perplexities they caused Hemingway is in Kenneth S. Lynn's *Hemingway* (New York: Simon and Schuster, 1987) 28–54.

5. Consider Gilles Deleuze, *Proust and Signs*, transl. Richard Howard (New York: George Braziller, 1972) 4: "Learning is essentially concerned with *signs*. Signs are the object of a temporal apprenticeship, not of an abstract knowledge. To learn is first of all to consider a substance, an object, a being as if they emitted signs to be deciphered, interpreted. There is no apprentice who is not 'the Egyptologist' of something. One becomes a carpenter only by becoming sensitive to the signs of wood, a physician by becoming sensitive to the signs of disease. Vocation is always predestination with regard to signs. Everything which teaches us something emits signs, every act of learning is an interpretation of signs or hieroglyphs."

6. Ernest Hemingway to Maxwell Perkins, 14 February 1927, *Letters*, 245. For my discussion I quote from the story as printed in *The Complete Short Stories of Ernest Hemingway* (New York: Scribner's, 1987) 250–53.

7. Joseph DeFalco, *The Hero in Hemingway's Short Stories* (Pittsburgh: U of Pittsburgh P, 1963), early detected the major's attempt to seduce his orderly and found in it a symbolic aberration symptomatic of war's unnaturalness, 131–32.

8. Sheridan Baker, *Ernest Hemingway: An Introduction and Interpretation* (New York: Barnes & Noble, 1967) 58.

9. See Sheridan Baker, *Ernest Hemingway*, 58–59; Jackson J. Benson, *Hemingway: The Writer's Art of Self-Defense* (Minneapolis: U of Minnesota P, 1969) 137; and, more recently, Kenneth G. Johnston, "'Hills Like White Elephants': Lean, Vintage Hemingway," *Studies in American Fiction* 10 (1982): 233–38; reprinted in his *The Tip of the Iceberg: Hemingway and the Short Story* (Greenwood: Penkevill, 1987) 125–34.

10. Characteristic is Arthur Waldhorn, *A Reader's Guide to Ernest Hemingway* (New York: Farrar, Straus and Giroux, 1972), who groups the major among "those whose sexual inclinations are aberrant" and for whom Hemingway has little tolerance: Waldhorn's rhetoric derides the major for having "too much unguent on his sunburned face and too much unction in his manner," 228–29.

11. Not a gratuitous remark, I add it to register my indebtedness to Lynn's psychobiographical penchant for finding androgynous signs laced throughout Hemingway's life and work, see, for example, 42, 110, 114, 136, 169, 181, 314, 389, 402, 417, 470, 512, and 539–44.

12. Umberto Eco, *The Role of the Reader: Explorations in the Semiotics of Texts* (Bloomington: Indiana UP, 1979) 47–66.

13. Robert Scholes, *Semiotics and Interpretation* (New Haven: Yale UP, 1982) 60, 30.

14. While germane to the larger matter of psychological universalities, I relegate to a footnote two triangles that require more space than my discussion allows: Freud's oedipal triangle, for the negative one—which signifies homosexuality—is clearly imprinted on the story; and Freud's "primal scene"—the imaging in a child (here the clerk) of the secret erotic combat behind parents' bedroom doors—for that triangle is visible too.

15. Admittedly, Hume's work is not among the lists of books in Hemingway's libraries, is catalogued in neither Michael S. Reynolds, *Hemingway's Reading, 1910–1940: An Inventory* (Princeton: Princeton UP, 1981) nor in James D. Brasch and Joseph Sigman, *Hemingway's Library: A Composite Record* (New York: Garland, 1981). But to look only to Hemingway's reading lists overlooks a broad intellectual milieu whose conversation provided much of his expatriated education.

16. I deliberately steer clear of adopting any single reader model lest *my* reader convict me of discipleship to one theoretician—Michael Riffaterre's "super-reader," Umberto Eco's "Model Reader," Jonathan Culler's "ideal reader," Norman Holland's "self-replicating reader," Wolfgang Iser's "implied reader," or a reader in one of Stanley Fish's "interpretive communities." For an excellent analysis of such theoreticians, see Elizabeth Freund, *The Return of the Reader: Reader-Response Criticism* (New York: Methuen, 1987).

17. *A Moveable Feast* (New York: Scribner's, 1964) 75.

18. For a sensible discussion of this process see Walker Percy, *Lost in the Cosmos: The Last Self-Help Book* (New York: Washington Square, 1983) 95–103.

19. For a fuller discussion of Hemingway's epistemological concerns, see my "From 'Sepi Jingan' to 'The Mother of a Queen': Hemingway's Three Epistemologic Formulas for Short Fiction" in Jackson J. Benson, ed. *The Short Stories of Ernest Hemingway: Critical Essays*, rev. edn. (Durham: Duke UP, forthcoming).

15

"Mais Je Reste Catholique": Communion, Betrayal, and Aridity in "Wine of Wyoming"

H. R. Stoneback

With "Wine of Wyoming," composed between October 1928 and May 1930, we move into the period of Winner Take Nothing, *Hemingway's third and final major anthology of short fiction. Although Kenneth Johnston has explored the story's Prohibition-era background in detail and Ann Putnam has recently revisited the short story, to date this atypical tale has received little extended attention. Here H.R. Stoneback argues that this "most infelicitous" neglect springs from the failure of Hemingway scholarship to recognize "Wine of Wyoming's" author as a "troubled but disciplined Catholic convert who finds the practice of his religion difficult in Protestant America." Stoneback goes on to illuminate the short story's Catholic context, and in so doing uncovers a fine* Waste Land *parable of communion and aridity. Stoneback not only refutes those biographers who have labeled Hemingway's Catholic conversion "bogus" but also prompts critics not to overlook the important influence of Catholic thought on Hemingway's fiction.*

"Wine of Wyoming," which carries one of Hemingway's most felicitous titles, has suffered the most infelicitous neglect. It is one of his finer stories, bringing together motifs and concerns that pervade his work from beginning to end and evoking subtle, complex responses in the engaged reader. Critical neglect of "Wine of Wyoming" may be, in part, a function of what some regard as the excessive use of the French language in the tale; more likely, the neglect springs from a general failure to come to terms with a Hemingway we have scarcely apprehended: the troubled but disciplined Catholic convert who finds the practice of his religion difficult in Protestant America.

It should also be noted that "Wine of Wyoming" illustrates amply Hemingway's considerable gifts as a comic writer—indeed, critics who insist on a humorless Hemingway would do well to look closely at this story. But my main purpose here is to consider the tale under the rubric of communion and prohibition, communion and dryness (in its several senses), to illuminate these categories of ritual concern in Hemingway and thus to clarify the subtle senses of betrayal and aridity with which "Wine of Wyoming" is most deeply concerned.

To judge from the early notices of the story, especially the reviews of *Winner Take Nothing* (in which the story was collected, after having appeared in *Scribner's Magazine* in August 1930), it would seem that "Wine of Wyoming" was well on its way toward a substantial reputation as one of the major stories in the Hemingway canon. For example, a brief, unsigned review in the *Kansas City Star* finds *Winner Take Nothing* pretty "raw stuff" and Hemingway "still pretty intimately concerned with the subjects of liquor, blood and sex." Yet, by way of pointing out the exceptions in the collection, the reviewer concludes, "At the same time Hemingway fans will tell you there are some of his finest stories in this collection, particularly 'Wine of Wyoming' and 'The Gambler, The Nun and the Radio.'"[1] In the same vein, the reviewer for the *Cincinnati Enquirer* viewed the collection with distaste—"food for strong stomachs only"—finding "plenty of meat" in *Winner Take Nothing* but asserting that most of it has "reached a somewhat advanced stage of mortification." Once again, the exception is "Wine of Wyoming," with its portrait of the "sweet and generous" Fontans contrasted with the "rudeness and vulgarity" of their American customers; moreover, there was "an expression of human sympathy" in this story.[2] Although the reviewer in the *London Times* found *Winner Take Nothing* a "somewhat gloomy book" overall, the happier mood of "Wine of Wyoming" was noted as an exception. The highest praise came from Horace Gregory, in the *New York Herald Tribune:* "There are two stories that show a sudden expansion of Hemingway's range, yet both are beautifully simplified and pure. These are 'Wine of Wyoming' and 'The Gambler, the Nun and the Radio.'" Gregory praises "Wine of Wyoming" in the highest terms: "I believe this piece to be one of the few instances in contemporary literature where the short story may be regarded as a superlative work of art. Hemingway is no longer content to present a situation and then let it answer for itself—it is his interpretation rising out of his experiences that makes a story."[3] Gregory's stress on the superlative art and interpretation is striking, all the more so since "Wine of Wyoming" is often taken to be an instance of mere reportage. In fact, few Hemingway stories interpret so much, so actively.

In spite of the early praise for "Wine of Wyoming" as one of the best stories in the otherwise dark and despairing *Winner Take Nothing*, the taste for despair of generations of Hemingway critics along with their indifference to, or will to ignore, the essentially Catholic Hemingway have held sway in subsequent criticism. For example, Arthur Waldhorn in *A Reader's Guide to Ernest Hemingway* devotes part of one sentence—and that in a footnote— to "Wine of Wyoming"; he labels it one of Hemingway's "most forgettable" stories.[4] Sheridan Baker, who finds evidence in *Winner Take Nothing* that Hemingway is "running down" and is close to "the edge of despair," also has one sentence on the story: it "has little to recommend it beyond the curiosity of American prohibition in rural form, and the fact that it seems to be almost straight Hemingway autobiography."[5] In fact, Hemingway critics, when they have bothered to mention the story at all, have shown a proclivity for the one-sentence dismissal of "Wine of Wyoming."[6]

Other standard critical sources, such as Linda Wagner's *Ernest Hemingway: Six Decades of Criticism* and Jackson J. Benson's *The Short Stories of Ernest Hemingway: Critical Essays*, offer not even a sentence on "Wine of Wyoming."[7] Indeed the checklist in the Benson volume makes it clear that even such neglected stories as "After the Storm," "Homage to Switzerland," "One Reader Writes," and "A Pursuit Race" have received more critical attention than "Wine of Wyoming." Jeffrey Meyers, who finds room in *Hemingway: A Biography* to comment on everything from "Banal Story" to "Wedding Day," utters not a word on "Wine of Wyoming," probably because the story so clearly works against the Hemingway-as-bogus-Catholic theme that informs the Meyers volume.[8] Even Carlos Baker fails under the one-sentence rubric—although, as usual, his passing remarks are on target: "Wine of Wyoming" is a "fine and subtle" story that provides evidence of Hemingway's "championship of the normal and the natural." Noting the general response that greeted *Winner Take Nothing* as the "poorest and least interesting" of Hemingway's volumes, Baker reminds the reader that "Wine of Wyoming" was the exception to that assessment; it was "generally admired," and it is a "character sketch full of cleanliness and order."[9]

There are, however, a few treatments of the story that go beyond the brief aside or the one-sentence dismissal. Sheldon Grebstein regards "Wine of Wyoming" as a "worthy" story and discusses it and "The Denunciation" as instances of Hemingway's skillful use of first-person narrators "who function significantly in the action and who convey an ethical norm which reflects the writer's own values."[10] Grebstein sees clearly that "Wine of Wyoming" is Hemingway's "effective indictment against his homeland," that the narrator and the Fontans "represent European values: the appreciation of good food and drink, friendship based on a shared ethos; individual freedom and responsibility; self-respect as evidenced by cleanliness, order, and pride in one's work."[11] These values are contrasted with American hypocrisy, irresponsibility, and messiness. Grebstein is right on the mark here, yet his discussion is somewhat vitiated by his failure to deal with the story's "catholique" theme and by his overstatement of the betrayal involved in the story's crisis. Wirt Williams, in a good, brief discussion of the story, sees that it is centered on the "sacramental wine" as "apotheosis of friendship and communion," but he, too, overstates Fontan's failure "in his roles as friend and as priest-guardian of the mysteries," just as he overlooks the precise thrust of the "catholique" theme and the role of the American narrator in the aborted communion.[12]

The only sustained critical commentary on "Wine of Wyoming" is found in Kenneth G. Johnston's article, "Hemingway's 'Wine of Wyoming': Disappointment in America," and in Joseph M. Flora's *Hemingway's Nick Adams*. Johnston is certainly correct about the story's expression of "disappointment" in America, but his approach, his angle of vision, is peripheral to the story's main concerns. It is not a story *about* the immigrant experience, "about the American 'melting pot.'" The story's focus is not on the failure of "the American Dream," as Johnston argues.[13] Rather, it might be said that the story demonstrates the *fulfillment* of the Protestant American Dream: the messy, confused individualism and legalism, the lack of discipline and ritual, the legal and spiritual dryness which, seen from a Catholic perspective, might be regarded as the natural and inevitable outcome of puritanism. While his essay provides some interesting background discussion, Johnston ignores the Catholic center of the story and completely misses the motif of communion and betrayal as well as the narrator's complicity in that movement.

The longest, and in some ways the most engaged discussion to date is Flora's *Hemingway's Nick Adams*. Flora understands the way the story is grounded in Catholicism and the "values of tradition and the Old World" and the importance of the narrator as protagonist in the tale.[14] Yet since his design requires consideration of "Wine of Wyoming" as a Nick Adams story—"as a part of a late Nick trilogy"—Flora is forced into insisting on some rather odd assertions, such as the "alarming nebulousness" of the narrator's wife, the view that the story is a suggestion of "what Nick's marriage had become," and the unnecessary belaboring of the narrator's "I-we" shifts.[15] Flora's case for "Wine of Wyoming" as an important Nick story is, if not compelling, wholly absorbing, and it deserves more attention than it has received. The net effect of his discussion, however, is to becloud the clarity and precision of "Wine of Wyoming" and its urgency as a single, separate tale that may or may not be about Nick Adams but is most certainly the key neglected Hemingway story, one of the most resonant stories dealing with the crucial matters of Hemingway's expatriation, his attitudes toward America, his code of values, and his Catholicism.

Since the question before us here is dryness, legal and spiritual, it might be useful to review a few background matters, to remind ourselves at the outset that Hemingway's Oak Park—fashionable and arid and Protestant suburb that it was—never had saloons. It was a community characterized as "righteously dry"; indeed, the boundary line between Chicago and Oak Park has been defined as "the point where the saloons ended and the churches began."[16] Ultimately, it might be argued, Hemingway's purpose is to bridge that abyss, to bring Chicago and Oak Park saloons and churches together in an inclusive and authentic sacrament. With this sense of the dry, puritanical community of Oak Park in mind, we may better appreciate the boldness of Hemingway's final column in his high school newspaper. In the course of general commentary on Oak Park social and political life, he writes, "A new party enters the [election] race next fall in the person of the anti-prohibition party. Its leaders . . . nominated the modest editor of these columns and announced their [campaign] slogan as 'Hemingway and a full Stein.'"[17] While we might simply attribute this humorous challenge to the morals of Oak Park to Hemingway's adolescent desire to shock his elders, we might also discern one source of his lifelong nickname—Hemingstein—as well as an early instance of what would become a major motif in his mature work: drink as symbolic act, drink as sign of life fully lived, drink as communion.

The other side of that coin, of course, is Prohibition as closure, as hypocrisy, as denial of communion. By the time Hemingway had his wartime experience of the way such matters were ordered in Europe, he would write scathing columns for the *Toronto Star* on the farce of American Prohibition. One such piece, dated 1921 and entitled "Chicago Never Wetter Than It Is Today," mocks Prohibition and suggests that it is a symbol of all that is wrong with America. This was written at a time when nearly everything he said evinced his determination to return to Europe to live. In ruminations on the so-called "lost generation," it is always useful to remember the exact role played by drink and Prohibition in the expatriate's and artist's credo. Many commentators on the 1920s have noted this; some few have seen that that role went beyond the mere accessibility of alcohol. Malcolm Cowley, for example, finds that a key article of faith for the American artist of those days was that, "by expatriating himself, by living in Paris . . . or the South of France, the artist can break the puritan shackles, drink, live freely, and be wholly creative."[18] Hemingway, then, shared the attitudes of many writers of his generation toward drink and the pervasive bad faith of Prohibition. For Hemingway, much more precisely and vividly, drinking was a matter of freedom and discipline and taste—aesthetic and moral, oenological and theological.

None of these exiled writers would make such bold use of drink in a literary work as Hemingway did in the novel that defined a period: *The Sun Also Rises*. It might be argued that the very structure of that novel derives from the ritual of drinking. At the most obvious level, there is not a single chapter without a drinking scene. Examination of the text reveals that there are at least 26 varieties of drink consumed in some 34 specific establishments. These facts have led some readers to regard the novel as a pointless chronicle of a group of rather tacky drunks. Some may even regard the novel as the best evidence *for* Prohibition. But it is nothing of the kind: it is, rather, a scrupulously orchestrated work bound together by four interwoven strands of ritual-centered activity, four precincts of the sacramental vision: drinking, fishing, the bullfight, and the Catholic church. This is not the place to launch a detailed discussion of the novel; I have argued elsewhere, in considerable detail, that the novel takes the form of quest, of a precisely structured Catholic pilgrimage.[19] It must suffice here to say that the matter of drinking is examined from various angles of vision: from the angle of taste and the formation of values, from the angle of moderation as well as necessary excess, and from the angle of communion. A brief look at one scene from the novel may be useful in demonstrating how the novel clarifies the focus of "Wine of Wyoming" and how the story illuminates central concerns of *The Sun Also Rises*.

Consider the hilarious yet intricately structured scene involving Jake and Bill after they have finished their first day of fishing. They are eating lunch by a trout stream in the Pyrenees. They have two bottles of wine that have been chilled in a spring.

> "Is this all we've got?"
> "Only the two bottles."
> "Do you know what you are?" Bill looked at the bottle affectionately.
> "No," [Jake] said.
> "You're in the pay of the Anti-Saloon League."
> "I went to Notre Dame with Wayne B. Wheeler."
> "It's a lie," said Bill. "I went to Austin Business College with Wayne B. Wheeler. He was class president."
> "Well," [Jake] said, "the saloon must go."
> "You're right there, old classmate," Bill said. "The saloon must go, and I will take it with me."[20]

Who was Wayne B. Wheeler?—the driving force of the Anti-Saloon League, the principal author of the Volstead Act, and one of the most feared political manipulators in American history. Self-described as one of "the champions of a sober America," Wheeler was widely celebrated and despised as the "Dry Boss."[21] Obviously, neither Jake nor Bill went to school with Wheeler, a nineteenth-century graduate of Oberlin (Hemingway's father's alma mater), a hotbed of Prohibition activities. Jake, a Catholic, observes ironically that he was with Wheeler at Notre-Dame—the last place where one would find a raving Protestant Prohibitionist. In fact, the deep form of this entire interlude, filled with humorous commentary on American life in the 1920s, leads the reader through the ritual of fishing in the good place in the mountains of Spain (with overtones of the Fisher King myth), through a sequence of rejections of American dryness, in every respect, through a prototypical communion scene with lunch and wine, to the ultimate business of the chapter, which reverberates in the question Bill asks Jake at the end of the scene: "Listen, Jake . . . are you really a Catholic?"

To examine this scene and others like it in *The Sun Also Rises* is to be reminded that the lay of the land is rendered not only through cafés and bars but through cathedrals and churches and that Jake, at least, spends almost as much time praying as he does drinking. Apparently one must read carefully to see this and to apprehend its significance, for it has generally been missed, but to see that the activities of the novel that matter most— drinking, bullfighting, and, yes, praying and fishing—are somehow prohibited, proscribed, or perverted in the pervasive dryness of America takes no great care. If specifically American aridity is one of the secondary motifs of *The Sun Also Rises*, it is the explicit theme, the exact center of "Wine of Wyoming."

"Wine of Wyoming" offers one of Hemingway's most satisfactory images of a clean, cheerful, bright place in the midst of a wasteland of dryness and desiccation. At the most obvious level, the story is a tale concerned with Prohibition. The Fontans, a French couple living in Wyoming, are bootleggers. They make and sell beer and wine in a dry country. They are arrested and fined for bootlegging under a bizarre puritanical system that they cannot comprehend. The American narrator, who lives in France and is on a hunting trip in Wyoming, eats and drinks with the Fontans several times; together they discuss such matters as Prohibition, the imminent Hoover-Smith election, and the Catholic church. The narrator finds the Fontans clean, vivid, and admirable characters. Monsieur Fontan urges him to come back with his wife, before they leave Wyoming, for some new wine, for a fête. The Americans, worn out from packing, do not come for the fête. That is the action of the story, yet this summary tells little about the tale's deeper movements.

The story begins with the American man, the unnamed I-narrator, drinking on the porch of Fontan's place. When someone drives up, he hides his beer under the table. The visitors ask for beer, and Madame Fontan informs them there is no more and sends them away. They stagger away; their car jerks and whirls on the road. Madame Fontan says, "Put the beer on the table. . . . What's the matter? Don't drink off the floor."[22] The narrator indicates his concern that the visitors might have been looking for Prohibition violators. Madame Fontan tells him they were just drunks, the kind that cause all the trouble. Such scenes recur; for example, there are the Americans who put whiskey in their beer:

> "No," I said.
> "Oui. My God, yes, that's true. Et aussi une femme qui a vomis sur la table!"
> "Comment?"
> "C'est vrai. Elle a vomis sur la table. Et après elle a vomis dans ses shoes. And afterward they come back and say they want to come again and have another party the next Saturday, and I say no, my God, no! When they came I locked the door."
> "They're bad when they're drunk." (460)

Then there are the teenagers who cruise in their cars and buy Fontan's beer and mix it with their moonshine. "They put whiskey in the beer," Madame Fontan exclaims in disbelief. "My God, I don't understand *that!*" The narrator explains, "They want to get sick, so they'll know they're drunk" (460). Then there are the Americans who put whiskey in wine, or the man in pajamas who slips out from under the watchful eyes of his wife to sneak some beer. In short, the behavior of Americans is characterized as messy, sneaky, hypocritical, and disgusting. They have no sense of the proper uses of wine and beer; they have no sense of decorum. They drink only to get drunk, vomit, and pass out. In contrast, the appropriately named Fontans run a bright, cheerful, orderly place and have room in their values for drinking as a life-affirming, joyful ceremony. This sense of things the narrator shares with the Fontans, but, as the story makes clear, that is because he is an American expatriate who lives in France.

This is the obvious theme: the messiness of Americans in general—at least the ones who have not lived in Europe—and their nasty drinking habits in particular. This theme in turn is linked directly with the Prohibition motif. Fontan, the proprietor, cannot understand why he has been arrested and heavily fined. The fines take all the money he makes working in the mines as well as the money Madame Fontan makes taking in washing. The narrator comments regarding the fines: "It's a crime." Madame Fontan points out that they charge very little for their wine and beer. "We never sell the beer before it's good. Lots of places they sell the beer right away when they make it, and then it gives everybody a headache. . . . They put Fontan in jail and they take seven hundred fifty-five dollars" (459). This time the narrator says, "It's wicked," thus acknowledging the correctness of the Fontan code and suggesting both Hemingway's exact view of Prohibition as well as the progression of the tale from the realm of the legal to the spiritual.

Legal, political, and spiritual questions are then woven together through a sequence of references to Al Smith. The time of the story is September 1928. Madame Fontan asks the narrator, "Schmidt ... if he's the President, you think we get the wine and beer all right?" "Sure," he replies. "Trust Schmidt" (458). Prohibition, of course, was one of the major issues of the 1928 campaign. While Americans were drinking more than ever, most public voices were preaching "purity" more stridently than ever. One historian has observed, "What Hoover was to call an experiment 'noble in purpose' represented the single most striking act of hypocrisy of the decade. Americans never drank so much, yet there was not a single major political figure of old ethnic stock to go on record as clearly opposing prohibition."[23] Smith, on the other hand, clearly opposed Prohibition. At the 1928 Democratic convention he fought for a stronger wet plank, without success. He was given a dry running mate. As one reporter observed, "The Democratic donkey has a wet head and wags a dry tail." A prominent Baptist minister declared, typically, that Smith represented "card playing, drinking, divorce, dancing, Darrow, nude art, and prize fighting." But the full demonic formula was Rum and Romanism, and by far the most vicious attacks were directed against Smith's Catholicism, which was *the* central issue of the campaign. As a Catholic, detractors said, Smith represented a "pernicious enemy of the American Dream," an "alien medieval Latin mentality."[24] If Smith won, they said, the pope would have a suite in the White House. Anti-Catholic literature inundated the country.

In spite of all this, and what we might surmise to be Hemingway's bitter personal reaction, as a Catholic, to such an anti-Catholic crusade, his use of the 1928 campaign in "Wine of Wyoming" is understated. At first, it seems little more than humorous counterpoint to the main business. Truly, however, it takes us to the heart of the matter; Smith is used as the inverted symbol of all that is wrong with America. He represents the positive forces that are persecuted or prohibited in America. Consider this crux:

> "The other day [Madame Fontan says] there was a little French girl here with her mother ... and she said to me, 'En Amérique. . . . It's not good to be catholique. The Americans don't like you to be catholique. It's like the dry law.' I said to her, 'What you going to be? Heh? It's better to be catholique if you're catholique.' But she said, 'No, it isn't any good to be catholique in America.' But I think it's better to be catholique if you are. Ce n'est pas bon de changer sa religion. My God, no." (456–57)

At this point Monsieur Fontan asks the narrator, "You go to the mass here?" "No," the narrator replies, "I don't go in America, only sometimes in a long while. *Mais je reste catholique.* It's no good to change the religion" (emphasis added). It is here, at the exact center of the story, textually as well as thematically, that the narrator, expatriate Catholic American, is involved directly in the story's deepest significations concerning order and chaos, communion and alienation, Catholicism and Protestantism. Al Smith is the focal point for the rest of this passage. Monsieur Fontan says, "On dit que Schmidt est catholique." Madame Fontan responds, "I don't think Schmidt is catholique. There's not many catholique in America." "We are catholique," the narrator says. "Sure but you live in France," Madame Fontan declares. "Je ne crois pas que Schmidt est catholique. Did he ever live in France?" Madame Fontan continues to assert, in the central, comic (yet deadly serious) repetition of the tale, her doubt that an American presidential candidate could be Catholic: "My God, Schmidt est catholique." "You think he'll be the president?" Monsieur Fontan asks the narrator. "No," the narrator says flatly, and this movement of the story ends (456–58).

The next day the narrator returns to Fontan's for a drink. Madame Fontan, looking "like Mrs. Santa Claus, clean and rosy-faced," brings him a beer and they discuss again the prospects for repeal of Prohibition if Smith is elected. Then the story progresses through anecdotes about messy, drunken Americans to the topic of the narrator's imminent departure. Before leaving Wyoming, he promises, they will return for the fête centered around Fontan's new wine. (Since the American sense of things tends to regard *fête* as a synonym for "party," it may be necessary to assert that the term means "feast"—in the religious sense—and no matter how social or cultural the fête, the resonance lingers, a resonance not present in the term "party.") When the time comes, weary from hunting and preparations to leave, the Americans, the narrator and his wife, do not make a presence at Fontan's fête. Profoundly disappointed, Fontan drinks up the new wine alone. This event hardly indicates, as Grebstein argues, that Fontan is a victim of "the same animal appetites he despises in those American *'cochons'* whom he bars from his table."[25] Nor is it, as Williams argues, "an act of self-destruction," an indication that Fontan is "destroyed in his roles as friend and as priest-guardian of the mysteries."[26] Rather, Fontan is seen here not so much as a failed priest in the wasteland, as a saddened, frustrated priest, a sorrowful hierophant who, in the absence of communicants who had given their word to attend the ceremony, must consume all the wine consecrated for that purpose. The next day, when the Americans stop by on their way out of town, Fontan tries to get more new wine from his storage place, but his worthless American daughter-in-law has gone off with the key. In an atmosphere of frustration and suspicion, as a neighbor watches the French bootlegger who is frantic at being locked out of his own building, the final possibility of communion, the last chance to share the new wine, is aborted.

The Americans bid farewell to the Fontans. Madame Fontan has tears in her eyes and Fontan is very sad: "'Good-by,' we said. We all felt very badly. They stood in the doorway and we got in, and I started the motor. We waved. They stood together sadly on the porch. Fontan looked very old, and Madame Fontan looked sad. She waved to us and Fontan went in the house. We turned up the road" (466). With flawless timing and subtlety, Hemingway modulates into the new key of betrayal, committed by the couple who, in the end, are all too American:

> "They felt so badly. Fontan felt terribly."
> "We ought to have gone last night."
> "Yes, we ought to have." (467)

But the merely personal has denied the formal, the meanest trivia and momentary weariness have led the American couple to break their word, to deny the ritual. As they drive out of the country that looks so much like Spain—"It looked like Spain, but it was Wyoming"—a repeated image that underlies the radical disparity, the absence in Wyoming of the rituals that make Spain and France the real old thing that Hemingway loved and for which he quested throughout his life and work, the narrator's wife hopes the Fontans will have "a lot of good luck." But the narrator knows they won't, "and Schmidt won't be President either."

The final passage reiterates the couple's knowledge of their betrayal of the Fontans, and echoes the notion introduced earlier in the story—the idea that while most things are wrong in Wyoming, it is at least a good country for fishing and hunting:

> "It's a fine country for la chasse, Fontan says."
> "And when the chasse is gone?"
> "They'll be dead then. . . ."
> "We ought to have gone last night."
> "Oh, yes. . . . We ought to have gone." (466–67)

Thus the final elegiac note of a tale concerned with Prohibition and betrayal in every possible sense, with a Waste Land where all things conspire against the slaking of thirst, rings the final change of the American couple's complicity in the general bad faith in a doomed land. It is "too late" for America, as Hemingway would explicitly assert in *Green Hills of Africa*, "too late" even for the very land, the spoiled country that had become a "bloody mess."[27]

A brief look at manuscript revisions will confirm the tale's design. The story is, of course, based rather directly on Hemingway's experiences in September 1928 with the Moncini family of Sheridan, Wyoming. In the original version he changed the name of the Moncinis to Pichot and the title was "Il Est Crazy Pour Le Vin." The effect of the change from Pichot— which Hemingway may have intended to suggest *pichet*, the familiar name for a wine pitcher—to Fontan is to evoke a rich cluster of associations with *fontaine*—fountain, spring, source—and *fonte*, thawing snow (a resonance underlined by the description of the melting snow on the high mountain peaks visible from Fontan's place). Fontan is in every way a more allusive and appropriate name, pinpointing the function that the Fontans perform admirably: the quenching of thirst, the provision of wine and beer and fellowship in a dry land. (Also, the suggestion of font, in the sense of baptismal font, is more than incidental, given the sacramental role the Fontans play.)

The change of title, from "Il Est Crazy Pour Le Vin" to "Wine of Wyoming," shifts the emphasis away from the possible misreading of Fontan as a kind of alcoholic, intoxicated with his role as bootlegger as well as his product (and that is how some readers have viewed the matter), to Fontan as a priestly figure. Of course, the title change also underlines the theme of American-European contrasts. Indeed most of the revisions shift the emphasis subtly in the direction of the sacramental vision, the patterns of significance analyzed in this essay. The references to Catholicism are reinforced and made more precise. (E.g., "it's better to be whatever you are" becomes "it's better to be catholique if you are.") The contrast of Wyoming with Spain is more effectively restated and reiterated. The telling line, "It looked like Spain, but it was Wyoming," replaces the less emphatic "It looked like Spain, but it was not Spain." The second assertion of this image—the mountains "looked more like Spain than ever"—is added in the final version. Finally, the bad faith of the American couple in failing to return for Fontan's fête is brought more sharply into focus. For example, Hemingway had originally written that the couple "should" have gone to the Fontans' fête; he changes this to "ought to," thus intensifying the sense of obligation and ritual duty in the emphatic four repetitions of the "We ought to have gone" line, knelling at the story's conclusion.

"Wine," as Hemingway said in *Death in the Afternoon*, "is one of the most civilized things in the world and one of the natural things of the world that has been brought to the greatest perfection."[28] This fundamental truth brings into proper perspective the appalling fact, the incomprehensible condition of being, known as Prohibition. Wine, the legacy of centuries of taste and cultivation, of creation and incarnation, was illegal in the desiccated states of America. It was forbidden, and the causes and consequences of that nay saying, that denial, were bound up with Protestantism and the burden of puritanism. "Wine of Wyoming" provides a searching examination of American spiritual dryness and its concomitant messiness and hypocrisy. The story develops a complex tapestry depicting Prohibition as spiritual aridity, a condition making communion extremely difficult even for those who long for it, those expatriate Americans or immigrant Europeans who, however wise they may be in the ways of tradition, are caught in the dry country. Betrayal breeds betrayal. Tradition and civilization, as anchored in the European-Catholic vision of the story, are betrayed. The land itself is betrayed. In the cumulative imagery of the mines, the reckless shooting, the cars whirling on the cement roads, there is more than a hint of the familiar machine-in-the-garden motif. Finally, the narrator betrays the very sacrament he celebrates. Like a good American, he hits the road, leaves Wyoming behind. Where will he go? Back to France? What person, what place, what grace is safe from betrayal?

On 31 May 1930, Hemingway sent "Wine of Wyoming" to Maxwell Perkins, with the comment: "Don't let anyone tell you it's not a good story or has too much French in it. . . . This is a 1st flight story I promise you."[29] A few weeks later Hemingway wrote to Archibald MacLeish, calling his attention to "Wine of Wyoming," saying, "Maybe you'll like the story."[30] Perhaps Hemingway wanted MacLeish's response to the story since it dealt with matter and themes very close to MacLeish's poem, "American Letter," which had recently appeared in print. Perhaps "American Letter" figured as a touchstone in Hemingway's process of composing the story. In any case, the well-known and important poem, which the editors of *The American Tradition in Literature* seem to think has something to do with "the spiritual defeatism to which the expatriate American writers in general succumbed" and represents MacLeish's "break with the expatriates of Paris," does indeed address the question of "the supposed aridity of American life." The poem, however, has less to do with some supposed rejection of expatriation, that question so urgent to Hemingway's and MacLeish's generation, than with a pattern of European-American contrasts and the heartsick pain of MacLeish's separation from France. The poem evokes, indeed celebrates, the quiet, traditional life of France—"They keep/The wise past and the words spoken in common. . . . They live together in small things"—and contrasts it with the lonely individualism of America: "America is West and the wind blowing/. . . America is alone and the gulls calling/It is a strange thing to be an American." Evoking the western sprawl of the American continent, MacLeish images Wyoming, "The smoke goes up from the high plains of Wyoming,"[31] and his heart longs for France. Perhaps Hemingway's story is, at least in part, a response to MacLeish's "American Letter," token

of a continuation of old discussions with an old friend, an old and very
Protestant friend, whose answers to all these matters diverged radically
from Hemingway's Catholic responses.[32] In "American Letter" MacLeish's
central question is, "How can a wise man have two countries?" In "Wine
of Wyoming" Hemingway replies, in effect, that perhaps a wise man, an
American, *must* have at least two countries. The shape of Hemingway's life
and work confirms the response.

Hemingway was right about "Wine of Wyoming." It is a good story—
"1st flight." And the resolution to the story's central theme—"it isn't any
good to be catholique in America"—is not *mais je reste américain;* rather,
in spite of all the difficulties involved, the voice reverberates in the American darkness, "Mais je reste catholique." The subtle terror of the betrayal
of the desired communion at the end of the tale, the aborted fête, does not
leave the engaged reader, the narrator and his wife, or the Fontans in
despair. Despair, as Hemingway observed in a letter, was the sin against
the Holy Ghost, a sin he had never committed.[33] Sadness and a lingering
sense of complexity and dislocation, yes; despair, no. Indeed, the communion has been present throughout the story; it is the ritual, incarnational
enactment of "the fête," the sacramental vigil that, quite necessarily and
appropriately for Protestant, Prohibition America, is denied.

The condition of aridity that obtains at the end of the story is one that,
in its deepest sense, Hemingway would know well from his reading of Saint
John of the Cross and Saint Teresa of Avila. To wit, aridity is a precise
theological term denoting the absence of satisfaction together with a "great
anxiety to please God." "All spiritual writers agree," continues *The Oxford
Dictionary of the Christian Church*, "in enjoining perseverance in prayer
despite the trial of aridity and they regard it, if patiently borne, as a means
of great advancement to the Christian soul."[34] "Wine of Wyoming," which
Hemingway said was one of his stories written "absolutely" as it happened—
a fact that does not preclude shaping imagination of the highest order—gets
as close to the heart of Hemingway's mature vision as any single story
does.[35] It deals profoundly with his country, his expatriation, his values, and
his religion. In spite of—perhaps *because* of—this "trial of aridity," the story
stakes out a terrain somewhere beyond the Waste Land and posts it with
the legend, "Mais je reste catholique."

Notes

1. Quoted in Robert O. Stephens, ed. *Ernest Hemingway: The Critical Reception* (New
   York: Burt Franklin, 1977) 140–41.

2. Quoted in Stephens, 141.

3. *London Times*, 9 February 1934, quoted in Stephens, 140.

4. Waldhorn's remark in his generally very solid and thoroughgoing *A Reader's Guide to Ernest Hemingway* (New York: Farrar, Straus and Giroux, 1972) has, I admit, haunted me for some time, along with other one-sentence dismissals by literary critics. Perhaps when a writer merely remarks that a story is "most forgettable" and offers no explanation, a reader is privileged to assume that the writer cannot remember the story or does not wish to remember. In any case, from 15 years' experience of teaching "Wine of Wyoming" to graduate seminars and undergraduate surveys, I have a distinct impression that this is one of Hemingway's most *memorable* stories. Scores of students have chosen to write papers on both the vivid comic richness of the story, which often—so they have said—reveals to them a Hemingway they had missed, as well as the sad or tragic or Catholic resonances of the story, which also lead them toward a deeper sense of Hemingway's work. This note amounts to an acknowledgment of what I have learned from their discussions. The story is beautiful to teach, and it engages students fully. If hundreds of students are an accurate indicator, then the two most memorable stories in *Winner Take Nothing* are "A Clean, Well-Lighted Place" and "Wine of Wyoming." The choice is hardly incidental, since the two stories are closely related. It is high time that we turn our attention, pedagogical and critical, from such overanthologized, overtaught, and overrated stories as "The Killers," for one, and pay heed to such stories as "Wine of Wyoming." "Wine of Wyoming" may be the most *forgotten* major short story, but it is certainly not the "most forgettable."

5. Sheridan Baker, *Ernest Hemingway: An Introduction and Interpretation* (New York: Rinehart, 1976) 84.

6. See Harold Bloom, ed. *Ernest Hemingway: Modern Critical Views* (New York: Chelsea House, 1985) 79; Joseph DeFalco, *The Hero in Hemingway's Short Stories* (Pittsburgh: U of Pittsburgh P, 1963) 52–53; Kenneth S. Lynn, *Hemingway* (New York: Simon and Schuster, 1987) 409; and Chaman Nahal, *The Narrative Pattern in Hemingway's Fiction* (Rutherford: Fairleigh Dickinson UP, 1971) 83–84.

7. See Linda W. Wagner, ed. *Ernest Hemingway: Six Decades of Criticism* (East Lansing: Michigan State UP, 1987) and Jackson J. Benson, ed. *The Short Stories of Ernest Hemingway: Critical Essays* (Durham: Duke UP, 1975).

8. Jeffrey Meyers, *Hemingway: A Biography* (New York: Harper & Row, 1985).

9. Carlos Baker, *Hemingway: The Writer as Artist*, 4th ed. (Princeton: Princeton UP, 1972) 141, and *Ernest Hemingway: A Life Story* (New York: Charles Scribner's Sons, 1969) 246, 191.

10. Sheldon Norman Grebstein, *Hemingway's Craft* (Carbondale: Southern Illinois UP, 1973) 60.

11. Grebstein, 65.

12. Wirt Williams, *The Tragic Art of Ernest Hemingway* (Baton Rouge: Louisiana State UP, 1981) 102.

13. Kenneth Johnston, "Hemingway's 'Wine of Wyoming': Disappointment in America," *Western American Literature* 9 (November 1974): 160, 166.

14. Joseph Flora, *Hemingway's Nick Adams* (Baton Rouge: Louisiana State UP, 1982) 224.

15. Flora, 232, 234.

16. Charles A. Fenton, *The Apprenticeship of Ernest Hemingway: The Early Years* (New York: Farrar, Straus, Young, 1954) 150.

17. Fenton, 30–31.

18. Malcolm Cowley, *Exile's Return* (New York: Viking, 1951).

19. H. R. Stoneback, "From the rue St.-Jacques to the Pass of Roland to the 'Unfinished Church on the Edge of the Cliff,'" *The Hemingway Review* 6 (Fall 1986): 2–29.

20. Ernest Hemingway, *The Sun Also Rises* (New York: Charles Scribner's Sons, 1926) 123.

21. Justin Stewart, *Wayne Wheeler: Dry Boss* (Westport: Greenwood, 1970) 299.

22. Hemingway, "Wine of Wyoming," *The Short Stories of Ernest Hemingway* (New York: Charles Scribner's Sons, 1966) 450. All subsequent references are to this edition.

23. Arthur M. Schlesinger, Jr., and Frederick Israel, eds., *History of American Presidential Elections* (New York: Chelsea House, 1971) 2589.

24. Schlesinger, 2590–97.

25. Grebstein, 65.

26. Williams, 102.

27. Hemingway, *Green Hills of Africa* (New York: Charles Scribner's Sons, 1935) 285.

28. Hemingway, *Death in the Afternoon* (New York: Charles Scribner's Sons, 1932) 10.

29. Hemingway to Maxwell Perkins, 31 May 1930, in *Ernest Hemingway: Selected Letters, 1917–1961*, ed. Carlos Baker (New York: Charles Scribner's Sons, 1981) 323.

30. Hemingway to Archibald MacLeish, 30 June 1930, *Letters*, 325.

31. Archibald MacLeish, "American Letter," *The Bookman* (28 January 1929), n.p.

32. See the incident recounted in Stoneback, 5–6.

33. In an unpublished letter to Robert Brown (8 August 1956), in the collection of the Humanities Research Center at the University of Texas.

34. F. L. Cross, ed., *The Oxford Dictionary of the Christian Church* (London: Oxford UP, 1957) 81–82.

35. Hemingway to Perkins, 16 November 1933, *Letters*, 400.

16

"That's Not Very Polite": Sexual Identity in Hemingway's "The Sea Change"

Warren Bennett

The 1986, posthumous publication of Hemingway's The Garden of Eden *should generate critical reassessment of long-published short stories treating sexual confusion and androgyny, stories now being recognized for the first time as parts of a larger trend in Hemingway's life and work. Here Warren Bennett provides such reassessment for "The Sea Change," composed between January and June of 1930. He reexamines every aspect of this short story: its oblique dialogue between Phil and the girl who is leaving him for a lesbian lover, its central allusion to Pope's "Essay on Man," and its descriptions of Phil's final encounters with the bartender, the bar's patrons, and his own reflection in the mirror. Bennett's thorough, close reading of "The Sea Change" in the light cast by* The Garden of Eden *leads to a wholly new and very persuasive interpretation of this short story. He challenges previous critics who have located "The Sea Change's" central conflict in Phil's need to accept or reject the girl's lesbianism. Instead, Bennett believes that the story pivots on Phil's recognition that "the nature and meaning of his relationship with the girl have been unmanly," a recognition that shatters his masculine identity. Seen through Warren Bennett's eyes, "The Sea Change" becomes more complex and more chilling than ever before.*

"The Sea Change" is among Ernest Hemingway's less appreciated stories, and it is also a story the full understanding of which has eluded critics. J. Bakker compares it to "Hills Like White Elephants" and finds that the "characters, especially of the girl, remain rather vague, and the dramatization of the change in the young man does not quite come off."[1] Sheldon Grebstein calls it "a more ambiguous and probably less successful story" than "Hills Like White Elephants" and ambiguously suggests that it "implies a general perversion of character, a deduction supported by the story's conclusion which hints at the man's degradation."[2] Joseph DeFalco suggests that the man, Phil, has "abnormal desires within him," but DeFalco does not clarify what he means by "abnormal desires."[3] H. Alan Wycherley is more specific and says that, "alas, [Phil] will embrace homosexuality so that he can understand" the girl's lesbian desires, an implied future action the logic of which is not clear.[4] J. F. Kobler also concludes that "there can be no question that [Phil] is moving toward a homosexual affair," but Kobler then asks, "Can we believe that Phil has by this one experience really been turned into a complete homosexual, whatever that is?"[5]

"The Sea Change," contrary to critical appraisal, is one of Hemingway's most artistically subtle and thematically complex stories. It is an early prototype of Hemingway's posthumously published *The Garden of Eden* with respect to the story's reflection of the relinquishment of masculine power and authority, Hemingway's use of mirror imagery, and the story's theme of confused sexual identity, which is Phil's psychic crisis of being. Although interpretation has centered on the conflict between Phil and the girl, the true conflict in the story is in the arena of Phil's mind, and the resolution of the story is not Phil's acceptance of the girl's lesbianism but Phil's ultimate conviction that the nature and meaning of his relationship with the girl have been unmanly, a conviction that marks the death of his masculine identity. The purpose here, therefore, is to reconsider the story in relation to, first, the relinquishment of masculine power; second, the insinuating dialogue between Phil and the girl; third, the full significance of Hemingway's allusion to Alexander Pope's *Essay on Man;* fourth, the significance of the two clients at the bar; fifth, the implications of the story's title, which incorporates allusion to T. S. Eliot's "Dans le Restaurant" and *The Waste Land* as well as allusion to Shakespeare's *The Tempest;* and sixth, the significance of Hemingway's shift of the center-of-consciousness from Phil to James, in relation to the mirror imagery, which creates a fateful irony as the story's resolution.

Hemingway's interest in variant sexual behavior as a subject that could be exploited in fiction was kindled, according to Michael Reynolds, in 1920 when Hemingway began reading Havelock Ellis's *Erotic Symbolism.* "In *Erotic Symbolism* he found detailed explanations of the female orgasm as well as copious analysis and examples of the Krafft-Ebing fetishes, including the erotic nature of hair, a fetish present in his fiction and in his private life."[6] Hemingway continued to read Ellis; he was so impressed that he began urging *Psychology of Sex* on his friends.

> In January [1921] he sent a copy to Hadley, whose first attempt at the catalogue of sexual behavior got no further than the chapter titles. But two weeks later she and Ernest were exchanging "essays" on male and female roles. . . . By April, Ernest had sent her three volumes of Ellis, which she said was too much; all those fetishes and inhibitions could intimidate a person.[7]

Such open discussion of sexuality and variant behavior—"only hinted at darkly by the preceding generation—were becoming the focus of Hemingway's age."[8] In Hemingway's words, "I thought that I had lived in a world as it was and there were all kinds of people in it and I tried to understand them, although some of them I could not like and some I still hated."[9] "The Sea Change" is only one of five stories written during the period from 1924–1932 that involve some aspect of variant sexual behavior. The other stories are "The Mother of a Queen," "Mr. and Mrs. Elliot," "The Battler," and "A Simple Enquiry."

In 1933 Hemingway told Max Perkins that "The Sea Change" was one of those stories that "I invent [*sic*] completely—Killers, Hills Like White Elephants, The Undefeated, Fifty Grand, Sea Change, A Simple Enquiry. *Nobody* can tell which ones I make up completely."[10] Whatever the degree of invention, Hemingway told Edmund Wilson in 1952 that "The Sea Change" was written from the knowledge he gained about lesbianism from Gertrude Stein in 1922.

> [Gertrude Stein] talked to me once for three hours telling me why she was a lesbian, the mechanics of it, why the act did not disgust those who performed it . . . and why it was not degrading to either participant. . . . It was this knowledge, gained from G.S., that enabled me to write A Sea Change, which is a good story, with authority.[11]

The mechanics of lesbianism may have given Hemingway the confidence needed to make lesbianism an explicit part of a story, but his familiarity with androgynous tendencies and lesbianism was not limited to Gertrude Stein and Alice B. Toklas, and one conversation with Stein would not seem to be the only source of information that "enabled" him to write "The Sea Change."

Hemingway's familiarity with androgynous tendencies began in his youth in Oak Park and involved Ruth Arnold, one of Grace Hemingway's voice students in 1907 who became a permanent resident in the house. In 1919, Dr. Hemingway ejected Ruth from the house. Grace wrote to the doctor, "no one in the world can ever take my husband's place unless he abdicates it to play at petty jealousy with his wife's loyal girl friend," and in

1920 Grace wrote two local gossips, "Ruth tells me that you have been misinformed by the repetition of an old malicious story. In the first place, Ruth never had such a thought."[12] Patrick Hemingway would later recall that "he was never allowed to visit Grandmother Grace because, Ernest told him, she was androgynous."[13]

Later, when Hemingway met Hadley Richardson, Hadley told him about her experience with the lesbian mother of her Bryn Mawr roommate. "She [the mother] managed to show me, Hadley related, how much pleasanter life was for women who loved women, and 'being very suggestible I began to imagine I had all this low sex feelin'' and she for me.'"[14] When Hemingway and Hadley went to Paris in 1922 they were immediately embroiled in the sexual turmoil of that city and Hemingway soon became acquainted with a number of lesbians in addition to Gertrude Stein and Alice B. Toklas: Natalie Barney, Sylvia Beach, Adrienne Monnier, Jane Heap, and Georgette Leblanc.[15] When Hemingway then met Pauline and Virginia Pfeiffer, divorced Hadley, and married Pauline, androgyny was again in the immediate vicinity of his interest.

> Like Pauline, Jinny was a woman who knew what she wanted—and high on her list was the loving companionship of other women. Although she was willing to go out with men, her sexual preferences were plainly lesbian and would remain so. About Pauline's preferences there are questions. . . . Pauline did have love affairs with several women following her divorce from Hemingway.[16]

Hemingway, however, in "The Art of the Short Story," written in Spain in 1959, cited a particular incident that took place in the summer of 1931, while he and Pauline were visiting Spain and France, as the source of his inspiration.

> In a story called "The Sea Change," everything is left out. I had seen the couple in the Bar Basque in St. Jean-de-Luz and I knew the story too too well, which is the squared root of well, and use any well you like except mine. So I left the story out. But it is all there. It is not visible but it is there.[17]

A signed typescript of "The Sea Change" is dated 22 September 1931.[18] It was then published in Paris by Edward W. Titus in the December issue of *This Quarter*. Nevertheless, the story does not seem to have been originally intended for Titus's magazine. Apparently it was intended to be one of three planned stories for a magazine called *The Forum*. At the John Fitzgerald Kennedy Library a pencil manuscript is headed, "Three Love Stories/by Ernest Hemingway."[19] Two titles are given, "The Sea Change" and "Unsuited to Our Needs." Three other stories are also listed under "The Sea Change": two drafts of one story, titled "Crime and Punishment," are about a man who has spent 20 years in San Quentin for sodomy; a fragment of another story is about a girl who is having sexual relations with her stepfather; and another fragment is about a Spanish town and sexual relations with a Spanish girl.[20] Also among the manuscript material is the following comment by Hemingway:

> The editor writes that as the Forum reaches not only trained readers but the general public the story must contain narrative or at least plot. . . .
> That would exclude the death of Angel C. Carratala which occurred yesterday morning at 10:15 in the infirmary of the Plaza Toros in the town Iuca on the island of Mallorca as that was completely without plot.[21]

Hemingway's disdain of *The Forum's* editor's insistence on plot is obvious in his comment. But he also wanted to be published, saying, "Let us see what we can do in 1260 words."[22] His solution to the contradiction between the demand for plot and his own artistic integrity is both subtle and ingenious. He establishes the appearance of a plot in the opening lines when the girl refuses to do what the young man is asking: "What about it?" he asks. "'No,' said the girl, 'I can't.'"[23] When the young man, Phil, says, "I'll kill her" (397), it becomes clear that Phil is attempting to stop the girl from going away with another woman. Phil says, "If it was a man——" (398). Hemingway has taken the conventional triangle plot—man versus man for girl—with its conventional resolutions and inserted a character in the triangle who should traditionally be ineligible: the other *woman.*

But even this is only the appearance of the plot, however central it seems to be on the surface. Phil has no real choice from the beginning but to let the girl go. He cannot challenge the other woman as he could challenge a man. What appears to be the plot consequently becomes only the story's *donnée* or given. Hemingway intends from the outset to establish the true conflict invisibly in the arena of Phil's mind, like dynamite hidden under a bridge, and to make the true resolution the psychic death—the ironic killing—of "poor old Phil" (398) which, like the death of Angel C. Carratala, is completely without plot.

When the story opens, Phil is attempting to maintain his traditional masculine authority over the girl, saying, "What about it?" (397), which, we learn later, refers to the girl's staying with him rather than going to the woman. The girl, however, refuses to agree to his proposal: "'No,' said the girl, 'I can't'" (397). Phil will not accept the girl's "I can't," which means to him a powerlessness in her to act otherwise. He says, "You mean you won't" (397), which implies that the girl is making a willful choice. The exchange is then repeated, the girl saying she "can't" and Phil insisting that the meaning of "can't" is more accurately "won't."

The exchange sets out two opposed philosophical views about the nature of man. Phil's view is neoclassical in its emphasis on the dominance of reason and man's ability to practice discipline and restraint, as my discussion of the allusion to Alexander Pope will presently show. The girl's view is late-nineteenth-century and holds that the actions of men and women may at times be determined by forces beyond the control of the will, or reason, such as heredity and environment, and particularly by the dark inner passions of sexuality. To the girl, a sexual relationship with "her" (397) is not a matter of rational choice but a matter of irrational desire, and she "can't" resist the powers of her own passions. Phil's position is that man's behavior is never determined by forces beyond his control; consequently, the girl is simply refusing to exercise restraint and is making a "choice" between him and the woman: she is choosing the woman.

The girl appears to acquiesce to Phil's position, saying, "You have it your own way" (397), but she has not changed her mind as to what she intends to do. Knowing this, Phil replies, "I don't have it my own way. I wish to God I did" (397). Phil's wishful appeal to God is consistent with his neoclassical position: God created man's reason to rule over his passions, just as He created the man first, then the woman, and commanded that the man should rule over the woman. When the girl replies, "You did for a long time" (397), she is simultaneously expressing a statement of fact and making the first of several insinuations. The fact is that Phil has exercised authority over her by virtue of his masculine power, but she is also insinuating that Phil's sexual preferences have taken priority and Phil has been preventing her, in one way or another, from fulfilling her own sexuality.

Phil does not refute either the fact or the insinuation, which by default establishes both the fact and the insinuation as accurate. Instead, he "look[s] at her" (397) and ironically succumbs to the irrational power of her attractiveness. He then retreats into typical masculine posturing and to a traditionally masculine solution. "I'll kill her" (397), he says. When the girl says "Please don't" (397), she is defending the woman, and her use of the word "please" suggests that all Phil would really do is create an embarrassing scene. Encouraged by the fact that the girl appears to have taken him seriously and still obsessed with the girl's attractiveness—her "fine hands . . . slim and brown and very beautiful" (397)—Phil repeats his threat and again appeals to God, this time on the assumption that he himself is on God's side: "I swear to God I will" (397). The girl calmly replies that killing the woman "won't make you happy" (397), which is the same as telling him that the problem is not inherent in the woman. The problem is inherent in her own sexuality, and the removal of the woman will not change the sexual feelings that Phil cannot satisfy.

Phil again relinquishes power to the girl's insight and tries to establish something less refutable. He now suggests that she has simply gotten herself into a "jam" (397), like any number of other possible jams, and he wishes she had "gotten into something else" (397). He has all but surrendered and it is now the girl who speaks with authority. She asks the crucial question that Phil initially asked: *"What* are you going to do *about it?"* (397: italics mine). When Phil says, "I don't know [what to do about it]" (397), he has, with that statement, lost all control over the circumstances, and he has lost all his power and authority over the girl. His final relinquishment of masculine power will come when he tells the girl, "Go on then" (400), and his conscious recognition of his true weakness and helplessness will occur after the girl is gone: "He was not the same-looking man as he had been before he had told her to go."

The story, which has been preoccupied with reality and the true meaning of things, then moves to the problem of "understanding."

> "I'm sorry," [the girl] said, "if you don't understand."
> "I understand. That's the trouble. I understand."
> "You do," she said. "That makes it worse, of course." (398)

The significance of this exchange is the suggestive insinuations inherent in what is said. Given the subject under discussion, which is the girl's lesbian desires, why would Phil imply that he understands the urge of that desire: "That's the trouble. I understand" (398). Even more ironic, on what basis can the girl be convinced that, "You do" understand, and that that "makes it worse" (398) for him, and perhaps for her? The girl says later, "when we do understand each other there's no use to pretend we don't" (398). Phil agrees, "I suppose not" (398). Then, after the girl has asked Phil to "be good" to her, "let [her] go," and "forgive" her (399), she says, "You don't think things we've had and done should make any difference in understanding?" (399). What could they have "had," and what could they have "done," that would enable Phil to understand the girl's lesbian desire? What is the girl insinuating?

Hemingway told Owen Wister, 25 July 1929, two years *before* writing "The Sea Change," "I try always to do the thing by three cushion shots rather than by words or direct statement. But maybe we must have the direct statement too. . . . Taste is all that can guide you."[24]

The suggestive and insinuating discussion between Phil and the girl about his understanding of her variant sexual desires, particularly the girl's comment that they have "done" things that should enable him to understand how she feels about the woman, is one of those "three cushion shots." The possible kinds of sexual activity in a heterosexual relationship are intercourse, cunnilingus, fellatio, and sodomy, and the one logical sexual activity in which Phil and the girl could have engaged that would enable Phil in any way to "understand" the girl's lesbian urges would be cunnilingus.[25]

The practice of oral sex as a form of heterosexual sexual variety, and its effect on the male's sense of sexual identity, is a subject Hemingway seems to have been working with again in his novel, *The Sea Chase*, edited and published posthumously as *Islands in the Stream*.[26] In one of the sections edited out of the novel, Thomas Hudson is remembering his first wife.

> [S]he had said, "I could love you very easily. But you are just too damn wholesome and then I would be bored."
> "But aren't you bored with those that are corrupt?"
> "You see what I mean? You see how stupid you are? I don't want you corrupt. Who mentioned corrupt? But it would be lovely if we could live together and not be too wholesome."

At night in bed, she says,

> "Now kiss me and be my girl."
> "I didn't know you wanted a girl."
> "Yes I do. Now and right away and my girl is you."
> "I don't know how to be a girl and I don't think it's good for you."
> "Yes it is. And my girl has to be a boy."
> "Did you ever have a girl before?"
> "No. You're my first girl and I love you. Do you hear?"
> "I hear." He felt weak through the base of his spine to his chest and back again. But the weakness was concentrated forward from the base of his spine. But he felt weak and destroyed inside himself. . . .
> "Did you like being my girl?"
> "Yes."[27]

Hudson's wife's demand, "Now kiss me and be my girl," leaves considerable ambiguity as to what she is asking of him, but when she later says, "Did you like being my girl?" the verb "being" clearly indicates that an action on the part of Hudson has taken place. And since to be a girl's girl implies a lesbian relationship, the implied action on the part of Hudson would seem to be an oral action.[28]

The holograph of "The Sea Change" also seems to indicate that Phil has engaged in the practice of oral relations. In the holograph, after the girl says to Phil: "You do [understand]. That makes it worse of course," Hemingway initially preceded Phil's bitter reply, "I'll understand all the time. All day and all night. I'll understand" with an omniscient author comment, perhaps because he thought he should "try to do the thing . . . by words" too.[29] The holograph reads, "'Sure,' he said, looking at her. <He still ate her up when he looked at her.> 'I'll understand all the time. All day and all night. . . . '"[30] The sentence, "He still ate her up when he looked at her," with its street euphemism "ate her," was "trop explicite."[31] Hemingway lined out "ate" and "up," and tried to be less direct by inserting "fed on," and "with his eyes": "He still ate <fed on> her up <with his eyes> when he looked at her."[32] But tinkering with the *inaccrochable* only made the line awkward, without solving the problem if its public acceptability.[33] With "taste all that can guide you," Hemingway omitted the entire sentence, preferring instead "to do the thing by three cushion shots rather than by words."[34]

Recognizing that what Phil and the girl have "had and done" refers to cunnilingus and to Phil's having been the girl's girl opens a new dimension in regard to Phil's attempt to quote a passage about "vice" from the neoclassic *An Essay on Man* by Alexander Pope.

After the girl has said, "You don't think things we've had and done should make any difference in understanding?" (399), Phil recalls a fragment of Alexander Pope's *Essay on Man*. The essay is characteristic of neoclassical faith in reason and authority, and its heroic couplets seem ironically appropriate to Phil as a heroic "young man" (401) who wants to "kill" his opponent in combat. Phil knows Pope's essay well, certainly well enough not only to remember the particular lines that characterize to him the nature of what he and the girl have "had and done" but also well enough to attempt to quote those lines. "'Vice is a monster of such fearful mien,' the young man said bitterly, 'that to be something or other needs but to be seen. Then we something, something, then embrace'" (399). The lines from Pope, which Phil is inaccurately quoting because he cannot "remember the words" (399), are from epistle II and read as follows: "Vice is a monster of so frightful mien,/As, to be hated, needs but to be seen;/Yet seen too oft, familiar with her face,/We first endure, then pity, then embrace."[35]

Pope says that vice is a monster whose mien is "frightful," a word that has connotations of alarm and revulsion. Phil changes the word to "fearful," which connotes not revulsion but anxiety and dread. Pope says that vice is at first hated, but that if it is seen too often, it is endured, then pitied, then embraced. Phil cannot remember this sequence; he remembers only "needs but to be seen" and "then embrace." The sense of the only words that Phil can quote suggests that vice in the contemporary naturalistic world is much less objectionable than in Pope's era. Vice is neither hated nor temporarily endured, and the process of initial revulsion, familiarity, toleration, and sympathy before it is finally accepted is no longer applicable. Vice is now simply seen and tried, and, although "something or other" (399) also takes place, if it is found pleasurable it is accepted. It is first "seen" as promising, and when it produces pleasure it is "embraced." "Vice," then, in the sense in which Phil is using the term, is specifically referring to what Phil and the girl have experienced together and embraced together. It is their vice.

The girl says, "Let's not say vice. . . . That's not very polite" (399), to which Phil replies, "Perversion" (399). Phil's use of the term "perversion" is in response to the girl, not to his own quoting of Pope, and it is directed at the girl's desire to carry their heterosexual vice to the extreme "embrace" of lesbianism. The idea of the "extreme," however, does not originate with Phil; it originates with Pope.

> But where th' Extreme of Vice, was ne'er agreed: .
> Ask where's North?[36]
>
> No creature owns it in the first degree,
> But thinks his neighbour further gone than he. . . . [37]
>
> What happier natures shrink at with affright,
> The hard inhabitant contends is right. . . . [38]
>
> And ev'n the best, by fits, [are] what they despise.[39]

Phil's reply, "Perversion," to the girl's "let's not say vice" indicates how well Phil knows epistle II of Pope's *Essay,* and it indicates that Phil is making a reasoned distinction between his relationship with the girl and the girl's relationship with "her." In doing so, Phil is defining both "vice" and "perversion." Vice is the indulgence in a practice that may be impure, but perversion is the willful disposition to go counter to what is natural, an abnormal condition of the sexual instincts. It is the same kind of reasoning that Phil has previously used when making a distinction between "can't" and "won't."

Phil's distinction between vice and perversion, which is derived from Pope's distinction between vice and the extreme, is structurally reinforced by Hemingway in another "cushion shot," which is the arrangement of the events of the story. The girl's comment about "things we've had and done" (399) immediately precedes Phil's quotation of Pope and therefore structurally determines that the word "vice" refers to Phil's sexual relationship with the girl. Similarly, Phil's statement, "Perversion," is immediately followed, not by a reply from the girl, but by a shift of scene to the two clients who have entered the bar: "'James,' one of the clients addressed the barman, 'you're looking very well'" (399). The clients are homosexuals, as we shall see shortly, and their introduction at this point in the story structurally determines that the word "perversion" refers to the girl's homosexuality. The story's "cushion shot" structuring defines each term.

Extratextual evidence for a distinction between vice and perversion can be found in *The Garden of Eden*. Catherine refers to masturbation as a "vice" when she accuses David of having a passion for reading his press clippings and of being unfaithful to her with them: "what are you to do if you discover the man is illiterate and practices solitary vice in a wastebasket full of clippings. . . ."[40] David, however, refers to Catherine's lesbian relationship with Marita as "perversion."

> "Don't you ever talk on any other subjects? Perversion's dull and old fashioned. I didn't know people like us even kept up on it."
> "I suppose it's only really interesting the first time one does it," Catherine said.[41]

In "The Sea Change," Phil's reasoned distinction between what he believes is their oral vice and the extreme of the girl's lesbianism is quintessential Pope, but Phil does not reckon on another aspect of Pope. Pope's logic in *An Essay on Man* is that man's mind is incapable of distinguishing for long between good and bad, black and white. "This light and darkness in our chaos join'd/[42] [They] oft so mix, the difference is too nice."[43] Consequently, man has a tendency to "into the notion fall/That Vice and Virtue there is none at all."[44] Such a "notion" is exactly the counterargument that the girl now mounts against Phil's distinctions.

> "I'd like it better if you didn't use words like that," the girl said. "There's no necessity to use a word like that."
> "What do you want me to call it?"
> "You don't have to call it. You don't have to put any name to it."
> "That's the name for it."
> "No," she said. "We're made up of all sorts of things. You've known that. You've used it well enough."
> "You don't have to say that again."
> "Because that explains it to you."
> "All right," he said. "All right." (400)

The debate here is pivotal and produces a reversal of fortune in both the surface argument and Phil's psychic drama. The girl's position is that reasoned distinctions are invalid. Human nature is "made up of all sorts of things" (400) and these things cannot be labeled good or bad, virtue or vice. People are the way they are. A sexual act is a sexual act, whether it is heterosexual or homosexual. The act itself cannot be judged in terms of gender. What was pleasurably appropriate for her and for Phil is pleasurably appropriate for her and for "her." There can be no distinctions, such as words like "vice" and "perversion." There is only the necessity of being socially "polite" (399). Again, the girl both accuses and convicts Phil on the basis of his own conduct with her. "You've known that," she accuses him, and insinuates more, perhaps that he is responsible for her present sexual needs. In Pope's words, "Self directs it still;/Each individual seeks a sev'ral goal."[45]

Phil's neoclassic logic is overthrown when faced with the girl's natural-istic logic supported by the fact of his own conduct. The girl has "explain[ed] it to [him]" (400), not in terms of the woman to whom she wants to go, but in terms of himself, and he cannot argue against himself. He has no alterna-tives, and he can do nothing "about it" (397), except to say, "All right," and "Go on, then" (400). But with those words there has been a sudden, dra-matic reversal in their fortunes. The girl is now "happy" (400) because she has won the contest, and she will go to her lesbian lover and "not look back at him" (400). She will also "come back" (400) to him later, and that will be "the hell of it" (400). The reversal for Phil is devastating. Once he has accepted what the "hard inhabitant contends is right,"[46] that "we're made up of all sorts of things" (400) and oral relations are oral relations—a rose is a rose, is a rose—his sexual identity as a masculine "brown young man" (401), king of land and sea, sun and water, is obliterated. Instead of seeing himself as the girl's masculine brown young man, he now has an image of himself as the girl's "first girl,"[47] and he now believes that by his own indulgences he has become the same as the woman to whom the girl is going. He believes that he is a man who has sexually acted as a girl, and like Thomas Hudson who has also sexually acted as a girl, he is "weak and destroyed inside himself."[48]

When Phil says, "Go on" (400) a second time, the girl detects something. She "look[s] at him quickly" (400). "You want me to go?" (400) she asks, and when he says, "Yes. . . . Right away. . . . Now" (400), she stands up and goes "out quickly" (400). Phil is left with the "two checks" (401), the barman, and the "two people" (399) who are "clients" (399).

The situation in the café has been tense, as demonstrated earlier in the story by the fact that Phil's argument with the girl has been carried on with such a raised voice and with such expressions of anger that the barman, James, "at the far end of the bar" (399), knows that they are going to "break up" (399). The "two people" enter the café. James says to them, "Yes, sir" (399), and takes their "orders" (399). The argument between Phil and the girl continues, with Phil "bitterly" (399) quoting Pope. When Phil says, "Perversion" (399), one of the two people who have entered the bar finally speaks, perhaps from discomfiture.

"James," one of the clients addressed the barman, "you're looking very well."

"You're looking very well yourself," the barman said.

"Old James," the other client said. "You're fatter, James."

"It's terrible," the barman said, "the way I put it on."

"Don't neglect to insert the brandy, James," the first client said.

"No, sir," said the barman. "Trust me."

The two clients are homosexuals, which is revealed in the language they use. One "addresses" the barman, which implies an affected formality; they keep repeating the barman's name, James, when he is otherwise referred to by Hemingway as "the barman" (399); they also force an affected familiarity by calling the barman "old James" and by discussing his appearance when James's "Yes, sir" does not indicate such a familiarity. The one client's instruction not to "neglect to insert" the brandy is a pretentious and exalted rhetoric similar to the language Hemingway uses in *The Sun Also Rises* when dramatizing the homosexuals with "white hands, wavy hair, white faces, grimacing, gesturing, talking" using rhetoric such as, "I do *declare*. There is an *actual* harlot," and "Don't you be *rash*" (italics mine), to which Jake responds, "I wanted to swing on one, any one, anything to shatter that superior, simpering composure."[49] The textual evidence of the language in the story is supported by a deleted manuscript fragment in which Phil refers to the "clients" as "punks," that is, catamites or male prostitutes. The fragment reads,

"What do the punks drink James? What can you recommend to a recent convert?"

"~~Do you want a~~

"~~What were you drinking?~~ Do you want another whiskey-soda?"

"Whatever the<y> ~~punks~~ drink, James. Take a look at me and mix whatever you like."[50]

In the story, when the barman responds to the homosexual's instruction about the brandy with "Trust me" (399), effectively ending the conversation, the attention of the two clients is again drawn to the discord between Phil and the girl. "The two at the bar looked over at the two at the table, then looked back at the barman again. Towards the barman was the comfortable direction" (399). What they have heard and no longer want to observe is an angry young man having an argument with a determined girl. The girl then gets up and walks out. The angry young man comes to the bar. He immediately says, "Vice is a very strange thing, James" (401), probably with considerable bitterness, since he spoke "bitterly" (399) when he brought the subject of "vice" up with the girl. The two at the bar then move farther down, or away, "to make room for him" (401). They move because the man's anger is apparently still being ventilated and his remark about "vice" seems a testy insult. Unaware of the true significance of Phil's remark, they observe only his displeasure. With the girl gone, he could be trying to pick a fight with them. When James says, "You're right there, sir" (401), agreeing with the angry young man that "Vice . . . is a strange thing" (401), the men at the bar move "down a little more so he would be quite comfortable" (401). They do not want to exacerbate this fellow's anger.

The scene at the bar with Phil, James, and the two homosexuals is charged with contradiction and conflict. It is not a scene of comforting friendliness, nor is it a scene of rapprochement between Phil and the homosexual clients. Phil's comment to James about "vice" expresses his still bitter anger, and his assertive "*I said* I was a different man, James" (401; italics mine), indicates an equally powerful determination to accept his fate. The scene reflects, as would a stirring of the waters, the psychic violence occurring in the depths of Phil as to his sexual identity. Having accepted as correct the girl's "logic" that "Vice and Virtue there is none at all"[51] and that a sexual act is a sexual act—distinctions in gender are invalid—Phil has changed from "brown young man" (401) to "a girl,"[52] no different from the woman to whom the girl is now going, and, by the same logic, no different from the male prostitutes—the girls—standing with him at the bar. The unresolvable contradiction for Phil, and the reason why he says that vice is a "very strange thing" (401), is that his sexual indulgences with the girl and his acceptance of the girl's logic have made him, in effect, one with the waiting lesbian and one with the homosexuals, when, in fact, he is not one with them and can never be one with them. "Ev'n the best, by fits, [are] what they despise."[53] It is the wrenching violence of this contradiction within himself that brings about the sea change, which is the death of "Poor old Phil" (398) and the emergence of the strange new Phil that he sees in the mirror.

The destruction of Phil's psychological self, his masculine sexual identity as a "brown young man" (401), is manifested in physical changes. "His voice sounded very strange. He did not recognize it . . . and his mouth was very dry. . . . He was not the same-looking man . . ." (400). The description suggests the symptoms of a man in shock: a partial paralysis of the throat, which affects the voice box; a drying of the mouth tissue; a glazed expression to the eyes; and a draining of the blood from the face. By omniscient author statement Phil is said to be "not the same-looking man" (401), and Phil knows that he is not the same person "he had been before he had told her to go" (401). The effects of his sudden loss of identity are both psychological and physical, and they are factual, not imaginary. Phil has unwittingly sailed into a tempest. His cargo of pleasures is too heavy, his rudder of neoclassic values has become useless, and his sail of authoritative self-confidence is torn to tatters. His good ship "Masculinity" goes to the sea bottom.

Phil has entered the whirlpool and will undergo what Hemingway calls, through the title of the story, his sea change. The allusion is to Shakespeare's *The Tempest* where the term "sea-change" appears in Ariel's song.

> Of his bones are coral made;
> Those are pearls that were his eyes:
>   Nothing of him that doth fade
>   But doth suffer a sea-change
> Into something rich and strange.
> Sea-nymphs hourly ring his knell.[54]

The difficulty with this original source of the allusion is that a complete application of a *Tempest*-like sea change to the story is elusive. The symbolic sense in which Hemingway appears to use the idea of sea change seems to be derived, not so much from Shakespeare as from T. S. Eliot. Eliot used the same Shakespearean allusion in *The Waste Land*, where Phlebas, the Phoenician sailor, enters the whirlpool in "Death by Water."

> A current under the sea
> Picked his bones in whispers. As he rose and fell
> He passed the stages of his age and youth
> Entering the whirlpool.
> . . . .
> Consider Phlebas, who was once handsome and tall as you.[55]

The Phoenician sailor Phlebas in "Death by Water" is the same Phlebas, le Phénicien [*sic*], who is the dirty waiter in Eliot's "Dans le Restaurant," a miserable man who tells a patron, on what he calls "le jour de lessive des gueux" (the washday of the beggars), about his earliest sex experience. "Mais alors," says the patron, "tu as ton vautour" (you have your lust). The patron is disgusted and angered, saying, "De quel droit payes-tu des expériences comme moi" (By what right do you pay for experiences like me), which establishes in the poem an ironic *dédoublement* of the personality. The patron then gives Phlebas "dix sous" for the washroom. The dirty waiter, however, receives his ultimate cleansing later, "pendant quinze noye" (during 15 days of drowning). "Figurez-vous donc, c'était un sort pénible" (Would you believe it was a painful fate). "Cependant, ce fut jadis un bel homme, de haute taille" (Yet, he was once handsome and tall as you).[56]

The basic elements of "Dans le Restaurant"—the café, the patron, the waiter, the revelation of lustful sexual experience, and the painful fate of a once handsome man—are all basic elements in "The Sea Change." In *The Waste Land*, Eliot added to the Phlebas story the element of recollection: "As he rose and fell/ He passed the stages of his age and youth." The process of recollection is also what Phil goes through in his debate with the girl, and it is his recollection of his past sexual experiences that precipitates his change. Hemingway's allusion to the sea change is Eliotic, not Shakespearean. Phil's sea change is a psychic purification in a symbolic death by water which will extinguish the fires of his sexuality. The lust of the flesh will be gradually washed away, as the sea washes the flesh from the bones.

Hemingway's use of the sea-change allusion to symbolize the psychic change that is the death of the "brown young man" who believes that he had the power and authority is more completely realized in the mirror imagery at the bar. When Phil goes to the bar in shock, he says to the barman, "I'm a different man, James. . . . You see in me quite a different man" (401). The change at this point is internal as the words "in me" suggest. He then looks "in the glass" behind the bar and believes that the feminization that he has undergone is confirmed in actuality by his mirror image: "he saw he was really quite a different-looking man" (401). The action in regard to the mirror is then repeated. "The young man saw himself in the mirror behind the bar. 'I said I was a different man, James,' he said. Looking into the mirror he saw that this was quite true" (401).

What the image in the mirror actually reflects and what Phil sees in the mirror are ambiguous, but a similar scene in *The Garden of Eden* where David Bourne also looks in a mirror suggests that the image Phil sees is a psychic self-image with physical manifestations.

> "You've done that to your hair and had it cut the same as your girl's and how do you feel?" . . .
> He looked at the mirror and it was someone else he saw but it was less strange now. . . .
> "You know exactly how you look now and how you are."
> Of course he did not know exactly how he was. But he made an effort aided by what he had seen in the mirror.[57]

Both David Bourne and Phil are seeing in their reflection other manifestations of an inner reality that makes each a "different man" (401), "someone else" other than the person he was before.

The ambiguity, however, as to precisely how different Phil has become as a result of the psychic death of his masculine self and the sea-change cleansing of his sexuality, still seems to remain. Phil's symbolic sea change, if considered by itself as a phenomenon separate from other elements in the story, may not, in J. Bakker's words, "quite come off."[58] But it does "come off," with powerful irony, when it is considered in relation to the Eliotic technique of *dédoublement* and the figure of James, the barman.

"The Sea Change" is written from the omniscient author point of view with Phil as the primary center of consciousness. Hemingway shifts the center of consciousness three times in the course of the narration. He shifts it when he tells us that the girl "could not believe him [Phil], but her voice was happy" (400), and again when the girl thinks, "He was settled into something" (400). The important shift, however, is the shift to the consciousness of James.

> The barman was at the far end of the bar. His face was white and so was his jacket. He knew these two and thought them a handsome young couple. He had seen many handsome young couples break up and new couples form that were never so handsome long. He was not thinking about this, but about a horse. In half an hour he could send across the street to find if the horse had won. (399)

If the barman is in the story simply to serve the two clients, to agree with Phil that vice is a strange thing, and to say that Phil looks very well, there is no reason to shift the center of consciousness to the barman. The reader already knows from earlier description that Phil and the girl are a handsome couple, and the reader already knows, from the girl's assertion, "I have to and you know it" (399), that she and Phil are going to "break up." If the barman is merely a stock character, there is certainly no reason for the digression about his preoccupation with a horse and a race. Either the story is artistically flawed, or the barman has some artistic function in relation to Phil. The latter is the case. The figure of James, the barman, is a further development of the mirror imagery and reflects, in an ironic *dédoublement*, the sea-changed Phil.

When the story begins, Phil and the girl are described as "both tanned, so that they looked out of place in Paris" (397). Now, in the ironic reversal of the unraveling, Phil is no longer "out of place in Paris." With the girl gone to her lesbian relationship and Phil "destroyed inside himself,"[59] "sea-changed," James's Paris has become Phil's appropriate "place." His standing at the bar with male prostitutes, as is James, marks the end of everything, including the end of the "brown young man" (401), and just as the girl has called him "old Phil" (398), the two homosexuals call the barman "old James" (399).

In the story's *denouement*, old James is the "embodiment" of the sea-changed self-image that old Phil sees reflected in the mirror behind the bar. The image that Phil sees is the image of a Paris man, an indoor man, a sunless man. The face is as "white" as a white "jacket" (399). He is getting "fatter" (399), a consequence of the loss of sexual powers, of becoming neutered, and it is "terrible . . . the way [he] put[s] it on" (399). Phil/James is the end product of disillusionment, a person who can observe a "handsome young couple" (399), watch them "break up" (399), and not even be "thinking about this" (399). In his feminization he will serve homosexuals and ask them to "trust" (399) him, as a female once asked him, "Don't you trust me?" (398). He may still agree that "Vice . . . is a very strange thing" (401), but since he no longer thinks about coupling—having lost his sexual identity and his lust—his one obsession or addiction will be gambling on the horses. He will pass the hours of his day waiting, not for a girl, but to find out if a "horse has won" (399). Sea nymphs will ring the knell of a man once handsome and tall.

The story's irony finds its ultimate expression in James's final words, "You must have had a very good summer" (401). Winner take nothing.[60]

Notes

1. J. Bakker, *Ernest Hemingway: The Artist as Man of Action* (Assen, N.V.: Van Gorcum, 1972) 144.

2. Sheldon Norman Grebstein, *Hemingway's Craft* (Carbondale: Southern Illinois UP, 1973) 114.

3. Joseph DeFalco, *The Hero in Hemingway's Short Stories* (Pittsburgh: U of Pittsburgh P, 1963) 177.

4. H. Alan Wycherley, "Hemingway's 'The Sea Change,'" *American Notes and Queries* 7 (January 1969): 68.

5. J. F. Kobler, "Hemingway's 'The Sea Change': A Sympathetic View of Homosexuality," *Arizona Quarterly* 26 (Winter 1970): 322. See also Robert Fleming, "Perversion and the Writer in 'The Sea Change,'" *Studies in American Fiction* 14.2 (Autumn 1986): 215–20. Fleming reads the story as a parable about the voyeurism of artists.

6. Michael S. Reynolds, *The Young Hemingway* (Oxford: Basil Blackwell, 1986) 120.

7. Reynolds, 184–85.

8. Reynolds, 184.

9. Ernest Hemingway, *A Moveable Feast* (New York: Charles Scribner's Sons, 1964) 19.

10. Hemingway to Maxwell Perkins, 16 November 1933, *Ernest Hemingway: Selected Letters, 1917–1961*, ed. Carlos Baker (New York: Charles Scribner's Sons, 1981) 400.

11. Hemingway to Edmund Wilson, 8 November 1952, *Letters*, 795.

12. Reynolds, 80, 132–33.

13. Reynolds, 81.

14. Kenneth S. Lynn, *Hemingway* (New York: Simon and Schuster, 1987) 143.

15. Lynn, 319–20.

16. Lynn, 301.

17. Hemingway, "The Art of the Short Story," *The Paris Review* 79 (Spring 1981): 88. Hemingway's repetition of the word "well," and the warning to use any "well you like except mine," is a Joycean form of pun, or word play, and the expression is suggestive of the vaginal symbolism of Radclyffe Hall's famous 1928 defense of lesbianism, *Well of Loneliness*, which Hemingway had read, and which is in his library at the Finca Vigía. See *Hemingway's Library: A Composite Record*, comp. James D. Brasch and Joseph Sigman (New York: Garland, 1981) 162, item 2879. For a more extensive study of the relationship between Hemingway and James Joyce, see Robert Gajdusek, *Hemingway and Joyce: A Study in Debt and Payment* (Corte Madera: Square Circle P, 1984).

18. Hemingway, mss. of "The Sea Change," Lilly Library, Bloomington, Indiana.

19. Item 681, John F. Kennedy Library, Boston.

20. Item 340, John F. Kennedy Library.

21. Item 681, John F. Kennedy Library.

22. Item 681, John F. Kennedy Library.

23. Hemingway, "The Sea Change," in *The Short Stories of Ernest Hemingway* (New York: Charles Scribner's Sons, 1966) 397. All citations in parentheses refer to this edition.

24. Hemingway to Owen Wister, 25 July 1929, *Letters*, 301.

25. Hemingway wrote a poem-letter to "Esteemed general [Ezra] Pound—" in December 1923 in which he described himself as "a man who likes to *drink* and *fuck* and *eat* and talk and read the papers and write something and keep clear of the shits." He then gives Pound a long catalogue of "the shits." The list includes "Buggary, sodomy . . . [and] cunt lapping (except among friends)." Hemingway to Pound, 9 December 1923, Pound mss., Lilly Library, Bloomington, Indiana. I want to thank the Lilly Library for permission to quote from this letter.

26. Kenneth S. Lynn also cites a scene in *The Sun Also Rises:*

> She kissed me cooly on the forehead.
> "Darling," she said. Then: "Do you want me to send him away?" . . .
> "What did you say to him?" . . .
> "Sent him for champagne. He loves to go for champagne."
> Then later: "Do you feel better, darling? Is the head any better?"

The passage includes a "Then" followed by a colon and a "Then later" followed by a colon. Both usages indicate a period of time elapsing and an omitted action. There is no way to be positive, of course, about Hemingway's meaning, for in order to keep Max Perkins's blue pencil still, an artful vagueness was essential. Nevertheless, the implication is fairly clear that, while the full extent of his injury is unspecified, Jake remains capable of achieving a degree of satisfaction through oral sex, and that Brett has been a most willing *mangeuse*. Jake and Brett had apparently made love in a fashion often associated with lesbian as well as heterosexual intercourse. See Lynn, 323–24.

27. I am indebteded here to Professor Bickford Sylvester, University of British Columbia, for drawing my attention to this scene while we were both doing research at the John F. Kennedy Library. Professor Sylvester discussed the scene in his paper, "The Strange

Case of the First Mrs. Hudson: Marriage and the Thing Left Out in *Islands in the Stream*," delivered at the 2nd International Hemingway Conference, Lignano Sabbiadoro, Italy. The scene is given more extensive consideration in Professor Sylvester's forthcoming study of extended vision in Hemingway's later works.

There are similar scenes in *The Garden of Eden;* for example, Catherine says to David: "You're my sweet dearest darling Catherine. You're my sweet my lovely Catherine. You're my girl my dearest only girl. Oh thank you thank you my girl . . ." (Hemingway, *The Garden of Eden* [New York: Charles Scribner's Sons, 1986] 56). I have cited the deleted passage from the *Islands in the Stream* manuscript because the scene has a greater clarity of purpose and a more definitive action consistent with "The Sea Change," whereas the scenes in *The Garden of Eden* are more complex and more ambiguous in relation to the different kinds of experimentation which may be taking place, and the *The Garden of Eden* involves the sexual changing of both David and Catherine, with Catherine's becoming a boy, "Peter" (Hemingway, *The Garden of Eden*, 17).

28. The same association between heterosexual oral relations and lesbianism is made by Hemingway himself in an entry he made in Mary Hemingway's diary, as recorded by Mary Hemingway in *How It Was* (New York: Ballantine, 1976) 466–67.

29. Hemingway to Wister, 25 July 1929, *Letters,* 301.

30. Item 679, John F. Kennedy Library.

31. Geneviève Hily-Mane, "Autour des manuscrits de 'The Sea Change,'" *Etudes Anglaises* 30.2 (1977): 208.

32. Item 679, John F. Kennedy Library.

33. Gertrude Stein told Hemingway that his story "Up in Michigan" was *inaccrochable:*

> "It's good," she said. "That's not the question at all. But it is *inaccrochable.* That means it is like a picture that a painter paints and then he cannot hang it when he has a show and nobody will buy it because they cannot hang it either."
> "But what if it is not dirty, but it is only that you are trying to use words that people would actually use? That are the only words that can make the story come true and that you must use them? You have to use them."
> "But you don't get the point at all," she said. "There is no point in it. It's wrong and it's silly." (Hemingway, *A Moveable Feast,* 15)

Hemingway complained that "I could have expressed myself more vividly by using an *inaccrochable* phrase that wolves used on the lake boats, 'Oh gash may be fine but one eye for mine.' But I was always careful of my language . . ." (*Moveable Feast,* 18–19).

34. Hemingway to Wister, 25 July 1929, *Letters,* 301.

35. Alexander Pope, "Essay on Man," *Alexander Pope: Selected Works,* ed. Louis Kronenburger (New York: Random House, 1948) II.iii.217–20.

36. Pope, II.iii.221–22.

37. Pope, II.iii.225–26.

38. Pope, II.iii.229–30.

39. Pope, II.iii.234.

40. Hemingway, *The Garden of Eden,* 216.

41. Hemingway, *The Garden of Eden*, 41.

42. Pope, II.iii.203.

43. Pope, II.iii.209.

44. Pope, II.iii.211–12.

45. Pope, II.iii.235–37.

46. Pope, II.iii.230.

47. Item 112, John F. Kennedy Library, 98.

48. Item 112, John F. Kennedy Library, 99. The central point here is not whether the girl's "logic" is logical or illogical, creditable or spurious, but that Phil believes it to be logical and succumbs to it because he is guilt-ridden about his "vice" and unsure of his manhood.

49. Hemingway, *The Sun Also Rises*, 20.

50. Item 681, John F. Kennedy Library.

51. Pope, II.iii.211–12.

52. Hemingway, mss. of "The Sea Change," Lilly Library, 99.

53. Pope, II.iii.211–12.

54. William Shakespeare, *The Tempest*, I.ii.400–405.

55. T.S. Eliot, "The Waste Land," *The Complete Poems and Plays of T.S. Eliot* (London: Faber and Faber, 1969) 71.

56. Eliot, "Dans le Restaurant," *Complete Poems*, 51.

57. Hemingway, *The Garden of Eden*, 84–85.

58. Bakker, 144.

59. Item 681, John F. Kennedy Library.

60. The epigraph to *Winner Take Nothing* in which "The Sea Change" was collected. Hemingway wrote the epigraph himself: "Unlike all other forms of lutte or combat the conditions are that the winner shall take nothing; neither his ease, nor his pleasure, nor any notions of glory; nor, if he win far enough, shall there be any reward within himself."

17

"A Natural History of the Dead" as Metafiction

Charles Stetler and Gerald Locklin

Charles Stetler and Gerald Locklin assert a theme that recurs in several places throughout this volume: many Hemingway short stories that remain neglected may be considered aesthetically inferior because they "have been viewed only in the light of realist or modernist criticism." Hemingway's most experimental stories, stories belatedly recognized as using postmodern techniques, fail to meet the formal expectations of older critical theories but may respond dramatically to methods evolved since the 1960s. Here Stetler and Locklin select "A Natural History of the Dead," composed between January 1929 and August 1931, as one example of a story ahead of its time or at least ahead of its criticism. While many previous scholars have rejected "A Natural History of the Dead" because of its combination of genres—the "story" is half satiric essay and half graphic fiction—Stetler and Locklin applaud its double identity as Hemingway's most effective use of metafiction. Their essay illuminates the many ways "A Natural History of the Dead" deliberately calls attention to its own status as an artifact and raises questions about the uneasy relationship of fiction and reality. Their approach not only revitalizes "A Natural History of the Dead" for today's readers but also reminds us of Hemingway's literary sophistication, a sophistication too often and too conveniently obscured by his unearned reputation as a "dumb ox."

In all likelihood the Hemingway short stories that remain neglected were, and perhaps are, considered aesthetically inferior because they have been viewed only in the light of realist or modernist criticism. In some of these works Hemingway seems to have made use of techniques we associate with postmodernism. It should be remembered that Hemingway established his reputation early. Almost from the start everything he wrote appeared in print exactly as he had conceived it. He experimented widely and chose to include in his short story collections works that left his editors wondering about precise terminology: vignettes? pieces? prose-poems? playlets? "A Natural History of the Dead" might head a list that could include "On the Quai at Smyrna," "Banal Story," "One Reader Writes," and "Homage to Switzerland" as works that could profit from reexamination in the light of experimentation that has taken place in fiction from the 1960s to the present.

Not only Hemingway's editors but his critics as well have had difficulty in deciding how to refer to "A Natural History of the Dead." Hemingway himself was never equivocal. Regarding the upcoming publication of *Winner Take Nothing*, Hemingway told Arnold Gingrich of his intention "to include 'A Natural History of the Dead' as it is a story."[1] Others have not agreed with that nomenclature. Sheldon Norman Grebstein feels the "work cannot properly be called a story at all; some such term as sketch would be better."[2] Robert O. Stephens includes the work in his volume, *Hemingway's Non-Fiction*, referring to it as a "seriously pedantic essay with a dramatized exemplum as part of his justification of bullfighting."[3] George Monteiro contends that Hemingway erred in "including his treatise—mocking naturalists, travelers, and humanists—as part of the story."[4] John A. Yunck objects to the combination of genres and to the fact that Hemingway used a short story "as a vehicle for miscellaneous criticism."[5]

Interpretative approaches are rare. According to Susan F. Beegel's calculation, prior to the appearance of her full-length study of four manuscripts,[6] fewer than 30 pages of Hemingway criticism had been devoted to "A Natural History of the Dead." Yunck and John Portz have spent considerable space explicating the story's allusions.[7] Beegel, however, has given the story its most thorough examination to date. She has traced all aspects of its genesis: as Hemingway's reaction against his childhood religious training, as satire of the natural historians, as attack on Humanist literary theory, and as overall aesthetic accomplishment, particularly in regard to Hemingway's decision to omit an autobiographical coda that fully explains the circumstances of his sighting of the dead while bicycling on the road from Fossalta di Piave. In effect, Beegel accepts the story on postmodernist grounds, and we quite agree with her conclusion that the omission of the coda "defies closure" and "opens the story by refusing to interpret it."[8] However, no one has yet viewed the story exclusively in its relationship to its use of techniques that are now associated with metafiction. This essay will focus on the story from that perspective.

Patricia Waugh has defined metafiction as writing "which self-consciously and systemically draws attention to its status as an artifact in order to pose questions about the relationship between fiction and reality."[9] Some specific characteristics include foregrounding; the entry of the narrator into the text; a parodic, playful style; defamiliarization; and the object of the work being language or other forms of discourse. There is the tendency in metafiction to operate "through exaggeration of the tensions and oppositions inherent in all novels: of frame and framebreak, of technique and counter-technique, of construction and deconstruction of illusion."[10]

Metafiction tends "to be constructed on the principle of a fundamental and sustained opposition: the construction of a fictional illusion . . . and the laying bare of that illusion."[11] The mixture is usually a running one. Hemingway's is not, but the two forms of discourse—essay and narrative—are eventually blended into a whole. The first part (about two-thirds of the whole) is an ironic essay on naturalist writing.[12] In keeping with this style, Hemingway makes it a personal essay and identifies himself as the narrator when he speaks of "persevering travellers like Mungo Park and me." The entry of the narrator into the text serves to foreground the entire piece. The second part is also an entity that, if printed by itself, could be referred to as a "typical" Hemingway short story. In fact, it employs one of Heming-way's favored structures: the immediate establishment of setting and conflict with the balance of the story developed primarily through dialogue. The narrator disappears. Both parts could stand alone, but Hemingway welds them into a contrasting whole and in the process has created one of his most amusing, but deadly serious, short works.

Metafiction employs parody self-consciously, often taking as its object languages of nineteenth-century realism, of historical romance, or of fairy tales. "The parody of these 'languages' functions to defamiliarize such struc-tures by setting up various counter-techniques to undermine the authority of the omniscient author, of the closure of the 'final' ending, of the definitive interpretation."[13] The reader is distanced from the language, but the defa-miliarization proceeds from a familiar base.

In the essay Hemingway mimics the style of nineteenth-century, natu-ralist writers. It is a style that differs from the clinicism employed by the pure scientist and leans more toward passionate appeal. It cloaks detach-ment under a tone that members at the club would use while exchanging reports of sightings in the field. It clearly derives from the British. In short, the botanist defines and describes accurately the hollyhock and its environs, but he also frequently displays considerable affection for the species. Hemingway employs this style to address the category of natural history least likely to inspire such warmth: the dead.

He begins formally with a question: can any branch of natural history be studied without increasing faith, love, and hope? What inspiration may we "derive from the dead"?[14] His phraseology could be mistaken for that of an ornithologist espying his favorite warbler: "An interesting aspect" or "On rare occasions I have seen." Hemingway makes frequent use of the impersonal "one," a practice he avoids in his usual journalistic or nonfiction prose. He also includes lengthy descriptions of the countryside. While he does not count all streaks in the tulips, he is quite detailed about the poplar-shaded roads and the blooming mulberry trees. The flora of Lombard sits in ironic contrast to its resident dead. To further reinforce his stylistic parody, Hemingway employs adverbs liberally. "Quite" and "clearly" appear often. His use of "proper" diction also enhances the tone. For example, the word "fragments" means one thing to the naturalist. Its connotation is considerably different when applied to the dead. On their search for "the complete dead," the members of the party collect "fragments." Scattered by their own weight, many "fragments" are found a "considerable distance away in the fields." This gathering of "fragments" is an "extraordinary business."

Important concerns for the naturalist are locale, shape, smell, and position. Thus we learn of the "beautiful burying grounds" for the dead in the mountains; we are told that the appearance of the dead changes daily, from white to yellow to yellow-green, and finally to black; the dead also grow "larger each day." The smell of a battlefield is "unlike the smell of a regiment," and the ultimate position of the dead "depends on the location of the pockets in the uniform."

Hemingway's use of a footnote is another amusing way of directing the reader's attention to form. Even his choice of the footnote number "two" is whimsical, for there is no number one. It is as if he is suggesting greater length and substance to his "scholarly-scientific" treatise, as well as mocking academic garrulity. The essay is Hemingway's public abnegation of the value of literary humanism, his declaration of disdain for academicians in general, particularly the likes of Irving Babbitt and Paul Elmer More and followers, who still thought in a pre-World War I mode and who wrote about death from a perspective just this side of Emerson but considerably nearer to the moral outlook of Hemingway's father. The parody of Marvell—equating pamphlets and footnotes with sterility—completes the attack.

The narrative in "A Natural History of the Dead" is reminiscent of "An Alpine Idyll," which appeared six years earlier in *Men Without Women*, but never to great acclaim, no doubt because it is intentionally so lacking in sentiment for the dead. The peasant who disfigures his wife's corpse by using it as a piece of furniture is generally viewed as an unfeeling individual. Hemingway seems to be assailing the priest who in a stock Victorian response chastises the old man for his irreverence for the dead. The peasant merely accepted the fact of death and realized the corpse could not be buried properly until spring. In "A Natural History of the Dead" Hemingway again makes mention of such practical problems of burial: "in the winter in the mountains you had to put them in the snow and when the snow melted in the spring someone else had to bury them."

The condition of the wounded man in "A Natural History of the Dead" is more repulsive than that of the peasant's wife. His head is "broken as a flower-pot may be broken, although it was all held together by membranes and a skillfully applied bandage now soaked and hardened, with the structure of his brain disturbed by a piece of broken steel in it." The man remains in this condition for two days and a night. There is controversy as to where the wounded man belongs. The stretcher-bearers want him placed outside the cave because they don't like to hear him breathing "in there with the dead." The doctor and the artillery officer resort to violence to settle the dispute over whether the man should be put out of his misery.

Hemingway chose to juxtapose the two parts—the essay and the narrative—with their offsetting tones to produce what those forerunners of postmodernism, the Russian formalists, designated as a defamiliarizing effect. The presence of the essay in the foreground distances the reader from the narrative. Thus the gruesome reality in the cave is set in sharper contrast to the romanticization of nature by Mungo Park (whose career underwent a parodic revival in *Water Music,* a metafictional novel by T. Coraghessan Boyle in 1983) and the insulated rhapsodies to the flora and fauna of Patagonia by W. H. Hudson (whose "sinister" book *The Purple Land* received derisive mention in *The Sun Also Rises*).

A popular theme of metafiction is, of course, art—often fiction itself. Metafiction regularly reminds the reader of the danger of art's dictating life. Kurt Vonnegut, Jr.'s *Breakfast of Champions* will serve as an example. Exploiting the technique of defamiliarization, Vonnegut has his ex-earthling narrator explain from his vantage point on another planet one of earth's problems: its people placed too much faith in "great" books. Hemingway plays on this metafictional theme by alluding to Goya, twice.

The first allusion is in the essay in reference to the practice of the Greeks in Smyrna where they broke the legs of all their baggage animals and pushed them off the quay to drown:

> The numbers of broken-legged mules and horses drowning in the shallow water called for a Goya to depict them. Although, speaking literally, one can hardly say that they called for a Goya since there has only been one Goya, long dead, and it is extremely doubtful if these animals, were they able to call, would call for pictorial representation of their plight but, more likely would, if they were articulate, call for some one to alleviate their condition.

The second allusion occurs when the doctor looks at the wounded man "once in daylight, once with a flashlight. That too would have made a good etching for Goya, the visit with the flashlight, I mean." This passage appears at the beginning of the narrative. The I-narrator is still present, but this is his last direct comment to the reader before exiting the text. The first reference to Goya foreshadows the second. A great artist like Goya would be hard pressed to find in this aspect of natural history—either in fact or in fiction—the solace that Mungo Park discovered in his moss-flower.

Thus it can be seen that rather than being two separate pieces, the two parts of "A Natural History of the Dead" are bound together by a number of ties: the presence of the author as narrator in the text, the two references to Goya, and the smooth transition from one style to another. The first sentence of the narrative sounds like a continuation of the tone of the essay: "In the mountains too, sometimes, the snow fell on the dead outside the dressing station on the side that was protected by the mountains from any shelling." Tone and content change after this, but the two parts remain linked by the "quality of unreality" about the dead. In the essay this is suggested by the wonder about the mortality of mules, by the confusion about the sex of the dead due to the short hair style of the women, and by the mutilated corpses ("fragments"). All anticipate the anonymity of the wounded man. His sex is determined, but not his identity. The dispute about where he belongs (among the dead or the wounded), the violence between the doctor and the officer, and the redundant announcement "the man in the dead-house is dead" (he was for all practical purposes dead all along) all reinforce the "quality of unreality."

Like his fellow modernists, Hemingway reacted against nineteenth-century realism that was based on a "firm belief in a commonly experienced, objectively existing world of history."[15] The modernists responded to the initial loss of belief in such a world with fiction that "signalled the first widespread overt emergence of a sense of fictiousness: a sense that any attempt to represent reality could only produce selective perspectives."[16] Metafiction extends this concept to "an even more thoroughgoing sense that reality and history are provisional: no longer a world of eternal verities but a series of constructions, artifices, impermanent structures."[17] Thus the forms that correspond to this ordered reality are rejected.

Stories within stories and plays within plays are as old as literature itself. But an essay cleverly attached to a narrative was different in its day. Hemingway loved to experiment with both form and content. He made use of an unreliable narrator in "Fifty Grand" and in "The Mother of a Queen." He anticipated the New Journalism in *Green Hills of Africa* and in *A Moveable Feast*. Both works, he tells us, may be read either as fiction or as nonfiction. It should, then not be surprising to find him exploiting some of the techniques of metafiction before the movement came into full bloom.

Notes

1. *Ernest Hemingway: Selected Letters, 1917–1961,* ed. Carlos Baker (New York: Charles Scribner's Sons, 1981) 393.

2. Sheldon Norman Grebstein, *Hemingway's Craft* (Carbondale: Southern Illinois UP, 1973) 77.

3. Robert O. Stephens, *Hemingway's Non-Fiction: The Public Voice* (Chapel Hill: U North Carolina P, 1968) 7.

4. George Monteiro, "Hemingway's Unnatural History of the Dying," *Fitzgerald/Hemingway Annual 1978,* 340.

5. John A. Yunck, "The Natural History of a Dead Quarrel: Hemingway and the Humanists," *South Atlantic Quarterly* 62 (Winter 1963): 33.

6. Susan F. Beegel, "'That Always Absent Something Else': 'A Natural History of the Dead' and Its Discarded Coda," in *Hemingway's Craft of Omission: Four Manuscript Examples* (Ann Arbor: UMI Research P, 1988) 31–49.

7. John Portz, "Allusion and Structure in Hemingway's 'A Natural History of the Dead,'" *Tennessee Studies in Literature* 10 (1965): 27–44.

8. Beegel, 47.

9. Patricia Waugh, *Metafiction: The Theory and Practice of Self-Conscious Fiction* (London and New York: Methuen, 1980) 2.

10. Waugh, 14.

11. Waugh, 6.

12. For the sake of clarity we will refer to the first part as "the essay" and to the second part as "the narrative"; however, our contention remains that together they add up to "the story."

13. Waugh, 13.

14. Hemingway, "A Natural History of the Dead," in *The Short Stories of Ernest Hemingway* (New York: Charles Scribner's Sons, 1966) 440–49. All quotations refer to this edition.

15. Waugh, 6.

16. Waugh, 6.

17. Waugh, 7.

18

"Homage to Switzerland": Einstein's Train Stops at Hemingway's Station

Michael S. Reynolds

"Homage to Switzerland," composed between March and June 1932, must rank as Hemingway's most cryptic short story, as incomprehensible to many critics as Einstein's theory of relativity to most lay people. The story is a triptych, featuring three different protagonists waiting for the Simplon-Orient Express at three different train stations at the same moment in time. Nothing much seems to happen in "Homage to Switzerland" except that each of the three protagonists participates in one of the mildly unpleasant, personally intrusive exchanges with strangers for which waiting rooms are notorious. The short story almost seems to predict Samuel Beckett's Waiting for Godot, *where "nothing happens, nobody comes, nobody goes, it's awful." "Homage to Switzerland" meets M.H. Abrams's definition of absurdist literature—it is "grotesquely comic as well as irrational" and "a deliberate parody of the traditional assumptions of Western culture." The short story also challenges the traditional assumptions of Western critics, and this may be one reason why Hemingway scholars have so long avoided it in favor of such straightforward narratives as "The Undefeated" and "Fifty Grand." Indeed, Hemingway could have had "Homage to Switzerland" in mind when he blasted his critics with "Gentlemen, you are criticizing my arithmetic when I am long ago into calculus."*

Here noted Hemingway biographer Michael Reynolds makes "Homage to Switzerland" more accessible by examining its historic context in detail and looking closely at its manuscripts, its autobiographical content, and even its weird and arcane jokes about the National Geographic. *In particular, Reynolds explores the story's striking experimentation with time and space, experimentation indebted to Einstein's unsettling discovery that these were not absolute values but relative to the speed of light. Reynolds con-*

vinces us that the story's "black comedy, chance encounters, failed relationships, misunderstandings, and communications gone astray in translation" constitute Hemingway's own disturbing proof that not love nor language nor time itself possesses absolute values in our time.

In 1932, when Hemingway first offered "Homage to Switzerland" to *Cosmopolitan* magazine, he called it "a new form for a story." He told the editor,

> The fact that the three parts all open the same way or practically the same is intentional and is supposed to represent Switzerland metaphysically where it all opens in the same way always and where a young man will not marry a young lady until she has had her original teeth out and her store teeth in since that is an eventual expense that the girl's father, not her husband, should bear. But, possibly, Mr. Lengel, you have been in Switzerland yourself. Anybody will have been there when they read the Homage.[1]

Mr. Lengel may or may not have visited Switzerland, but he was unimpressed with Hemingway's humor and his experimental "new form," for he rejected the manuscript. Since 1933, when "Homage" was finally published by *Scribner's* magazine (which could hardly refuse it), this curious triad of stories has attracted little critical attention, which some might say is more attention than it deserves. Our record as scholars has been less than splendid in the rigorous study of Hemingway's nonce stories. If the story does not fit our pattern, we are not interested. We ignore or dismiss as Hemingway mistakes anomalies that do not fit our view. Rather consistently we judge to be failures whatever we do not understand. If "Homage" is the failure that it appears, perhaps even from a Hemingway failure we may learn something useful.

The parts of Hemingway's triptych are set in similar train stations at three points along Lake Geneva: Montreux, Vevey, and Territet. In each section an American male is waiting to catch the Simplon-Orient Express to Paris. The train is an hour late in all three stories, which appear to begin simultaneously about 9:25 P.M. The first story ends with the train's arrival about 11:30 P.M. in Montreux. The second or central section at Vevey ends at 10:45 P.M. before the train arrives. The last story at Territet also ends before the train arrives.

Because Hemingway seldom uses geography carelessly, we should be aware that the three geographical points in his story are out of their proper order. The sequence should be Territet, Montreux, and Vevey. The train should arrive at Territet a few minutes before Montreux, which is less than a mile away, and at Montreux perhaps 10 minutes before Vevey, which is not more than five miles down the line. To arrange this sequence with

Vevey at the center is to distort geography and to emphasize that the Vevey incident is the most important of the three stories. Moreover, we might notice that the actual Simplon-Orient Express did not stop at either Vevey or Territet, for both were minor stations. The Express stopped only at Montreux, where in fact it does arrive in the story. Presumably the men at Vevey and Territet are still waiting for their overdue train.

All of which is to say that "Homage to Switzerland" is about time and space, themes central to much of Hemingway's fiction, and themes of great interest to the most important physicist of the century, Albert Einstein, in whose mind-experiments time and space were relative in a universe whose only constant was the speed of light. In Einstein's now classic mental experiment, two men—one on a passing train and the other standing on the platform—each carry a clock and a measuring rod. The train moves at the speed of light; the man on the platform is stationary. As the train passes the platform, each man measures the window on the train. The measurement the man on the platform makes is shorter than the measurement the man on the train makes. The man on the train measures a stationary window; the man on the station platform measures a window passing at the speed of light. Both measurements are relatively correct, but neither measurement is correct for both men. The length of the window varies depending upon the position of the measurer in time and space relative to it. Moreover, the two clocks appear to run at different rates: to the platform observer, the train clock runs more slowly than his stationary clock.

In the early part of this century, the Newtonian world of fixed, certain, mechanical processes broke irrevocably down, leaving us no more absolutes except one: the speed of light. All else became relative. In March 1922, while Hemingway was learning his way about Paris, Albert Einstein was in town delivering a series of lectures. Einstein, whose first theoretical paper on relativity was published in 1905, had, by 1932 when "Homage to Switzerland" was written, become a world celebrity whose picture needed no caption. His name and his ideas were bandied about in the popular press as frequently as they appeared in scientific journals. From 1922 to 1928, the *New York Times* carried 172 stories about Einstein and his ideas; during the same period almost a hundred articles about Einstein appeared in English and American periodicals. There is no evidence that Hemingway ever read anything that Einstein wrote, but the young author could not have avoided a general understanding of the physicist's ideas.

In the film *The Third Man,* Orson Welles told us that in five hundred years of peace Switzerland produced only the cuckoo clock. Welles's exaggeration ignored, among other Swiss contributions, those of Albert Einstein, whose major papers on relativity were written in Switzerland while he was working in the Patent Office. It is, therefore, altogether fitting that Hemingway's "Homage to Switzerland" should develop its tripartite story at three interchangeable Swiss railway stations, each with its three porters and one waitress. Each story begins in exactly the same manner, but each takes its own curious twist. That they are happening simultaneously in a relative universe is neither accidental nor whimsical. Each of the three male characters—Mr. Wheeler at Montreux, Mr. Johnson at Vevey, and Mr. Harris at Territet—has a problem with relationships. Each man has a chance encounter with what seem to be the same characters.

Had they read the first draft of "Homage to Switzerland," Hemingway's readers would have been even more bewildered, for he initially intended the stories to be happening to the same man—Mr. Wheeler—all stories taking place simultaneously in Montreux.[2] Early in the experiment Hemingway decided to set the stories in three adjacent towns, but only after completing the first draft did he divide Mr. Wheeler into three characters by simply changing his name. Hemingway was trying the limits of the short story genre, still learning, still growing as an artist. Had he followed his initial idea for the experiment, "Homage to Switzerland" would have read more like a Jorge Luis Borges story than one by Hemingway.

We, Hemingway's critical readers, were not much interested in such an experiment. If James Joyce had written "Homage to Switzerland," its study would have produced a book, 15 articles, and 30 dissertations, all finished 10 years ago. Some bright physicist would have worked out the time problem that runs through the triptych. Because Hemingway wrote it, we have simply read past the time references, because they did not seem important. As a result, no one has yet asked the simple question: when is the story taking place? Because Mr. Harris, the last character, tells us that his father recently committed suicide in 1928, the biographical trap offers an easy solution. If we take that carefully planted bait, we have to ignore references to specific *National Geographic* articles and pictures that are the half-comic heart of the third section. There, you remember, Mr. Harris is approached by an old man whose opening lines rank with the strangest in all of Hemingway's fiction. He says, "I beg your pardon if I intrude . . . but it has just occurred to me that you might be a member of the National Geographic Society."[3] Mr. Harris and his readers have just encountered the absurd.

During the following three pages of reminiscences about *National Geographic* articles, Harris asks: "Do you remember the panorama of the Sahara Desert?" The old man replies, "The Sahara Desert? That was nearly fifteen years ago" (433). The two men continue to discuss the panorama and whether the Arab was kneeling toward Mecca or standing. The picture they both recall so fondly appeared in the April 1911 issue of *National Geographic* as a fold-out; readers could order special uncreased copies "printed on very heavy mat art paper suitable for framing" for only 50 cents. The panorama was called "The Hour of Prayer: In the Sahara Desert," and the magazine called it "the most extraordinary desert scene that has ever been published."[4]

Mr. Harris remembered the Arab kneeling toward Mecca, but the old man says he was standing. The memories of Mr. Harris and his odd interlocutor were reinforced by the December 1911 *National Geographic* whose lead article, "The Sacred City of the Sands," ran several desert pictures of Arabs, camels, and sand, one of which shows two Arabs kneeling, beside their camel, praying toward Mecca.[5] A third reference to the 1911 *National Geographic* appears in the men's discussion of George Shiras the Third, or "Three" as the old man calls him. The November 1911 issue ran a clever article by George Shiras, III, in which he took night flash photos of an albino porcupine and a hungry racoon.[6]

Just when 1926 looked like a firm date for the story—that is, 1911 plus 15 years—Hemingway adds to the temporal confusion by introducing T. E. Lawrence to the conversation. Harris says that he confused the 1911 kneeling Arabs with those found standing in Colonel Lawrence's book (434). Hemingway's reference here is to T. E. Lawrence's *The Revolt in the Desert* which was not published until 1931 and which Hemingway bought that September, which would place the story in either 1931 or early 1932.[7]

In five pages, Hemingway has given us more internal dating for this story than we have any right to expect, but the dates are in conflict. If we take the biographical dating of Hemingway's father's suicide, the story takes place in 1929: "he died last year. Shot himself, oddly enough" (434). If we take the T. E. Lawrence reference, the story takes place in 1931–32, when Hemingway actually wrote it. If we follow the clue of 15 years after the 1911 *National Geographic,* Mr. Harris's railway station interlude takes place in 1926. What is a reader to do?

First, we should stop taking ourselves so seriously. Like Herman Hesse's Steppenwolf, we must learn to laugh, or, at the very least, to giggle, for perhaps, just perhaps, Hemingway is having ironic fun with his story and with us, his readers. Let us give him the benefit of the doubt. Maybe he actually knew what he was doing when he wrote this story. As much as we like having it both ways, we cannot praise Hemingway's subtle touches in stories we favor and then say that he did not know what he was doing with "Homage to Switzerland." That time references do not correlate is perfectly appropriate in a universe in which time is relative.

As I write these words, I can hear the groans of the recalcitrant: they will not be moved, certain that Hemingway was still making mistakes, that he was unaware of the time references. But perhaps they have been to Switzerland and know how it all opens the same way. And perhaps they are certain always of time and location. And of course Hemingway never expected his American readers to know where the Express stopped or where the towns were located along the lake. These readers might see little humor in a paying of "Homage to Switzerland" by an author who had once paid "Homage to Ezra" and who sat beneath the Picasso painting "Homage to Gertrude Stein."[8]

For the unconvinced, let me suggest that Hemingway not only knew what he was doing but was also performing on at least two or three levels simultaneously in this story. First, the story is a triptych: a central story framed by two slightly shorter stories, all happening simultaneously just as they do in a medieval triptych, where the side panels may comment or enlarge upon the central issue. Hemingway saw plenty of triptychs, the most impressive, perhaps, being those of Hieronimous Bosch in the Prado, including "Garden of Earthly Delights."

The central panel of "Homage to Switzerland" develops the depressed condition of Mr. Johnson, an American whose wife has decided to divorce him. At the Vevey station Mr. Johnson tries to interest three porters in his situation. In a mixture of English, French, and German, the resulting scene could have come from a Marx Brothers movie. Mr. Johnson is, in fact, deeply hurt by his wife's action, but the comedy of the three porters undercuts his bathos. At the end the good sport leaves the three porters with an unopened bottle of "Sportsman" champagne, but through the window Mr. Johnson sees them trade it back in with the waitress. "That makes three francs something apiece, Johnson thought" (430). Feeling nasty, Mr. Johnson strolls off in the dark to pass the time.

In manuscript Hemingway wrote past his ending with a long paragraph describing how hollow Mr. Johnson felt and how his wife had never understood how the dark affected him. We are told that Mr. Johnson's heart is gone:

> She had his heart and it was lost now. She couldn't help it. She could never help anything. He knew it and he did not blame her but his heart was gone. He would live without his heart because he had to and everything went on but he did not care. But he could not write without his heart. It was all hollow like this story.[9]

Realizing that this pathetic ending detracted from the irony and absurd humor of his central panel, Hemingway cut it.

Hemingway then framed his central panel with Mr. Wheeler's heartless propositioning of the waitress at Montreux, a sexual joke, for Mr. Wheeler knows there is no place at the station to carry out a rendezvous. Mr. Wheeler, we are told, "never took chances." Mr. Wheeler, in fact, is a homosexual who "did not care for women" (425). His brief interlude is a joke but a bitter one. In the other framing panel is Mr. Harris's absurd encounter with the old *National Geographic* man who wants to nominate Harris to the society. There is a good deal of humor in this absurd interchange: the old man finally decides that he will nominate T. E. Lawrence instead. But there is also something pathetic, strange, a little weird. I am reminded of the bottle-green eyes of the old josher in Joyce's "An Encounter," a tale of perversion. If the old man is not making a strange sexual advance to Mr. Harris, he is, at very least, the loneliest man we meet, doomed to approaching railway strangers in the night of Territet, looking for conversation. Black comedy, chance encounters, failed relationships, misunderstandings, and communications gone astray in translation: homage to Switzerland, famed for its timepieces and the man who destroyed time.

On another level, Hemingway had his private and literary reasons for writing "Homage to Switzerland." It was at Chamby sur Montreux that he and Hadley twice wintered so innocently, and it was in Switzerland that he lost Hadley through his affair with Pauline Pfeiffer. He also knew of at least one strange relationship that centered at Territet: it was there that Bryher Ellerman lived with H.D. and where Bryher's pseudo-husband Robert McAlmon would occasionally visit. Like his characters, Hemingway waited more than once to catch the Simplon-Orient Express. The bitterest wait, of course, was for the Express back to Paris to check on the loss of his early manuscripts.

On the literary level, Hemingway was having a kind of intellectual fun that we seldom allow him in our critical readings. Without exploring all the implications, I will suggest a few associations. First, one cannot say "Vevey" without thinking of Henry James's *Daisy Miller.* Hemingway had already done his addendum to that classic when he wrote "A Canary for One," where the American mother confides that her daughter fell in love with an unacceptable European at Vevey.[10] Another literary association is loosely connected with Territet, the closest railway stop to the Castle of Chillon, which Hemingway visited and which has Byron's name scratched into the stone pillar of the dungeon. It was in that dungeon that Byron set his "Prisoner of Chillon," the narrative of three brothers doomed for following the values of their father. At Territet, oddly enough, we learn that Mr. Harris's father has shot himself, a difficult example for Mr. Harris to follow. And as a final fillip, one cannot think of Lake Geneva on whose shore the three towns are set without remembering that this is the same lake on which Eliot finished the first draft of *The Waste Land,* a bleak sexual comedy of failed relationships: "By the waters of Leman I sat down and wept."

But no weeping here, good friends, for as I write these words, two curious and very different versions of this essay are being written in other rooms not unlike the one in which I sit. One of these three is quite comic, one mendacious. It will be said that the other writers bear some resemblance to me in all but name.

Notes

1. *Ernest Hemingway: Selected Letters, 1917–1961*, ed. Carlos Baker (New York: Charles Scribner's Sons, 1981) 367.

2. Hemingway Collection, items 476, 476a, 476b, John F. Kennedy Library.

3. Hemingway, "Homage to Switzerland," *The Short Stories of Ernest Hemingway* (New York: Charles Scribner's Sons, 1966) 432. All page references in parentheses refer to this edition.

4. "Our Desert Panorama," *National Geographic* 22 (April 1911): 409–10. Whether the Arab was standing or kneeling in the panorama cannot be settled until someone finds the fold-out, which was missing from the volume I used.

5. Frank E. Johnson, "The Sacred City of the Sands," *National Geographic* 22 (December 1911): 1062.

6. George Shiras, III, "A Flashlight Story of an Albino Porcupine and of a Cunning but Unfortunate Coon," *National Geographic* 22 (May 1911): 572–95.

7. Michael S. Reynolds, *Hemingway's Reading, 1910–1940: An Inventory* (Princeton: Princeton UP, 1981) 146.

8. Ernest Hemingway, "Homage to Ezra," *This Quarter* 1.1 (Spring 1925): 221–25.

9. Hemingway Collection, item 476b, John F. Kennedy Library.

10. See Lois P. Rudnick, "Daisy Miller Revisited: Ernest Hemingway's 'A Canary for One,'" *Massachusetts Studies in English* 7 (1978): 12–19.

19

Repetition as Design and Intention: Hemingway's "Homage to Switzerland"

Erik Nakjavani

Erik Nakjavani attacks the riddles of "Homage to Switzerland" with an array of postmodern critical methods related to the story's own disturbing view of language. His interest in "Homage to Switzerland" resides in what J. Hillis Miller would call the story's "complex tissue of repetitions and of repetitions within repetitions, or of repetitions linked in chain fashion to other repetitions, making up the structure of the work within itself, as well as repetitions determining its multiple relations to what is outside it." Nakjavani inquires minutely into how the numerous repetitions of the tripartite "Homage to Switzerland" conspire to produce its intention, and he discovers an intricately constructed tale of "universal homelessness and the isolation of the individual," of "mutual incomprehension ... in the midst of ... human community."

> *Recollection is the pagan lifeview,*
> *repetition is the modern.*
>
> —Søren Kierkegaard,
> *Repetition: An Essay in Experimental Psychology*

> *Pain joins the rift of the difference.*
> *Pain is the difference itself.*
> —Martin Heidegger, *Poetry, Language, Thought*

In his biography of Hemingway, Carlos Baker remarks that

"Homage to Switzerland" went back in time to Ernest's visit to Switzerland in 1927, just before his divorce from Hadley. It was a humorous and ironic three-part story about Mr.

Wheeler, Mr. Johnson, and Mr. Harris in Montreux, Vevey, and Territet. Anyone acquainted with Ernest's marital history could easily recognize that all three men were himself, attempting to recover from the trauma of separation from his first wife, Hadley.[1]

Elsewhere, Baker considers this story less biographically and classifies it as one of a group of stories that "explore the predicament of divorce."[2] Joseph DeFalco follows this thematic approach, enlarges it, and treats the story within a new but related group of stories that deal with marriage and marital problems in Hemingway's stories.[3]

Can it be that the dismaying paucity of scholarship on this highly complex and innovative story is due mainly to this biographical and narrow thematic approach? It may well be so, because the aim of such studies always appears to be total and exhaustive. In any case, let us acknowledge the truth and usefulness of the limited existing studies on the themes of marriage, separation, and divorce.

Having done so, we pose the following questions: Doesn't the story provide a ground of possibility to go beyond the existing studies of it? Cannot one offer, for example, a new reading that would draw solely and directly from the text of the story itself and interweave the various strands of themes and structures in it? I propose a reading of "Homage to Switzerland" as a short story that deals with the universal and fundamentally ambiguous problem of individual identity as difference and the overwhelming human desire to do away with the loneliness that difference or otherness engenders.

"Homage to Switzerland" consists of a triptych of events unfolding simultaneously, occupying proximal spatial dimensions, and evolving more or less contiguously in plot, characters, narrative structures, and dialogue. However, within these elements of fiction and structures unfolds a hermetic and experimental work of short fiction whose surface accessibility, as in many other Hemingway short stories, is highly deceptive. Consequently, a sort of fundamental ambiguity in form and content appears to hover over its apparent simplicity. For me, this ambiguity constitutes the unusual design and the central intention that affect the signifying structures of this story.

A close scrutiny of the story reveals an expansive pattern of narrative discourse, where the smooth, bright surfaces and their deep, dark intimations are interwoven into a tapestry of design and intention. The inescapable and dazzling array of repetitions of certain elements of fiction and narration in each of the three parts of the story create this opening.

J. Hillis Miller's statement about the significance of repetition in English novels provides an appropriate point of departure for a study of the patterns of repetitions in "Homage to Switzerland." Miller writes, "Any novel is a complex tissue of repetitions and of repetitions within repetitions, or of repetitions linked in chain fashion to other repetitions determining its multiple relations to what is outside it." He concludes these reflections by posing a necessary question: "What controls the meaning these repetitions create?"[4] In other words, how do repetitions create the intention of a novel?

Miller's observations on the role of repetition in the novel may be applied to the short story inasmuch as the genres differ in their internal economy of development and its exigencies. Otherwise, the two forms share common elements. Therefore, one may ask how these repetitions emerge and function in "Homage to Switzerland," both self-referentially within the particular world of the narrative text itself and referentially in relation to that other text, the world outside the text, that one may call the text of the human condition in general. What intention in the short story do these repetitions serve? These questions can only be answered by developing a typology of repetitions and their corresponding morphology in this story.

Descriptive Repetitions and Binary Oppositions as Their Constituents

The first category of repetitions in "Homage to Switzerland" consists of those involving what I would designate as the space-time coordinates of each of the three parts of the story. These repetitions establish the descriptions of the railroad station cafés at Montreux, Vevey, and Territet and set the stage for the drama that follows. Each of these initial descriptions, in turn, provides a backdrop against which plot, characters, patterns of dialogue, and internal monologue evolve in each of the three parts of the story. As a result, together, they provide a basis for understanding how this story produces its meaning. They set up a dialectical relationship between this universal background and the particular life of the individual human being presented in each of the three sections. The individual and the background in which he appears become, then, part of a series of concentric spheres of interactions. The dialectical relationship between the universal and the individual results at the same time in what Martin Heidegger calls the "mood" or of "'how one is, and of how one is faring'" in each cluster of the spheres of human interactions that sketch out each main character in the three parts of the story.[5]

I consider the temporal coordinate in each of the three parts of the short story as an "arrested" case of repetition insofar as it reaches the category of simultaneity. The train in each station is an hour late *at the same time,* so time in the story reveals itself as a repeated pattern in each of the three parts. This shared temporal pattern of repetition reinforces the impression of an equally shared and unavoidable universal human condition that the story as a whole imparts.

However, the spatial coordinate of the three parts is not and cannot be coincidental. The coincidence of both the temporal and the spatial coordinates in each descriptive repetition would have pushed the three parts of the short story beyond the plane of simultaneity onto that of identicalness and would have undone its intentional triangular division. The spatial coordinate of the three parts varies inasmuch as the three train station cafés represent three different reference points in space. They are localized; therefore, they are clearly specified. Similarly, they vary from one part to another—slightly but importantly. Thus, whole spatial characteristics remain essentially the same and predetermined, each of them functions in such a way as to offer the most appropriate background for the indeterminate free play of the development of a particular character. That is their singularly important function in the story.

Within these repetitions of time-space coordinates, I now find an ensemble of what I would term "essential transversal repetitions." They appear to derive as a series from a set of primary, inside versus outside binary oppositions (so common in Hemingway's fiction): warm versus cold, light versus darkness, movement versus stasis, manmade world versus natural world, order versus disorder, predictable versus unpredictable, known versus unknown, female versus male, heterosexual versus homosexual, young versus old, employee versus customer. The objective narrative point of view provides these dualities as the organizing and controlling principle of the beginning descriptive repetitions in all three parts of the story. I believe that this primary series of binary oppositions sets up a dialectic that provides the perspective from which all ensuing events in the story flow in parallel lines and, eventually, in a specific sense, *in parallel lines but in reverse directions*.

Let us begin at the beginning and consider the first sentence of the first paragraph in part 1: "INSIDE [capitalized in the original] the station café it was warm and light."[6] What is this "inside" but the human space? Is it not human space fashioned by human hands—carved out of the infinite space at its threshold, a space within space, a shelter against the cold and the dark of the night, a kind of second human skin? Is it not a space appropriated and shaped by human bodies to suit their needs, its outer layers secreted from human toil like a crust or a shell to protect them against the menacing "outside" ("Outside the window it was snowing")? This shell is not illuminated by the sun, the moon, or the stars. Its light and warmth derive from a constellation of human efforts. Indeed, all that lies beyond this bright and warm "inside" is nonhuman. And what is nonhuman is nature: a state of cold, wild, dark profusion of matter against a background of silent nothingness and empty space. In its most pure, uncompromising, and primitive state, the outside is a place of suffering, death, and disappearance. Yet the outside remains immensely attractive to human beings at the same time, like an incurable obsession. The call of the outside is a constant appeal to the deepest instincts in mankind to approach the nonhuman and to deal with it. In contrast, the inside defines itself as a known but limited sanctuary.

This first sentence only prefigures the four following sentences, which intensify the sense of communal living in this created human space. At least, the human space incorporates a provisional order into the seemingly amorphous and incomprehensible world of matter and makes human life possible. One reads, "The wood of the tables shone from wiping and there were baskets of pretzels in glazed paper sacks. The chairs were carved, but the seats were worn and comfortable. There was a carved wooden clock on the wall and a bar at the far end of the room" (422). Nature has been conquered and domesticated here, and the undeniable stamp of this conquest and this domestication is to be found everywhere. The wood has been made into tables and seats by human hands for the satisfaction of human needs and desires that have rendered them shining, well worn, and comfortable by continual usage. They almost appear to be extensions of the human body. In any case, they are thoroughly invested with the human presence in the world and bear witness to it. There is also transformation of natural substances by human hands into bread in the form of "pretzels in glazed paper sacks" and wine and spirits at the bar that completes the sacred and the domestic nature of the scene. "INSIDE," time, too, has been reduced to human scale in evanescent bits of eternity. Time is segmented in predetermined, mechanized movements by that intricate human invention that is the clock ("There was a carved wooden clock on the wall").

However, this sheltering and nurturing human world can and does break down periodically. One reads that "Two of the station porters sat drinking new wine under the *clock*" (my emphasis) while "Another porter came in and said the Simplon-Orient Express was an hour late at Saint Maurice" (422). Invented, fabricated, and operated by man, trains may fail and may be late, as their generic creators sit under the mechanical measuring rod of time to learn of its lateness and drink "new wine." The Express may be and is late. In this world the predictable and the unpredictable coexist. Rapid movement and stasis can be and are combined in a binary opposition that brushes against the boundaries of the absurd and yet remains curiously within the domain of the human and the comprehensible. Chaos cannot always be kept at bay. The unknown stubbornly defies the known at every juncture. Order often breaks down, usually more often than is desirable.

In general, however, this commonly created human space, in contrast to what lies outside its domain, is reassuring. One discovers, for instance, that after the announcement that the Express is an hour late, "The waitress came over to Mr. Wheeler's table" in order to ask him, "Can I bring you some coffee?" (422). She attempts to remedy in one part of the human space what has gone wrong in another. The comforting and nurturing female figure completes the picture of the station café, which the narrative discourse now has symbolically raised to the level of that quintessential human space, a home, which is a particularly significant space in Hemingway's fiction.

This series of primary and secondary binary oppositions structure the first two paragraphs of part 1 in such a way as to allow an interpretation of the "INSIDE," the human space or the manmade world, as hospitable and sheltering. Hemingway essentially repeats these series of binary oppositions in the beginning, descriptive paragraphs of part 2 and part 3. These series of binary oppositions initiate the process of production of meaning in the last two parts of the story as they do in part 1.

It should be noted and understood that these space-time coordinates along with their attendant primary and secondary binary oppositions in the three parts of the story are not limited to what I call "synchronic repetitions," which are repetitions that take place within the time of the story as it develops. There is also another less apparent but equally crucial pattern of repetitions that is always present in the synchronic repetitions and infuses them with a dimension that goes beyond the time of the story. I refer to them as "diachronic repetitions." They contain all the silent and invisible history of the incalculable number of times that the finite and indeterminate human world has touched upon the infinite and seemingly predetermined, unknown, nonhuman world. The diachronic repetitions involve the genesis and the history of the development of the "synchronic repetitions" in the story. Consequently, each "synchronic repetition" in the story finds itself by implication and evocation within a considerably longer chain of "diachronic repetitions" as its inherent historical background.

These contacts, so common in Hemingway's fiction, wherever and whenever they occur, plunge human beings atavistically into the long saga of regressive repetitions of their development back into the dawn of human existence on earth. They bear witness to the struggle—against the chaos, the dark night, and the nonhuman—that makes up the story of the human emergence and presence in the world. They sketch the story of human consciousness prowling an alien world like a ghost in search of a home, finding the possibilities of fulfillment of this desire everywhere and nowhere. That is the universal given of the human condition as we know it.

As a result, these initial passages in the three parts of "Homage to Switzerland" represent a network of "repetitions within repetitions," which are of considerable significance in their historical and universal implications.

The evolution of the dialectic between inside and outside, or human space and natural space, is no less than the sum total of human history, both in reality and in fiction. It is our common experience that wherever one encounters this dialectic one touches upon that enormous spider's web of history that reaches from the present far into the past.

On the level of synchronic repetitions, the modified and repeated elements function in each of the three parts in two related ways. First, they establish a common ground of the emergence and unfolding of events; second, they establish the source from which the "mood" in each one of the three parts derives. Examined from this perspective, the sentences in the first two paragraphs of part 1 reveal certain significant functional qualities. For the sake of clarity, I shall quote these paragraphs in their entirety.

> INSIDE the station café it was warm and light. The wood of the tables shone from wiping and there were baskets of pretzels in glazed paper sacks. The chairs were carved, but the seats were worn and comfortable. There was a carved wooden clock on the wall and a bar at the far end of the room. Outside the window it was snowing.
>
> Two of the station porters sat drinking new wine at the table under the clock. Another porter came in and said the Simplon-Orient Express was an hour late at Saint Maurice. He went out. The waitress came over to Mr. Wheeler's table. (422)

The sentences in these two paragraphs may all be more or less short, staccato, and declarative. The objective narrator's eyes establish no more connection among them than their visual contiguity as images in space. Each sentence outlines the existence of an underlying autonomous act of perception related to an equally autonomous cluster of images. Each contains a world of its own. Their very contiguity betrays their separateness. even though contiguity lexically signifies touching at a point or along a line, points and lines are always signs of demarcation and separation. The human gaze recognizes the void, the nothingness of space that permeates such lines and points that define the boundaries of the visible as such.

As a consequence, the human world, that of Mr. Wheeler, which the first two paragraphs of part 1 prefigure, attempts to become an integrated whole but does not achieve its end. The sentences in these two paragraphs aim at creating a harmonious and uninterrupted world, but this world is assailed everywhere by the vacuum brought into it by the consciousness of the objective narrator. This vacuum enters abruptly; it draws up sharp and unbridgeable boundaries, fragments the whole into parts, and differentiates and names the parts. The human eye has become here merely a camera, functioning automatically, reducing everything to sharp visual images, without the mediation of other faculties.

Thus, a sense of irreconcilable difference and separation exists at the heart of the contiguity of images in these two paragraphs. The separation brings recognition and differentiation to their various constituents. In due course, this recognition of difference permeates all the events of part 1 in their entirety and sets the mood as Mr. Wheeler's attempts at hiding his own personal difference, his homosexuality, are shown to be doomed to failure. (The recognition of difference as an absolute, incidentally, may be considered in itself as a mode of internal repetition in each of the three parts.)

An examination of the initial descriptive passage in part 2 reveals that the main modification of the two initial paragraphs in comparison with those of part 1 issues from an attempt to combine as well as to differentiate at the level of the sentence and of the paragraph. Here are the initial paragraphs of part 2.

> Inside the station café it was warm and light; the tables were shiny from wiping and on some there were red and white striped table cloths; and there were blue and white striped table cloths on the others and on all of them baskets with pretzels in glazed paper sacks. The chairs were carved but the wood seats were worn and comfortable. There was a clock on the wall, a zinc bar at the far end of the room, and outside the window it was snowing. Two of the station porters sat drinking new wine at the table under the clock.
>
> Another porter came in and said the Simplon-Orient Express was an hour late at Saint-Maurice [*sic*]. The waitress came over to Mr. Johnson's table. (425)

In comparison to the first sentence in part 1, the first sentence of the opening paragraphs of part 2 is longer and richer in details. The first sentence in part 2 involves a series of dependent clauses joined by semicolons. The narrator's eye seemingly no longer seeks to impart only crisply delineated visual images by incorporating the nothingness of space into their boundaries to make sharp distinctions among them. The eye attempts rather to accentuate the proximity of images beyond mere contiguity. Semicolons, rather than periods, as well as the conjunction "and" serve as bridges that span from one image to another. There is a sense of one sentence's reaching out to another and a consequent juxtaposition, if not merging, of the two. A proclivity for connection rather than fragmentation is manifest here.

Even on the level of the paragraph, a portion of the second paragraph in part 1 has been added to the first paragraph in part 2. The act of fusion of sentences and paragraphs takes place subtly, legato. The apparent inclination toward communication and unity, toward common affinities, toward a state of togetherness at the syntactic level in this paragraph also extends to the entire narrative text of part 2 as a whole. As the central panel of the triptych which mediates between part 1 and part 3, these two paragraphs anticipate the appearance of Mr. Johnson, whose main desire is also to reach out to others for shared understanding and communion.

Finally, extending the same method of examination to the first paragraph of part 3, what I would call the "combinative desire" is once again in operation.

> In the station café at Territet it was a little too warm; the lights were bright and the tables shiny from polishing. There were baskets with pretzels in glazed paper sacks on the tables and cardboard pads for beer glasses in order that the moist glasses would not make rings on the wood. The chairs were carved but the wooden seats were worn and quite comfortable. There was a clock on the wall, a bar at the far end of the room, and outside the window it was snowing. There was an old man drinking coffee at a table under the clock and reading the evening paper. A porter came in and said the Simplon-Orient Express was an hour late at Saint Maurice. The waitress came over to Mr. Harris's table. Mr. Harris had just finished dinner. (430–31)

The objective narrator once more welds together sentences in this paragraph, bringing together their separate spatial worlds. There is a keener sense of mediated observation in the objective narrator's descriptions. Aside from the repeated elements common to the opening paragraphs of the two previous parts, there is the discovery here that "In the station café at Territet it was *a little too warm*" and that "the lights were *bright*" (emphasis added). Or that there were "cardboard pads for beer glasses in order that the moist glasses would not make rings on the wood" (430). These observations, however, do not greatly augment the overall sense or intention of the paragraph as a whole. Quite the contrary, they appear gratuitous.

I should add that the combinative desire in part 3 is more expansive on the level of paragraphs. It fuses into one the two sets of paragraphs that appear in each one of the preceding parts and incorporates into it "an old man drinking coffee at a table under the clock and reading a paper" (430). The whole is reminiscent of Cézanne's portraits ("Head of an Old Man" or "Man in a Blue Cap," for example), in which a touch of ineffable loneliness and otherness always supervenes. As I shall discuss presently, this sense of mystery or ineffability, too, carries through the narrative text of part 3 in Mr. Harris's conversation with the waitress and the "old man."

The presence of these essential patterns of descriptive repetitions, *which never become a duplication,* in "Homage to Switzerland" is a part of its unusual design. They make it possible for the reader not only to perceive each part of the story anew but also to interpret it afresh.

A New Series of Binary Oppositions
and the Repetition of the Commonplace

With the conversation between the waitress and Mr. Wheeler in part 1 of the story a new series of binary opposition becomes suddenly surface. It creates a quiet and yet profound drama of much consequence that may well go unnoticed. The initial, binary opposition of inside and outside now asserts itself in a new mode and deepens its human sense and direction. It radicalizes its operation and moves further inward. The social human world in itself now becomes the outside world for the individual. The result is that what constituted the inside in the paragraphs that precede the dialogue between the waitress and Wheeler now has to be considered as the outside world in relation to the inner world of the individual.

At this point, the human skin itself defines the threshold of the boundaries of the two inside and outside realms. Hence, there is a reversal of the parallel dialectic of the former, binary opposition of inside and outside. Or the reversal may be regarded as the regressive application that substitutes the social world for the natural world as it tries to integrate the collective with the individual world. Additionally, the protective and nurturing human world of the station café may now be regarded as coextensive with the world of the "commonplace," which can only masquerade as a zone of human communion, solidarity, and peace. As Jean-Paul Sartre has pointed out in his preface to Nathalie Sarraute's *Portrait of a Man Unknown:*

> This excellent word [the commonplace] has several meanings. It designates, of course, our most hackneyed thoughts, inasmuch as these thoughts have become the meeting place of the community. It is here that each of us finds himself as well as the others. The commonplace belongs to everybody and it belongs to me; in me, it belongs to everybody, it is the presence of everybody in me. In its very essence it is generality; in order to appropriate it, an act is necessary, an act through which I shed my particularity in order to adhere to the general, in order to become generality. Not at all *like* everybody, but to be exact, the *incarnation* of everybody. Through this eminently social type of adherence, I identify myself with all the others in the indistinguishableness of the universal.[7]

In this sense, the binary opposition of inside and outside within the station café can now be equated with the dual, Sartrean terms, universal and individual, and the two sets of binary oppositions may be used interchangeably.

In this perspective, the commonplace provides the negation of the individual as an authentic mode of being. The world of the commonplace integrates the individual into its enormous body by reifying him, to borrow a term from Karl Marx. The claim that to be everyone is to be no one carries an experiential truth. To be "the *incarnation* of everybody" is, therefore, to enter into the "indistinguishableness of the universal," an endless, faceless repetition of an equally universal essence of humanity, stretching out in a straight line without deviation into the socially governed conventions of a given culture. The metamorphosis of the particular individual into the "*incarnation* of everybody" only accomplishes itself in terms of the individual's unrecognizability from others. Such universality, if ever completely achieved, transforms the reality of individual lives into an amorphous mass that is the primary characteristic of the undifferentiated collectivity known as the crowd or the mob. Such incarnation designates precisely the process through which human subjectivity is made into an object that merely occupies space among other objects.

Yet the desire for what Sartre calls the "communion of the commonplace" is obsessive, incessant, and often fierce. The crushing loneliness of the experience of individual life as an ensemble of differentiating attributes, which remains for the most part incommunicable in its uniqueness, is for the majority of individuals intolerable and incessantly pushes them toward this "eminently social type of adherence" that is the commonplace, even though its objective is the annihilation of the individual as an autonomous subject.

Is it not this obliteration of the individual as an autonomous subject that precisely constitutes the intention of Mr. Wheeler's dialogue with the waitress in part 1 of "Homage to Switzerland"? After being asked by the waitress if he wishes some coffee, Wheeler attempts a kind of mild pleasantry and responds, "If you think it won't keep me awake" (422). The waitress is uncomprehending, either because of a lack of mastery of the English language or because of the slightly American cultural and idiomatic context of the remark. How else could Mr. Wheeler's response be interpreted but as an appeal to the "union of the commonplace"? From my point of view, his request that the waitress "take a cigar" (422) or have a "drink of something" (422) with him and his subsequent repeated and increasing offer of money to her "to go upstairs with him" (423) for sexual favors are no more than desperate attempts to escape the prison of the unique self, its inherent loneliness, and the exorbitant price that it exacts. The price of being oneself is crushing. As Emmanuel Levinas observes, "To revert to oneself is not to settle oneself at home. . . . It is to be like a stranger, hunted down even in one's home, contested in one's identity. . . ."[8]

The eventual discovery (through the mediation of the omniscient narrative point of view) that Mr. Wheeler "was very careful about money and did not care for women," or that "He had been in that station before and he knew there was no upstairs to go to," and that "Mr. Wheeler never took chances" (424–25) in no way negates the urgency and the seriousness of his effort. The discovery only strengthens that urgency and seriousness and gives the effort more credence. Mr. Wheeler may be a miser and a homosexual, but these facts do not attenuate his desire not to be different from the majority and to belong to its socially accepted and sanctioned values; they make his desire resonate with greater urgency and intensity.

Mr. Wheeler's attempted conversation is laced with falsehood, insensitivity, even cruelty. He can smile to himself for some time after this conversation. The discomfiture of the Swiss waitress offers him a chance to be somewhat amused. The whole thing is a mild joke to him. But there is a truth to the psychoanalytic teaching that such jokes have a subjacent reality far more serious than their surface manifestations. And it is equally true that even cruelty itself is, in a strict sense, a mode of communication.

However, Mr. Wheeler's appeal to the "union of the commonplace" clearly fails. His effort operates and remains at the level of a "very inexpensive sport" (424) because he plays a sort of verbal cat-and-mouse game. This homosexual never quite carries off the heterosexual chitchat or "idle talk" that is the coin of the "commonplace." The waitress remains baffled by his remarks. "He is ugly," she thinks, "ugly and hateful. Three hundred thousand francs for a thing that is nothing to do. How many times have I done that for nothing. And no place to go here." She concludes, "What people these Americans" (424).

The "irony and pity" of part 1 are not limited to the reader's feeling of sympathy for the working-class woman (however justified that may be), but extend to sympathy for the inevitable failure of a man whose sense of individuality and isolation is heightened and perhaps overly determined by his homosexuality, his seeking to be provisionally "indistinguishable" from anyone else by attempting to dissolve his identity—that is, his difference—in heterosexual patter. After all, what is identity but difference? And this identity, this frightening otherness, can only be established and maintained in that perpetual, agonizing freedom that represents the meaning of the individual's life as an indeterminate text for him and for the society in which he lives to interpret, morally or in any other way.

Mr. Wheeler's idle talk closes off the possibility of any disclosure, even that of the commonplace, a field of clichés, where all the thoughts are frozen in prejudgment and prejudice, where all notions and concepts are prejudiced, preconceived, and foreunderstood. "For what is said," as Heidegger tells us, "is always understood proximally as 'saying' something—that is, as uncovering something. Thus by its very nature, idle talk is a closing-off, since to go back to the ground of what is talked about is something which it *leaves undone*."9

The intention in Mr. Wheeler's dialogue with the waitress consists of a paradoxical combination of efforts at concealment as well as a desire for communication. The inner contradiction of such a combinatory act destroys it from within as an authentic conversation. The dialogue between Mr. Wheeler as the speaker and the waitress as the listener and respondent lacks that crucial third ingredient of a dialogue that is the disclosure of a world that the speaker and the listener create. The potential for such a disclosure is already negated by the deceptive premise of the dialogue initiated by Mr. Wheeler and the waitress's intimation of it throughout the dialogue.

Mr. Wheeler's desire to act in such a way as to become a meeting place of the "general" in order to escape what particularizes him as an individual, even provisionally, is dismally unsuccessful as an act. His action is doomed to disappointment because it relegates itself to the plane of play-acting and dissimulation.

The result of this failure is that he is barred from the communion of the commonplace, that inauthentic but fervently sought zone of warmth and acceptance. There is no fleeing from the self for him. He is to remain himself in a vastly heterosexual world, defining in himself his otherness or difference in relation to the sameness of the heterosexual world. He is the symbol of an alienation for which the inside world of the station café embodies the outside and offers no promise of a home. I read the portrait of Mr. Wheeler in Montreux as the portrait of difference and otherness as concealed everywhere.

In my opinion, the analysis of the dialectic of the binary opposition of inside and outside and the application of that analysis to the sphere of human social interactions, the commonplace, and the world of the individual in part 1 offer a paradigm of a pattern of repetitions in part 2 and part 3 of the story as well. I reiterate that these repetitions are *essentially* the same as ensembles that produce similar, identifiable effects, but their particular signification differs in the three parts of the story.

In part 2, for instance, one encounters Mr. Johnson at the station café at Vevey in settings and in circumstances comparable to Mr. Wheeler's. Mr. Johnson is another one of "those Americans" who so puzzle and confuse the waitress at the station café at Montreux. As a character, he is a modified repetition of Mr. Wheeler insofar as his nationality and common present situational attributes are concerned. Mr. Johnson shows the same tendency toward "small talk" as Mr. Wheeler does in part 1. When asked if he wants some coffee, he tries to enter the zone of the commonplace by using a form of common courtesy in an ironic way under the circumstances and responds, "If it's not too much trouble" (425). However, the slightly comic irony of the response escapes the waitress, possibly because of both cultural differences between the two and her limited mastery of the language. Just as the waitress at Montreux is observed in part 1, the reader finds the waitress at Vevey bringing "the coffee from the kitchen" while Mr. Johnson, like Mr. Wheeler, looks "out the window at the snow falling in the light from the station platform" that delimits the outer horizon of this microcosmic human world. Furthermore, Mr. Johnson asks the waitress to have a "drink of something with him" and, like Mr. Wheeler, offers her a cigar, the offer perhaps, foreshadowing his punning question, "You wouldn't like to play with me?" (245–46).

All of this is a virtual repetition of the situation and the dialogue in part 1. However, one important absent dimension is Mr. Wheeler's homosexuality. Even though it still embarrasses the waitress and makes her blush, Mr. Johnson's request that they "make up a party and see the night life of Vevey" (426) is one not of repulsion but of common sense. She simply replies, "I must work" (426).

The odd but interesting aspect of the dialogue between Mr. Johnson and the waitress is his jocular insistence on assaulting her with his idle talk; it breathes life into the "commonplace" but can only be understood in the context of the educated, middle-class American culture. His suggestion that the woman get a "substitute" to work in her place so that she would be free to leave with him is based on the premise that "They used to do that in the Civil War" (426). It is, of course, a ludicrous remark under the circumstances and is intended to be so. But the humor of it cannot be appreciatd by the Swiss working woman, who responds, "Oh, no, sir. I must be here myself in the person." The mixture of humor, irony, and suppressed melancholy that characterizes Mr. Johnson's dialogue reaches its absurd peak in the following exchange between the two:

> "Where did you learn your English?"
> "At the Berlitz school, sir."
> "Tell me about it," Johnson said. "Were the Berlitz undergraduates a wild lot? What about this necking and petting? Were there many smoothies? Did you ever run into Scott Fitzgerald?
> "Please?"
> "I mean were your college days the happiest days of your life? What sort of team did Berlitz have last fall?" (426)

Mr. Johnson here is mimicking precisely the kind of vaguely pretentious, American, prep-school or cocktail-party chatter of his time that in the United States would have allowed him to relax in the luxurious lap of the commonplace and lose himself. In Switzerland it does not work. It cannot take the edge off his spleen. The commonplace is primarily a social and cultural phenomenon. Every society and culture produces and controls its own mode of the commonplace at a given time in the history of its development. The commonplace cannot as easily serve transients such as Mr. Johnson.

Mr. Johnson is not a homosexual, but, like Mr. Wheeler, he too carries a secret that results in a certain psychic intensity and dislocation. This emotional upheaval in him gives whatever he says a cutting edge. Nevertheless, he seeks to communicate and to be consoled. Mr. Wheeler's secret can only be revealed in the narrative by the omniscient narrator after his attempt at concealment. It makes for a desultory sort of duplicity and deception that can only bring him an ironic smile. Mr. Johnson's secret, his divorce, on the contrary, need not necessarily provoke strong social sanctions. He has no need to deceive. He soon reveals his problem through his desire to cauterize it in a genuinely salutary human dialogue that would allow him to break through his feeling of isolation and separateness. He hopes that the disclosure of his secret burden to others will bring him a kind of psychic closure and peace. Obviously, his dialogue with the waitress represents a superficial effort at distraction that does not reach its goal. But his conversation with the three old porters is a sincere, if ironic and fruitless, cry for understanding. It eventually degenerates into the trivialities of the commonplace which the three porters, meticulously observing the social code, cannot help but indulge.

Striking up a conversation with the porters is made even more complicated for Mr. Johnson by the incongruities of their social and national backgrounds and the humorous vagaries of speaking in foreign languages. The ritual of offering a drink somewhat facilitates entry into the commonplace. However, Mr. Johnson's rather extravagant and ironic suggestion that they drink the best champagne confuses the porters, who conclude that this must be a festive occasion for him, perhaps "the gentleman's birthday." "No," Mr. Johnson replies, "It's not a fête. My wife has decided to divorce me" (427).

In conversation with the porters, at first Mr. Johnson tries to situate his problem within the domain of the universal in order to get rid of its particular poignancy for him. "It is doubtless a common experience," he says, "like the first visit to the dentist or the first time a girl is unwell, but I have been upset" (427). The understated comparisons combine the anxiety of anticipation of pain and change of state with a sense of resignation in the common nature of divorce. "It is understandable," responds the oldest porter, "I understand it" (426). There is no doubt politeness, sociability, perhaps even sympathy, in this statement and yet there is no discernible sign of understanding in it. The commonplace does away with any hope for such an understanding. The individual and the particular cannot attempt to dissolve their defining features in the universal and still remain the same.

The porters, one of whom is appropriately "a little deaf" (427), converse in different languages during the conversation, and are not to be moved by Mr. Johnson beyond the limits of the commonplace. One porter's understanding of widespread divorce in America is based upon what he has read "in the paper" (428). None of the porters is divorced—one of them for the excellent and indisputable reason that he has never been married and that "It would be too expensive" anyway (429). The following humorous passage sums up so succinctly the hopelessness of this dialogue among the "deaf" that it merits quoting in its entirety:

"You like being married?" Johnson asked one of the porters.
"What?"
"You like the married state?"
"Oui. C'est normale."
"Exactly," said Johnson. "Et vous, monsieur?"
"Ça va," said the other porter.
"Pour moi," said Johnson, "ça ne va pas."
"Monsieur is going to divorce," the first porter explained.
"Oh," said the second porter.
"Ah ha," the third porter said.
"Well," said Johnson, "the subject seems to be exhausted. You're not interested in my troubles. . . ." (429)

Mr. Johnson's accurate observation is also a statement of the failure of the whole venture that he has initiated. It is interesting to note that the two married porters seem not to have been following the conversation at all. Johnson, then, perceptively tries to change the subject of the conversation. Understandably, one of the porters wishes to speak about sports, that quintessential subject of the commonplace.

For Mr. Johnson indeed *"ça ne va pas."* "Inside the café he had thought that talking about it would blunt it; but it had not blunted it; it had only made him feel nasty" (420). Like the objective narrator in the initial paragraph of part 2, who tries to bring together autonomous worlds of various sentences through the partial mediation of semicolons, he has tried, through an attempt at dialogue, the foundation of oneness and unity, to bridge the chasm that separates individuals. Oneness has proved to be unattainable in reality. It simply represents an illusion of human solidarity that can rarely take place beyond the communion of the commonplace. For Mr. Johnson, there is no longer a distinction to be made between the sheltering inside and the threatening outside. In both spheres his problems of separation, divorce, and loneliness remain. In this sense, the two spheres somehow lose their identity and merge. Outside, the snow is now falling heavily. Inside, the deaf talk *at* one another. Isolation and incomprehension reign everywhere. As a writer, Mr. Johnson no doubt is more vulnerable to this absence of communication. He may well write, "Mr. Johnson Talks about It at Vevey but No One Hears It or Understands It."

Finally, in part 3, the transversal repetition of the commonplace and its intersection with the subjacent individual reality occur suddenly once more and for the last time. Again, the familiar ritual of the preceding two parts of the short story reoccurs. After the announcement that the Simplon-Orient Express is an hour late at Saint Maurice, which by now has acquired an incantational dimension, the waitress at the station café at Territet offers to bring Mr. Harris (another American on his way back to the United States through Paris and Le Havre), some coffee. Again, the waitress, as in the two previous parts, cannot comprehend Mr. Harris's slightly idiomatic and ironically polite response, "If you like," and again there is a discussion of the waitress's knowledge of various languages spoken in Switzerland and the inevitable offer by Mr. Harris, in the manner of his two other compatriots, that she take "a drink of something or a coffee" or a cigar and the Swiss waitress's by now formulaic refusal (431). This time, however, the attempt at ironic pleasantries as an approach to the commonplace becomes much more abstract, opaque, even baffling. The following dialogue, which concludes Harris's conversation with the waitress, plays this abstraction in a new key, an apparent semantic discontinuity worthy of Gertrude Stein:

> "You wouldn't take a cigar?"
> "Oh, no, sir," she laughed. "I don't smoke, sir."
> "Neither do I," said Harris, "I don't agree with David Belasco."
> "Please?"
> "Belasco. David Belasco. You can always tell him because he has his collar on backwards. But I don't agree with him. Then, too, he is dead now." (431)

I can only characterize Mr. Harris's part in this dialogue as a "voiced" interior monologue. After the first brief foray made into the zone of the commonplace, Harris is no longer talking to the waitress. He is pursuing a highly private trend of thought that is merely inflicted upon the waitress. Mr. Harris's conversation here is akin to that of Mr. Wheeler's with the waitress in part 1: its intention is concealment rather than disclosure; in other words, it is no dialogue at all. The world that it opens up closes in upon itself in the process and destroys the conversation's purpose. The conversation emerges at the intersection of the commonplace and its subjacent reality, which is Mr. Harris's inner life, and subsequently evaporates into the nothingness of inscrutable abstraction—a mystery. This intimation of the mystery of the self remains silent not because it has nothing to disclose but, rather, because it has a considerable depth that does not lend itself easily to lucidity. It cannot be easily deciphered by the well-known but rigid codes of idle talk.

This so-called dialogue prefigures another equally puzzling and gratuitous one that an old man initiates with Mr. Harris. "I beg your pardon if I intrude," says the old man in English, "but it has just occurred to me that you might be a member of the National Geographic Society" (432). A long, pointless, and somewhat humorous conversation about the National Geographic Society, one of its presumably prominent members Frederick J. Roussel, a few issues of the Society's publication of particular interest to Mr. Harris and the old man and, finally, an expressed desire by the old man to nominate Lawrence of Arabia for membership in the society constitute

the essentials of the discourse between the two. The interchange culminates
in the revelation of the suicide of Mr. Harris's father the previous year.

The old man's loneliness and desire to find someone with whom he may
talk takes this unusual but assuaging form. The communion of the commonplace for him appears to be successful. His desire to communicate is satisfied
in this social place that belongs to everyone and to no one. Not unlike that
other old gentleman in "A Clean, Well-Lighted Place," this old man comes
after dinner to the station café at Territet, where the "lights are bright" and
where he can drink a cup of coffee and read the paper and be a communicant
of the commonplace in his own fashion. He is walled in the prison of old
age, but his "certificate of membership" (432) in the National Geographic
Society provides him with a sanctioned mode of entry into this world where
everyone is someone in general and no one is anyone in particular. The text
refers to him first as "an old man," then as "the old gentleman," and
eventually as a name on a card that declares him to be "DR. SIGISMUND
WYER, PH.D./Member of the National Geographic Society" (435). Nothing
beyond certain social classifications makes him stand out in any way. He has
been assigned the status of a member of a recognizable social group and
made into an object as an "old man." Because he manifests certain accepted
social graces, he is then called the "old gentleman," fundamentally "un-
distinguishable" from any other in such a group.

One may point out here that for Dr. Wyer "*ça va,*" but for Mr. Harris,
not unlike Mr. Johnson, "*ça ne va pas.*" The tone of Mr. Johnson's conversation is a curious mixture of politeness and sarcasm, impatience and restraint,
reticence and volubility. For Mr. Harris, the conversation is largely barren.
For him idle talk gets nowhere; it is a "closing-off." As Heidegger has
pointed out, "This closing-off is aggravated afresh by the fact that understanding of what is talked about is supposedly reached in idle talk. Because
of this, idle talk discourages any new inquiry and any disputation, and in a
peculiar way suppresses them and holds them back."[10] It is only by chance
that at a given moment the conversation between Mr. Harris and the "old
gentleman" becomes more personal by the disclosure of the suicide of Mr.
Harris's father.

It is clear that Mr. Harris has not yet fully accepted his father's death
and is preoccupied with it. He refers to his father in the present tense. He
tells Dr. Wyer that he is not a member of the National Geographic Society
and adds "my father is. He's been a member for a great many years" (432).
Presently, however, he reveals his father's suicide and declares that he
"Shot himself, oddly enough" (434). Mr. Harris, too, carries a heavy inner
burden: the suicide of a father that weighs upon him like a corpse refused
burial. There is a sense in which the dead never die and haunt the living
constantly. A conversation about membership in the National Geographic

Society does not offer the possibility of getting rid of such a problem. Mr. Johnson's private grief finds no consolation in the world of the commonplace. "I am very truly sorry," says Dr. Wyer, upon hearing of the suicide of Mr. Harris's father, but he immediately shifts from this privative declaration to a more public statement: "I am sure his loss was a blow to science as well as to his family" (434). "Science took it awfully well" is Harris's acerbic, concise, and truthful response.

So ends "Homage to Switzerland," a tale of universal homelessness and the isolation of the individual as individual, unique and different, and the consequent mutual incomprehension of individuals in the midst of the human world and the human community. The nature of this desperate world is intimated in three bright and warm station cafés in a peaceful country. Three travelers pass through this idyllic land, leaving no trace but three disturbing epiphanies, each offering a glimpse of an isolated human life in which the satisfaction of belonging and communion appears only as an ever-receding horizon. The three men do so "without quite breaking through into a void of hysteria," Marvin Mudrick's qualified remark to the contrary notwithstanding.[11] The actions and utterances of these three travelers are forlorn efforts to communicate the incommunicable: the ancient, profound, deeply ambiguous, indeterminate world of the individual. The communication of this reality requires a miraculous operation, that of approximating and then comprehending in a new way through art the opacity of the other as other. A truly genuine work of fiction, no matter how short, having appropriated the truth of this ambiguity and this indeterminacy and having taken responsibility for it, should intimate it without trying to explain it away. "Homage to Switzerland" is indeed such a work.

Notes

1. Carlos Baker, *Ernest Hemingway: A Life Story* (New York: Charles Scribner's Sons, 1969) 238.

2. Baker, *Ernest Hemingway: The Writer as Artist,* 4th edn. (Princeton: Princeton UP, 1972) 138.

3. Joseph DeFalco, *The Hero in Hemingway's Short Stories* (Pittsburgh: U of Pittsburgh P, 1963): 179–83. For other references to the theme of family, marriage, and marital problems in "Homage to Switzerland," see Joseph M. Flora's *Hemingway's Nick Adams Stories* (Baton Rouge: Louisiana State UP, 1982) 210–59. For a more biographical treatment of the story see Richard Hovey's *Hemingway: The Inward Terrain* (Seattle: U of Washington P, 1968) 11–12.

4. J. Hillis Miller, *Fiction and Repetition: Seven English Novels* (Cambridge: Harvard UP, 1982) 2–3.

5. Martin Heidegger, *Being and Nothingness*, trans. J. McQuarrie and Edward Robinson (New York: Harper & Row, 1962) 173.

6.   Ernest Hemingway, *The Short Stories of Ernest Hemingway* (New York: Charles Scribner's Sons, 1954) 422. All subsequent quotations are from this edition and are cited by page number in my text.

7.   Jean-Paul Sartre, *Situations*, trans. Benita Eisler (Greenwich: Fawcett, 1965) 137.

8.   Quoted by Mark C. Taylor in *Alterity* (Chicago: U of Chicago P, 1987) 206.

9.   Heidegger, 213.

10. Heidegger, 213.

11. Marvin Mudrick, "Hudson Review," *Hemingway: The Critical Heritage*, ed. Jeffrey Meyers (London, Boston, and Henley: Routledge & Kegan Paul, 1982) 504.

20

Myth or Reality:
"The Light of the World" as Initiation Story

Robert E. Fleming

The human community in "The Light of the World," another short story composed during the spring and summer of 1932, consists of two boys, a couple of whores, a dead fighter, a homosexual cook, and "any number of lumberjacks and Indians." According to Robert Fleming, critical fascination with this cast of grotesques has distracted attention away from "the true core of the story . . . which really focuses on the two young protagonists and their possible initiation." Using newly uncovered evidence, Fleming builds a strong case for our reading this story as "an ironic tale of how initiations go wrong in a world where the loss of youthful illusions may be too painful to bear." Fleming's essay sheds new light on "The Light of the World" and poses a persuasive solution to a problem story.

When he wrote his introduction to his collected stories in 1938, Ernest Hemingway referred to "The Light of the World" as one work "which nobody else ever liked."[1] There was good reason for Hemingway to write such a remark in the late 1930s, as he was undoubtedly still smarting over Alfred Dashiell's rejection of the story. Dashiell, the editor of *Scribner's* magazine, had had his troubles with Hemingway during the serialization of *A Farewell to Arms* and apparently felt that "The Light of the World" was unsuitable for a respectable family magazine.[2] Maxwell Perkins, in suggesting the "The Light of the World" not be used as the first story in *Winner Take Nothing*, had compounded the insult.[3] Some critics have liked the story to the extent of writing essays about it, but only in the past few years has it become possible to see three pieces of evidence that might help account for Hemingway's fondness for it and his implicit suggestion that there was more to the story than meets the eye.

The chief new evidence consists of, first, a fact contributed by Michael Reynolds in his biography of the young Ernest Hemingway; second, Hemingway's essay "The Art of the Short Story"; and third, the manuscripts of the story in the Hemingway Collection of the John Fitzgerald Kennedy Library. These pieces of evidence suggest that, while previous critics have been investigating interesting questions, they have strayed from the true core of the story, which really focuses on the two young protagonists and their possible initiation rather than the two whores, the dead fighter, the homosexual cook, or any number of lumberjacks and Indians.

The mysteries that have interested previous critics center on three questions. The most important concerns the identity of the fighter referred to as Steve Ketchel and the truthfulness of the two whores who claim to have loved him. Carlos Baker stated the opinion of the majority when he suggested that the story was a "very complicated defense of the normal [Alice] against the abnormal."[4] Baker and others have pointed out the obvious flaws in the story told by the peroxide blonde prostitute—its sentimentality and its failure to match the facts of Stanley Ketchel's life.[5] A second question that has not much concerned critics is why the homosexual cook is the only person in the waiting room to identify Stanley Ketchel correctly.[6] Nor has anyone been greatly interested in the first episode of the story, which takes place in a tavern. A minority of the critics have concerned themselves with the incidental question of the number of Indians in the train station, wondering whether Hemingway might have been indulging in a sort of cryptographic humor, perhaps at the expense of his readers.[7]

This last question can be disposed of quickly, thanks to the availability of the manuscript. Hemingway's original, corrected typescript identified the people in the railway waiting room as five whores, six white men, and four Indians. He cancelled "four" and changed it to "three," and the second reference to the Indians (two sitting and one standing) conformed to his revised number.[8] Unaccountably, the typescript used as setting copy for the story[9] fails to show the correction, and Hemingway apparently did not see the error when he read proof for *Winner Take Nothing*, in which the story first appeared.

Central to the meaning of the story are the biblical sources to which the title alludes. Two sources refer to Jesus and a third to his followers. In John 8:12, Jesus says, "I am the light of the world: he that followeth me shall not walk in darkness, but shall have the light of life." In John 9:5, Jesus states, "As long as I am in the world, I am the light of the world." Finally, in three verses, Matthew 5:14–16, Jesus tells his followers,

> Ye are the light of the world. A city that is set on a hill cannot be hid. Neither do men light a candle, and place it under a bushel, but on a candlestick; and it giveth light unto all that are in the house. Let your light so shine before men, that they may see your good works, and glorify your Father which is in heaven.

Since "light of the world" can refer either to Jesus Christ or to Christians, the phrase is ambiguous, and it is this ambiguity that has helped to make "The Light of the World" a difficult story to interpret.[10]

It is here that Michael Reynolds's *The Young Hemingway* offers important new evidence. Carlos Baker, in a note to his biography of Hemingway, had suggested a possible link between a Holman Hunt painting and "The Light of the World," based on Grace Hall Hemingway's use of a reproduction of the painting in a scrapbook she kept for her son.[11] During his research, however, Reynolds found a story in *Oak Leaves*, an Oak Park, Illinois, newspaper, that described the painting and implied the personal significance the painting had to Hemingway when he was growing up, for his mother had given a copy of it to the church that Hemingway attended, and the author saw it regularly as a boy:

> In memory of her father, Ernest Hall, whose death occurred May 10, 1905, Mrs. Grace Hall Hemingway has presented to the Third Congregational Church a copy of Holman Hunt's "The Light of the World." . . . The artist has represented Christ standing in the dead of night before a door. The hinges are rusted and the doorway is overgrown with ivy. Before the threshold is a tangle of weeds. A bat driven from the shadows is circling about. The Savior bears a lantern in His left hand. His right is raised in the act of knocking. Upon his head is a crown of thorns.[12]

The existence of this picture would suggest that, to Hemingway, the identification of Christ with the phrase "the light of the world" would be the more natural one.

A second piece of evidence that bolsters that of the Holman Hunt painting is Hemingway's essay, "The Art of the Short Story." In the late 1950s, Hemingway wrote the essay to serve as an introduction to a collection of his short stories intended for college classes. The anthology was never published, and the essay remained unpublished until *The Paris Review* printed it in 1981.[13] In this essay, Hemingway said of "The Light of the World," "I could have called it 'Behold I Stand at the Door and Knock' or some other stained-glass window title, but . . . actually 'The Light of the World' is better." He also warns that the story is "about many things and you would be ill-advised to think it is a simple tale" (92). The references to stained-glass windows and to knocking at a door clearly refer to the remembered painting at his own church in Oak Park.

Finally, there is the evidence of the manuscripts of the story. Item 548 in the Hemingway Collection, a holograph pencil manuscript, includes two alternate endings rejected by Hemingway. In the first, the homosexual cook's interest in the two young protagonists is more pointed than in the story as published.

"Come on," Tom, said. "Let's go."
"I'll come with you," the cook said.
"No," Tom said. "Not with us."[14]

In the second alternate ending, Alice offers to introduce the narrator to sex without charging him.

"What do you say son," Alice said to me in that nice voice.
"We have to go," I said.
"You can stay for nothing," Alice said.
"We really have to go. I'm much obliged."
"Come on," said Tom. "Let's go."
"You're [sic] friend don't want to stay?"
"Thanks very much," Tom said.

The boys leave the station and talk about the experience:

"Why didn't you stay with her?" Tom said.
"Why didn't you?"
"She liked you," he said. "She just asked me to be polite."
"I didn't want to."
"You were afraid of her."
"No I wasn't."
"Sure you were."
"You want to go back?"
"All right."
We went back a little way and I stopped. "I don't want to go," I said. "I like her but I'm spooked."[15]

With these three new pieces of evidence in mind, the reader can now go back to the story and see some features that have not been adequately treated. The story is primarily about the two young boys, the only characters who appear both in the tavern scene and in the railway station scene that follows.[16] In the first scene of the story, the boys have a quarrel with a bartender when they attempt to sample the "free lunch" at the tavern. The scene serves to establish the unnamed town as a hostile place—"What the hell kind of place is this?" says Tommy to the narrator as they leave the bar (385). The first scene is also important because it provides the essential clue to the focus and significance of the second scene; the clue lies in the bartender's calling the boys "punks," 1920s slang that can mean that they are young and inexperienced, but which can also mean that they are either homosexuals or catamites, boys used by a pederast. The latter meaning sets up a tension that is resolved only on the last page of the story, where the boys reject the cook.

After leaving the bar, the boys go to the railroad station, where they meet a lumber camp cook, whose sexual preference is clearly indicated by the cumulative evidence of the narrator's observations and the broad jokes of the other men in the station. His face is pallid, his hands are thin and white, and his manner of speaking is almost femininely delicate. One of the men asks the boys if they would like to "interfere" with the cook, who would appreciate the activity;[17] then the man tells the boys that the cook's hands are white because he bleaches them with lemon juice; finally he refers to the cook as a "sister" (385–86, 388). The cook might seem just a curious piece of local color were it not for the fact that he seems to know more about the historical Steve Ketchel than anyone else at the station, more even than either of the two whores who claim to have been intimate with Ketchel. The cook alone knows Ketchel's real name—"Wasn't his name Stanley Ketchel?" he asks (388)—and he inserts a note of realism into Peroxide's glowing account of the fighter when he reminds everyone that Ketchel was knocked out by Jack Johnson (389).

The peroxided whore's account, on the other hand, presents a mythic depiction of Steve Ketchel. Linking him with Christ in her first reference to him, she states that Ketchel's father was responsible for his death: "Yes, by Christ, his own father. There aren't any more men like Steve Ketchel" (388). He was "no Stanley," she erroneously says, perhaps because she feels Steve is a more manly name, or, it has been suggested, because "Steve" recalls Saint Stephen, the first Christian martyr.[18] Steve Ketchel was "clean," "white," and "beautiful," "moved just like a tiger," and was a free spender. She "loved him like you love God." After the cook points out that Jack Johnson beat Ketchel in his most famous fight, Peroxide tells the story in mythic terms: Johnson, who was black, is cast as a satanic figure, while Ketchel, the white, represents goodness. Johnson was only able to beat Ketchel when, after Ketchel had knocked the heavyweight champion down, he stopped to smile at Peroxide, who was sitting at ringside. Johnson treacherously took advantage of the romantic act to knock Ketchel out.

Peroxide's story is full of misinformation. Although he did use the name Steve professionally, Ketchel, the middleweight Michigan Assassin, was really named Stanley; his birth certificate, in fact, spelled the name Stanislas Kiecal. Far from being saintly, Ketchel had probably been part of a sordid fixed fight in which Johnson was to carry him for most or all of the fight. Both fighters would thus cash in on the gate and the motion picture proceeds generated by a fight between a hated black champion and a "white hope" who was an underdog because he weighed some 45 pounds less than Johnson. Ketchel apparently decided to doublecross Johnson, but after his surprise knockdown, the champion got up and knocked out the lighter man easily. Ketchel followed the fight with a short period of drunkenness, drug use, whoring, and possible fight fixing before being shot by a hand on a Missouri farm where he had gone to dry out and get back into shape.[19]

Peroxide's story is debunked, however, not by any of these facts, but by the huge prostitute Alice, who counters by saying that *she* is Ketchel's true love. She offers little evidence except the observation that Steve did not talk the way Peroxide has said. Alice's Ketchel, it is true, speaks more like a prizefighter: "You're a lovely piece, Alice" (390). Beyond this, Alice is convincing only because of her own Michigan origins, her manner of swearing—"God can strike me dead if it isn't true" and "it's true, true, true, to Jesus and Mary true" (390)—and by her apparent contentment with her memories near the end of the story. Indeed, Alice's story is perhaps the most appealing version of what happened to Steve Ketchel. Nevertheless, because of the flimsiness of her case, one recent critic has expressed reservations about Alice's truthfulness.[20]

Both women share a view of Steve Ketchel that stresses his mythic nature. Although Peroxide recalls a polite, godlike man who might have been the hero of a romantic novel and Alice a godlike man in the mold of Ezra Pound's Christ in his "The Ballad of the Goodly Fere," neither differs with the other on "Steve's" basic nature. Both link him to God in their statements. Yet of the two, Alice's is the closer to reality.

On the other hand, the homosexual cook, discredited because he belongs to a despised minority, convinces no one in his attempt to present the real Stanley Ketchel. Ironically, in rejecting the cook's homosexuality, the boys also reject his truth. Indeed, they are so caught up in the myth that Tommy can no longer credit what he has seen with his own eyes. After Peroxide tells her version of the Johnson fight, he tells her that he has seen the "moving pictures" of the bout (389). However, the fight films, which are still in existence, make a liar of Peroxide; apparently Tommy is so taken in by Peroxide's story that he accepts the myth rather than reality.

It is this gullible reaction of Tommy and the narrator that would seem to be at the heart of the story's meaning. Both Matthew Bruccoli and Joseph DeFalco have treated the story as an initiation story, and up to a point, it is. However, the discarded fragments of manuscript show Hemingway working toward a different effect at the very end of the story. In the first fragment, which is the basis for the ending of the story as printed, the boys forcefully reject the cook. In the second, the narrator regretfully refuses Alice. The rejection of the cook could be seen as a rejection of his homosexuality, but when the two pieces of manuscript evidence are linked, another possibility opens up. Both the cook and Alice represent reality. Both have rejected the make-believe world of Peroxide, whose nickname underscores the pretense with which she is identified.

The double rejection of the cook and Alice in the manuscript suggests that the initiation of the two boys has been an utter failure. Both still prefer the mythic Steve Ketchel who can play the role of Christ figure in their lives—not a less-than-heroic Stanley Ketchel. The boxer, then, is a touchstone in this story; in effect, the responses of characters to Ketchel provide the reader a way to judge them. Offered an entry into the real world, these two boys flinch from accepting the burdens of adulthood and settle instead for remaining in the world of illusion—or innocence—that they have inhabited during their childhood. Childhood has no place for homosexual men who may prey on boys nor for realistic boxers like the real Ketchel. The cook is rejected vehemently and Alice regretfully, but both pose problems of adulthood that are too big to be faced at the moment. Like Nick Adams at the end of "Indian Camp" or "The Three-Day Blow," the boys prefer to avoid the pain of dealing with the truth about how real people function in a less-than-perfect world. "The Light of the World" is indeed an initiation story, but it is an ironic tale of how initiations go wrong in a world where the loss of youthful illusions may be too painful a process for the initiate to bear.

Such an interpretation not only adds one more level of irony to a story that already contains an abundance of ironies, but is also the probable key to Hemingway's liking for the story and his remark that it is not simple. Bruccoli has noted the first level when he suggested that it is ironic that a scoundrel such as Steve Ketchel should become a latter-day light of the world; DeFalco has called attention to the further irony that in John 8:12 Jesus is speaking to the woman taken in adultery. The final irony unites both scenes of the story: the two would-be initiates, who in the first scene are trying to appear more mature than they really are, come finally in the second scene to prefer Peroxide's obvious lies to an unmistakable but unpleasant truth.

Notes

1. Ernest Hemingway, *The Short Stories of Ernest Hemingway* (New York: Charles Scribner's Sons, 1966) v. References to "The Light of the World" employ this edition and are inserted parenthetically in the text.

2. Carlos Baker, *Ernest Hemingway: A Life Story* (New York: Charles Scribner's Sons, 1969) 238.

3. Baker, *Life*, 241.

4. Carlos Baker, *Hemingway: The Writer as Artist*, 4th edn. (Princeton: Princeton UP, 1972) 140.

5. Besides Baker's, some of the best studies are James F. Barbour, "'The Light of the World': The Real Ketchel and the Real Light," *Studies in Short Fiction* 13 (1976): 17–23; Matthew J. Bruccoli, "'The Light of the World': Stan Ketchel as 'My Sweet Christ,'" *Fitzgerald/Hemingway Annual 1969*: 125–30; Joseph DeFalco, *The Hero in Hemingway's Short Stories* (Pittsburgh: U of Pittsburgh P, 1963) 81–88; Peter Thomas, "A Lost Leader: Hemingway's 'The Light of the World,'" *Humanities Association Bulletin* 21 (Fall 1970): 14–19; and Richard B. Hovey, *Hemingway: The Inward Terrain* (Seattle: U of Washington P, 1968) 18–20.

6. James J. Martine, "A Little Light on Hemingway's 'The Light of the World,'" *Studies in Short Fiction* 7 (1970): 465–67. See also Peter Thomas on the cook as scapegoat or sacrificial lamb.

7. See William J. Schaefer's tongue-in-cheek essay, "Ernest Hemingway: Arbiter of Common Numerality," *Carleton Miscellany* 3 (Winter 1962): 100–104 and James Barbour's "'The Light of the World': Hemingway's Comedy of Errors," *Notes on Contemporary Literature* 7.5 (December 1977): 5–8.

8. Item 549, 2. The Finca Vigía Edition of Hemingway's short stories (New York: Charles Scribner's Sons, 1987) corrects two accidentals in the 1966 edition but does not change the four Indians to three.

9. Item 222, 1.

10. Probably the best interpretation of biblical allusions is Peter Thomas's.

11. Baker, *Life*, 606.

12. Quoted in Michael S. Reynolds, *The Young Hemingway* (Oxford: Basil Blackwell, 1986) 104. Originally published in *Oak Leaves* 4 (November 1905). See also Reynolds's earlier "Holman Hunt and 'The Light of the World,'" *Studies in Short Fiction* 20 (1983): 317–19.

13. "The Art of the Short Story," *The Paris Review* 79 (Spring 1981): 85–102. References are inserted parenthetically in my text.

14. Item 548, 23.

15. Item 548, 24, 25–26.

16. See DeFalco, 82 on this point.

17. Item 549, 2 offers a cruder reading of this joke: "Ever buggar a cook? . . . You can buggar this one. . . . He likes it." [*sic*]

18. Barbour, "Real Ketchel," 18.

19. Barbour, "Real Ketchel," 18–20.

20. William J. Collins, "Taking on the Champion: Alice as Liar in 'The Light of the World,'" *Studies in American Fiction* 14 (1986): 225–32.

21

Up and Down: Making Connections in "A Day's Wait"

Linda Gajdusek

Between March and July 1933, Hemingway wrote a short story called "A Day's Wait," the last story collected in the 1933 anthology Winner Take Nothing *to be discussed in this volume. Here Linda Gajdusek postulates that the story has been overlooked because critics have misinterpreted its superficially simple plot as "an easy, seemingly trivial amusement." Gajdusek takes a closer look at the complex relationship of father and son in "A Day's Wait," peeling back this short story's multiple layers of misunderstanding to reveal a work that is far from trivial. She uncovers a "deeply involved and involving" story about "the need to reconcile opposites, the danger of unbridged schism, and the hero-father engaged in the healing task of establishing vital connections," revealing a short story that deserves reconsideration.*

Hemingway's very short story "A Day's Wait"[1] has failed to attract much serious attention to itself, perhaps for the reason that it offers us such an easy, seemingly trivial amusement. A young boy mistakes his temperature, reported in Fahrenheit degrees, for degrees Celsius and spends one long, lonely day bravely awaiting what he takes to be his inevitable death. His father, unaware of what his son is thinking, does all he can to make the sick boy comfortable and then passes several hours hunting quail in a snow-covered landscape. The pleasure of the story is that as readers we only realize the boy's mistake and consequently the nature of his ordeal at the end of the story, when the father himself realizes what his son has been thinking and gently explains away his misunderstanding. We enjoy the joke that Hemingway has played on us; what we thought to be the case as we read wasn't exactly the case. And so we go back and, with our new information, examine the boy's behavior and see that indeed he has comported himself (to borrow Arthur Waldhorn's terms) like an "exemplary" (albeit "Lilliputian") Hemingway hero, confronting his assumedly inevitable death with control and even a measure of concern for others.[2] ("You don't have to stay in here with me, Papa, if it bothers you" [437], he tells his father.) A good joke, another image of the Hemingway hero—in miniature—and on to the next story.

So it is that the criticism of "A Day's Wait" does not often help us explore or experience the story. Even some of Hemingway's most enthusiastic readers have not been able to find the merits of this story, calling it charming but "sentimental," "almost straight journalism," even "one of Hemingway's worst."[3] T. S. Matthews's quip that "all *Penrod* enthusiasts should be made to read 'A Day's Wait'" hardly qualifies as praise.[4] In fact, among the 11 reviews included by Stephens in his survey of critical reaction to *Winner Take Nothing* (where the story was first published in 1933), this quip by Matthews was the only mention the story received.[5] The comprehensive biographers who mention the story merely note the biographical incident on which the story seems to have been based: Bumby's bout with influenza in Piggot in December 1932.[6]

An overview of the more interpretive criticism reveals that even when the story has not been completely overlooked, commentators often allude to "A Day's Wait" only in support of a large pattern or framework that they are pursuing through the Hemingway canon and that they find echoed or supported in the story. As a result, they do not explore the story from within to discover its unique structure and value. That is not their purpose. In some cases their approach may point the way to a more rewarding reading, while other readings seem merely to exploit the text to buttress a particular theory or philosophy. I agree with Bakker that Killinger's existential reading of the piece suffers from this weakness.[7] Killinger presents the boy's behavior after his ordeal—"he cried very easily at little things that were of no importance" (437)—as Hemingway's demonstration of our existential need to repeat the death experience so that life will continue to have meaning. Killinger writes:

> The significant thing is that facing death (or so he thought) made the little things unimportant to him and that when death was removed as an imminent threat he relapsed into ordinary childishness. To perpetuate the existentialist attitude it is necessary to continue to experience death and violence.[8]

J. Bakker, bringing judgment and human experience to bear, questions: "Does not the ordinary observation of human nature, that the aftermath of intense mental strain in people is weakness, imbalance, and edginess, explain Schatz's reactions?"[9]

John Atkins cites "A Day's Wait" in a chapter on "The Mechanics of Fear," speculating that "[the story] may all be based on a vast cosmic misunderstanding," that we may all be like Schatz, "fooling ourselves all the time."[10] This may be true, but does it help us understand more about the story? Bernard Oldsey, considering patterns of snow and light imagery in Hemingway, begins to redress the critical balance. He naturally turns to the snowy landscape of "A Day's Wait," which he calls "one of the most unjustly overlooked of Hemingway's short pieces."[11] Bringing to bear on the piece his concern with the match between "structural design" and "narrative technique," Sheldon Norman Grebstein helps us to begin to appreciate some of the story's structural subtlety. He demonstrates the movement from inside to outside to inside, from stasis to action to stasis, showing how the story's action "straightforwardly narrates a commonplace sequence of events yet is highly suggestive."[12]

Joseph DeFalco, reading with an emphasis on the boy and *his* experience, discusses the story among other "Initiation Experiences" and sees the boy winning a "victory over the inner forces of the self."[13] DeFalco's reading raises an important question, one that is at the center of a critical controversy that this little story has managed to generate: Who (and therefore what) is the story really about? The controversy also involves the identity of the unnamed narrator-father. Is he, in fact, a grownup Nick Adams, now dealing with a son of his own? Commentators who see the narrator as Nick Adams tend to focus their reading on the father-narrator's experience. As early as 1963, Carlos Baker, examining the theme of the father-son relationship in the stories, refers to "Nick's unspoken sympathy for his own son 'Schatz' in a little story called 'A Day's Wait.'"[14] Baker takes the narrator's identity for granted and does not stop to defend or even explain his assumption. Richard Hovey, without naming the narrator, continues to focus his attention on the narrator-father and treats the story within the framework of fathers who "bring disillusionment" to their sons.[15] He concludes with a criticism of the narrator: "We still feel somehow that Schatz could and should have been spared, that somehow between him and his father the lines of communication could have been clearer."[16] But not until Joseph Flora's careful reading of the text and explication of the misunderstanding that lies at its core does anyone answer or explain Hovey's criticism of the narrator.[17] Significantly, each of these three readers responds to the story with appreciation and an involved reading. Indeed, Hovey's criticism of the father is *not* a criticism of the story, but rather an emotionally involved response to it.

Although Waldhorn includes the story in a chapter entitled "Nick Adams, Master Apprentice," he focuses more on the boy's experience than the father's.[18] However, when he refers to the narrator, it is as "Nick." The question of interpretation becomes more a controversy when Philip Young, invited by Scribner's to select materials for *The Nick Adams Stories*, chooses not to include "A Day's Wait."[19] Although he too concedes that Schatz is the child that Helen of "Cross-Country Snow" was going to have ("that child . . . was born—a son called Schatz in "A Day's Wait"), he goes on to say that "A Day's Wait" is "a story which could have been included in this book [*The Nick Adams Stories*], except that it is really about the boy."[20] Bakker, in spite of his fully expressed disagreement with Young's method of interpretation, nevertheless seems to second Young's opinion in this case. Bakker writes, "'A Day's Wait' easily fits in the Nick Adams stories, with the difference that . . . the story is rather about his son than about Nick himself."[21] But in contrast with Young, Bakker does not fail to appreciate the piece. He praises its "stylistic economy," Hemingway's "ability to transfer the right emotional effect to the reader without having to sentimentalize or without even having to mention the emotions at play."[22] However, it is Flora who finally begins to read the story with the sympathy and appreciation that it deserves. He calls it a "generally underprized story" and argues that it is "far from . . . journalism."[23]

Flora begins his careful reading by first addressing some important minor issues in the piece. After succinctly dealing with the problem of the wife, who is only referred to once by plural pronoun reference in the first line ("Hemingway chose not to emphasize any sense of parental separation in 'A Day's Wait,'"), Flora uses the text itself to argue the importance of the father and the father-son relationship: "Hemingway chose to tell the story in first person because he wanted to put emphasis on that relationship. If the point were merely the lad's brave wait for death, third person would have done just as well."[24] I would additionally suggest that the decision to employ a first person and therefore *limited* point of view is necessary to the plot development. The reader only knows what the narrator-father knows and so shares the father's misunderstanding—the misunderstanding that Flora does such a fine job of articulating.

Indeed, that this is primarily a story about misunderstanding—*breakdown* in communication—is central. Not only does Hemingway have us experience a misunderstanding of our own (i.e., our initial misreading of the boy's words and actions), but the occasion for the boy's heroic conduct is, also and ironically, a misunderstanding (his misunderstanding about temperature scales). Not only does Hemingway make us participate in the experience of our own misunderstanding (initial misreading) of the boy's words and actions, but ironically, the occasion for the boy's heroic conduct *is* his misunderstanding. Many of the stylistic or structural elements of the piece gain significance from and give significance to this controlling theme. As noted above, Grebstein has commented on the inside-outside-inside pattern that does draw attention to a schism (one that leads to misunderstanding) between what is inside (the boy's mind) and what is outside (facts or reality). But the more central movement of action and settings in this story is a regular up-down alternation. As we examine this movement in relation to the congruent patterns of up-down, hot-cold, and red-white images that structure the story, we uncover Hemingway's deeper theme, as well as the identity of the authentic Hemingway hero in the piece.

Misunderstanding is a particularly troublesome breakdown in communication because, by its very nature and even more than the Hemingway iceberg, it lies hidden. Until other "clues" in the situation (confusion, or the feeling that something does not make sense) reveal that the same knowledge is not shared or referred to by both people, the misunderstanding remains in place. The significant fact is that *neither* party suspects the mismatch of assumed knowledge—knowledge on which both depend to make sense of the relatively few words (facts) that are actually exchanged. As a result, the same words mean different things to each speaker.

As he has done so often before, Hemingway relies on pronouns to make the point:

> "You don't have to stay in here with me, Papa, if it bothers you."
> "It doesn't bother me."
> "No. I mean you don't have to stay if it's going to bother you." (437)

The father, and therefore the reader whose access to the event is through the perception of the first-person narrator-father, assumes that the boy's "it" refers to "stay[ing] here with me." That is what the father's "it" means in his reply, "It doesn't bother me." The son tries once more to clarify his meaning—"if it's *going* to bother you" (emphasis mine). Clearly the future tense leaves no question that the boy refers to his impending death, not the present inconvenience of staying with and caring for him. But there is not yet enough of a clue for the father to discover the mismatch—in this case the faulty pronoun reference. This is how all misunderstanding works. This misunderstanding will remain in place until one of the speakers receives a message that simply does not fit with his other assumptions (which must include the assumption of a match of relevant background information). Even at this early point in the story, the father senses that something is wrong, but since the clue is not strong enough to reveal the misunderstanding, he explains away his sense of something not quite right in terms of the boy's fever, which he assumes has made his son "a little lightheaded."

Once more before the dénouement, Hemingway indulges in the same pronoun play:

> "Don't think," I said. "Just take it easy."
> "I am taking it easy," he said, looking straight ahead. (438)

Again, there is no specific referent for the father's "it"; this "it" is part of an idiom, "take it easy," "take things easy," while the "it" in the son's response can only refer to the death he has so bravely awaited all afternoon.

Shortly after this last pronoun exercise, the boy asks the question that reveals the mismatch: "What time do you think I'm going to die?" (438). Finally the father (and reader) have enough of a clue, and the father immediately acts to supply the necessary information, bringing reality to correct the boy's mistaken illusion: "You aren't going to die. . . . It's like miles and kilometers" (439).

This almost expository study of the dynamics of misunderstanding is further developed by and controls the structure and patterns of imagery. Hemingway economically uses reference to a change in time or place to economically delineate eight scenes. Although the larger controlling pattern of action may move from inside (the house) to outside (the hunting scene) and back to inside (the house again), a more detailed, scene-by-scene account will establish the regular, up-down movement that is crucial not only to the plot complication but to the developing metaphoric pattern. The story opens upstairs in the father's bedroom. We infer this from the transitional "When I came downstairs" (436), which marks the beginning of the second scene in the kitchen by the fire. The third scene is upstairs in the boy's room ["you go up to bed" (436)], where the doctor examines him and mentions his temperature of 102 degrees. The fourth scene moves "downstairs" (436) again. This is the movement that is crucial to the plot complication. Here (downstairs) the doctor reassures the father that the illness is not serious— but the boy, lying in bed upstairs, hears none of this conversation. In the fifth scene the father goes back upstairs "back in the room" (436) to be with and care for his sick son. In the sixth scene, having done all he can to make the boy comfortable, the father goes down and outside, hunting in the cold, white, snow-covered world. In the seventh scene the father returns to the house, and after a brief interchange with someone downstairs he "[goes] up" (438) to the boy's room for the last, eighth scene. There is an abrupt stylistic shift in the final three lines of the story. Here the narrator talks *about* the boy's behavior the following day in general terms, no longer rendering the situation in concrete, dramatic scenes, so we are neither up nor down; the duality that had structured the tension of the piece has been resolved—or, at least, has disappeared.

As we have already seen, this movement is crucial on the level of plot complication. It explains how the misunderstanding could have happened in the first place. But the *break* between what is up and what is down is really more significant—that, and the contrast between *who* moves, making connections between what is up and what is down, and who remains up, a contrast between the one who is active and the one who lies in deathlike inactivity.

A reinforcing series of hot-cold images sustains this controlling pattern: The main problem is fever—temperature that is up. The boy is afraid he will die of too high a fever. The fever is not serious if it does not go above 104 degrees. The medicine, in order to restore health, will bring down the fever. In this story "up" and "hot" seem dangerous.

Further, the boy in the upper room is out of contact with the reality expressed below (that the fever is not dangerous). He is the one whose first act in the story was to "shut the windows" (436), breaking yet another connection—between inside and out. It is not surprising that he is described as "very detached" (437). It is this break, this detachment from reality (outside and below) that is life threatening. What he needs is not only a medicine to bring down the fever but a way of reestablishing the broken connections. And who is the one who keeps making the connection between the boy upstairs, isolated by his *imagined* forthcoming death, and reality below? It is the father, moving up and down throughout the story.

Lest we fail to appreciate the significance of this constant, up-down movement, Hemingway introduces reinforcing images into the hunting scene that seem, in the context of this pattern, almost blatant. In this scene, he swiftly sketches a vivid winter landscape and conveys the action of a whole afternoon's hunting in 111 words (five sentences). The passage merits our special attention, for it is not only a splendid example of Hemingway's taut, evocative, descriptive prose but the catalyst that makes the story resonant, more than just an exercise in the dynamics of human communication:

> It was a bright, cold day, the ground covered with a sleet that had frozen so that it seemed as if all the bare trees, the bushes, the cut brush and all the grass and the bare ground had been varnished with ice. I took the young Irish setter for a little walk up the road and along a frozen creek, but it was difficult to stand or walk on the glassy surface and the red dog slipped and slithered and I fell twice, hard, once dropping my gun and having it slide away over the ice.
>
> We flushed a covey of quail under a high clay bank with overhanging brush and I killed two as they went out of sight over the top of the bank. Some of the covey lit in trees, but most of them scattered into brush piles and it was necessary to jump on the ice-coated

mounds of brush several times before they would flush. Coming out while you were poised unsteadily on the icy, springy brush they made difficult shooting and I killed two, missed five, and started back pleased to have found a covey close to the house and happy there were so many left to find on another day. (437–38)

Oldsey, too, quotes the passage in its entirety, praising its "succinctness" and commenting that it is "somehow the precise counterpoint or imagistic correlative needed in balancing the feverish boy back in the room believing himself in death's grip."[25] This is the real achievement of the passage, not just the evocative prose but the way the passage functions within the piece. It makes the boy's character and behavior more plausible, permitting us to assume that death is a meaningful concept for this nine-year-old boy, who may have accompanied his father on other such expeditions. At the least, he would have seen the dead game his father brought back to the house.

A more important function of the scene within the story is to provide contrast, even relief. The other scenes, which occur inside the house, are also correlatives, but for the boy's experience. They are spare, lacking the weight of much concrete physical description, realized through limited dialogue or flat description of mundane activities. Against this reduced vision of reality, the father's world of the hunting scene is rich with the beauty of glistening landscape and the vitality of movement, even clumsiness, clatter, sliding, slithering. In fact, compared with the astonishing control demonstrated by his young son, this father, who slips and falls and drops his gun and misses half his shots, seems not all that much in control of things. Certainly, he is, at this point, unaware of his own son's ordeal and therefore powerless to do anything about it; he even, ironically and unintentionally, prolongs it as he hunts.

But even as we enjoy the contrasts provided by the father's world, accept the respite it offers from the stifling inside heat and tension in the humorous image of a man, precariously poised, jumping up and down on slippery ice-coated mounds, we notice that, while the images and tone contrast with the rest of the story, the same metaphoric patterns persist. Here we have the father making the same connections between up and down (jumping is an up-and-down motion) on ice-coated mounds (ground that goes up and down). Consistent with the style of this passage, the up-down motif is here objectified in a single image—one of physical movement. We also note that the birds are safe as long as they remain down under the brush and only die when they fly up over the top of the bank. Such details seem to declare that in both worlds of this story "up" is a detached and dangerous place.

The hunting scene also functions to associate cold with vitality and life while, in consistent contrast, heat threatens death—whether by fever or from a very real, hot bullet.[26] Of course, the thermometer, which is at the center of the original misunderstanding, perfectly integrates these two sets of metaphors: on a thermometer "up" or "higher" means "hotter."

Having labored to articulate this intricate pattern of up-down, hot-cold images, however, we sense that something is not quite right. Normally, we associate death with cold, not with heat, while warmth seems a quality of life. So we must ask why these "normal" patterns are inverted in this story?[27] The answer might be that in this story about misunderstanding Hemingway has inverted the normal pattern of things so that we may experience the confusion, the misunderstanding on yet one more level.

The young boy has gotten things separated and mixed up, turned around. He suffers from a split, a detachment of imagination from reality, and it is the father, the true Hemingway hero, who practices the fine art of moving back and forth, up and down, creating necessary connections and restoring health. It is at this point that we see how fully this slight story participates in the essence of Hemingway's vision and art. We recognize the recurrent theme of necessary connections throughout the Hemingway canon. Robert Gajdusek has long argued the importance of connections and bridging in Hemingway:

> In the work of Ernest Hemingway the image of the bridge becomes the central, dominating and obsessive metaphor. In all of the novels, crossing over to the other side or making connections—a bridge—with the other side is the most significant act, controlling the larger action and determining the outcome: the novels cannot be resolved until the proper connections are made.[28]

Surely the last sentence explains the action and resolution of this story as well.

Thus, I would argue that "A Day's Wait" is not really about the boy's experience, but about the father's. He is the first-person narrator, and he is the one who learns and teaches us the more profound lesson. The boy learns about two temperature scales and, perhaps, something about his inner resources. The father learns how hard it is to be one with, to share the thoughts of another person, even someone as close as a much-loved young son. Once having discovered the boy's misunderstanding, the father cannot but immediately sense how painful his son's ordeal must have been, and while *we* can intellectually understand *how* it happened, the father cannot escape his own guilt, the feeling of failure that he let it happen. The last sentence of the story, which describes the boy's fatigue and loss of control the following day, conveys to us not the boy's "regression" but the father-narrator's painful sense of just how much energy his son must have expended during his long, lonely day's wait.[29] The narrator's pained realization that the boy "had been waiting to die all day" (439) and his sympathetic, twice-repeated "You poor Schatz" (439) reveal just how bad he feels about having failed to be more perceptive. He must *feel* (as Hovey) "that somehow Schatz should have been spared . . . that somehow . . . the lines of communication could have been clearer."[30]

Thus the story, for all of its light tone, is also an act of confession or expiation. Although different in degree, tone, and weight, this little piece of storytelling proceeds from a source, a need, not unlike that which moved Frederic Henry, whose guilt and sense of responsibility for Catherine's death bring him to tell (confess) the story that we read as *A Farewell to Arms*. We can make the comparison without losing sight of the fact that the scale of this story is everywhere miniature, understated. Bakker notes the extraordinary "stylistic economy" of "A Day's Wait," and that in this story Hemingway does not have to "mention the emotions at play."[31] But the reduction in scope does not change the fact that the components, the psychic dynamics, perfectly replicate patterns that exist in broader, more deeply involved and involving terms in the larger works. That we smile as we discover, with the narrator-father, the boy's misunderstanding is not to say that we need dismiss the piece as a joke. Our smile is an acknowledgment—a "recognition of the other"—of our connection with the boy, his father, and their experience.[32]

This narrator, who had earlier taught his son modes of "holding tight" under pressure, now teaches him about different temperature scales. He, and through him the reader, learns something about the dynamics of misunderstanding. And Hemingway uses these easier lessons to show us something harder about the need to reconcile opposites, the (deadly) danger of unbridged schism, and the father-hero engaged in the healing task of establishing vital connections.

Notes

1. All references to "A Day's Wait" in parentheses are from *The Short Stories of Ernest Hemingway* (New York: Charles Scribner's Sons, 1966) 436–39. The text in the more recent Finca Vigía edition (New York: Charles Scribner's Sons, 1987) is identical, with the exception of one additional paragraph break at the beginning of the hunting scene.

2. Arthur Waldhorn, *A Reader's Guide to Ernest Hemingway* (New York: Farrar, Straus and Giroux, 1972) 71.

3. See Peter Hays, "Self-Reflexive Laughter in 'A Day's Wait,'" *Hemingway Notes* (1980): 25; Sheridan Baker, *Ernest Hemingway: An Introduction and Interpretation* (New York: Rinehart, 1967) 88; and Jackson J. Benson, introd. and ed., *The Short Stories of Ernest Hemingway: Critical Essays* (Durham: Duke UP, 1975) xii.

4. T. S. Matthews, "Fiction by Young and Old," *New Republic* (15 November 1933): 25.

5. Robert O. Stephens, *Ernest Hemingway: The Critical Reception* (New York: Burt Franklin, 1977).

6. See Gerald B. Nelson and Glory Jones, *Hemingway: Life and Works* (New York: Facts on File, 1984) 81; Carlos Baker, *Ernest Hemingway: A Life Story* (New York: Charles Scribner's Sons, 1969) 236; and Kenneth S. Lynn, *Hemingway* (New York: Simon and Schuster, 1987) 410. Philip Young offers the further biographical explanation that Scott Fitzgerald's similar confusion about centigrade and Fahrenheit may have provided "the germ of [this] story." See *Ernest Hemingway: A Reconsideration* (University Park: Pennsylvania State UP, 1966) 286n.

7. J. Bakker, *Ernest Hemingway: The Artist as Man of Action* (Assen, N.V.: Van Gorcum, 1972) 253n and John Killinger, *Hemingway and the Dead Gods: A Study in Existentialism* (Lexington: U of Kentucky P, 1960) 25.

8. Killinger, 25.

9. Bakker, 253n.

10. John Atkins, *The Art of Ernest Hemingway: His Work and Personality* (London: Spring, 1964) 144.

11. Bernard Oldsey, "The Snows of Ernest Hemingway," in *Ernest Hemingway: A Collection of Criticism*, ed. Arthur Waldhorn (New York: McGraw-Hill Paperbacks, 1973) 66.

12. Sheldon Norman Grebstein, *Hemingway's Craft* (Carbondale: Southern Illinois UP, 1973) 9–10.

13. Joseph DeFalco, *The Hero in Hemingway's Short Stories* (Pittsburgh: U of Pittsburgh P, 1963) 54.

14. Baker, *Life*, 133–34.

15. Richard B. Hovey, *Hemingway: The Inward Terrain* (Seattle: U of Washington P, 1968) 43.

16. Hovey, 44.

17. Joseph Flora, *Hemingway's Nick Adams* (Baton Rouge: Louisiana State UP, 1982) 215–24.

18. Waldhorn, *Reader's Guide*, 52–71.

19. This collection of the Nick Adams stories, arranged chronologically with respect to Nick's age, was published by Charles Scribner's Sons in 1972.

20. Young, "Big World Out There: The Nick Adams Stories," in Benson, 43.

21. Bakker, 40.

22. Bakker, 40.

23. Flora, 216, 220.

24. Flora, 218.

25. Oldsey, 66.

26. A pattern of red-white color imagery works to reinforce this complex structure. Although the sick boy's face is, indeed, twice described as "white," the death-threatening fever

turns the "tops of his cheeks" red. Hemingway describes them as "flushed by the fever," repeating for the third time within 15 lines the word "flush." This time he uses it with its color denotation, while the two preceding occurrences denote the action of drawing the quail from their protected positions under the brush, out and up to their real deaths. This flushing involves the narrator and his hunting dog ("We flushed a covey of quail" [437]). and it is significant that this dog, a "young Irish setter" whom we would associate with hunting and, thus, with the real deaths of the quail, is the only touch of color—"the red dog" in the robust "frozen," white ("varnished" and "coated" with ice) landscape. Red flushed cheeks, red hunting dog helping to flush the quail: red is associated with heat and death—real or imagined—in sharp contrast to the energy and movement of the white landscape.

27.   Usually white is the color of death, not only in Hemingway (e.g., the image of Catherine Barkley as a statue at the end of *A Farewell to Arms*, the hills like white elephants, or the high, white, square top of Kilimanjaro), but in general. Red usually suggests health and robust life. Here that pattern has been inverted.

28.   Robert E. Gajdusek, "Bridges: Their Creation and Destruction in the Works of Ernest Hemingway," in *Up in Michigan: Proceedings of the First National Conference of the Hemingway Society*, ed. Joseph Waldmeir and Joseph Marsh (Traverse City: The Hemingway Society, 1983) 75.

29.   DeFalco, 53.

30.   Hovey, 30.

31.   Bakker, 40.

32.   Louis H. Stewart and Charles T. Stewart, "Play, Games, and Affect: A Contribution Toward a Comprehensive Theory of Play," in *Play as Context*, ed. A.T. Cheska (Westpoint: Leisure, 1981) 42–52.

22

Illusion and Reality: "The Capital of the World"

Stephen Cooper

"The Capital of the World," written between November 1935 and February 1936, was collected for the first time in Hemingway's 1938 omnibus anthology, The Fifth Column and the First Forty-nine Stories. *Like "A Day's Wait," "The Capital of the World" centers on a boy's confrontation with death. A game of bullfighting becomes suddenly, horrifyingly real for the reader when young Paco, playing at matador, is fatally gored by the carving knife horns of a kitchen-chair bull. Stephen Cooper speculates that critics have neglected this short story because of its deceptive simplicity and its failure to fit neatly into a schematic reading of Hemingway's work. He discusses how "The Capital of the World" treats many of the author's supposedly characteristic subjects (the bullfight, life in Spain, initiation into manhood, the disillusionment that comes with experience, the nature of fear, the necessity of facing death alone) in uncharacteristic ways and suggests that this short story serve as "a warning against simplistic interpretations" of Hemingway's fiction.*

The relative neglect of "The Capital of the World" is puzzling because the story deals with some of Hemingway's most characteristic subjects and themes: the Spanish bullfight, life in Spain, the initiation into manhood, the disillusionment with life that comes with experience, the nature of fear, and the necessity of facing death alone. Perhaps the reason for the neglect is the seemingly simple moral of the story's main action: the boy Paco is killed because of his own naïveté. Perhaps the story suffers from comparison with the two masterpieces Hemingway composed at about the same time, "The Short Happy Life of Francis Macomber" and "The Snows of Kilimanjaro."

And perhaps the story simply does not fit very well with a schematic reading of Hemingway's work.

Probably the most schematic reading of the story is Stephen A. Reid's "The Oedipal Pattern in Hemingway's 'The Capital of the World.'"[1] Reid imposes a rigid Freudian framework on the story. He sees bullfighting as acting out the oedipal struggle with the matador as son and the bull as father. Reid bases much of his interpretation on the statement in the story's first paragraph that Paco "had no one to forgive him."[2] Thus, Paco fails at the symbolic, oedipal bullfight because he has never undergone a real oedipal conflict. Reid also emphasizes Paco's innocence of the world's danger in contrast with the disillusionment of the other characters. Sheldon Norman Grebstein has also emphasized the split between Paco, who is full of illusions, and the rest of the characters in the story.[3] He blames Paco's failed initiation into manhood on a lack of technical skill. Paco possesses sufficient courage but lacks craft in his confrontation with the kitchen-chair "bull." Recently, Bernard Oldsey has focused on the cinematic techniques of the story and its movie allusions, both explicit and implied.[4] He relates the allusions to the theme of illusion and disillusion in the story. Although Oldsey suggests the story proposes a balance between illusion and disillusion, he describes a familiar dichotomy between the uninitiated Paco and the rest of the characters. These critics provide valuable and provocative insights into "The Capital of the World." They also tend toward either/or dichotomies—characters are full of illusions or totally disillusioned—which obscure the ironies and ambiguities of the story. This tendency is not confined to "The Capital of the World" (e.g., Hemingway's women characters are subject to similar either/or descriptions), but a fresh look at this story can remind us of the dangers of a reductive reading of Hemingway's works.

"The Capital of the World" gives a different twist to most of Hemingway's familiar themes. This difference is most obvious in his treatment of Spain and the bullfight. Hemingway's love of Spain and the bullfight is well known. For him the values of the bullfight embody the values of the "real" Spain: courage, honor, pride, and a tragic view of life. Whether one finds Hemingway's portrayal of bullfighting a juvenile romanticization or an insightful analysis,[5] one cannot deny his admiration for the figure of the matador.

In "The Capital of the World," however, Hemingway presents three matadors and one would-be matador who all fall short of the ideals of bravery, honor, and craftsmanship that he described in *Death in the Afternoon* and embodied in the character of Pedro Romero in *The Sun Also Rises*. The three bullfighters staying at the Pension Luarca when the story opens are all failures. One has failed because he is a coward, although we are told that "until he had received a peculiarly atrocious horn wound in the lower abdo-

men at the start of his first season as a full matador, [he had] been exceptionally brave and remarkably skillful" (30). The second matador at the pension
was also a promising performer in his youth, but his career has been destroyed by illness, by the blood he quietly coughs into his handkerchiefs.
The last matador has had a brief vogue as a novelty because "he was so short
that he could barely see over the bull's withers" (30). But despite his real
courage and ability, the short matador does not draw people to the ring with
his old-fashioned style and colorless personality.

Hemingway's portrait of the bullfighting world in this story is not romantic or glamorous. What we are given is the mundane, even seedy side
of the sport. Public attention is usually focused on the famous, highly paid
stars of the ring, but for every Belmonte there are dozens of matadors like
those in the Pension Luarca. Hemingway had portrayed the other side of
the sport in an earlier, more widely read story, "The Undefeated." That
story presents vividly the humiliating treatment of Manuel García, a bullfighter whose career is in decline. Suitcase in hand, García must beg the
promoter Retana for the chance to fight in a second-rate nocturnal fight after
the burlesque bullfights, the "Charlie Chaplains." Like the matadors in
"The Capital of the World," García is no longer in demand, the waning of
his career partly the result of bad luck. But he does get the chance to
perform and to rise above his dismal surroundings. Although he is gored and
his performance is unappreciated by either the audience or the bullfight
critic of *El Heraldo*, García fights courageously and remains undefeated
when the story ends, one of the earliest examples of Hemingway's dictum
that a man may be destroyed but not defeated.

What makes "The Capital of the World" a much bleaker story than
"The Undefeated" is that the matadors of the Pension Luarca never get the
chance that Manuel García has to prove themselves. They are not even
given the dignity of names. We see them only as destroyed and, in large
measure, defeated. The cowardly matador has his advances rejected by
Paco's sister and even loses the whore he buys drinks for to a picador. The
sick bullfighter attempts to hide his illness and preserve his dignity, but he
is fighting a losing battle. The short matador also preserves an outward
dignity, but his chances of real success as a bullfighter are gone. As the
narrator tells us at the beginning of the story, "There is no record of any
bullfighter having left the Luarca for a better or more expensive hotel;
second-rate bullfighters never became first rate; but the descent from the
Luarca was swift . . ." (30).

While the real matadors at the Luarca never get the chance to prove
their courage in the story, the would-be matador Paco does—with disastrous
results. When Paco, a waiter at the Luarca, enacts some passes with an
imaginary bull in the hotel's kitchen, the dishwasher Enrique tells him he

would be afraid of a real bull and unable to perform. Responding to a suggestion by Enrique, Paco insists that they stage a mock bullfight using a chair with sharp knives tied to the legs so he can prove his courage. During one of Enrique's charges with the chair, Paco steps two inches too close, and a knife slips into him "as easily as into a wineskin" (37), severing his femoral artery and causing him to bleed to death. Because he is young and innocent, it is tempting to call his death tragic, but in reality his death is more absurd than tragic. Hemingway had insisted throughout *Death in the Afternoon* that the bullfight was a tragedy, but without a real bull and without the dignity bestowed by ritual and tradition, Paco's "bullfight" is nothing more than a parody. There is a vast difference between being killed while making a pass with a real bull in the *plaza de toros* and being killed while making the same pass with a chair in the kitchen of a second-rate hotel.[6]

In explaining the meaning of Paco's death, commentators tend to focus on his illusions—his detachment from reality. Grebstein has said, "The cause of Paco's death is the excess of courage and illusion."[7] Similarly, Reid says that "Paco died *because* of his illusions" (emphasis in original), and then goes on to contrast him to the rest of the characters in the story: "Paco is different from all the other characters in the story. Each of them is disillusioned; Paco stands apart from them."[8] Both Grebstein and Reid see the theme of the story revolving around a necessary disillusionment or an initiation into life's unpleasant realities. That Paco has many illusions and only a slight grasp of the realities of life is clear from the story. The narrator tells us that Paco "would like to be a good Catholic, a revolutionary, and have a steady job like this, while, at the same time, being a bullfighter" (32). The theme is spelled out in the story's last paragraph: "He died, as the Spanish phrase has it, full of illusions" (38). Does the story thus resolve itself into a simple dichotomy between Paco with his fatal illusions and the rest of the characters with their disillusioned wisdom? Oldsey has suggested (without developing the idea in much depth) that the story is about the need for a balance between illusion and disillusionment.[9] A closer look at the story shows the wisdom of Oldsey's suggestion.

One of the titles Hemingway considered for the story—"The Capitol of Illusion" [*sic*]—indicates that the illusions of the story are not confined to Paco.[10] From the beginning of the story we are told that illusion plays an important part in the lives of the supposedly "disillusioned" matadors, who live at the Pension Luarca not only because it is cheap but also because its address is impressive: "It is necessary for a bullfighter to give the appearance, if not of prosperity, at least of respectability, since decorum and dignity rank above courage as the virtues most highly prized in Spain, and bullfighters stayed at the Luarca until their last pesetas were gone" (29–30).

The effort to maintain a certain decorum and dignity is illustrated by the sick matador who carefully launders his own blood-soaked handkerchiefs in an effort to hide his illness. The cowardly matador tries to maintain the illusion of his early success by retaining "many of the hearty mannerisms of his days of success" (30). Thus, the difference between Paco and these matadors is not that they do not live their lives according to certain illusions but that to some degree they try consciously to create and manipulate their illusions, whereas Paco's illusions are largely unconscious.

The passage quoted above also makes it clear that the matadors epitomize a typically Spanish trait. In *Death in the Afternoon* Hemingway had defined *pundonor*, the Spanish word for honor, as "honor, probity, courage, self-respect and pride in one word."[11] Given this oft-quoted and high-sounding definition of Spanish honor, it is startling to hear him say "decorum and dignity rank above courage as the virtues most highly prized in Spain." This statement implies that saving face—maintaining a certain appearance or illusion—is more important to Spaniards in general and bullfighters in particular than cultivating a more substantial virtue like courage. The preference for a decorous or romantic illusion is also illustrated by the intense disappointment of all Madrid with Greta Garbo's *Anna Christie*—a realistic film that showed Garbo "in miserable low surroundings" (37). Just as *Anna Christie* showed Greta Garbo in a new way, "The Capital of the World" shows Spain and bullfighting in a less romantic, less heroic way than Hemingway's earlier writing had. Thus, with the possible exception of some passages from *For Whom the Bell Tolls,* this story is Hemingway's most negative portrait of Spain.

The timing of the story may help explain his negative view. "The Capital of the World" was completed by spring 1936 and was first published in *Esquire* (June 1936) as "The Horns of the Bull." What Hemingway perceived as the decay of bullfighting and the corruption and inefficiency of the new Spanish Republic seem to have tainted slightly his view of Spain in the early and middle 1930s.[12] The growing decadence of the bullfight had been an underlying theme of *Death in the Afternoon.* During a 1933 visit to Spain, Hemingway wrote to his mother-in-law, Mrs. Paul Pfeiffer, that "Spain is in what is called a state of confusion. All the idealists now in power have their fingers in the pie and they have gotten down to where the plums are pretty small. When they run out of pie there will be another revolution."[13]

On the eve of the Spanish Civil War, Hemingway's irritation with the changes in the bullfight world and the follies of Spanish politics found expression in "The Capital of the World." As one would expect, Hemingway did not express his view of Spain in political or sociological pronouncements but embedded it in the tone and atmosphere of the story and illustrated it by a large and vivid cast of characters. In a sense, this story is another illustration of Edmund Wilson's view of Hemingway: "His whole work is a criticism of society: he has responded to every pressure of the moral atmosphere of the time, as it is felt at the roots of human relations, with a sensitivity almost unrivaled."[14] Of course, with the outbreak of the Spanish Civil War in the summer of 1936, the moral atmosphere of Spain would undergo a drastic change that would be reflected in Hemingway's writing over the next four years.

Although "The Capital of the World" is very much a portrait of Madrid and Spain in the 1930s, it is also the story of a young man's confrontation with the real world. As a sort of initiation story, it bears comparison to Hemingway's other initiation stories. Once again, "The Capital of the World," although dealing with a familiar Hemingway theme, stands apart from his other stories, for it is an aborted initiation into manhood.

Hemingway's best stories about coming of age are undoubtedly the Nick Adams stories. In stories like "Indian Camp," "The Battler," and "The Killers," Nick is confronted by a violent, disturbing world that he must come to terms with. In these stories he is mostly an observer rather than a participant, and he must try to make sense out of what he sees and hears. Even in the war stories, such as "Now I Lay Me" and "A Way You'll Never Be," the focus is on Nick's reactions to his experience and on what he has learned and how it has affected him. Despite the violence of these stories, they tend toward reflection on experience, which leads to self-knowledge and understanding of the world.

In contrast, Paco never has a chance to reflect on experience and to learn: he faces a violent reality, and it kills him. Actually, his situation is extremely ironic because he faces a violent illusion of reality—Enrique pretending to be a bull with a chair and a pair of knives—and it kills him. His initiation into manhood—the chair episode is a sort of parody of a primitive rite complete with totemic bull—is cut off, and Paco never even enjoys the short, happy life that was granted to that middle-aged initiate, Francis Macomber. Even after the accident, Paco continues to think in terms of his illusionary bullfight world. As he tries to stop his bleeding, he says to Enrique, "'There should be a rubber cup,'" because "he had seen that used in the ring" (37). As Enrique runs off to get help, Paco's mind again reverts to the bullring: "In the ring they lifted you and carried you, running with you, to the operating room. If the femoral artery emptied itself before you reached there they called the priest" (37). Paco's only other reactions are disbelief ("He could not believe that this had happened to him" and fear ("He was frightened"). His feelings are normal and understandable, and they are also in line with the experiences of many characters in Hemingway's fiction. Certainly shock and fear are central to Nick Adams's growth. But before Paco has a chance to reflect on his feelings and experience, his life goes "out of him as dirty water empties from a bathtub when the plug is drawn" (37).

Of course, it is questionable whether Paco would have matured as Nick did even if he had lived. His simplicity and innocence seem almost complete, and in the story we do not see indications of the kind of intelligence and reflectiveness that Nick Adams possessed. Goodness and innocence are not enough to make Paco a success in the world. "The Capital of the World," Grebstein has argued, "advances the mordant conclusion that to be brave, good, and innocent is to be unfit for life."[15] Stated another way, perhaps Hemingway's theme will seem less mordant: innocence and goodness do not equal wisdom.

Although Paco's innocence and basic goodness are fairly obvious, the nature of his courage seems questionable to me. Grebstein assumes that Paco is brave, based on the story's assertion of his lack of fear, and argues Paco's downfall is the result of too much courage and not enough craft or skill in his bullfighting technique.[16] While his technique is certainly defective, I would argue that Paco does not possess courage but simply lacks fear. Having never faced real danger, he simply does not know enough to be afraid.

A comparison with other Hemingway stories that deal with fear and courage is helpful here. In perhaps his best-known story on the subject, "The Short Happy Life of Francis Macomber," Francis undergoes tremendous fear, running from the lion, before he develops the courage to face the charging buffalo. The realities of danger and fear must be faced before true courage can develop. All of Hemingway's truly courageous characters have a realistic sense of the world's dangers and know the taste of fear. For example, Robert Jordan in *For Whom the Bell Tolls* performs his duties bravely, but his interior monologues make it clear that he knows the risks he is facing, and he confronts the issue of fear squarely. Hemingway outlined a growth process in *Death in the Afternoon* that seems to apply to Jordan. He said bullfighters usually are devout at the start of their careers and then become cynical, but the best of them then "become devout again by cynicism."[17] In contrast, Paco's "courage" is born of ignorance. In his reading of "The Capital of the World," Stephen Reid makes a similar point: "Paco fails to have fear. The contrast Hemingway makes is between the needed, disillusioning recognition of fear and the failure of Paco to get that far in his understanding."[18]

While there is something pathetic about Paco's death because he dies before he has the chance to grow and mature, his death also saves him from the difficult and painful process of disillusionment. After Hemingway's wounding in 1918, he wrote, in a letter to his family, "And how much better to die in all the happy period of undisillusioned youth, to go out in a blaze of light, than to have your body worn out and old and illusions shattered."[19] Although Paco does not "go out in a blaze of light," he does avoid the disillusionments of growing old. In his works and in his life Hemingway often advocated the value of worldly experience and an insider's knowledgeable view, but he also demonstrated the pain and effort and cost of acquiring that knowledge. The vividly presented anguish of so many of his characters raises the question of whether that knowledge, or even life itself, is worth the suffering it entails. Seen from this point of view, there are more ironies in Paco's story than most commentators realize. Paco is killed because of his illusions about life and his lack of experience, but his death also saves him from the pain of disillusionment and the fate of the residents of the Pension Luarca, who in their disillusionment seem to "survive as if because of their imperfections."[20]

The history of Hemingway criticism is filled with many examples of reductive or schematic readings of his works. These readings often rely on a selective reading of his fiction. For example, I have often felt that "The Short Happy Life of Francis Macomber" is anthologized not because it is a fine story but because it can be read as a paradigm of many clichés about Hemingway. It can be seen as an example of the tyro-tutor motif or as an instance of Hemingway's macho attitudes toward male-female relations. But it can be read in these ways only by ignoring many inconvenient ironies and ambiguities.[21]

A story like "The Capital of the World," which gives a different twist to many familiar Hemingway themes, should serve as a warning against simplistic interpretations of his work. In addition, the complexities of the story itself and the ambiguities surrounding such a seemingly simple character as Paco should remind us of the danger of taking Hemingway's work at face value. In "The Capital of the World," as in his best fiction, Hemingway used a lucid style to create an illusion of simplicity that conceals an emotional and thematic complexity.

Notes

1. Stephen A. Reid, "The Oedipal Pattern in Hemingway's 'The Capital of the World,'" *Literature and Psychology* 13 (Spring 1963): 37–43

2. Ernest Hemingway, "The Capital of the World," *The Complete Short Stories of Ernest Hemingway*, Finca Vigía edn. (New York: Charles Scribner's Sons, 1987) 30. Subsequent references to this edition are in the text in parentheses.

3. Sheldon Norman Grebstein, "Hemingway's Dark and Bloody Capital," in *The Thirties: Fiction, Poetry, Drama*, ed. Warren French (Deland: Everett Edwards, 1967) 21–30.

4. Bernard Oldsey, *"El Pueblo Español:* 'The Capital of the World,'" *Studies in American Fiction* 13 (Spring 1985): 103–10.

5. The classic exposition of the negative view of Hemingway on bullfighting is Max Eastman's 1934 essay "Bull in the Afternoon," reprinted in *Ernest Hemingway: The Man and His Work,* ed. John K. M. McCaffery (Cleveland and New York: World, 1950) 66–75. A positive view can be found in James A. Michener's introduction to Hemingway's *The Dangerous Summer* (New York: Charles Scribner's Sons, 1985) 3–40.

6. Grebstein has said that Paco's death is "different only in detail from the hundreds of deaths which Hemingway tells us occurred in Spain each year in provincial towns staging their own informal town-square bullfights *(capeas),* when local men and youths faced the bull under the most hazardous conditions." See Grebstein, 24. Even at the level of the informal *capeas,* the difference between a real bull and a chair would seem to be more than mere detail.

7. Grebstein, 23.

8. Reid, 37.

9. Oldsey, 108.

10. Letter to Arnold Gingrich, 5 April 1936, in *Ernest Hemingway: Selected Letters, 1917–1961,* ed. Carlos Baker (New York: Charles Scribner's Sons, 1981) 441.

11. Hemingway, *Death in the Afternoon* (New York: Charles Scribner's Sons, 1932) 91.

12. Carlos Baker, *Ernest Hemingway: A Life Story* (New York: Bantam, 1970) 313–14.

13. *Letters,* 398.

14. Edmund Wilson, "Hemingway: Gauge of Morale," *The Wound and the Bow* (1941) (New York: Farrar, Straus and Giroux, 1978) 195.

15. Grebstein, 25.

16. Grebstein, 25.

17. Hemingway, *Death in the Afternoon,* 59.

18. Reid, 39.

19. *Letters,* 19.

20. Grebstein, 25.

21. Kenneth S. Lynn has recently argued that Wilson is not the honorable hunter he seems to be, and thus not much of a tutor. See *Hemingway* (New York: Simon and Schuster, 1987) 432–36. Kenneth G. Johnston has provided a strong defense of Margot Macomber, supposedly the quintessential Hemingway bitch, in *The Tip of the Iceberg: Hemingway and the Short Story* (Greenwood: Penkevill, 1987) 207–11.

23

Hemingway's Spanish Civil War Stories, or the Spanish Civil War as Reality

Allen Josephs

Sadly, the 1938 publication of The Fifth Column and the First Forty-nine Stories *may be said to mark the true end of Ernest Hemingway's career as a short story writer. With the exception of* The Old Man and the Sea *(a short story that attained novella length),* "The Short Happy Life of Francis Macomber" *and* "The Snows of Kilimanjaro," *both completed in 1936 and collected in* The First Forty-nine, *are his last acknowledged masterpieces in the genre. In the anthology's preface Hemingway expressed hope that he would live long enough to write 25 more stories, but the 23 years between 1938 and his suicide in 1961 did not allow him to fulfill that ambition. The distractions were manifold: the Spanish Civil War, World War II, the Castro rebellion, two divorces, two marriages, two plane crashes, multiple injuries and illnesses, one Nobel Prize, and deteriorating mental and physical health. Hemingway had somewhat better success as a novelist, publishing* For Whom the Bell Tolls *in 1940 and* Across the River and into the Trees *in 1950. More often than not, however, he was involved in desperate, Laocoon-like struggles with long manuscripts that would not "come right"—* The Garden of Eden, Islands in the Stream, *and* The Dangerous Summer. *Nevertheless, a great deal remains to be said about some of the short stories Hemingway did write during these final years.*

Allen Josephs provides a detailed consideration of five stories about the Spanish Civil War—"The Denunciation," "The Butterfly and the Tank," "Night Before Battle," "Under the Ridge," and "Landscape with Figures"— all composed between May 1938 and February 1939 but uncollected until after Hemingway's death. Josephs points out that Hemingway's service as a war correspondent in Spain, his role as pioneer of the new journalism and the nonfiction novel, and his professed method of creating fiction by "in-

venting from experience" all combine to produce a blurring of fact and fiction in his writings about the Spanish conflict. The essay builds a strong case for ranking these short stories with Hemingway's dispatches and political articles rather than with For Whom the Bell Tolls, for considering them as writings about the "real" rather than the "invented" war. Story by story, Josephs demonstrates how each records Hemingway's own political and emotional responses to actual war experiences. He shows too how these stories may be read as a group to appreciate the changes in those responses as the Loyalist cause lost ground. Under Josephs's treatment, the Spanish Civil War stories garner significance as "a kind of cathartic fictional memoir," an emotional purgative that would cleanse Hemingway for the task of inventing For Whom the Bell Tolls.

> A lot of people went there that I did not like, the same as at The Stork, say, but I was never in Chicote's that it wasn't pleasant. One reason was that you did not talk politics there.
>   —"The Denunciation"

> It would be a most interesting story if Hemingway would write a book based upon his experiences while in Spain working on the film [The Spanish Earth]. He has not and says he will not. . . .
>   —Jasper Wood

The only positive "cause" Ernest Hemingway ever really supported was the Spanish Republic. For a while his devotion to the Republic did have, as Scott Fitzgerald wrote to Max Perkins, "something almost religious about it."[1] Although Hemingway eventually became disgusted by the "carnival of treachery and rotten-ness," as he put it in 1938, also in a letter to Perkins,[2] he probably wrote more about the Spanish Civil War than any other single topic. The list is impressive: some 30 syndicated news dispatches for the North American Newspaper Alliance (NANA); miscellaneous pieces for New Masses; one for Pravda; 12 pieces for Ken magazine; the narration for the film, The Spanish Earth; his play, The Fifth Column; a half-dozen short stories; and, of course, his largest novel, For Whom the Bell Tolls. To put it succinctly, the Spanish Civil War dominates the middle period of Hemingway's writing.

Although Hemingway wrote about the war as fact and as fiction, distinguishing between his fact and his fiction is not always a simple matter. For Whom the Bell Tolls was, for example, mostly fiction, and the news dispatches were largely factual. Yet even here, there is a crossing over of fact and fiction. André Marty (the French commissar who was chief of the International Brigades, to pick one, well-known example) and a number of the general officers for the Republic appear in *For Whom the Bell Tolls*, while a good deal of opinion, even political opinion or propaganda, as well as rich descriptions that read like fiction make their way into the news dispatches. One of the best examples of this blurring of fact and fiction is "Old Man at the Bridge." Originally cabled from Barcelona on Easter Sunday of 1938— only a few hours after the events it portrays—as a piece for *Ken* magazine, it was subsequently published as the last "story" in *The Fifth Column and the First Forty-nine Stories.*[3]

Hemingway was a kind of pioneer in new journalism and the nonfiction novel, as books such as *Death in the Afternoon* and *Green Hills of Africa* demonstrate, so his crossing of genre comes as no surprise. Since his self-professed method of writing, "inventing from experience," is a kind of oxymoronic negation of any absolute categories of fact and fiction in the first place, it may be more accurate to speak of the real war and the invented or imagined war in Hemingway's writings than to attempt to distinguish too closely between fact and fiction, a distinction that much recent criticism has, in any case, made rather suspect.

The writing about the real war, by which I mean the Spanish Civil War as Ernest Hemingway actually saw it, includes the political articles and war dispatches, the play, and the five short stories about to be considered—"The Denunciation," "The Butterfly and the Tank," "Night Before Battle," "Under the Ridge," and the recently published "Landscape with Figures." In the play and in these stories, Hemingway was writing from actual experience, and, although he was to some extent inventing from that experience, these pieces were largely crafted from events in which Hemingway himself took part. He even made his own hotel room the setting for the play and, in part, for the story "Night Before Battle," and his favorite bar, Chicote's, the locale for "The Denunciation," "The Butterfly and the Tank," and the beginning of "Night Before Battle." When he sent the last of these to Arnold Gingrich in October 1938, for publication in *Esquire*, he called it "the third Chicote story."[4]

These stories of the Spanish Civil War have two characteristics in common. The first-person narrator is clearly Ernest Hemingway himself—correspondent, filmmaker, writer, raconteur, personage. There is no making himself up as in the Nick Adams stories, and the occasional use of a fictional name—Mr. Emmunds in "The Denunciation" and Edwin Henry in "Night Before Battle" and "Landscape with Figures"—only makes the real identity more obvious. Young Jasper Wood, rushing the script of *The Spanish Earth* into publication in May 1938, spoke too soon about Hemingway's reluctance to write about his experiences "while in Spain working on the film."[5]

The second characteristic is that the real subject of all these stories, sometimes overtly, sometimes subtly, is the political nature of the conflict at hand. The narrator's remark about not talking about politics at Chicote's refers to the old days before the war and is therefore meant ironically. An examination of these two characteristics in these stories makes us keenly aware of Hemingway's increasing personal distaste for politics as the 1930s and the Spanish Civil War came to a close. In so doing, such an analysis also helps us understand how *For Whom the Bell Tolls* would become an invented world where politics was largely a remembrance of nights past at Gaylord's.

My grouping of the stories is not entirely arbitrary. Not only do they all deal with the Civil War, but they formed something of a group in Hemingway's mind at the time of their composition. In February 1939, less than four months after the publication of *The Fifth Column and the First Forty-nine Stories*, Hemingway wrote to Max Perkins from Key West about the possibility of a new book of stories:

> I ought to have enough new stories for a book in the fall or do you think that is too soon for another book of stories? I have
> The Denunciation   Esq.
> The Butterfly and the Tank   Esq.
> Night Before Battle   Esq.
> Nobody Ever Dies   Cosmo. *Read it in March No.*
> Landscape With Figures—not sent out yet.[6]

On 25 March 1939, just as he was beginning *For Whom the Bell Tolls*, he wrote Perkins from Key West about a new story about the war which "Pauline thinks among best I've ever written, called Under the Ridge."[7] In this letter he reiterates the new grouping of stories in the same order, now including "Under the Ridge": "So it looks like we will have a book of stories and a novel. Have five new stories so far. The Denunciation. The Butterfly and The Tank. Night Before Battle. Nobody Ever Dies. Landscape With Figures. And this new one Hell, that makes six."[8]

Although Hemingway did not pursue this project, Mary Hemingway and Scribner's pursued it when they published *The Fifth Column and Four Stories of the Spanish Civil War* in 1969. Not accidentally the stories appear in the same order in which Hemingway had arranged them. "Nobody Ever Dies" was not included in the volume, probably because the story takes place in Cuba and does not actually deal with the Spanish Civil War. For the same reason, I am not considering it here. "Landscape With Figures" was not included either, I assume because it had not been previously published. Since it has now come out in the so-called Finca Vigía Edition of the stories, since Hemingway did include it in the group, and since it fits perfectly with the other stories, in style, in setting, and in the character of the narrator, Edwin Henry, I consider it here.

The project for the Civil War stories occurred to Hemingway in February and March of 1939, just as he was about to begin and was beginning *For Whom the Bell Tolls*. The connection between these stories and the germination of the novel is important to bear in mind. They are not really separable, as the two Key West letters cited above reveal quite vividly. In fact, it may well have been his shift from the stories to the novel that precluded the project to bring out the book of stories. Swept up in the excitement of writing the novel, Hemingway surely lost enthusiasm for these stories that simply could not measure up to the big book.

In the first letter to Perkins, Hemingway lists the stories, then goes on to describe three more long stories he wants to write. One is about an "old commercial fisherman who fought the swordfish all alone in his skiff for 4 days and four nights," one is about the battle of Teruel, and the last is about the "storming of the Guadarrama pass by the Polish lancers." Creative energy fairly radiates from this letter. But the most important comment for our purposes comes at the end as Hemingway relates to Perkins his bad dreams about Spain: "Last night I was caught in this retreat again in the goddamndest detail. I really must have a hell of an imagination. That's why should *always* make up stories—*not* try to remember what happened."[9]

Hemingway's insistence on the importance of imagination to his fiction is a point he would reiterate in his second letter to Perkins on 25 March. Instead of the three stories he had gone to Cuba to write, Hemingway finished "Under the Ridge" and "started on another I'd had no intention of writing for a long time and working steadily every day found I had fifteen thousand words done; that it was very exciting; and that it was a novel." The novel, of course, was *For Whom the Bell Tolls*, and Hemingway was obviously very pleased with it: "It is 20 times better than that Night Before Battle which was flat where this is rounded and recalled where this is invented."[10] From this point on the novel absorbed him completely, and the project to publish a book of Spanish Civil War stories disappeared from view.

Bearing this history in mind, we can return to the examination of the two characteristics these stories have in common: their straightforwardly autobiographical narration and their unavoidably political characterization of the Spanish Civil War. In "The Denunciation," the first of the Chicote stories, we learn that the narrator—Mr. Emmunds, and in Spanish, Enrique, from which we can deduce without too much trouble that his name is Henry Emmunds—is one of a group referred to as "us," staying at the Hotel

Florida in November of 1937. Emmunds knows Spain well and has spent a good deal of time there in prewar days. In the second Chicote story, "The Butterfly and the Tank," the nameless narrator also lives in the Hotel Florida in the winter of 1937–38, is a well-known writer, and heads home from the censorship office, a sure indication that he is a foreign correspondent.

In the third Chicote story, which takes place "in a shell smashed house that overlooked the Casa del Campo,"[11] in the Gran Vía restaurant where foreign correspondents ate, and again at the Hotel Florida, the narrator is Edwin Henry. Edwin Henry and Henry Emmunds, E. H. and H. E., are obviously heads and tails of the same coin. The time is now April 1937, and Edwin Henry is making a film, the money from which "all goes for ambulances." He describes the film: "We've got the Twelfth Brigade in the counter-attack at the Arganda Bridge. And we've got the Twelfth again in the attack last week by Pingarrón. We've got some good tank shots there" (116). The Arganda Bridge and nearby Pingarrón (heights on the Jarama front) were undoubtedly not household place-names for the average *Esquire* reader, but they correspond exactly to the places the real E. H. worked on the film, *The Spanish Earth*. And the long metal bridge over the Jarama River, fictionally transposed later into the Guadarrama Mountains, would become Robert Jordan's target of demolition. For the present, however, Hemingway was content to write stories about the bridge in its real location.

The narrator in "Under the Ridge" is not called by name, but we find him, again in April 1937, at a "long ridge above the river" (140), where he is with Spanish troops. An attack is "being made by an International Brigade" (141; the Twelfth was an International Brigade), and the narrator and his companions had come "to film the attack" (142). To see just how much Hemingway is himself in these stories, it is interesting to compare his comments in "Night Before Battle" about "the good tank shots" and certain descriptions from "Under the Ridge" with one of his news dispatches. Here is the beginning of "Under the Ridge": "In the heat of the day with the dust blowing, we came back, dry-mouthed, nose-clogged and heavy-loaded, down out of the battle . . ." (140). At the end of the story he tells us, "But the oddest thing about that day was how marvelously the pictures we took of the tanks came out. On the screen they advanced over the hill irresistibly, mounting the crests like great ships, to crawl clanking on toward the illusion of victory we screened" (151). Also in "Under the Ridge" there is a long discussion of thirst. The key line is spoken by the narrator in response to a discussion about wine versus water: "Yes. But for the thirst, water" (141).

Now compare those descriptions with this news dispatch by Hemingway, dated 9 April 1937: "The first [attack] was in the grey olive studded broken hills of the Morata de Tajuña sector [i.e., Pingarrón] where we had gone with Joris Ivens to film infantry and tanks in action, going over behind the infantry and filming the tanks as they ground like ships up the steep hills and deployed into action. A high cold wind blew the dust the shells raised into your eyes and caked your nose and mouth. . . . Your correspondent is always thirsty, but that attack was the thirstiest I've ever been. But the thirst was for water."[12] The details are remarkably alike.

Hemingway wrote a short memoir of *The Spanish Earth* for *Verve* in 1938, and his memory of the filming is exactly like the story and the news dispatch: "you ran with the cameras, sweating, taking cover in the folds of the terrain on the bare hills. There was dust in your nose, and dust in your hair and in your eyes, and you had the great thirst for water, the real dry-mouth that only battle brings." Toward the end he wrote, "So now when it is all over you sit in a theater and suddenly the music comes and then you see a tank coming riding like a ship and clanking in the well remembered dust and your mouth dries again."[13]

I have not begun to exhaust the coincidences between fact and fiction in this story, nor is that my purpose. Rather, I have quoted these last details at some length because they show us to what extent Hemingway himself was, quite without pretense, the narrator of these stories, and also because they afford us what I think is a rather rare glimpse of fact and fiction being virtually identical in Hemingway's work. These details are not so much invented from experience as they are lifted from reality.

"Landscape with Figures" is the most autobiographical story of the group. The narrator, Edwin Henry again, is clearly Hemingway himself. The two Dutch film makers are clearly Joris Ivens and his cameraman, John Ferno. The Old Homestead, the building on the Paseo de Rosales which they—both the real people and the story's characters—used as a vantage from which to film the battle in the Casa del Campo, is clearly exactly that, the same "Old Homestead" that "Dos Passos, Matthews, Sid Franklin, Tom Delmer, Martha Gellhorn, and Virginia Cowles" in the words of Carlos Baker, "converged on" in real life.[14] It is also clearly the same building from which Edwin Henry was filming at the beginning of "Night Before Battle." And, finally, the American woman journalist, Elizabeth, whom the narrator addresses as "daughter," who walks "with a long loose stride" and whose "hair, which was dusty yellow in the fading light, hung over the collar of her short, fur-collared jacket,"[15] is so clearly Martha Gellhorn that one wonders, in fact, why Hemingway even bothered to invent names for these "characters."

"Landscape with Figures" seems rather unfinished, beginning with its odd title. "Landscape with Well-Known People" would have been more accurate. It is the least developed "story" of the group and the least overtly political, at least from a self-contained, fictional point of view. If, however, we take it for what it really is, a slice of life from a *roman à clef* to be, then it becomes potentially quite political. *A Handbook to Literature* gives *The Sun Also Rises* as a "notorious" example of the *roman à clef*, yet *The Sun Also Rises* is as pure fiction compared to "Landscape with Figures."[16] Thus if we disregard the fictionality of the piece, the real subject—looking beyond the incomplete moments of comedy and pathos—is the filming of *The Spanish Earth*, Hemingway's single most political venture.

One important difference between "Landscape with Figures" and the other stories is that in the others the narrator is an observer who tells a story about other people. He is always involved in it, but the story is never just about him. In "Landscape with Figures," however, the narrator and the girl, the ironically titled "figures," stand center stage with the other characters revolving around them, and the ending, with its protective sentimentality about not letting the girl see a battle too closely, is Hemingway at his most self-indulgent. I think Scribner's was wiser not to include this story in the 1969 volume of Civil War Stories than it has become more recently, yet "Landscape with Figures" does illustrate very well Hemingway's probably inescapable self-involvement, both personally and politically, at the time.

The other stories are less self-conscious and more consciously involved with the political problems of the war. At the beginning of "The Denunciation," Emmunds informs us that Chicote's was "the best bar in Spain, certainly, and I think one of the best bars in the world" (90). The waiter who eventually denounces the fascist pilot, Luis Delgado, "was an old man with a bald head and very old-fashioned manners which the war had not changed" (92). The waiter at first shows reluctance to denounce Delgado because he had been an old client: "Only the old waiters know him and the old waiters do not denounce" (93), he tells Emmunds.

Now in the war, however, things have changed. Politics is very much discussed at Chicote's. Pedro Chicote himself, whom Emmunds compares to the chasseur at the Ritz in Paris, was caught by the revolt in San Sebastian and now runs "the best bar in Franco's Spain" (90). The waiters have taken over the bar; the liquor is gone; and the old waiters do, in fact, eventually denounce old clients. After all, the old waiter has a son at the front and, as he says, "Certainly such a man [as Delgado] is dangerous to our cause" (93).

"The Denunciation" reveals Hemingway at his most ironically antipolitical. Not only does Delgado, the fascist, become the most sympathetic character in the story, but this same old waiter will confess in "Night Before Battle" that he belongs to no party (121). One way or another everyone in the story is undone by the necessities of the war. The old waiter betrays his own values; Emmunds accuses himself of "impartiality, righteousness and Pontius Pilatry" (97) for having given the telephone number of Pepe, the chief of counterespionage, to the old waiter (Pepe is obviously Pepe Quintanilla, the real such person); and Delgado will be shot for his bravado. The only solace, again ironic, is that Emmunds takes responsibility for the denunciation because he did not want Delgado "to be disillusioned or bitter about the waiters" before he died (100). Especially not the old waiters in the best, clean, well-lighted bar in the capital of the world, one might add. As John, Emmunds's Greek comrade, tells Emmunds, "Is a trouble with a war. Is a too many people crazy" (99).

Probably all these stories are based on real occurrences, but we know positively that the central incident of "The Butterfly and the Tank" actually occurred because Langston Hughes also reported the meaningless killing of the "flit king" in Chicote's.[17] Hemingway had already used this pathetic affair in *The Fifth Column.* In the play it is reported as one of the stupid, brutal vagaries of war, but it has no particular, political significance. In the story, however, there are several levels of political implications, each more ironic than the previous.

After the flit king is killed, the narrator remarks, "I told the forceful girl I thought the whole thing was a pretty good story and that I would write it sometime." She objects that it would be "prejudicial to the cause of the Spanish Republic," and the narrator explains that it had nothing to do with politics but thinks, "probably a lot of other people will say I shouldn't too" (106). Obviously Hemingway was already keenly aware of the kind of political criticism that would haunt everything he wrote about the war.

The next day the manager of Chicote's, using what the narrator calls "relentless Spanish logic" (106) and "the real Spanish metaphysics" (107), insists the narrator must write the story and that it must be called "The Butterfly and the Tank" to symbolize the "gaiety" of the flit king which "comes in contact with the seriousness of the war" (108). Neither the symbolism of the title nor the insistence of the manager please the narrator any more than the idea he ought not write the story, although ironically both the corny title and the story itself survive, in part as a kind of monument to insensitivity and inept political symbolism.

Finally the narrator thinks about the flit king's wife's saying, "Pedro. *Pedro,* who has done this to thee, Pedro?" (109). Disregarding the obvious bathos, the narrator thinks in the closing phrase, "And I thought that the police would never be able to tell her that even if they had the name of the man who pulled the trigger" (109). In one sentence, the petty politics, the simplistic symbolism, and the bathetic sentimentality of the story give way to the historical and ever-political, fratricidal reality of the Spanish Civil War. Who killed the flit king indeed? I cannot help being reminded of Larra's grimly prophetic remark, written exactly a century before: "Here lies half of Spain; it died of the other half"; or of Antonio Machado's famous verses to a newborn Spaniard: "One of the two Spains/will have to freeze your heart."

"Night Before Battle"—a long, rambling story about the impending death of an American communist tank driver in the offensive the Republic mounted in the Casa del Campo—is built around the same battle Hemingway and company had witnessed from the "Old Homestead" and which Hemingway described in detail in his NANA dispatch of 11 April 1937.[18] The narrator and Al Wagner, the tank man, both tell us the attack is a failure. An officious little man in Chicote's, evidently a knowledgeable party member, then explains in some detail why it will fail, blaming it on "An S.O.B. named Largo Caballero" (113), who was then the prime minister of the Republic. "The first time they let him look through a pair of field glasses he became a general. This is his masterpiece," the officious man informs us, to conclude: "Largo Caballero is liable to be shot. He ought to be shot" (113). In fact, the communists despised him and in March 1937 "resolved to destroy Largo Caballero once and for all."[19]

Discussion of the in-fighting between the socialists and the communists, regardless of its veracity as political history, does not, however, make for Hemingway's most brilliant fiction. The story was indeed "flat," as Hemingway had remarked to Max Perkins. Al Wagner's dilemma—having to attack when he knows he will probably be killed and having to do so essentially for political rather than military reasons—is poignant and believable, but along the way the story gets mired in too much political subtextuality. We understand the narrator's frustration at the end when he identifies with Al Wagner's plight and thinks, "You get angry about a lot of things and you, yourself, dying uselessly is one of them. But then I guess angry is about the best way that you can be when you attack" (139). The vicarious anger and frustration in "Night Before Battle" are typical of Hemingway's attitude at this time and consistent with the other stories, but the drawn-out expression of these emotions here does not translate into very effective fiction. "Night Before Battle" is the weakest of the Chicote stories.

The political dimensions of the battlefield story, "Under the Ridge," on the other hand, reach far beyond the actual subject matter of the story. The Frenchman's desertion—he makes his own peace, walks away from the war, and is shot by the Russians—forms the nucleus of the story, around which many negative charges are grouped. Among other things are the matter of the boy named Paco who is executed by the Russians as an example to discourage self-inflicted wounds; the matter of the hatefulness of the Russian military police; the matter of the failure of the tanks to advance and the French tank commander's drunkenness and impending execution; the matter of the narrator's good friend, the Hungarian general who was killed two months after the events in the story take place (obviously based on

Hemingway's friend, General Lucasz); the matter of the Hungarian general's necessary censorship of events; and, finally, the minor matter of filming the battle. But all these are secondary to the matter of the Extremaduran's virulent politics, which underscores in blood this catalog of the problems of the Republican Army and the International Brigades in early 1937.

When the narrator asks the belligerent Extremaduran what his politics are, he replies, "I hate all foreigners" (143). Being more specific he says, "I hate the Moors, the English, the French, the Italians, the Germans, the North Americans and the Russians" (143). When he adds that he hates the Russians most, the narrator wonders aloud if he is a fascist. "No," he replies, "I am an Extremaduran and I hate foreigners" (143).

This mock-xenophobe, who is not as crazy as he sounds, has specific historical reasons for his hatred: "I am from Badajoz. In Badajoz we have been sacked and pillaged and our women violated by the English, the French and now the Moors. What the Moors have done now is no worse than what the English did under Wellington. You should read history. My great-grandmother was killed by the English. The house where my family lived was burned by the English" (145; Wellington took Badajoz in 1812). The Extremaduran hates North Americans because "My father was killed by the North Americans in Cuba while he was there as a conscript," and he hates the Russians because he considers them "the representatives of tyranny and I hate their faces" (145). He does not bother to explain why he hates the Germans and the Italians, because they are obviously the enemy.

Hemingway has created or observed (or both) in this strange being a kind of historical compendium of centuries of violence perpetrated on the Spanish people by foreign powers. In the eighteenth and nineteenth centuries a devastating proportion of European wars was fought on Spanish soil, not the least of them—as Goya so horrifyingly recorded—the Napoleonic conflict. Now in 1937, Russia was squared off against Italy and Germany, rehearsing for the coming world war on Spanish soil. The Extremaduran surely had a perverse kind of right to his fierce politics.

Beyond all those historical concentricities, there is also the matter of the "Massacre of Badajoz" as it is usually called, to which the Extremaduran only alludes with the phrase "what the Moors have done now." After the town fell to the insurgents, many civilians were rounded up and executed in the bullring. The *New York Times* headline of 17 August 1936 read, "Rebels Slaughter Badajoz Leftists, Execute 1,200." Later estimates put the figures at 4,000 for the period between 14 and 24 August.[20] Of all the grim realities of the Spanish Civil War, this one, which Hemingway treated almost indirectly, was one of the grimmest. As the narrator prepares to leave, the Extremaduran asks him if he understands his hatred, and the narrator replies, "I understand your hatred" (150).

Because of the brutality at Badajoz and because of all the historical atrocities the Extremaduran enumerates, I find it hard to accept Warren French's idea that "It is difficult to imagine how a story could more directly indict the Communists."[21] It does indict the communists, of course, but it also indicts the fascists and the English and the French and the Americans and by extension anyone who ever wielded force over or usurped political power from anyone else. In his sympathy with the Extremaduran and his brief identification with the Frenchman who deserts, the narrator makes it clear that almost anything is preferable to such usurpation and force. It is here, perhaps more than anywhere else in these stories, that Hemingway's own disgust with the political treachery of the war comes closest to the surface. Angel Capellán has observed that "Under the Ridge" "is the story in which Hemingway best conveys the multifaceted implications of Spain at war."[22] Hemingway himself put it this way in a letter to Ivan Kashkin in March 1939: "in stories about the war I try to show *all* the different sides of it."[23]

In "Under the Ridge," as at the end of "The Butterfly and the Tank," we get a fleeting glimpse across the abyss of Spanish history. The flit king dead on the floor at Chicote's, not like a butterfly but, as the narrator thinks, more like "a dead sparrow" (109); the boy, Paco, shot in the head from behind by the Russians; the Extremaduran standing "straight up in his rage" (147) despite the bullets coming over—these scenes, these new *desastres de la guerra*, seem somehow familiar, as though one had seen them before hanging in the Prado.

Regardless of these memorable moments, however, the Spanish Civil War stories cannot be considered among Hemingway's finest ("Landscape with Figures" and "Night Before Battle" might more properly be considered among the worst), and John Steinbeck surely overestimated "The Butterfly and the Tank" when he wrote to Hemingway that it was "one of a very few finest stories in all time."[24] Hemingway himself seems to have recognized that they were not his best. In 1958, when *Esquire* wanted to reprint the three Chicote stories in *The Arm Chair Esquire*, he said that two of the stories "were not as good as I wanted them and I wanted to revise them before letting them go into book form."[25] It is quite probable, as Angel Capellán has suggested, that the autobiographical and political aspects of these stories were precisely what determined Hemingway to block their reprinting.[26]

Regardless of their literary merit, the stories as a group do have a function which I alluded to at the beginning. For better or worse, these stories present the real war as Hemingway experienced it, an experience that included being on the losing side. As he expressed it to Max Perkins in the first Key West letter, "Well we've lost another war."[27] There is no doubt Hemingway was disillusioned about the state of affairs. As he wrote to Arnold Gingrich in October 1938, "Things here are so foul, now, that if you think about it you go nuts."[28] Just a week later he would write to Perkins about the "carnival of treachery and rotten-ness."[29] What these stories did, I believe, precisely because they were autobiographical and political, was to purge the real war and the real loss of the Spanish Republic from Hemingway's fiction. Perhaps nothing could really purge such a loss personally, but literarily at least he got the dreadful reality of the war as he had experienced it out of his system. The stories as a group became a kind of cathartic, fictional memoir.

That catharsis led straight into the writing of *For Whom the Bell Tolls*, which was rounded rather than flat, invented rather than recalled, and exciting and 20 times better than "Night Before Battle." Whether the inventing was altogether a good idea is another question, but had Hemingway not written these stories, it might have taken him as long to get to *For Whom the Bell Tolls* as it did to write *A Farewell to Arms* after the First World War. Remember that letter to Perkins in which Hemingway says that after writing "Under the Ridge," the last and most cathartic story in the group, he had "started on another I'd had no intention of writing for a long time."[30] Martin Light has written that these stories "can be seen as part of Hemingway's search for a true way to recreate the Spanish experience."[31] I think they are that and more: they also readied him to write the great romantic war novel he so badly wanted to do. As Hemingway wrote to Tommy Shevlin on 4 April 1939, "it is the most important thing I've ever done and it is the place in my career as a writer I have to write a real one."[32]

Years later, looking back, he would write to Charles Poore, "Dr. Tolstoi was at Sevastopol. But not at Borodino. He wasn't in business in those days. But he could invent from knowledge we all were at some damned Sevastopol."[33] Hemingway was not at the Guadarrama offensive (he was in Bimini at the time,[34] just as he had not been in the retreat from Caporetto. But he knew the territory, and, as the Civil War stories show so well, he was in the Casa del Campo and in the heights at Pingarrón and at the Arganda Bridge. These stories about the Spanish Civil War—the real war—were Hemingway's Sevastopol.

Notes

1. Carlos Baker, *Ernest Hemingway: A Life Story* (New York: Charles Scribner's Sons, 1969) 316.

2. *Ernest Hemingway: Selected Letters, 1917–1961*, ed. Carlos Baker (New York: Charles Scribner's Sons, 1981) 474.

3. William B. Watson, "'Old Man at the Bridge': The Making of a Short Story," *The Heming-way Review* 7.2 (Spring 1988): 164.

4. Ernest Hemingway to Arnold Gingrich, 22 October 1938, *Letters*, 472. "The Denuncia-tion" appeared in the November 1938 issue of *Esquire*, "The Butterfly and the Tank" in the December 1938 issue, and "The Night Before Battle" in the February 1939 issue. "Under the Ridge" appeared in the October 1939 issue of *Cosmopolitan*. "Landscape with Figures" was published for the first time in *The Complete Short Stories of Ernest Hemingway*, Finca Vigía edn. (New York: Charles Scribner's Sons, 1987).

5. Jasper Wood, "Introduction" to Ernest Hemingway, *The Spanish Earth* (Cleveland: J. B. Savage, 1938) 9–16.

6. Hemingway to Maxwell Perkins, 7 February 1939, *Letters*, 479. I have kept Hemingway's typographical idiosyncrasies throughout.

7. Hemingway to Perkins, 25 March 1939, *Letters*, 482.

8. Hemingway to Perkins, 25 March 1939, *Letters*, 482.

9. Hemingway to Perkins, 7 February 1939, *Letters*, 479.

10. Hemingway to Perkins, 25 March 1939, *Letters*, 482.

11. Ernest Hemingway, *The Fifth Column and Four Stories of the Spanish Civil War* (New York: Charles Scribner's Sons, 1969) 110. Subsequent references to this edition appear in parentheses in the text.

12. "Hemingway's Spanish Civil War Dispatches," ed. William Watson, *The Hemingway Review* 7.2 (Spring 1988): 24.

13. Hemingway, "The Heat and the Cold," *Verve* 1.2 (Spring 1938): 46.

14. Carlos Baker, *Ernest Hemingway: A Life Story* (New York: Charles Scribner's Sons, 1969) 308.

15. Hemingway, "Landscape with Figures," 595.

16. William Flint Thrall and Addison Hubbard, *A Handbook to Literature* (New York: Odys-sey, 1960) 422.

17. Martin Light, "Of Wasteful Deaths: Hemingway's Stories about the Spanish War," in *The Short Stories of Ernest Hemingway: Critical Essays*, ed. Jackson J. Benson (Durham: Duke UP, 1975) 71.

18. Watson, "Dispatches," 27–28.

19. Hugh Thomas, *The Spanish Civil War* (New York: Harper & Row, 1977) 650. Within weeks Largo was replaced by Negrín.

20. Peter Wyden, *The Passionate War: The Narrative History of the Spanish Civil War, 1936–1939* (New York: Simon and Schuster, 1983) 135–39.

21. Warren French, *The Social Novel at the End of an Era* (Carbondale: Southern Illinois UP, 1966) 93.

22. Angel Capellán, *Hemingway and the Hispanic World* (Ann Arbor: UMI Research P, 1985) 250.

23. Hemingway to Ivan Kashkin, 23 March 1939, *Letters*, 480.

24. Baker, *Life*, 337.

25. Light, 66. Hemingway did allow reprinting of "The Butterfly and the Tank."

26. Capellán, 303.

27. Hemingway to Perkins, 7 February 1939, *Letters*, 478.

28. Hemingway to Gingrich, 22 October 1938, *Letters*, 474.

29. Hemingway to Perkins, 28 October 1938, *Letters*, 474.

30. *Letters*, 482.

31. Light, 77.

32. Hemingway to Tommy Shevlin, 4 April 1939, *Letters*, 484.

33. Hemingway to Charles Poore, 23 January 1953, *Letters*, 800.

34. Baker, *Life*, 313.

24

The Hunting Story in *The Garden of Eden*

James Nagel

As best we can tell from Scribner's heavily edited text of The Garden of Eden, *the novel's protagonist, David Bourne, drifts helplessly through Hieronymus Bosch-like nightmares of hysteria, madness, fornication, infidelity, and androgynous metamorphoses at the soul-destroying whims of a demoniac wife. Bourne's only source of strength, the only "clean, well-lighted place" in his otherwise passive and troubled character, is his integrity and discipline as a writer. Begun in 1946 and finally abandoned in 1958,* The Garden of Eden *contains an untitled short story that James Nagel identifies here as the "heart" of this unusual novel and "one of the finest stories" Hemingway ever wrote. Nagel explores precisely how Bourne can create significant art by "using present emotions to capture the feelings of the past" even as his marriage disintegrates around him, and in the process he demonstrates why* The Garden of Eden *"contains some of Hemingway's most intriguing observations about the creative process." An out-of-control novel about an out-of-control life and its destruction of a writer,* The Garden of Eden *seems Hemingway's elegy for Hemingway, the hunting story at its center the dying flare of a meteoric career.*

It is comforting to reflect, in the wake of the publication of Ernest Hemingway's long awaited *The Garden of Eden* in May of 1986, that the reviews of this novel have not been dramatically more insightful than those of his first novel 60 years earlier.[1] Despite a history of progressively more perceptive criticism on Hemingway's work during the intervening decades, the reviewers of the present novel, with very few exceptions,[2] have failed to come to terms with it as a work of art on any but the most superficial of levels.

Whatever the root cause of this phenomenon, whether it results from the subtlety of Hemingway's craft or from the limitations of the review as an interpretive form, the sad fact is that the initial reactions indulged in little beyond Papa-bashing and a quick read of the more sensational aspects of the sexual games on the surface of the plot. To be sure, on this level Wilfrid Sheed's observation that "*The Garden of Eden* is a bore. It needs a good snake"[3] has its merits. But there are other aspects of this novel that deserve consideration and, in fact, relate this novel to the central thematic strains of the best of Hemingway's fiction, including his finest short stories and novels.

The romance plot of the novel is not, in itself, of particularly great moment, but there is a good deal more to it than "Catherine's inserting her finger in a naughty place" and the "laughable" consideration that "love shall die and the best and the brightest hopes of earth depart because of some silly talk and some jiggery-pokery under the covers," to quote from Rhoda Koenig.[4] Catherine is certainly a more complex character than a simple "bitch destroyer" and Marita more than a "comfy sleeping bag,"[5] epithets that harken back to the simplistic readings of Hemingway's women typical of early Hemingway criticism. David Bourne, as the troubled writer who lives through a painful episode in his marriage at the same time he writes a short story about an agonizing memory in Africa, is actually one of Hemingway's most intriguing characters, certainly on a par with Harry, the dying protagonist in "The Snows of Kilimanjaro," a story with a good many parallels to *The Garden of Eden*. Lorian Hemingway's dismissal of him in the observation that "once in a while he puts on a clean fishing shirt and a pair of shorts. It may be noted that he never puts on a hat and a pair of Groucho Marx glasses and forgets to put on his shorts,"[6] surely ignores the most complex dimensions of the character, as does Sheed's assessment of David and of Jake Barnes, as "passive, rueful, flawed, and much more dominated than dominating."[7] David Bourne, in many respects, is more like Frederic Henry, who, a decade after Catherine died in Switzerland, narrates his novel still acutely aware of the pain of his loss. Similarly, David writes of the elephant hunt nearly two decades after the fact, and even then the emotions of it are difficult for him to contain.

At the heart of *The Garden of Eden* is the African hunting story David writes during the last half of the novel. The story is based on an experience he had as a young boy of about eight when he accompanied his father on a hunting trip that led not only to the death of an elephant but to the end of Davey's respect and love for his father and of the close ties between them. It is evident in every chapter of the novel that David is a committed and serious writer and that the best of his work springs from deeply felt emotions from his own experience transformed into imaginative constructs that convey the feelings, if not the exact people and circumstances, that evoked them. Despite his dedication, and despite the smoldering memories that urge themselves into his consciousness, he has never been able, has never had the courage, to write the African story. The central issue in the novel, far overshadowing the more sensational romance intrigue, is how and why he can now face the painful memory of the elephant hunt and write what comes to be a truly great work of short fiction. The answer lies in the interrelationship of the two lines of plot in the novel.

The deeper significance of these plot developments rests not so much on who ends up sleeping with whom but on the interrelated matters of how the earlier experience in Africa affects David's behavior toward Catherine on their honeymoon and how the dissolution of their relationship contributes to his ability at last to write the story that has been in him for many years. On this level David's story has parallels to the story of Ike McCaslin in William Faulkner's "The Bear" in that it is the maturation ritual of the hunt that allows Ike to develop morally to the point at which he repudiates his inheritance to expiate the family guilt of wealth derived from slavery. Without the experience of the hunt, the implications are, Ike would not have been capable of the somber reflections that lead to his most significant decisions. Although Faulkner's fiction is artistically dense and complex, these implications are basically inescapable. Hemingway's fiction is nearly the reverse: its method is simple and understated, and its implications are imbedded in suggestion and nuance and in much that is never spoken.

The suggestion in *The Garden of Eden* is that the African experience changed David at the tender age of eight in ways that still manifest themselves on his honeymoon two decades later. That he still feels the emotions of that experience keenly is everywhere apparent in the novel, particularly in the story itself and in the reflections that follow his episodes of composition. The central point, of course, is that what David is as a person, his level of sensitivity and awareness, his capacity to explore his experience and write about it, have been shaped by the experiences of his youth, and the formative event of his youth was the African hunting trip with his father. After that, things were never the same again, for instead of finding adventure and an opportunity to win his father's respect, he found, for the first time in his life, the emotional power of betrayal, disillusionment, and estrangement. That he still feels these emotions powerfully is evident in the fact that he knows that this is the best story he has to tell but he has never had the courage to tell it, to delve into the painful territory and live it all again. Not even for his art, which means nearly everything to him, is he willing to go through it again. However, as his relationship with Catherine deteriorates, and since he must deal with betrayal and estrangement in his marriage, he finds the strength to go back and confront precisely the same themes in his story.

What is interesting in all of this is how the boyhood experience of the hunting invests the romantic conflict with special values and, conversely, how the painful realities of the dissolution of the marriage make it possible for David, as artist, to explore the material he had always avoided.

In one sense, there is never really any suspense about David's relationship with Catherine. It is clear from the beginning that she is emotionally unstable and self-destructive and that it is only a matter of time until their marriage must end, despite the fact that they are still on their honeymoon. At the end of the first chapter, for example, even as he holds Catherine in his arms in the night, "his heart said goodbye Catherine goodbye my lovely girl goodbye and good luck and goodbye" (18). This awareness dominates their relationship throughout, despite David's attempts to hang on to it, and their marriage deteriorates through a series of painful stages to a final separation. In Madrid, for example, on the morning that Catherine visits the Prado, David reflects that "it lasted a month, he thought, or almost" (57).

Catherine, too, senses that the marriage is over: in chapter 13, in response to David's toast "here's to us," she answers, "there isn't any us . . . not any more" (117). It is not surprising, therefore, that Catherine comes to advocate that David marry Marita, since she seems genuinely to care for him on some level and to wish to spare him the loneliness and despair she knows are coming (144–45).

Since he must deal with betrayal and estrangement in the present, David is in a position to confront the same kinds of issues in the story he writes. His reflections about his writing reveal a consistent pattern of interaction between his feelings at the time of composition and the emotions he portrays in his fiction. For example, at a key juncture in the novel, just after Catherine has insulted David's writing, there is a revealing passage:

> What Catherine had said about the stories when she was trying to hurt him had started him thinking about his father and all the things he had tried to do whatever he could about. Now, he told himself, you must try to grow up again and face what you have to face without being irritable or hurt that someone did not understand and appreciate what you wrote (211).

In a deleted portion of the manuscript, David thinks that his marital problem "is as useless <to go into> as to {wonder} think what would have happened if you and Kibo had not learned to hunt at night with the full moon."[8] It is not until the relationship with Catherine is irreparably shattered, when she tears up one of his stories and tells him she hates him (157–58), that he is finally able to write about the elephant hunt.

The hunting story starts innocently enough but intensifies through each of its five sections. In the first (159–60), Davey and his dog are tracking the old bull elephant in the moonlight while his father waits back at camp. There is a heavy emphasis on the close relationship between Davey and Kibo: the boy strokes the dog often, and Kibo recognizes the need for silence and quietly pushes his muzzle into the hollow of Davey's knee to announce his presence. When they first encounter the elephant, what impresses Davey is the animal's smell and his size, with his "great ears" slowly moving and his tusks that reach almost to the ground. Although this is positive imagery, faintly similar to the description of the noble lion in "The Short Happy Life of Francis Macomber," Davey does not yet associate any deeper values with the elephant, although there is naturally a sense of foreboding about what will happen now that he has been discovered and they can begin the pursuit.

After David writes this section of the African story, he and Marita swim together, openly displaying their burgeoning affection (161–63). For her part, Catherine has had a quiet respite at the hotel reading the first section of the hunting story, which frightens her. She confesses that she has never liked David's father and that she is worried about the dog. Although there is plenty to worry about in this scene, with the marriage slipping away and with Catherine on the edge of sanity, the tone is one of restraint and quiet foreboding. These values also invest the next installment of the African story (164–66), during which it becomes clear that Davey should not have been brought along on the strenuous hunt through the broken country of Africa. Juma and David's father treat him with concern but remain determined to push ahead after the elephant. As Davey awakens in the night he thinks of the elephant and only begins to realize the full emotional investment he has in the animal his father regards only as prey:

> Then he woke once with the moonlight on his face and he thought of the elephant with his great ears moving as he stood in the forest, his head hung down with the weight of the tusks. David thought then in the night that the hollow way he felt as he remembered him was from waking hungry. But it was not and he found that out in the next three days. (166)

What is fascinating in this scene is that the boy in the story is on the edge of a recognition of his true feelings about the elephant, a realization that will change his life, just as David is about to admit that his marriage is over. He is also aware that as writer he uses the feelings of his present situation to enrich the story he is developing. He thinks to himself, "So you must write each day better than you possibly can and use the sorrow that you have now to make you know how the early sorrow came" (166). David will use the anguish of the marriage to deepen the emotion of the hunting story.

After he writes this second segment of the story, David reflects on his life and art and realizes that the only thing he truly has is his writing. He has good fun in the suggestive banter with the proprietress of the hotel, later makes love with Catherine, and then discovers that Marita is reading his novel. More and more, Marita is moving into the role of loving and supportive wife just as Catherine is moving away from it. As the relationships in the marriage begin to darken, so do the relationships in the African story.

As the action moves to the third of the five episodes of the hunting story, Davey's feelings have progressed to a sense of betrayal and regret and the sinking realization that there is no turning back, no way to save the elephant from his father. Even as he writes this the emotions are difficult for him to control: "But his feeling about the elephant had been the hardest part . . ." (174). The conflicts begin to mount as the chase becomes more strenuous and as Davey's values begin to diverge from those of his father and their African guide, Juma. Juma "had always been David's best friend and had taught him to hunt," but now Juma does not let him carry the rifle, indicating to Davey that it is going to be a rough day. Just before dark Davey kills two fowl with a slingshot, graphically introducing death into the scene, and he wins, at least temporarily, his father's approval. He does not welcome the news that five years before Juma killed the friend of this elephant not far from where they are, and his reflections are rather grim: that Juma and his father are not really proud of him and that they will be able to kill the elephant now only because he had found the elephant and had endured the pace well enough so that they could sustain the pursuit. He is ambivalent about whether he is glad he ever discovered the elephant or not (174). As he finishes writing this part of the story, David reflects on the problems of handling the emotion: "The hardest to make truly was how he had felt and keep it untinctured by how he had felt later," particularly about the elephant.

As he leaves his room he sees Marita still reading in a chair, and he is reminded of the impossible circumstances of his domestic life. Catherine convinces David that they should both get another haircut, an event that progressively complicates their problems of identity throughout the novel, and Catherine says that they are both damned now: "David looked at her eyes that he loved and at her dark face and the incredibly flat ivory color of her hair and at how happy she looked and he began to realize what a completely stupid thing he had permitted" (178). The next morning he has difficulty in resuming the story, suggesting that he is no more eager to move toward the conclusion of the hunt than he is to move to a dissolution of the marriage.

On the hunt they are drawing closer to the elephant now, and they find the skeleton of the kill from five years ago. Juma smiles in satisfaction, remembering how he had dispatched the bull with a shot in his ear. Davey's concerns are for other matters:

> "How long do you suppose he and his friend had been together?" David asked his father.
> "I haven't the faintest idea," his father said. "Ask Juma." (180)

When Davey is told that Juma does not care, he realizes that he himself *does* care, and the rest of the fourth section of the story is essentially a record of Davey's boyish reflections:

> The bull wasn't doing anyone any harm and now we've tracked him to where he came to see his dead friend and now we're going to kill him. It's my fault. I betrayed him. . . . Kibo and I found him and I never should have told them and I should have kept him secret. . . . I'm going to keep everything a secret always. I'll never tell them anything again. (181)

It is interesting that the boy who vowed to keep everything a secret becomes the writer who devotes his life to revealing everything through his art, even his most agonizing memories.

Before David writes the final section of the hunting story, in which the elephant is brutally killed, his relationship with Catherine also moves into its final stage. David and Marita make love again, and their relationship improves as the marriage deteriorates. Catherine insists that David return to writing the narrative of their journey and abandon the African story, and when she then insults his father he knows that the relationship is over:

> "Well write it then. It's certainly much more interesting and instructive than a lot of natives in a kraal or whatever you call it covered with flies and scabs in Central Africa with your drunken father staggering around smelling of sour beer and not knowing which ones of the little horrors he had fathered."
> "There goes the ball game," David said. (189)

Catherine insists that David's stories are simply his means of avoiding his duty, and she says that she has no further need of either David or Marita (191). David's realization that the marriage is over paves the way for his writing the conclusion of the story.

The final section of the story is rich in the emotions of loss. Davey misses Kibo, who has been left behind. He turns against Juma for killing the elephant's friend, and he feels himself the brother of the elephant that is about to be killed. David can smell the elephant and hear him feeding in the brush just before he hears the rifle shot. Juma has wounded him, but the elephant bolts, and they follow him to the deep forest where he is dispatched in a brutal scene. The elephant looks directly at the father before he is shot, and after he falls his eyes still look at David. When David's father instructs him to kill the elephant, Davey refuses, and Juma finishes him. But all is lost, for Davey's father realizes the way Davey feels just as Davey knows that there is now a permanent break between them. (Indeed, later, as a grown man, he will entitle one of his novels about his father *The Rift.*) Davey knows that his father is perceptive and sees at once the shift in his son's attitudes: "He is not stupid. He knows all about it now and he will never trust me again" (182).

In the final scene of the killing of the elephant, Davey comes to think of the elephant as his brother, as Santiago thought of the great marlin in *The Old Man and the Sea,* and he is sickened by the elephant's suffering and despair and by his death near the bones of his old friend. Not only does Davey refuse to shoot the downed animal, he comes to hate elephant hunting (200), to love the elephant, and to admire his courage and dignity: "The elephant was his hero now as his father had been for a long time and he had thought, I did not believe he could do it when he was so old and tired" (201). It is a death on two levels: the death of the elephant and the death of Davey's love for his father.

It is all rather too much for a boy his age, just as Nick Adams observed and felt rather too much in his youth, as when he observes death in "Indian Camp," feels romantic betrayal in "Ten Indians," and is shocked by violence and senseless destruction in the war, as in "In Another Country" and "A Way You'll Never Be." As the story "Fathers and Sons" reveals, even nearly three decades later Nick still feels the emotions of these events keenly, particularly those involving his father, and the only way he knows to deal with them is in his art: "Now, knowing how it had all been, even remembering the earliest times before things had gone badly was not good remembering. If he wrote it he could get rid of it. He had gotten rid of many things by writing them. But it was still too early for that."[9] So it is with David: having once lived through a painful episode of betrayal, disillusionment, and estrangement, he is not at all eager to do so again, even though it seems inevitable from the first. What appears to be passivity and ineffectuality on his part is actually, given the insights of the hunting story, a reluctance to enter once again into the painful emotional territory he knew as a boy. Indeed, he never does act decisively on Catherine's behavior, even when she burns his stories. It is she who finally leaves him.

The story concludes in agony and emptiness, with irreparable loss and searing emotion. David's life is forever changed as he moves emotionally away from his father and away from youth, and he has been unable to come to terms with the incident over the intervening two decades. Now, through the telling of it, he seems able to face it and deal with it, if not to expiate the emotion. These realizations in the story correspond to the final events of the novel, as the marriage finally terminates. The petty quarrels between Catherine and David and her jealousy about his art lead not only to her burning of his stories but inevitably to their separation and impending divorce (214, 223, 233). What is most significant about the conclusion, however, is not that the marriage has come to its predictable end but rather that David has been able to transform the difficulties of his present life into significant art by using present emotions to capture the feelings of the past. As David realizes more and more as the novel progresses, it is only in his writing that he truly lives.

The Garden of Eden is certainly a flawed novel. As a heavily edited text it belongs in the Hemingway canon in only a qualified sense, but it is, nevertheless, a valuable document that contains some of Hemingway's most intriguing observations about the creative process along with one of the finest stories he ever wrote. That these things occur in the context of a bisexual *ménage à trois* is less intriguing than the fact that there is an essential thematic relationship between the marriage plot and the African hunting story.

It is not until David can come to terms with the painful realities of his marriage that he has the maturity and wisdom to understand fully and write about his earlier break with his father. Creativity, as David pursues it, exacts its price, but the result is deeply moving art. Through it all David Bourne emerges as Hemingway's most artistically committed protagonist, one who finds strength in his craft under the most difficult of circumstances and who uses the crisis of his personal life as a means of exploring the best of his material. David learned early that love can have painful dimensions, that estrangement comes hard; what gives him extraordinary strength as a character is his dedication to his craft and to those who can appreciate his work. For David, it is art that is the forbidden fruit that leads to knowledge of oneself and the way out of the Garden of Eden.

Notes

1.   Ernest Hemingway, *The Garden of Eden* (New York: Charles Scribner's Sons, 1986). All references are to this edition.

2.   Perhaps the most insightful of the reviews is that by Allen Josephs in *The Hemingway Review* 6 (Fall 1986): 112–14.

3.   Wilfrid Sheed, "A Farewell to Hemingstein," *The New York Review of Books* (12 June 1986): 5.

4.   Rhoda Koenig, "Adam and Eve on a Raft," *New York* 19 (12 May 1986): 137.

5.   Koenig, 137.

6. Lorian Hemingway, "Ernest Hemingway's Farewell to Art," *Rolling Stone* 5 (5 June 1986): 42.

7. Sheed, 5.

8. Folder 23, John F. Kennedy Library.

9. Ernest Hemingway, "Fathers and Sons," *The Short Stories of Ernest Hemingway* (New York: Charles Scribner's Sons, 1954) 491.

25

Hemingway's Tales of "The Real Dark"

Howard L. Hannum

Put out the light, and then put out the light. Howard Hannum has elected to perform that function for this volume with a fine essay on "Two Tales of Darkness," the last of Hemingway's stories published during his lifetime. "Get a Seeing-Eyed Dog," composed between March 1954 and 1956, and "A Man of the World," written in May and June of 1957, are often dismissed, as Carlos Baker dismisses them, as "rough and unfinished . . . rambling and pointless," evidence that Hemingway's "judgment was slipping." According to Hannum, those few critics who have given them serious consideration have endeavored to inflate these stories' reputations, arguing unconvincingly that "Get a Seeing-Eyed Dog" and "A Man of the World" are a fitting capstone to a career that produced "Big Two-Hearted River" and "The Snows of Kilimanjaro." Hannum's approach is more realistic. He makes no preposterous claims for the quality of the tales of darkness, but instead sets about demonstrating how "Get a Seeing-Eyed Dog" and "A Man of the World" represent grim reworkings of "characters and themes that were virtual clichés in [Hemingway's] fiction, even to the point of self-parody." There are no clean, well-lighted places in these stories, their blind protagonists experience nothing but darkness within and without, and finally their importance resides in their graphic depiction of "mind[s] whose creative light has failed," as Hemingway's own was failing.

Only a few critics (and not very many more readers) have ever tried to rescue Ernest Hemingway's "Two Tales of Darkness," his last stories published during his lifetime, from the obscurity into which they almost immediately fell. Written for the November 1957 centennial issue of *Atlantic Monthly*, "A Man of the World" and "Get A Seeing-Eyed Dog" formed a puzzling combination of brutality and near sentimentality, the story of the blind barroom brawler and the story of the blind writer.[1] The average reader shared Carlos Baker's estimate, that if Hemingway really thought the first was a good story, "his judgment was slipping."[2] Set against the fiction of Hemingway's prime, the stories simply seemed like evidence of the writer's decline. But Hemingway's artistic impulse in publishing only these two out of six stories he had before him in 1956–57 should not pass unnoticed. And in view of his usual genius for titles, the two tales and their "darkness" merit further analysis.

In most broad-range studies of Hemingway's fiction, these stories have drawn scant attention. Julian Smith, in the first full analysis of them, saw the two as the capstone of Hemingway's fiction, as treatments of his most powerful and typical theme: endurance under pressure. Smith saw "A Man of the World" and Blindy's acceptance of his fate *happily*, as an example of "grace under pressure."[3] Smith suggested that Philip, the blind writer in "Get a Seeing-Eyed Dog," assumed aspects of the dying Harry, in "Snows of Kilimanjaro," and of Hemingway himself. "A Man of the World," Smith claimed, plus *A Moveable Feast*, marked the geographical range of Harry/ Hemingway's uncompleted art: the western mountains whose stories he had never told and the Paris about which he had never written. The lucky rediscovery, in November 1956, of notebooks and manuscripts stored at the Paris Ritz since 1928, allowed Hemingway to depict the Paris of his prime. But, Smith argues, with his great memory failing, after his air crashes in 1954, Hemingway/Harry soon thereafter died.

Delbert Wylder also saw the "two tales" as the capstone of Hemingway's fiction—as the fusion of Hemingway's mastery of naturalistic detail with his long development of a romantic sensibility. The stories of Blindy and Philip showed both, Wylder felt. He linked Hemingway with Edgar Allan Poe, Nathaniel Hawthorne, and Herman Melville as a writer haunted by the symbols of an inner world in which self-treachery threatened to betray the human character, as it had betrayed Blindy and threatened to betray Tom and Philip.[4]

Thirty years after publication, "Two Tales of Darkness" do not indeed seem like the capstone of Hemingway's fiction, though they surely were a late effort to reformulate his art.[5] The stories covered a broad spectrum of the experience he had fashioned into his best fiction, from *In Our Time* to the tales of Macomber and Harry in Africa. Smith's caution against reading self-parody into the tales might actually have diverted criticism from a clear assessment, for Hemingway surely was reworking characters and situations that were virtual clichés in his fiction—the physical brute in his triumph (or perhaps, the artist observing him) and the uneasy lover on the verge of crisis—but his treatment carried well beyond the cliché in what would prove his final disposition of them.

The "Two Tales" are a grim reworking of the two familiar patterns, with all of the worst possibilities already realized for Blindy in the first and inevitably implied for Philip in the second. If Philip assumed aspects of Harry, he also assumed aspects of many other Hemingway lover-writers, and Blindy was the final, hopeless extension of a figure who had begun with Jim Gilmore, the brutal lover in "Up in Michigan." It seems significant that this violent figure was a central one in Hemingway's "first" completed story, and again in what was to be his "last." Violence, threatened or accomplished, is the chief trait not only of Gilmore, but also of Dick Boulton, in "The Doctor and the Doctor's Wife," of Al and Max in "The Killers," and of Ad Francis and Bugs in "The Battler." All but Boulton are seen in darkness—actually, in light set against darkness—and, considering the prominence of boxers in Hemingway's stories, the oft-repeated image suggests that he was constantly redramatizing the fight Dr. Adams had backed down from with Boulton, or one his own father had not fought the day Hemingway "found out he was a coward."[6] In the long run, this violent character emerges as pathetic.

Certain key details and the actual boxing references suggest that Hemingway wrote "A Man of the World" against the background of the Nick Adams stories. The fight between Blindy and Willie Sawyer surely relates to the one between Dr. Adams and the arrogant Boulton, the Indian lumberjack who had come to *saw* logs for him.[7] The surname Sawyer, seemingly fashioned as well from the Sawtooth Mountains outside Ketchum, Idaho, suggests Boulton, as does the Old Forester whiskey the men are drinking at the Pilot bar. Blindy's loss of both eyes of course relates to Ad Francis's loss of both ears during his career in the boxing ring. Blindy's high voice, the result of his castration, recalls the cook in "The Light of the World"; in fact, the Pilot's status as an "old days bar" recalls the dark one with free lunch in the same story. The brakeman's brutality toward Nick as well as Bugs's toward Ad in "The Battler," is of a piece with that shown in "A Man of the World."

Hemingway drew upon his early memories of boxing in the apparent model for Blindy—bantamweight champion Pete Herman (Peter Gulotta), who was gouged and blinded in the right eye by an opponent's thumb in May of 1917.[8] In his remaining fights, as Hemingway wrote to Sherwood Anderson in 1922, Herman's vision was often clouded: "He's blind in one eye you know and sometimes blood or sweat gets into the other one and they cuff him all over the place—but he must have been seeing well the night you lamped him."[9] Herman was legally blind when he retired from the ring in 1922, as the boxing world knew. Hemingway might well have taken the names of the patrons in the Pilot bar, Al Chaney and Hollis Sands, from the same sport. Pete Herman fought Young (Andy) Chaney in May 1918, and Hemingway had joined fans everywhere in regret at the accidental death of Dave Sands, the Australian aborigine, in 1952, at the height of his career.

Rather than a figure of "grace under pressure," as Julian Smith saw him, Blindy seems to be Hemingway's final, sardonic comment on the boxer-brawler he had so often watched in the ring and used in his fiction. As J.M. Ferguson notes, Blindy "thrives on the narrowness of his experience."[10] The almost unbearably brutal fight between Blindy and Willie is the final stage of such violence. Blindy is the net result, motivated only by revenge, and alive only in the adulation of those who remember his fight.

Criticism has gone astray in the analysis of "A Man of the World," which is actually Tom's story, to a large extent. Apparently the artist Thomas Hudson, whose ties to "the ranch" are well established in *Islands in the Stream*,[11] Tom wants no part now in idolizing brutality, but when the young man in the Pilot responds to it, Tom is drawn into the process all over again. Smith and Wylder are correct: the meaning of the story is in the reactions of the patrons,[12] but the chief significance is in the dynamic responses of Tom and the young man.

Philip, the lover-writer of "Get a Seeing-Eyed Dog," can also be traced back to *In Our Time:* the prominence of "the kittens" and the rain in this last story recalls the obtuse, young husband in "Cat in the Rain." Like Philip, he sits in bed, but smugly reading and unaware of his wife's deep need for "that kitty" (which she goes out into the driving rain for), unaware that her need may in some way be met. Both stories are set on the stormy Italian seacoast, and Philip twice echoes the young wife's desire for spring. The basic character Philip of course appears again in many variations in Hemingway's fiction, with a good deal more awareness of his situation, but it is as Macomber or Harry of the African stories that he relates most closely to the blind lover of this last appearance. Harry's wife, rummaging the book bag, anticipates the review of *New Yorkers* by Philip's wife. The former cannot take dictation for Harry's "dying" stories, and Philip's wife needs practice with the voice recorder. She doesn't need much practice with the rifle, though, having killed her lion, which is presumably on the way back from the taxidermist. The basic Harry character is weakening, and this wife does things on her own now.

Hemingway wanted the "Two Tales" to relate not only to his earlier fiction but also to each other, as the many complementary details in the stories make plain. The verbal tricks familiar in early stories have become black humor in the "Two Tales": Blindy waits until it is "good and dark" (489) before starting for Jessup, and Philip refers to doing "such wonderful things in the dark" (492) as if he actually distinguished it. With "small pus icicles out of both eyes," says Tom, "[Blindy] didn't look really very good" (493). The gruesome account of the gouging and stomping (castration) borders on the fantastic humor of the American frontier. Philip's wife blunders, being unable to wait until "we see" her lion (488). Ironically, while Blindy's growing "strong" is disgusting, Philip's doing so is a hopeful sign, and where Blindy feels Willie's face out of hatred, Philip feels his wife's out of love. Blindy and Willie have destroyed each other by violence; Philip and his wife are destroying each other by intended kindness (which he knows cannot last).

Blindy has come from The Flats to Jessup, just as Philip left "the flats" in Africa to return to Venice and contemplate "the flats" on the way to Torcello. Each of the victims has returned to a place familiar before his blinding, so that he has some orientation to the scene, but from memory, rather than current observation.

Each of the tales is a monologue by an artist comtemplating blindness as an ultimate condition,[13] either to behold in his material or to endure in himself. Each narrator is on the verge of internal treachery, as Wylder observes, about to betray himself and another into moral darkness. Both narrators are victims of memory: Tom's is all too clear about the horror he avoids, and Philip's is rapidly returning with an unspoken horror that he does not seem to sense. In each case, a story within a story contains the horror.

Seated at the Pilot bar as Blindy enters, Tom records the little drama of Blindy and the young man's playing the slot machines in powerful naturalistic detail, even to Blindy's plaguing him for quarters and rubbing each one. Tom's physical and moral revulsion for Blindy reflects his own guilt at having watched, and enjoyed, the fight with Willie. The horror that threatens Tom is that he might again betray himself into the same lust for brutality. Thus, he twice lies to avoid involvement with Blindy, and calls him "Blackie" when he does order him a drink. Blindy also lies, about why Willie put him out of his car, until the young man's curiosity to know his story puts him back into the limelight. Then he admits that he felt Willie's face in revenge. Tom, the lifelong fan of brutality in sports, struggles to suppress approval of Blindy in front of the young man, whose heavy shoes (Oregon Cities) mark him as a modern successor to Nick Adams. Like Nick (or Jack London or Stanley Ketchel the boxer—both heroes of Hemingway's youth), he is hiking or making his way through "the world."[14]

In Blindy, Hemingway has drawn the substance of horror. Of all the boxers he had left in hopeless conditions: Ole Andreson awaiting "the mob," Ad Francis in the "care" of Bugs, and Jack Brennan with "a busted gut," in "Fifty Grand," Blindy is the most repulsive and least sympathetic. In his entrance to the Pilot, he recalls a classic of American folklore, the "dog-dirty miner" of Robert Service's "The Shooting of Dan McGrew." The miner and Dan had fought over the love of "a gal named Lou"; obviously, the unrevealed motive for Blindy's fight with Willie could have involved a woman, but, if so, neither has retained her, in this world without women. Blindy also recalls another grotesque of American literature, John Steinbeck's whimpering junk-yard worker with the ugly, squirming eye socket in *The Grapes of Wrath,* which perhaps supplied the image of Blindy's eye as a grape. Like Blindy, Steinbeck's character sleeps in a shack behind the yard.

It is Tom who halts the exodus from the Pilot and thus sets up both the young man's involvement and the renewal of his own involvement with Blindy. Tom at first disclaims memory of Blindy's fight, but his resistance collapses as the young man becomes captivated by the gory account. Not only does Tom order Blindy's drink, but he joins the conversation: "'You don't want to see him,' I told the stranger" (495). Tom's self-treachery starts the cycle again, and the young man is caught up.

Shadows of horror beset Philip, seated in bed, as he tries to firm up his romantic resolve to send his wife on a vacation from her "nurse's" chores for him. His guilt at having "hurt her so much" prompts a "Plan" (490) to relieve her, since she has been so good and "she was not built to be . . . this sort of good" (488). But her loyalty is unwavering. She is attempting to be a seeing-eye dog to Philip, but he sees that she cannot sustain this. In the analogy, his blindness (or anyone's) would require a "seeing-eye*d*" dog, one with the dogness previously trained out of it, not a dog that would have to submit to the process *after* it had known a full life. Beneath the conscious love, however, loom ominous threats to the pair. His wife's caution not to remember too much today suggests that Philip may one day dredge up details of horror. And the similarities to the Macomber situation subtly suggest that the two elements moving toward each other, his memory and her lion, may destroy Philip. The manner and the cause of his blinding still seem lost in his memory, in "the real dark," from which he is emerging. Indeed, the blunt words of the hunter Robert Wilson to Macomber may hold the key: "In Africa no woman ever misses her lion and no white man ever bolts."[15] The coincidence of an injury or wound to the head, in the safari situation, with the wife a very capable shot, would start suspicions in the reader's mind, Hemingway certainly saw. He has Philip living in a corridor, which grows shorter as memory opens doors into it: "the real dark" might live in front of him.

Disgust suddenly flashes beneath the wife's love, when she tells him not to be "so bloody noble" about their condition, but she quickly repents and kisses him (489). She senses his sexual fears about her vacation, as Wylder has noted.[16] The masculine crew of the dhow in Africa, the gulls and terns on the flats toward Torcello, and the talk of sleeping with "any old pillow" signal the couple's fears. His impotence, or feeling of inadequacy in their sex "in the dark now," shows through to her, and she seems to fear her own self-treachery in being sent away.

Wylder's contention that Philip shows a new, long-developing, romantic sensibility in Hemingway's fiction (in the attempt to show generosity toward the wife) does have merit, but it is undercut by Philip's own excesses: "in lots of ways we couldn't have it better" (489), and "I must learn to take good care of her in every way I can" (490). In the last several paragraphs of the story, Hemingway introduces the pillow and the kittens that would later disturb many readers of *Islands in the Stream.* It is clear that the wife will not long survive mawkish luncheons "by the fire in our old fine place" (491).

Philip is a final, futile stage of the romantic. A counterpart to Blindy, he is reduced to the state of Jake Barnes, introducing Brett Ashley to Romero, despite what will follow, because he cannot prevent it. Philip sees that he will have to risk nearly all of his wife to preserve even a small part worth saving. His self-treachery is urging her to become "a woman of the world."

In these last two stories published during his lifetime, Hemingway certainly attempted an artistic statement. His chronological rearrangement of the pair alone would indicate this. The original situations and their characters look like simple metaphors of his early fiction, at first reading, but he has given them a symbolic complexity that seems to speak for his whole career. This final view of life is devastating—Philip could well have brought it back from "the real dark." Neither brutality nor sentiment, life without women nor life with women can escape the pervading darkness. Both the shadow and the substance of horror stalk humanity, which seems to have lost ground everywhere in its fight for "grace." The autumn darkness of Nick Adams has become winter darkness, and the glamor of a Stanley Ketchel has yielded to the despair of a Blindy, who retires to "the back" of the Pilot bar. This is what the young man will ultimately find in the world. Where death waited for Macomber and Harry, it is life, ironically, that waits for Philip.

The really frightening darkness—what Philip called "the real dark"—seems to be out in front of the characters and their author, as well as behind them. The rare renewal of Blindy's triumph will not last longer than the drink in his hand: the story ends on that irony. Tom has relapsed into worship of the horror that he lied to avoid and has condoned it for the young man. Philip's escape from amnesia, only a matter of time apparently, threatens to reveal facts about the safari that will destroy him.

What the stories suggest about Hemingway is alarming. The physical brutality that had long been a natural part of his fiction had been escaping control in later years in both his life and his writing. Tom's response to Blindy is really an extension of Thomas Hudson's approval of the severe beating Roger gave the drunken boat owner in *Islands in the Stream* [17] and Colonel Cantwell's senseless battering of two drunken sailors in *Across the River and into the Trees.*[18] Hudson even had a "literary" justification for Roger, "If he could write the way he fought on the dock, it could be cruel, but it would be very good."[19] Hemingway's aggressive streak, loosed by alcohol, did not really fit a context. The flow of alcohol for Cantwell and for Hudson (at the Floridita) is unrealistic. The obliging headwaiter at the Gritti keeps the wine and martinis flowing at such a rate that Cantwell need make no moral choice, but Hudson does have Eddy to reassure him that even two beers with breakfast do not constitute alcoholism.[20] Although the drinking is under much better control in the "Two Tales," both Tom and Philip are headed toward another drink at the end.

Philip Young saw Thomas Hudson the painter and Roger the writer as "the authorial ego [grown] so great it took two characters to contain it" in *Islands in the Stream.*[21] The same ego appeared to be fragmenting by 1956– 57. Although Hemingway had artistic control over Tom and Philip in the final versions of the "Two Tales," Philip did remain "Tommy" as late as the last typescript of "Get a Seeing-Eyed Dog."[22] The four stories of World War II present a central figure who is really two additional characters: a tough military commander of "irregulars" and a self-centered war correspondent—with the one personality too quickly shifting into the other. Arranged in a chronological sequence, from the liberation of Paris in August 1944 to the 22nd Infantry Regiment's assault on the Siegfried Line in September, the stories are sad evidence of Hemingway's failing genius.[23]

A sudden reversal in Hemingway's relations with Mary helped motivate the "romantic sensibility" that Wylder saw in "Get a Seeing-Eyed Dog." The story dramatizes the reversal, which followed the airplane crashes in Africa in 1954, as the wealth of autobiographical detail suggests. Philip's apartment is a composite of the familiar Gritti Palace Hotel, Venice, and the fireplace in the inn at Torcello ("the fine old place by the fire"). Philip's blindness was both Hemingway's erysipelas in 1949 and his loss of sight after the second crash. The injured Hemingway might well have had distrustful thoughts about Mary's shopping trip to London during his recuperation, and of course the irony of "don't count on a wife" was implied in the need for the dog, at one level. But in fact, Hemingway threw a romantic coloring over the incidents. His artistic reworking of relations with Mary seems quite predictable in retrospect. His public abuse of her and his "flirtations" with other women became Philip's concern for his wife, and Mary's hasty departure became the wife's staunch loyalty.

The reversal in his relations with Mary was only one of a number that began to appear in Hemingway's life, as well as his fiction, at this time. If he stayed at home and waited for Mary in Venice, he would do so much more often now, everywhere, and would depend upon others to drive cars and manage daily tasks for him. Hemingway, of all people, turned against skiers (his own incapacity and his jealousy of Mary no doubt fueled this).[24] Joyce's eye shade was no longer funny when Philip/Hemingway had to wear it. And some things had begun happening to him in ways that he had made them happen to his whipping boys, such as Scott Fitzgerald and Macomber, in his earlier fiction. Cantwell's death, after all, was essentially "that rummy Fitzgerald's," but by late 1953 Hemingway's own drinking had brought a severe reprimand from Philip Percival. Then too, Hemingway had just stumbled through something like Macomber's disgrace, gut-shooting a lion that Denis Zaphiro had to kill off in the grass for him, though Hemingway was given a triumphal ride by the native boys.[25] He did not indeed *bolt* before a charging lion, as Macomber had, but he walked away from the wounded animal. Robert Wilson's words, and the code they reflected, surely came back to Hemingway. Nevertheless, he would claim, most ungraciously, in a *Sports Illustrated* article, "Miss Mary's Lion," to have broken the back of her lion on 7 December 1953.[26] Outwardly unembarrassed by all of this, during a holiday plane trip in January 1954, he showed Mary where Pauline "got" her first lion on the Serengheti Plain in 1933. He was apparently impervious to the disparity in his own conduct, generously letting Pauline have "his" lion 20 years earlier but meanly claiming "Miss Mary's" (Denis's) on the present occasion.

In the spring of 1954, and for much of his remaining life, Hemingway was a good deal more like Philip than he was like Tom. Like the central figures of his last two completed stories, Hemingway was on the verge of "the real dark," that unarticulated horror worthy of Poe, Hawthorne, or Melville. Tom had watched Blindy slip into it, Philip held his vague recollection of it, and Hemingway lived in dread of it. Even as he was telling George Plimpton at about this time, "Once writing has become your major vice and greatest pleasure only death can stop it,"[27] he had to see that something other than death had stopped it for him. The corridor of time in which he had left Philip had its own special application to him. More than just his memory, Hemingway had lost his great capacity to bring art and life together on the page—he who had taught an era to do so now stared at the blank page. The four war stories and the uncompleted long narratives defied his waning skills; the two stories he did ready for the press were depressingly negative. The darkness that haunted Hemingway's final years was in the mind whose creative light had failed. Like Philip, he awaited "the real dark," but for him it was in death.

Notes

1. Ernest Hemingway, "Two Tales of Darkness," *The Atlantic Monthly* 200.5 (November 1957): 64–68. Parenthetical notes in this article refer to the texts of the stories in *The Complete Short Stories of Ernest Hemingway*, Finca Vigía edn. (New York: Charles Scribner's Sons, 1987).

2. Carlos Baker, *Ernest Hemingway: A Life Story* (New York: Charles Scribner's Sons, 1969) 538.

3. Julian Smith, "Eyeless in Wyoming, Blind in Venice: Hemingway's Last Stories," *Connecticut Review* 4 (April 1971): 12.

4. Delbert E. Wylder, "Internal Treachery in the Last Published Short Stories of Ernest Hemingway," in *Hemingway In Our Time*, ed. Richard Astro and Jackson J. Benson (Corvallis: Oregon State UP, 1974) 54.

5. Kenneth G. Johnston in *The Tip of the Iceberg: Hemingway and the Short Story* (Greenwood: Penkevill, 1987) 250, calls the stories "a pair of disappointing 'tales of darkness' that give melancholy evidence of [Hemingway's] diminishing power and judgment."

6. See Philip Young, *Ernest Hemingway: A Reconsideration* (University Park: Pennsylvania State UP, 1966) 33n, and Jeffrey Meyers, *Hemingway: A Biography* (New York: Harper & Row, 1985) 212

7. Ernest Hemingway, "The Doctor and the Doctor's Wife," *The Nick Adams Stories*, ed. Philip Young (New York: Charles Scribner's Sons, 1972) 22–23.

8. Peter Heller, *"In This Corner . . . !"* (New York: Simon and Schuster, 1973) 52, and Bert Randolph Sugar, *The 100 Greatest Boxers of All Time* (New York: Bonanza, 1984) 129.

9. Hemingway to Sherwood Anderson, 9 March 1922, *Ernest Hemingway: Selected Letters, 1917–1961*, ed. Carlos Baker (New York: Charles Scribner's Sons, 1981) 63.

10. J. M. Ferguson, "Hemingway's Man of the World," *Arizona Quarterly* 33 (1977): 116–20.

11. Delbert Wylder's identification of Tom as Thomas Hudson seems quite plausible and natural to the reader of the Hemingway canon, since the character would fit Hudson, removed to the West he loved, after the deaths of his sons (which would partly motivate his interest in the young man, as well). Tom's resistance to the fight suggests that he is a man of some sensitivity, as does his narrative skill. His gift for perspective, implied throughout the story, argues his identity as a painter. The physical circumstances of Tom's sitting in the bar echo those in the Floridita Bar in *Islands in the Stream*.

12. Smith, 10; Wylder, 58.

13. As Julian Smith observes, "It is almost as though Hemingway had written the story in the first-person and at the last moment substituted "he" for "I". Smith, 14.

14. In his first typescript of this story, Hemingway crossed out "Whitey" seven times and substituted "Blackie." See item 565, John F. Kennedy Library. Perhaps he even considered suggesting a relationship between Blindy and Stanley Ketchel, whose "whiteness" had been so stressed by the prostitute, Peroxide, in "The Light of the World," but

decided against it. At any rate, a relationship between the young man in the Pilot and Nick "on the road" seems to emerge.

15. Hemingway, "The Short Happy Life of Francis Macomber," *The Short Stories of Ernest Hemingway* (New York: Charles Scribner's Sons, 1966) 7. The flashback technique of the story allows for the repetition of the word "bolt," to Macomber's embarrassment.

16. Wylder, 63.

17. Hemingway, *Islands in the Stream* (New York: Charles Scribner's Sons, 1970) 38–41.

18. Hemingway, *Across the River and into the Trees* (New York: Charles Scribner's Sons, 1950) 283–84.

19. Hemingway, *Islands in the Stream*, 98.

20. Hemingway, *Islands in the Stream*, 100.

21. Young, 235.

22. Items 424 and 425, John F. Kennedy Library.

23. Hemingway's "irregulars" are shown resting at the Paris Ritz in "A Room on the Garden Side," in skirmishes with retreating Germans in "Indian Country and the White Army" and "Black Ass at the Cross Roads," and then in the approach to the Siegfried Line in "The Monument." "A Room on the Garden Side" and "Black Ass at the Cross Road" are far better integrated than the other two stories, which fall into digressions too often to advance the narrative. Hemingway's eye for detail was still good, but he could no longer organize his material. The narrator's confused identities rob the sequence of unity; so too does the focus, which shifts from the apparent narrative to the narrator far too often. The sequence is never really brought to a climax. See "A Room on the Garden Side," item 764, John F. Kennedy Library; "Indian Country and the White Army," item 496b; and "The Monument," item 580a. "Black Ass at the Cross Roads" appears in *The Complete Short Stories of Ernest Hemingway*, 579–89.

24. In item 565, John F. Kennedy Library, a typescript of "The Man of the World," Hemingway identified the "dudes" of the published version as "ski dudes," who ski by fixed dates, rather than by actual conditions on the slopes. Again, in a letter to John Dos Passos, 29 May 1949 (Outgoing Correspondence Box 3, John F. Kennedy Library), he wrote, "What makes the skiers so fragile now is the funiculars and the telefericas, which keeps them from ever having to climb." Mary's skiing trips (often without him) upset him.

25. Under the cover of Mary's loyal silence, Hemingway claimed the kill on this lion, 10 September 1953, as he was claiming other kills not his own (see note 26). He repeated the claim in a letter to Bernard Berenson five days later, but placed the kill "Yesterday" (15 September 1953, *Letters*, 825). Bernice Kert formed the unflattering inference of Hemingway's deceit. (See *The Hemingway Women* [New York: W.W. Norton, 1983], which Baker had stopped short of in 1969 [*Life*, 515].) Zaphiro confirmed in a letter to Jeffrey Meyers that Hemingway had not killed a lion on the 1953 safari (Meyers, 502).

26. Hemingway's public version of incidents on the safari no doubt was substantially that which appeared in *Sports Illustrated* 35 (20 December 1971): 5, 40–45, 57–66; 36 (3 January 1972): 24–46; and 37 (10 January 1972): 22–30, 43–50. The articles give the kill on Mary's lion to Hemingway ("You broke his back," 36: 42b) and demean Mary as "too small to shoot a lion," having gotten this one under "tarnished circumstances" (36: 24–46; 37: 23). Mary supported this version for many years, but later told Bernice Kert that

Denis had killed "her" lion. See Kert, 473. Mary also revealed in *How It Was* (New York: Ballantine 1976) 357, that she had protested to her husband about the morality of his posing, on 1 October 1953, for Earl Theisen, a *Look* magazine photographer, with a leopard that might well have been killed by Mayito Menocal (who was completely out-shooting Ernest on the safari). Both Meyers (501) and Kenneth S. Lynn (*Hemingway* [New York: Simon and Schuster, 1987] 570) cite evidence that Hemingway's excessive drinking ruined his shot and that his jealousy of Menocal's marksmanship completely unsettled him—Hemingway claimed other hunters' kills, but *did not shoot a lion* (italics added).

27. George Plimpton, "An Interview with Ernest Hemingway," *Paris Review* 18 (Spring 1958): 85–108.

Contributors

Susan F. Beegel earned her Ph.D. in 1986 from Yale University, where she studied as a Ruth Ingersoll Goldmark Fellow in English literature. Beegel is the author of a book, *Hemingway's Craft of Omission: Four Manuscript Examples*, and of essays on Ernest Hemingway, Herman Melville, Edgar Allan Poe, Thomas Hardy, and Dante Gabriel Rossetti, as well as on composition pedagogy. A member of the board of the Ernest Hemingway Foundation, Beegel has taught English and American Studies on Nantucket Island for the University of Massachusetts at Boston.

Warren Bennett is Professor of English at the University of Regina in Regina, Canada, where he teaches American literature. Bennett is best known among Hemingway scholars for his ground-breaking essay, "Character, Irony, and Resolution in 'A Clean, Well-Lighted Place,'" published in *American Literature* (March 1970).

Gerry Brenner is Professor of English at the University of Montana. He is the author of *Concealments in Hemingway's Works* and, with Earl Rovit, the co-author of *Ernest Hemingway*. Among his many articles on Ernest Hemingway, "Are We Going to Hemingway's *Feast?*," *American Literature*, December 1982, is particularly noteworthy. A former Fulbright Senior Lecturer on American literature in Yugoslavia, Brenner has also published on Chaucer, Shakespeare, Austen, Browning, Cooper, Thoreau, Fitzgerald, Updike, and Morrison.

Lawrence Broer, Professor of English at the University of South Florida, earned his Ph.D. from Bowling Green State University. The author of two books, *Hemingway's Spanish Tragedy* and *Sanity Plea: Schizophrenia in the Novels of Kurt Vonnegut*, Broer has also edited a study of contemporary writers called *Counter Currents*. In 1981 and 1984, he served as Fulbright Lecturer at the University of Paris. His numerous essays on twentieth-century literature have appeared in such journals as *Modern Fiction Studies,* *Studies in Short Fiction,* and *The Southern Humanities Review.*

ROBERT COLTRANE has been a member of the English department at Lock Haven University of Pennsylvania since 1983, having previously served as Director of Public Relations since 1969. He is currently a Ph.D. candidate at Pennsylvania State University, specializing in twentieth-century American literature. His most recent publication, a study of William Styron's collection of nonfiction pieces, *This Quiet Dust,* appeared in the special Styron issue of *Papers on Language and Literature* (Fall 1987).

STEPHEN COOPER is Assistant Professor of English at Troy State University in Troy, Alabama, and assistant editor for reviews of the *Alabama Literary Review.* He earned his B.A. from the University of Delaware and his M.A. and Ph.D. from the University of North Carolina at Chapel Hill. His book, *The Politics of Ernest Hemingway,* was published by UMI Research Press in 1987. His most recent publication is "Politics over Art: Hemingway's 'Nobody Ever Dies,'" *Studies in Short Fiction* (Spring 1988).

SCOTT DONALDSON, Cooley Professor of English at William and Mary, is a biographer and critic who has served on the board of editors of *American Literature,* written the annual Fitzgerald-Hemingway chapter in *American Literary Scholarship,* and published a number of books, among them *By Force of Will: The Life and Art of Ernest Hemingway* (1977), *Fool for Love: F. Scott Fitzgerald* (1983), and *John Cheever: A Biography* (1988).

ROBERT E. FLEMING is a Professor of English at the University of New Mexico. He has published articles on Ernest Hemingway in *Arizona Quarterly,* *The Hemingway Review,* *North Dakota Quarterly,* *Studies in American Fiction,* and *Notes on Modern American Literature.*

LINDA GAJDUSEK has an M.A. in Literature from Columbia University, where she studied as a Woodrow Wilson Fellow, and a second M.A. in Teaching English as a Second Language from San Francisco State University, where she currently teaches ESL. Her article, "Toward Wider Use of Literature in ESL: Why and How," recently published in *TESOL Quarterly,* and her ESL textbook, *Literary Contexts for ESL Writers: Connecting Form and Meaning,* co-authored with Deborah van Dommelen, attempt to build a new bridge between these currently separate disciplines.

ROBERT E. GAJDUSEK is Professor of English at San Francisco State University. The author of two books, *Hemingway's Paris* and *Hemingway and*

Joyce: A Study in Debt and Payment, Gajdusek has also published articles and book reviews in such journals as *The Hemingway Review, The D. H. Lawrence Miscellany, The D. H. Lawrence Review, American Imago,* and *The American Scholar.* He is currently at work on a pair of books, *Hemingway's Italy* and *Hemingway in Key West and Cuba.*

MIMI REISEL GLADSTEIN has served as Chair of the English and philosophy departments at the University of Texas at El Paso. She is the author of *The Ayn Rand Companion* and *The Indestructible Woman in Faulkner, Hemingway, and Steinbeck.*

HOWARD L. HANNUM earned his M.A. and Ph.D. from the University of Pennsylvania. Associate Professor of English at La Salle University, he has published articles in *Studies in Short Fiction, The Hemingway Review,* and *Arizona Quarterly,* as well as in *Up in Michigan: Proceedings of the First National Conference of the Hemingway Society.* Hannum is currently at work on a study titled "Nick Adams on the Road—to War," an analysis of eight short stories, and on "Hemingway's Unpublished Stories of World War II."

BRUCE HENRICKSEN teaches composition, literature, and theory at Loyola University in New Orleans. The Criticism and Theory Editor of the *New Orleans Review,* he has also edited a book entitled *Murray Kreiger and Contemporary Critical Theory.* Henricksen has published widely in a number of distinguished journals. Particularly noteworthy are two essays on Conrad: "The Construction of the Narrator in *The Nigger of the Narcissus,*" *PMLA,* October 1988, and "*Heart of Darkness* and Gnostic Myth," printed in Harold Bloom's anthology, *Modern Critical Interpretations: Joseph Conrad's* Heart of Darkness.

ALLEN JOSEPHS is University Research Professor at the University of West Florida. An internationally recognized scholar of Spanish culture, he has published more than 50 articles on Spain in scholarly journals as well as in *The New Republic, The Atlantic Monthly,* and *The New York Times Book Review.* Josephs has translated Federico García Lorca, and is the author of *White Wall of Spain: The Mysteries of Andalusian Culture,* with a foreword by James A. Michener. He is currently at work on a book about Hemingway and Spain.

GERALD LOCKLIN teaches at California State University, Long Beach. The essay in this volume is the tenth resulting from his collaboration with Charles Stetler on the works of Ernest Hemingway. Locklin has also published on Nathanael West, Charles Bukowski, Gerald Haslam, John Fante, and others. He is the author of over a thousand poems, stories, reviews, articles, and interviews in periodicals and anthologies. Three of his books have appeared in translation in West Germany, with a fourth in progress. His poetry can be found regularly in *The Wormwood Review* and *Poetry/LA*.

GEORGE MONTEIRO, Professor of English at Brown University, is a scholar-critic, translator, and poet. His most recent books are *Robert Frost and the New England Renaissance, Self-Analysis and Thirty Other Poems by Fernando Pessoa,* and *Double Weaver's Knot. Poems.*

JAMES NAGEL is Professor of English at Northeastern University in Boston. He is also the founder and editor of the scholarly journal *Studies in American Fiction,* now in its seventeenth year. Among his publications are ten books and more than thirty articles on American literature, among them *Stephen Crane and Literary Impressionism* and *Ernest Hemingway: The Writer in Context.* He is a past president of the Hemingway Society.

ERIK NAKJAVANI is Professor of Humanities at the University of Pittsburgh/Bradford. His recent articles on Hemingway include "The Aesthetics of Silence: Hemingway's 'The Art of the Short Story'," "The Aesthetics of the Visible and Invisible: Hemingway and Cezanne," "Knowledge as a Mode of Power: Robert Jordan as an Intellectual Hero," "Ernest Hemingway's Robert Jordan and Carlos Fuentes' Lorenzo Cruz: An Intertextual Study," "Intellectuals as Militants in Hemingway's *For Whom the Bell Tolls* and Malraux's *L'Espoir:* A Comparative Study," and "Hemingway on Non-Thinking."

ANN PUTNAM teaches English at the University of Puget Sound. She has published essays in *The Hemingway Review, The Western American Literature Quarterly,* and *The South Dakota Review,* and is currently at work on a book treating Ernest Hemingway's short fiction.

MICHAEL S. REYNOLDS is Professor of English at North Carolina State University. He is the author of numerous works on Ernest Hemingway, including such books as *Hemingway's First War: The Making of A Farewell to Arms, Hemingway's Reading, 1910–1940, The Young Hemingway,* and The Sun Also Rises: A Novel of the Twenties. Reynolds is presently completing a biography of Hemingway's Paris years.

PHILLIP SIPIORA is an Assistant Professor of English at the University of South Florida, where he has taught a variety of courses in the history of rhetoric, critical theory, and American literature since earning his Ph.D. in English from the University of Texas at Austin. He has published on classical rhetoric and American literature, with articles on the relationship between classical rhetoric and contemporary applications, and essays on Hemingway and D. H. Lawrence. Sipiora is currently completing a study, *Kairos: A Rhetoric of Time and Context,* which attempts to integrate classical rhetorical theory with contemporary rhetorical practice.

PAUL SMITH is Goodwin Professor of English at Trinity College, Connecticut, and has published articles on Melville, Shelley, critical theory, and the English curriculum, as well as on the short stories of Ernest Hemingway. He is the author of *A Reader's Guide to the Short Stories of Ernest Hemingway,* and the co-author, with Robert Foulke, of *An Anatomy of Literature.* Smith served as the first president of the Hemingway Society.

JAMES STEINKE teaches writing at Boston University. He is a Fellow of the South Coast Writing Project in Santa Barbara and formerly taught literature and composition at the University of California at Santa Barbara. Steinke has won two first prizes for Best Essay from *Spectrum* with articles on "Cat in the Rain" and *The Sun Also Rises.* In various papers and articles he has conducted extensive explorations of inferable states of feeling in Hemingway's characters, and has two books on the subject now in progress.

CHARLES STETLER teaches at California State University, Long Beach, and has written ten articles on Ernest Hemingway in collaboration with Gerald Locklin. Stetler specializes in modern American and modern British literature. He has published on James Purdy and e.e. cummings, and co-authored an article on Richard Brautigan. His other publications include two books of poetry and more than 200 poems in little magazines.

H. R. STONEBACK is Professor of English at the State University of New York/New Paltz. He has published numerous essays on Durrell, Faulkner, Hemingway, and O'Connor, as well as his own fiction, poetry, and song. Stoneback is the editor of *Selected Stories of William Faulkner,* the first major translator into Chinese of Faulkner's work, and the author of *Cartographers of the Deus Loci,* a volume of poetry. Stoneback has lectured on Hemingway and Faulkner around the world, and been a Senior Fulbright Professor at Peking University, and a Visiting Professor at the University of Paris.

SUSAN SWARTZLANDER earned her Ph.D. in December 1988 from Pennsylvania State University, where her doctoral dissertation treated James Joyce's use of history. Now a Visiting Assistant Professor at Bucknell University, she is at work with Marilyn Mumford co-editing a collection of essays on May Sarton, and "challenging the canon" with a study of Norah Hoult, an Irish author who produced 30 novels between 1928 and 1982. Swartzlander has published articles in such journals as *Southern Studies, Studies in Short Fiction, Studies in American Fiction, James Joyce Quarterly,* and *Shaw: The Annual.*

BICKFORD SYLVESTER teaches at the University of British Columbia and has just completed a critical study of Hemingway's later fiction. His early Hemingway publications were on *The Old Man and the Sea,* and he is now preparing the volume on that novel for the new explication, commentary, and interpretation series on Hemingway's major works to be published by Southern Illinois University Press. Sylvester is also at work editing an anthology of essays reflecting critical recognition of Hemingway's allusive method. For fifteen years he has guided sports fisherman on the coastal waters of Washington and British Columbia.

Bibliography

Principal Collections

Bancroft Library. University of California. Berkeley, California.
Charles Scribner's Sons Archives. Princeton University Library. Princeton, New Jersey.
Ernest Hemingway Papers. John Fitzgerald Kennedy Library. Boston, Massachusetts.
Humanities Research Center. University of Texas. Austin, Texas.
Lilly Library. Indiana University. Bloomington, Indiana.
University of Wisconsin Library. Milwaukee, Wisconsin.

Published Works by Ernest Hemingway

Across the River and into the Trees. New York: Charles Scribner's Sons, 1950.
"African Journal." *Sports Illustrated* 35 (20 December 1971): 5, 40–52, 57–66; 36 (3 January 1972): 26–46; 37 (10 January 1972): 22–30.
"The Art of the Short Story." *The Paris Review* 79 (Spring 1981): 85–102.
By-Line: Ernest Hemingway, Selected Articles and Dispatches of Four Decades. Ed. William White. New York: Charles Scribner's Sons, 1967.
The Complete Short Stories of Ernest Hemingway. Finca Vigía edn. New York: Charles Scribner's Sons, 1987.
The Dangerous Summer. New York: Charles Scribner's Sons, 1985.
Dateline Toronto: Hemingway's Complete Toronto Star *Dispatches, 1920–1924.* Ed. William White. New York: Charles Scribner's Sons, 1985.
Death in the Afternoon. New York: Charles Scribner's Sons, 1932.
Ernest Hemingway: On Writing. Ed. Larry Phillips. New York: Charles Scribner's Sons, 1984.
Ernest Hemingway: Selected Letters, 1917–1961. Ed. Carlos Baker. New York: Charles Scribner's Sons, 1981.
A Farewell to Arms. New York: Charles Scribner's Sons, 1929.
The Fifth Column and the First Forty-nine Stories. New York: Charles Scribner's Sons, 1938.
The Fifth Column and Four Stories of the Spanish Civil War. New York: Charles Scribner's Sons, 1969.
For Whom the Bell Tolls. New York: Charles Scribner's Sons, 1940.
The Garden of Eden. New York: Charles Scribner's Sons, 1986.
Green Hills of Africa. New York: Charles Scribner's Sons, 1935.
To Have and Have Not. New York: Charles Scribner's Sons, 1937.
"The Heat and the Cold." *Verve* 1.2 (Spring 1938): 46.
Hemingway. Ed. Malcolm Cowley. New York: Viking, 1944.

The Hemingway Reader. New York: Charles Scribner's Sons, 1953.

"Hemingway's Spanish Civil War Dispatches." Ed. William B. Watson. *The Hemingway Review* 7.2 (Spring 1988): 4–92.

"Homage to Ezra." *This Quarter* 1.1 (Spring 1925): 221–25.

in our time. Paris: Three Mountains Press, 1924. Facs. edn. Bloomfield Hills: Bruccoli Clark Books, 1977.

In Our Time. 1925. New York: Charles Scribner's Sons, 1955.

Islands in the Stream. New York: Charles Scribner's Sons, 1970.

Men at War: The Best War Stories of All Time. Ed. Ernest Hemingway. 1942. Rpt. New York: Bramhall House, 1979.

Men Without Women. New York: Charles Scribner's Sons, 1927.

A Moveable Feast. New York: Charles Scribner's Sons, 1964.

The Nick Adams Stories. Ed. Philip Young. New York: Charles Scribner's Sons, 1972.

The Old Man and the Sea. New York: Charles Scribner's Sons, 1952.

Preface to *The Torrents of Spring. Fitzgerald/Hemingway Annual* (1977): 112.

The Short Stories of Ernest Hemingway. New York: Charles Scribner's Sons, 1954, 1966.

The Spanish Earth. Introd. Jasper Wood. Cleveland: J. B. Savage, 1938.

The Sun Also Rises. New York: Charles Scribner's Sons, 1926.

Three Stories and Ten Poems. Paris: Contact, 1923.

The Torrents of Spring. New York: Charles Scribner's Sons, 1926.

Winner Take Nothing. New York: Charles Scribner's Sons, 1933.

Secondary Sources

Abrams, M. H. *A Glossary of Literary Terms.* 3rd edn. New York: Holt, Rinehart, & Winston, 1971.

Ackroyd, Peter. *T. S. Eliot.* London: Hamish Hamilton, 1984.

Adams, Richard P. "Sunrise Out of the Wasteland." *Tulane Studies in English* 9 (1959): 119–31.

Anderson, Charles R. "Hemingway's Other Style." *Modern Language Notes* 76 (May 1961): 434–42.

Anderson, Sherwood, *Dark Laughter.* 1925. Cleveland: World, 1942.

———. *Letters of Sherwood Anderson.* Ed. Howard Mumford Jones and Walter B. Rideout. Boston: Little, Brown, 1953.

Aristotle. *The "Art" of Rhetoric.* Trans. J. H. Freese. 1926. Cambridge: Harvard UP, 1975.

Armistead, Myra. "Hemingway's 'An Alpine Idyll.'" *Studies in Short Fiction* 14 (Summer 1977): 255–58.

Astro, Richard and Jackson J. Benson. *Hemingway In Our Time.* Corvallis: Oregon State UP, 1974.

Atkins, John. *The Art of Ernest Hemingway: His Work and Personality.* London: Spring, 1964.

Austen, Jane. *Jane Austen: Letters, 1796–1817.* Ed. R. W. Chapman. London: Oxford UP, 1975.

Bahktin, Mikhail. "Discourse in the Novel." In *The Dialogic Imagination.* Ed. Michael Holquist. Austin: U of Texas P, 1981. 259–422.

———. *Problems of Dostoevsky's Poetics.* Trans. Caryl Emerson. Minneapolis: U of Minnesota P, 1984.

Baker, Carlos. *Ernest Hemingway: A Life Story.* New York: Charles Scribner's Sons, 1969. Paperback edn., New York: Bantam, 1970.

———. *Hemingway: The Writer as Artist.* 4th edn. Prince-ton: Princeton UP, 1972.

———, ed. *Ernest Hemingway: Critiques of Four Major Novels.* New York: Charles Scribner's Sons, 1962.

_____, ed. *Hemingway and His Critics*. New York: Hill & Wang, 1961.

Baker, Sheridan. *Ernest Hemingway: An Introduction and Interpretation*. New York: Rinehart, 1976.

Bakker, J. *Ernest Hemingway: The Artist as Man of Action*. Assen, N.V.: Van Gorcum, 1972.

Balassi, William. "The Writing of *The Sun Also Rises*, with a Chart of Its Session-by-Session Development." *The Hemingway Review* 6.1 (Fall 1986): 65–78.

Barbour, James. "'The Light of the World': Hemingway's Comedy of Errors." *Notes on Contemporary Literature* 7.5 (December 1977): 5–8.

_____. "'The Light of the World': The Real Ketchel and the Real Light." *Studies in Short Fiction* 13 (1976): 17–23.

Barnes, Daniel R. "Traditional Narrative Sources for Hemingway's *The Torrents of Spring*." *Studies in Short Fiction* 19 (Spring 1982): 148–49.

Barthes, Roland. *Image, Music, Text*. Trans. Stephen Heath. New York: Hill & Wang, 1977.

Beegel, Susan F. *Hemingway's Craft of Omission: Four Manuscript Examples*. Ann Arbor: UMI Research P, 1988.

Behr, Caroline. *T. S. Eliot: A Chronology of His Life and Works*. New York: St. Martin's P, 1983.

Belsey, Catherine. *Critical Practice*. London and New York: Methuen, 1980.

Bennett, Tony. *Formalism and Marxism*. London and New York: Methuen, 1979.

Benson, Jackson J. *The Writer's Art of Self-Defense*. Minneapolis: U of Minnesota P, 1969.

_____, ed. *The Short Stories of Ernest Hemingway: Critical Essays*. Durham: Duke UP, 1975.

_____, ed. *The Short Stories of Ernest Hemingway: Critical Essays*. Rev. edn. Durham: Duke UP, 1989.

Benveniste, Emile. *Problems in General Linguistics*. Trans. Mary Elizabeth Meek. Coral Gables: U of Miami P, 1971.

Berg, A. Scott. *Max Perkins: Editor of Genius*. New York: Pocket Books, 1978.

Bloom, Harold, ed. *Ernest Hemingway's The Sun Also Rises: Modern Critical Interpretations*. New York: Chelsea House, 1987.

_____, ed. *Ernest Hemingway: Modern Critical Views*. New York: Chelsea House, 1985.

Booth, Wayne. *The Rhetoric of Fiction*. Chicago: U of Chicago P, 1961, 1983.

Brasch, James D. and Joseph Sigman. *Hemingway's Library: A Composite Record*. New York: Garland, 1981.

Brenner, Gerry. *Concealments in Hemingway's Works*. Columbus: Ohio State UP, 1983.

Brickell, Herschell. Rev. *In Our Time. New York Evening Post*. 17 October 1925: 3.

Bruccoli, Matthew J. "'The Light of the World': Stan Ketchel as 'My Sweet Christ.'" *Fitzgerald/Hemingway Annual 1969*: 125–30.

Bryer, Jackson, ed. *The Short Stories of F. Scott Fitzgerald: New Approaches in Criticism*. Madison: U of Wisconsin P, 1982.

Callaghan, Morley. *That Summer in Paris*. New York: Penguin, 1963.

Capellán, Angel. *Hemingway and the Hispanic World*. Ann Arbor: UMI Research P, 1985.

Carr, David. *Time, Narrative, and History*. Bloomington: Indiana UP, 1986.

Catalog of the Ernest Hemingway Collection at the John F. Kennedy Library. Boston: G. K. Hall, 1982.

Collins, William J. "Taking on the Champion: Alice as Liar in 'The Light of the World.'" *Studies in American Fiction* 14 (1986): 225–32.

Cope, Edward M. *An Introduction to Aristotle's Rhetoric with Analysis Notes and Appendices*. London: Macmillan, 1867.

Cornides, A. "Concelebration." In *New Catholic Encyclopedia*. Washington, D.C.: Catholic U of America P, 1987: 103–5.

Cowley, Malcolm. *Exile's Return*. New York: Viking, 1951.

———. "Introduction." *The Portable Hemingway*. Ed. Malcolm Cowley. New York: Viking, 1944. vii–xxiv.

Cross, F. L., ed. *The Oxford Dictionary of the Christian Church*. London: Oxford UP, 1957.

Dahiya, Bhim. *The Hero in Hemingway*. Atlantic Highlands, N.J.: Humanities, 1982.

DeFalco, Joseph. *The Hero in Hemingway's Short Stories*. Pittsburgh: U of Pittsburgh P, 1963.

Dekker, George and Joseph Harris. "Supernaturalism and the Vernacular Style in *A Farewell to Arms*." *PMLA* 94 (March 1979): 311–18.

Deleuze, Gilles. *Proust and Signs*. Trans. Richard Howard. New York: Georges Braziller, 1972.

Dolch, Martin. "A Day's Wait." In *Insight I: Analyses of American Literature*. Ed. John V. Hagopian and Martin Dolch. Frankfurt: Hirschgraben, 1962: 104–5.

Donaldson, Scott. *By Force of Will: The Life and Art of Ernest Hemingway*. New York: Penguin, 1978.

———. "Preparing for the End: Hemingway's Revisions of 'A Canary for One.'" *Studies in American Fiction* 6 (Autumn 1978): 203–11.

———. "The Wooing of Ernest Hemingway." *American Literature* 53.4 (January 1984): 691–710.

Eagleton, Terry. *Literary Theory: An Introduction*. Minneapolis: U of Minnesota P, 1983.

Eco, Umberto. *The Role of the Reader: Explorations in the Semiotics of Texts*. Bloomington: Indiana UP, 1979.

Eliot, T. S. *The Complete Poems and Plays: 1909–1950*. New York: Harcourt Brace, 1950.

———. *The Complete Poems and Plays of T. S. Eliot*. London: Faber & Faber, 1969.

———. "Ulysses, Order, and Myth." *Dial* 75 (November 1923): 480–83.

———. *The Waste Land and Other Poems*. New York: Harcourt, 1934.

Elliott, Emory, ed. *The Columbia Literary History of the United States*. New York: Columbia UP, 1988.

Ellmann, Richard. *James Joyce*. Rev. edn. New York: Oxford UP, 1982.

Evans, Oliver. "'The Snows of Kilimanjaro': A Revaluation." *PMLA* 76 (December 1961): 601–7.

Fenton, Charles A. *The Apprenticeship of Ernest Hemingway: The Early Years*. New York: Farrar, Straus, Young, 1954. Paperback edn., New York: Viking, 1958; rpt. New York: Octagon, 1975.

Ferguson, J. M. "Hemingway's Man of the World." *Arizona Quarterly* 33 (1977): 116–20.

Fitch, Noel. "Ernest Hemingway—c/o Shakespeare and Company." *Fitzgerald/Hemingway Annual 1977*: 175.

Fitzgerald, F. Scott. *The Great Gatsby*. New York: Charles Scribner's Sons, 1925.

———. *The Letters of F. Scott Fitzgerald*. Ed. Andrew Turnbull. New York: Charles Scribner's Sons, 1963.

Flanagan, John T. "Hemingway's Debt to Sherwood Anderson." *Journal of English and Germanic Philology* 54 (October 1955): 507–20.

Fleischer, Nathaniel. *The Ring Record Book and Boxing Encyclopedia 1982*. New York: Ring/Atheneum, 1983.

Fleming, Robert. "Perversion and the Writer in 'The Sea Change.'" *Studies in American Fiction* 14.2 (Autumn 1986): 215–20.

Flora, Joseph M. *Hemingway's Nick Adams*. Baton Rouge: Louisiana State UP, 1982.

Fontana, Ernest. "Hemingway's 'A Pursuit Race.'" *The Explicator* 42.4 (Summer 1984): 43–45.

The Forum 72 (October 1924).

The Forum 73 (February 1925).

The Forum 73 (June 1925).

The Forum 74 (August 1925).

Foucault, Michel. *The Order of Things.* New York: Vintage, 1973.

French, Warren, ed. *The Thirties: Fiction, Poetry, Drama.* Deland: Everett Edwards, 1967.

———. *The Social Novel at the End of an Era.* Carbondale: Southern Illinois UP, 1966.

Freund, Elizabeth. *The Return of the Reader: Reader-Response Criticism.* New York: Methuen, 1987.

Friar, Kimon. "Notes." *Modern Poetry: American and British.* Eds. Kimon Friar and John Malcolm Brinnin. New York: Appleton-Century-Crofts, 1951. 472–97.

"Frush Knocked Out by Mascart in 2D." *New York Times* (28 January 1925): 11.

Gajdusek, Robert E. *Hemingway and Joyce: A Study in Debt and Payment.* Corte Madera, Calif.: Square Circle P, 1984.

Genette, Gérard. *Narrative Discourse: An Essay in Method.* Ithaca: Cornell UP, 1980.

Gordon, Lyndall. *Eliot's Early Years.* Oxford: Oxford UP, 1977.

Grebstein, Sheldon Norman. *Hemingway's Craft.* Carbondale: Southern Illinois UP, 1973.

Griffin, Peter. *Along with Youth: Hemingway, The Early Years.* New York: Oxford UP, 1985.

Grimes, Larry E. *The Religious Design of Hemingway's Early Fiction.* Ann Arbor: UMI Research P, 1985.

Gurko, Leo. *Ernest Hemingway and the Pursuit of Heroism.* New York: Crowell, 1968.

Hackett, Francis. "Hemingway: *A Farewell to Arms.*" *Saturday Review of Literature* (6 August 1949): 32–33.

Hanneman, Audre. *Ernest Hemingway: A Comprehensive Bibliography.* Princeton: Princeton UP, 1967.

———. *Supplement to Ernest Hemingway: A Comprehensive Bibliography.* Princeton: Princeton UP, 1975.

Hattam, Edward. "Hemingway's 'An Alpine Idyll.'" *Modern Fiction Studies* 12 (Summer 1966): 261–65.

Hauger, B. A. "First Person Perspective in Four Hemingway Stories." *Rendezvous* 6 (1971): 29–38.

Hays, Peter L. "Self-Reflexive Laughter in 'A Day's Wait.'" *Hemingway Notes* (1980): 25.

Heidegger, Martin. *Being and Nothingness.* Trans. John McQuarrie and Edward Robinson. New York: Harper & Row, 1962.

———. *Poetry, Language, and Thought.* Trans. A. Hofstadter. New York: Harper & Row, 1971.

Heller, Peter. *In This Corner . . . !* New York: Simon and Schuster, 1973.

Hemingway, Lorian. "Ernest Hemingway's Farewell to Art." *Rolling Stone* 5 (5 June 1986): 42.

Hemingway, Mary. *How It Was.* New York: Alfred A. Knopf, 1976. Paperback edn., New York: Ballantine, 1976.

Hily-Mane, Geneviève. "Autour des manuscrits de 'The Sea Change.'" *Etudes Anglaises* 30.2 (1977): 207–9.

Hovey, Richard B. *Hemingway: The Inward Terrain.* Seattle: U of Washington P, 1968.

———. "*The Torrents of Spring*: Prefigurations in the Early Hemingway." *College English* 26 (March 1965): 460–64.

Iser, Wolfgang. *The Implied Reader: Patterns of Communication in Prose Fiction from Bunyan to Beckett.* Baltimore: Johns Hopkins UP, 1974.

Jackson, Paul R. "Hemingway's 'Out of Season.'" *The Hemingway Review* 1.1 (Fall 1981): 11–17.

Johnson, Frank E. "The Sacred City of the Sands." *National Geographic* 22 (December 1911): 1062.

Johnston, Kenneth G. "Hemingway's 'Out of Season' and the Psychology of Errors." *Literature and Psychology* 21 (1 November 1971): 41–46.

———. "Hemingway's 'Wine of Wyoming': Disappointment in America." *Western American Literature* 9 (November 1974): 159–67.

———. *The Tip of the Iceberg: Hemingway and the Short Story.* Greenwood: Penkevill, 1987.

Josephs, Allen. Rev. *The Garden of Eden. The Hemingway Review* 6 (Fall 1986): 112–14.

———. "*Toreo:* The Moral Axis of *The Sun Also Rises.*" *The Hemingway Review* 6 (Fall 1986): 88–99.

Joyce, James. *Dubliners.* 1914. New York: Penguin, 1967.

Kenner, Hugh. *Joyce's Voices.* Berkeley: U of California P, 1978.

Kert, Bernice. *The Hemingway Women.* New York: W. W. Norton, 1983.

Kierkegaard, Søren. *Repetition: An Essay in Experimental Psychology.* Trans. W. Lowrie. Princeton: Princeton UP, 1964.

Killinger, John. *Hemingway and the Dead Gods: A Study in Existentialism.* U of Kentucky P, 1960.

Kobler, J. F. "Hemingway's 'The Sea Change': A Sympathetic View of Homosexuality." *Arizona Quarterly* 26 (Winter 1970): 318–24.

Koenig, Rhoda. "Adam and Eve on a Raft." *New York* 19 (12 May 1986): 137.

Krause, Sydney J. "Hemingway's 'My Old Man.'" *Explicator* 20 (1962): item 39.

Kronenburger, Louis, ed. *Alexander Pope: Selected Works.* New York: Random House, 1948.

Kvam, Wayne E. "Hemingway's 'Banal Story.'" *Fitzgerald/Hemingway Annual 1974:* 181–91.

———. *Hemingway in Germany.* Athens: Ohio UP, 1973.

Lacan, Jacques. "Of Structure as an Inmixing of Otherness Prerequisite to Any Subject Whatever." In *The Structuralist Controversy.* Ed. Richard Macksey and Eugenio Donato. Baltimore: Johns Hopkins UP, 1972. 186–95.

Lanford, Ray. "Hemingway's 'My Old Man.'" *Linguistics in Literature* 1 (1976): 11–19.

Lewis, Robert W., Jr. "Hemingway's Lives: A Review." *The Hemingway Review* 3.1 (Fall 1987): 45–62.

———. *Hemingway on Love.* Austin: U of Texas P, 1965.

Lynn, Kenneth S. *Hemingway.* New York: Simon and Schuster, 1987.

———. Interview. "Hemingway Heretic." *Johns Hopkins Magazine* 30.2 (April 1988): 22–29.

Lyotard, Jean-François. *The Postmodern Condition: A Report on Knowledge.* Trans. Geoff Bennington and Brian Massumi. Minneapolis: U of Minnesota P, 1984.

McCaffery, John K. M., ed. *Ernest Hemingway: The Man and His Work.* Cleveland and New York: World, 1950. Rpt. New York: Cooper Square, 1969.

McComas, Dix. "The Geography of Ernest Hemingway's 'Out of Season.'" *The Hemingway Review* 3.2 (Spring 1984): 46–49.

MacLeish, Archibald. "American Letter." *The Bookman* (28 January 1929): n.p.

Mahoney, Patrick J. "Hemingway's 'A Day's Wait.'" *Explicator* 27 (November 1968): Item 18.

Mailer, Norman. *The Long Patrol: 25 Years of Writing from the Works of Norman Mailer.* Ed. Robert F. Lucid. New York: World, 1971.

Martine, James J. "A Little Light on Hemingway's 'The Light of the World.'" *Studies in Short Fiction* 7 (1970): 465–67.

Matthews, T. S. "Fiction by Young and Old." *New Republic* (15 November 1933): 24–25.

———. *Great Tom: Notes Towards the Definition of T. S. Eliot.* New York: Harper, 1974.

Messinger, Christian K. *Sport and the Spirit of Play in American Fiction: Hawthorne to Faulkner.* New York: Columbia UP, 1981.

Meyer, John M. "Myths of Socialization and of Personality." In *Reconstructing Individualism: Autonomy, Individuality, and the Self in Western Thought.* Ed. Thomas C. Heller, Morton Sosna, and David E. Wellbery. Stanford: Stanford UP, 1986. 208–21.

Meyers, Jeffrey. *Hemingway: A Biography.* New York: Harper & Row, 1985.

————, ed. *Hemingway: The Critical Heritage*. London, Boston, and Henley: Routledge & Kegan Paul, 1982.

Miller, J. Hillis. *Fiction and Repetition: Seven English Novels*. Cambridge: Harvard UP, 1982.

Monteiro, George. "Hemingway's Unnatural History of the Dying." *Fitzgerald/Hemingway Annual 1978*: 339–42.

Montgomery, Constance Cappel. *Hemingway in Michigan*. New York: Fleet, 1966.

Nagel, James. "Literary Impressionism and *In Our Time*." *The Hemingway Review* (Spring 1987): 17–26.

————, ed. *Ernest Hemingway: The Writer in Context*. Madison: U of Wisconsin P, 1984.

Nahal, Chaman. *The Narrative Pattern in Hemingway's Fiction*. Rutherford: Fairleigh Dickinson UP, 1971.

Nakajima, Kenji. "*Lacrimae Rerum* in 'My Old Man.'" *Kyushu American Literature* 22 (1981): 18–23.

Nelson, Gerald B. and Glory Jones. *Hemingway: Life and Works*. New York: Facts on File, 1984.

Nelson, Raymond S. *Hemingway: Expressionist Artist*. Ames: Iowa State UP, 1979.

Nietzsche, Friedrich. *On the Genealogy of Morals*. Trans. Walter Kaufman and R. J. Hollingdale. New York: Vintage Press, 1968.

O'Banion, John D. "Narration and Argumentation: Quintilian on *Narratio* as the Heart of Rhetorical Thinking." *Rhetorica* 5 (1987): 325–51.

O'Connor, Frank. *The Lonely Voice*. New York: Harper & Row, 1963.

Oldsey, Bernard. "*El Pueblo Español*: 'The Capital of the World.'" *Studies in American Fiction* 13 (Spring 1985): 103–10.

"Our Desert Panorama." *National Geographic* 22 (April 1911): 409–10.

Parker, Dorothy. *The Portable Dorothy Parker*. New York: Penguin, 1978.

Parrott, Thomas Marc, ed. *Shakespeare: Twenty-three Plays and the Sonnets*. New York: Charles Scribner's Sons, 1953.

Peden, William. "The American Short Story in the Twenties." *Studies in Short Fiction* 10 (Fall 1975): 368.

Pedoto, Constance. "*Il Gioco del Nulla*: Ernest Hemingway and Italo Calvino's Construction of Nothingness." Dissertation, U of South Florida, 1988.

Percy, Walker. *Lost in the Cosmos: The Last Self-Help Book*. New York: Washington Square, 1983.

Peterson, Richard. *Hemingway: Direct and Oblique*. Paris: Norton, 1969.

Plimpton, George. "An Interview with Ernest Hemingway." *Paris Review* 18 (Spring 1958): 85–108.

Pontes, Mário, trans. "Aconteceu em Michigan." *êla ela* 1.2 (March 1970): 99–105.

Portz, John. "Allusion and Structure in Hemingway's 'A Natural History of the Dead.'" *Tennessee Studies in Literature* 10 (1965): 27–44.

Potts, Willard, ed. *Portraits of the Artist in Exile*. Seattle: U of Washington P, 1979.

Putnam, Ann. "Dissemblings and Disclosures in Hemingway's 'An Alpine Idyll.'" *The Hemingway Review* (Spring 1987): 27–33.

————. "'Wine of Wyoming' and Hemingway's Hidden West." *Western American Literature* 22 (May 1987): 17–32.

Quintilian. *The Institutio Oratoria of Quintilian*. Trans. H. E. Butler. 4 vols. Cambridge: Harvard UP, 1958.

Reid, Stephen A. "The Oedipal Pattern in Hemingway's 'The Capital of the World.'" *Literature and Psychology* 13 (Spring 1963): 37–43.

Reynolds, Michael S. *Hemingway: The Paris Years* (London and New York: Basil Blackwell, 1989).

_____ . *Hemingway's First War: The Making of* A Farewell to Arms. Princeton: Princeton UP, 1976.

_____ . *Hemingway's Reading, 1910–1940: An Inventory.* Princeton: Princeton UP, 1981.

_____ . "Holman Hunt and 'The Light of the World.'" *Studies in Short Fiction* 20 (1983): 317–19.

_____ . *The Young Hemingway.* Oxford: Basil Blackwell, 1986.

_____ , ed. *Critical Essays on Ernest Hemingway's* In Our Time. Boston: G. K. Hall, 1983.

Richards, I. A. *Practical Criticism: A Study of Literary Judgment.* New York: Harcourt, Brace, & World, 1929.

Rovit, Earl. *Ernest Hemingway.* Boston: Twayne, 1963.

Rudnick, Lois P. "Daisy Miller Revisited: Ernest Hemingway's 'A Canary for One.'" *Massachusetts Studies in English* 7 (1978): 12–19.

Sartre, Jean-Paul. *Situations.* Trans. Benita Eisler. Greenwich: Fawcett, 1965.

Schaefer, William J. "Ernest Hemingway: Arbiter of Common Numerality." *Carleton Miscellany* 3 (Winter 1962): 100–104.

Schapiro, Leonard. *Turgenev: His Life and Times.* New York: Random House, 1978.

Schlesinger, Arthur M., Jr. and Frederick Israel, eds. *History of American Presidential Elections.* New York: Chelsea House, 1971.

Scholes, Robert. *Semiotics and Interpretation.* New Haven: Yale UP, 1981.

_____ . *Textual Power: Literary Theory and the Teaching of English.* New Haven: Yale UP, 1985.

Scholes, Robert and Robert Kellogg. *The Nature of Narrative.* 1966. London: Oxford UP, 1976.

Schroeter, James. "Hemingway via Joyce." *Sewanee Review* 10.1 (January 1974): 95–114.

Service, Robert W. *The Shooting of Dan McGrew and the Cremation of Sam McGee.* New York: William R. Scott, 1969.

Sheed, Wilfrid. "A Farewell to Hemingstein." *The New York Review of Books* (12 June 1986): 5.

Shepherd, Allen. "Hemingway's 'A Day's Wait': Biography and Fiction." *Indiana English Journal* 4 (Spring 1970): 31–36.

Shiras, George, III. "A Flashlight Story of an Albino Porcupine and of a Cunning but Unfortunate Coon." *National Geographic* 22 (May 1911): 572–95.

Silber, John. "Our Hellenic Heritage." *Bostonia* 62.6 (November-December 1988): 26–29.

Smith, Chard Powers. *Along the Wind.* New Haven: Yale UP, 1925.

Smith, Julian. "Eyeless in Wyoming. Blind in Venice: Hemingway's Last Stories." *Connecticut Review* 4 (April 1971): 9–15.

Smith, Paul. "Hemingway's Apprentice Fiction: 1919–1921." *American Literature* 58.4 (December 1986): 574–88.

_____ . *A Reader's Guide to the Short Stories of Ernest Hemingway.* Boston: G. K. Hall, 1989.

_____ . "Three Versions of 'Up in Michigan,' 1921–1930." *Resources for American Literary Study* 15.2 (Autumn 1985): 163–77.

Solomon, Barbara Probst. "Where's Papa?" *The New Republic* (9 March 1987): 30–34.

Somers, Paul P., Jr. "The Mark of Sherwood Anderson on Hemingway: A Look at the Texts." *South Atlantic Quarterly* 73 (Autumn 1974): 487–503.

Spenko, James Leo. "A Long Look at Hemingway's 'Up in Michigan.'" *Arizona Quarterly* 39.2 (Summer 1983): 111–21.

Stein, Gertrude. *The Autobiography of Alice B. Toklas.* New York: Harcourt Brace, 1933.

_____ . *Selected Writings of Gertrude Stein.* Ed. Carl Van Vechten. New York: Vintage, 1962.

Steinbeck, John. *The Grapes of Wrath.* 1939. New York: Penguin, 1976.

_____ . *Journal of a Novel: The* East of Eden *Letters.* New York: Viking, 1969.

Steinke, James. "Hemingway's 'Cat in the Rain.'" *Spectrum* 25 (1983): 36–44.

Stephens, Robert O. *Hemingway's Non-Fiction: The Public Voice* Chapel Hill: U of North Carolina P, 1968.

———, ed. *Ernest Hemingway: The Critical Reception.* New York: Burt Franklin, 1977.

Stephens, Rosemary. "'In Another Country': Three as Symbol." *University of Mississippi Studies in English* 7 (1966): 87–96.

Stewart, Justin. *Wayne Wheeler: Dry Boss.* Westport: Greenwood, 1970.

Stewart, Louis H. and Charles T. Stewart. "Play, Games, and Affect: A Contribution Toward a Comprehensive Theory of Play." In *Play as Context.* Ed. A. T. Cheska. Westpoint: Leisure, 1981. 42–52.

Stoneback, H. R. "From the rue Saint-Jacques to the Pass of Roland to the 'Unfinished Church on the Edge of the Cliff.'" *The Hemingway Review* 6 (Fall 1986): 2–29.

Sugar, Bert Randolph. *The 100 Greatest Boxers of All Time.* New York: Bonanza, 1984.

Sutherland, Fraser. *The Style of Innocence: A Study of Hemingway and Callaghan.* Toronto and Vancouver: Clark & Irwin, 1972.

Sylvester, Bickford. "Winner Take Nothing: Development as Dilemma for the Hemingway Heroine." *Pacific Coast Philology* 31 (November 1986): 73–80

Taylor, Mark C. *Alterity.* Chicago: U of Chicago P, 1987.

"Test Cricket Game Stirs All London." *New York Times* (23 January 1925): 16.

Theweleit, Klaus. *Male Fantasies.* Vol. 1. Trans. Stephen Conway. Minneapolis: U of Minnesota P, 1987.

Thomas, Hugh. *The Spanish Civil War.* New York: Harper & Row, 1977.

Thomas, Peter. "A Lost Leader: Hemingway's 'The Light of the World.'" *Humanities Association Bulletin* 21 (Fall 1970): 14–19.

Thrall, William Flint and Addison Hubbard. *A Handbook to Literature.* New York: Odyssey, 1960.

Turgenev, Ivan. *The Torrents of Spring.* Trans. Constance Garnett. 1916. Freeport: Books for Libraries, 1971.

Wagner, Linda W., ed. *Ernest Hemingway: Six Decades of Criticism.* East Lansing: Michigan State UP, 1987.

Waldhorn, Arthur. *A Reader's Guide to Ernest Hemingway.* New York: Farrar, Straus and Giroux, 1972.

———, ed. *Ernest Hemingway: A Collection of Criticism.* Contemporary Studies in Literature. New York: McGraw-Hill Paperbacks, 1973.

Waldmeir, Joseph and Joseph Marsh, eds. *Up in Michigan: Proceedings of the First National Conference of the Hemingway Society.* Traverse City: The Hemingway Society, 1983.

Watson, William B. "'Old Man at the Bridge': The Making of a Short Story." *The Hemingway Review* 7.2 (Spring 1988): 152–65.

Watts, Emily Stipes. *Ernest Hemingway and the Arts.* Urbana: U of Illinois P, 1971.

Waugh, Patricia. *Metafiction: The Theory and Practice of Self-Conscious Fiction.* London and New York: Methuen, 1980.

Weber, Horst, ed. *Hemingway.* Darmstadt: Wissenschaftliche Buchgesellschaft, 1980.

Weeks, Robert P., ed. *Hemingway: A Collection of Critical Essays.* Englewood Cliffs, N.J.: Prentice Hall, 1962.

White, Ray Lewis. "Hemingway's Private Explanation of *The Torrents of Spring.*" *Modern Fiction Studies* 13 (Summer 1967): 262–63.

Wilkinson, Myer. *Hemingway and Turgenev: The Nature of Literary Influence.* Ann Arbor: UMI Research P, 1986.

Williams, Wirt. *The Tragic Art of Ernest Hemingway.* Baton Rouge: Louisiana State UP, 1981.

Wilson, Edmund. "The Sportsman's Tragedy." *The New Republic* 53 (14 Dec. 1927): 102–3.

———. *The Wound and the Bow.* 1941. New York: Farrar, Straus, and Giroux, 1978.

Wycherley, H. Alan. "Hemingway's 'The Sea Change.'" *American Notes and Queries* 7 (January 1969): 67–68.

Wyden, Peter. *The Passionate War: The Narrative History of the Spanish Civil War, 1936–1939.* New York: Simon and Schuster, 1983.

Wylder, Delbert E. *"The Torrents of Spring." South Dakota Review* 5 (Winter 1967–68): 23–35.

Yannella, Phillip R. "Notes on the Manuscript, Date, and Sources of Hemingway's 'Banal Story.'" *Fitzgerald/Hemingway Annual 1974.* Ed. Matthew J. Bruccoli and C. E. Frazer Clark, Jr. Englewood: Microcard, 1975: 175–79.

Young, Philip. *Ernest Hemingway.* New York: Rinehart, 1952.

————. *Ernest Hemingway.* Pamphlets on American Writers, 1. Minneapolis, U of Minnesota P, 1959.

————. *Ernest Hemingway: A Reconsideration.* University Park: Pennsylvania State UP, 1966.

Young, Philip and Charles W. Mann. *The Hemingway Manuscripts: An Inventory.* University Park: Pennsylvania State UP, 1969.

Yunck, John A. "The Natural History of a Dead Quarrel: Hemingway and the Humanists." *South Atlantic Quarterly* 62 (Winter 1963): 29–43.

Index